ENVIRONMENTAL LAW
FOR NON-LAWYERS
SECOND EDITION

ENVIRONMENTAL LAW FOR NON-LAWYERS
SECOND EDITION

by

DAVID B. FIRESTONE, ESQ.
Professor of Law
Vermont Law School

DR. FRANK C. REED
Research Director
Environmental Law Foundation

SoRo Press
South Royalton, Vermont

Library of Congress Catalog Card Number 93-92673
ISBN 0-9625463-1-3

SoRo Press
RR 2, Box 151
South Royalton, VT 05068
(802) 763-2116

Printed in the United States of America on recycled paper.

PREFACE

Some years ago, I became interested in communicating an understanding of the law to people who are not lawyers but whose professional work involves substantial contact with certain areas of the law. It is my belief that there is no need for law to be a mystery understood only by lawyers, and that an understanding of the law by non-lawyers would provide a healthier climate for critical analysis of the law. Sound critical analysis and an understanding of the objectives of the law would hopefully lead to meaningful changes where the law is not doing a good job, as well as less resistance to compliance with the law where it is doing a good job. These beliefs have led me to participate in various educational activities for non-lawyers during the last twenty years.

My primary teaching area, as a law school professor and as a teacher of non-lawyers, has been environmental law. I have presented numerous seminars and lectures to non-lawyers from industry and government whose jobs involve environmental law. The feedback from these people has indicated that they have benefited greatly from being exposed to environmental law in language that non-lawyers can easily understand. I hope this book will further my goal of providing an understanding of environmental law to those who administer it or live under it. Although Frank and I believe this book will also be useful to lawyers who do not specialize in the practice of environmental law and who want an overview of the area, our primary addressees are those people who have not had formal legal training. The book will therefore provide the reader with a basic discussion of some general legal concepts as well as environmental law topics. These concepts will be discussed in the context of specific environmental subject areas, e.g., solid waste disposal; however, the reader should be aware that a legal concept discussed in a solid waste context may also be applicable to other subject areas, such as noise pollution or control of radiation hazards.

Before beginning, let me note what we will not be doing in this work. Our role will be that of teachers rather than of advocates. We do not view our job as an effort to convince the reader of what is the right or wrong position on any environmental issue. Our job will be to present arguments for the alternative positions, and, although it is inevitable that our biases will make themselves known, we do not crusade for a particular point of view.

David B. Firestone

A long time ago, I used to go and play in the woods near our house. Today, those woods are covered by tract homes, and the forest floor is now lawn. Every time I pass by this area, I wonder why my childhood playground had to be developed. Then I remember that there are more people on earth now than there were back then, and people do have to live someplace. But, I wonder when this growth will level off so some forest playgrounds will remain.

Later in my life (1969), while visiting Buffalo, New York, I stopped to buy some gasoline. The ''rotten egg'' odor of hydrogen sulfide was at once recognizable in the air, so I asked the gas station attendant how he could stand the smell, and he said, ''What smell?'' This encounter, along with many other experiences, left me aware of the fact that environmental problems do exist and that something ought to be done to control or eliminate them.

Over the years, I came to understand what could be done about such problems. The ''answer'' appeared to lie in environmental law coupled with environmental awareness. What is presented here is an attempt to pass along to you the awareness of, and the reasoning behind, the current regulation of perceived environmental problems. It is hoped that this effort will give you a perspective on the issues.

Frank C. Reed

ACKNOWLEDGMENTS

The authors wish to express their thanks to Vermont Law School for its cooperation and assistance in the preparation of this book. Special thanks go to Laura Gillen, without whose help this project would never have been completed, to Vermont Law School Librarians, Diane Frake, Christine Ryan, Victoria Weber, Carl Yirka, and Susan Zeigfinger for their invaluable research assistance, and to Leann Cushman, Arlene Elderd, Mary Fisk, and Linda Winter for their highly competent work on the manuscript.

David B. Firestone is Professor of Law at Vermont Law School, where he has been specializing in the field of Environmental Law for twenty years. Prior to teaching law, he was an attorney with the United States Department of Housing and Urban Development. He was also an engineer with the Ford Motor Company and Douglas Aircraft. Mr. Firestone has presented numerous seminars and lectures before industry and professional groups and is thus experienced in providing knowledge of law to non-lawyers. He is a member of the Vermont and Massachusetts Bars and received his JD from Harvard Law School and a BS in Mechanical Engineering from Wayne State University.

Frank C. Reed received his BS from the State University of New York at Oswego. He then taught high school biology, chemistry, earth science, genetics and geometry in Central Square, New York. Subsequently, he received an MS in Biology and a PhD in Botany from Michigan State University. Dr. Reed has authored numerous papers in ecological journals and has recently authored papers concerning acid precipitation and clean air. He is currently Research Director of the Environmental Law Foundation.

To our parents for the
environment they provided.

CONTENTS

CHAPTER 1

ENVIRONMENTAL LAW—To What Does It Apply?
Do We Need It? Where It Comes From.
How To Find the Law.

A. TO WHAT DOES IT APPLY?

The environment can be defined in many ways, some highly formal, some very informal. The environment could be said to be the occupation of space through time by definables, or the environment could be defined as that which is around us throughout our lifetime. The environment includes air, water, land, buildings, flowers, snakes, snails and even puppy dog tails. The environment is everything. Most people have a general sense of what the environment is and agree that it should be protected. What are most often the subjects of dispute are what is the appropriate extent of protection and how fast environmental controls should be implemented. The question which needs to be addressed first is how the environment is organized, since that must be examined prior to taking any steps to control or influence the environment.

For our purposes, let us consider the individual of a species as the least complex unit of organization. This is like saying that the person sitting next to you is an individual of the species called humans. All the individuals of the species called humans taken collectively constitute a unit called the species population. The aggregate of all species populations is called the community, while the community with the attendant abiotic factors (things that aren't alive) is called the ecosystem. This scheme is presented diagrammatically in Figure 1. Also, at this point, it might be helpful to realize that as the complexity of any system increases, the ability to define cause-effect relationships decreases. For example, with respect to the economy and the issue of acid rain, it is easier to define the economic cause-effect relationship between acid rain and an individual farmer raising a specified crop than the economic cause-effect relationship between acid rain and all

1

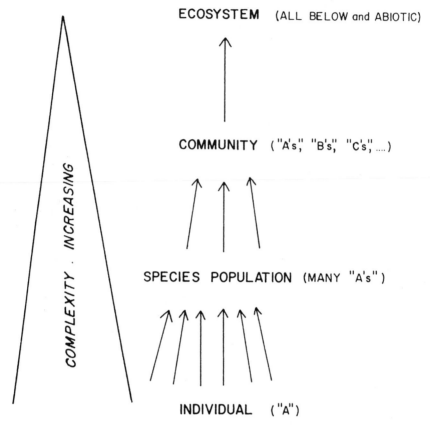

Figure 1.   A scheme to help understand one view of how the environment is put together.

farmers raising all crops. In the first case, the question of cause-effect is at the individual level, while the second cause-effect relationship is sought at the species population level. In addition, it would be easier to define the cause-effect relationship between acid rain and farming than to define the cause-effect relationship between acid rain and all business enterprises which would include not only farming, but also steel production, fishing and automobile manufacturing. The greater the diversity of any system, the more difficult it becomes to define ultimate cause-effect relationships that may be detrimental, since what may cause a negative effect on one population may cause a positive effect on another. Furthermore, the effect that is being investigated will often greatly influence any policy decision being made. In other words, if we want to know the effects of acid rain on the economy, the answer may be much different from the effects of acid rain on human

health and survival, and, therefore, any decisions for action will probably
be different depending on what effect is being investigated.

At this point, an example of what one might consider the environment
to be is in order. To illustrate this, consider Figure 2, along with the following
narrative. Suppose you are A, alone (notion 1), and you generate a waste
to an external environment, rather than "your" environment. If there are
not too many A's, then no one will notice, or it will be someone else's
problem. Now suppose that all the A's together (species population) collectively send a waste to an external environment (notion 2). If there are
not too many A's, the "problem" will go unnoticed by the A's until there
are a lot of A's. If the A's together with all the species populations (community) produce a common waste, the waste could still go to an external
environment and not be a "problem" if a large enough external environment
exists (notion 3); however, if we take into account all the species populations,
it is highly unlikely that there can be an external environment. The A's,
B's and all the other species are no longer able to find an external environment
and consequently are putting a common waste directly into the environment

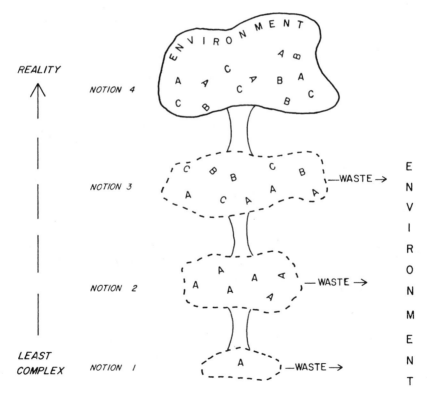

Figure 2.   Waste Disposal? You can't always put everything someplace else.

of which they are a part—the ecosystem (notion 4). It is in this sense, the ecosystem as a whole, that the definition of environment and the questions of whether or not to control or influence it must ultimately be considered.

B.   DO WE NEED IT?

1.   The "Early" Years

A phenomenal expansion of governmentally imposed environmental controls began in the late 1960's. The degree of regulation with respect to the environment has multiplied many times and has expanded to cover many, many subject areas since then, and the pace of government's environmental involvement shows no signs of slowing down in the 1990's. This portion of the chapter will consider why there has been this tremendous surge of interest in environmental matters and whether the massive network of governmental regulation which has resulted is justified. We will then continue by setting aside, in part, the question of what the involvement of the law should be with respect to the environment, and devote the bulk of this book to an analysis of what the law is and what it means to business, to industry, to people who work for governmental bodies, and to individuals in their everyday lives.

Our analysis of what the law is will include both private law and public law control mechanisms. The private law mechanisms usually consist of the bringing of lawsuits by individuals or corporations. These suits ask a court for relief without the request for relief being based on any action of a legislative body. For example, property owners might ask a court to prohibit a factory from polluting the air in their neighborhood because such pollution constitutes a nuisance which a court will act against even in the absence of federal or state air pollution control statutes. The public law mechanism, on the other hand, operates when a governmental body takes some form of initiative, such as enacting legislation. The spectrum of governmental initiatives includes actions such as prohibitions, permit requirements and educational efforts. Examples include: Congress prohibiting the manufacturing of a chemical; a state legislature requiring that a permit be obtained before a factory may discharge a pollutant into a river; or a city council establishing a publicity campaign to educate the public to voluntarily recycle glass and paper.

Having noted some types of environmental control mechanisms which are available for use, let's begin by moving back a step and considering one series of arguments for and against strict governmental control of the environment in an attempt to see how people have reached different conclusions when answering the question: Do we need environmental controls at all and, if so, to what degree?

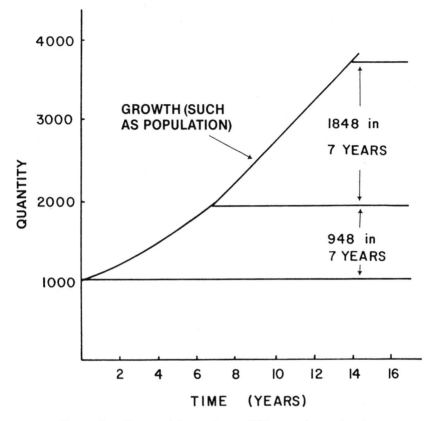

Figure 3. Exponential growth at a 10% annual growth rate.

A study that helped spark widespread interest in environmental protection is called *The Limits to Growth*.[1] A group of researchers from MIT used system dynamics computer technology to attempt to predict what future patterns of growth might look like, what limits there might be on such growth, and what the results of various patterns of growth might mean to humans. Concerning patterns of growth, the study found that parameters such as population and industrial production exhibit the characteristic of exponential growth, i.e., growth which increases at a constant percentage rate and therefore increases numerically faster and faster (Figure 3). As one example, consider the meaning of Figure 3, assuming a 10% growth rate and an initial quantity at the beginning of Year 1 of 1000 units:

---

1. Meadows, D.H., et al., *The Limits to Growth* (New York: Signet, 1972).

End of Year 1	$1000 + 10\%$ of 1000	$=$	1100
(Year 1 Growth = 100)			
End of Year 2	$1100 + 10\%$ of 1100	$=$	1210
(Year 2 Growth = 110)			
End of Year 3	$1210 + 10\%$ of 1210	$=$	1331
(Year 3 Growth = 121)			
* * *	* * *		* * *
End of Year 7	$1771 + 10\%$ of 1771	$=$	1948
(Year 7 Growth = 177)			

Thus, in seven years, 1000 units has become nearly 2000 units and, in another seven years (the doubling period for a 10% growth rate), we end up with nearly 4000 units. If the growth rate were reduced to 4%, the doubling period would be increased to eighteen years.

The second part of the "Limits to Growth" thesis is that some necessary resources are finite, for example, arable land or the pollution absorption ability of a medium like the air. When those finite resources (limits) are imposed on an exponential growth pattern, the "Limits to Growth" model predicts that the actual behavior of the growth parameters would be in the nature of catastrophic decline. Thus, to use population as an example, when exponential population growth reaches the finite limit of arable land, the result is famine and a massive population decrease (Figure 4). In addition, because of the overuse of the arable land resource by the increasing population as the time of a famine is approached, the capacity of the land to sustain population in the future may be severely reduced. If catastrophe is the result of reaching the finite limit rapidly (exponentially), what remedy is prescribed by those who agree with the "Limits" study? The remedy is to have strict control of variables such as population, pollution, and use of natural resources, and, since growth is taking place very quickly (exponentially), strict controls must be implemented very quickly.

The need for early action to avert catastrophe is best illustrated by a children's riddle: A lily plant grows in a pond and the plant doubles in size every day. If allowed to grow freely, it would completely cover the pond in 30 days, killing off all other forms of life. You decide not to worry about checking its growth until it covers half the pond. On what day will that be?[2] With the answer being the twenty-ninth day, there is only one day left for action to avert disaster. Maybe one could effectively control the lily plant in one day, but could population growth or pollution or petroleum use be effectively brought under control in a short time period? And, even if last minute control were possible, the drastic nature of the measures which would

2. Ibid., p. 37.

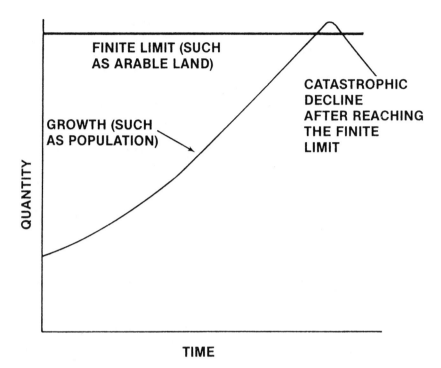

Figure 4.   Catastrophic decline in growth after reaching the finite limit.

be necessary to achieve control and the consequences of such measures would be unpalatable and would argue in favor of taking less drastic action at an earlier time.

We should note in passing that the above discussion isolated variables like population and pollution; however, the "Limits" model does consider interrelationships of variables in great detail. Among the dozens of parameters built into the model are land yields, nonrenewable resources, industrial capital availability, pollution generation, and pollution absorption rates. As an example of the effects of the interrelationships of variables, consider population and pollution together. Increasing population might cause increasing pollution, but increasing pollution may cause a decrease in the rate of population growth due to possible deaths or shortened life spans from pollution-related diseases. The "Limits" model attempts to account for the interrelationships among variables and to present a "net behavior pattern" for each parameter evaluated.

Based on their evaluations, the proponents of the "Limits to Growth" hypothesis conclude that, with current growth trends, the limits on growth will be reached within one hundred years, and the likely result of reaching these limits will be a sudden, uncontrollable decline in population and industrial capacity. Furthermore, to return to our lily plant analogy, the point of no return (control possible without needing to use extremely drastic control measures) may occur very soon. Those who accept the "Limits to Growth" type of reasoning would argue in favor of strict governmental controls with respect to the environment and would contend that implementation of those controls should not be delayed.

Having considered one theory with conclusions favoring strict environmental control, let's give equal time to those who are not convinced of the need for massive governmental regulation of our environment by presenting some of the arguments which characterize the "Limits" advocates as "prophets of doom."[3]

One challenge to the "Limits" theory attacks the concept of finite limits. For example, it may be argued that arable land is not finite in amount since technology can increase not only the number of arable acres (by methods such as irrigation), but also technology can increase productivity through means such as the use of new fertilizers or new varieties of plants. Similarly, technology can increase the availability of resources—petroleum from oil shale; freshwater from seawater. The concept of finite limits may thus be said to be illusory.

The "Limits" proponents might contend that while technology can indeed increase the magnitude of the limits, there still are finite limits, just at a higher level. The result is merely a brief delay in reaching the crisis point (Figure 5). The critics' response might be that if the growth parameters increase exponentially, technology can also make the limiting parameters increase exponentially. If a "limiting" parameter increases at a rate faster than growth increases, the result is divergence between the limiting parameter and the growth parameter such that no crisis point is ever reached (Figure 6). If the limiting variable increases more slowly than growth demands, then convergence occurs and there is a crisis; however, the crisis point would only be reached when the curves converge, which may be in the very distant future and beyond the level of reliability of our tools of prediction (Figure 7). Thus, those who do not accept a "Limits to Growth" type of reasoning would contend that there is no coming environmental catastrophe to worry about, and, while environmental concerns and the effects of growth should be considered, there is no need for strict governmental controls in areas such as pollution, use of natural resources, or population.

A second challenge to the "Limits" theory might be to attack the concept of catastrophe itself. It may be argued that there are social mechanisms which work in a manner such that as the "limit" is approached, natural decreases

---

3. Kaysen, C., "The Computer That Printed Out W*O*L*F," *Foreign Affairs*, 50:660–668 (1972).

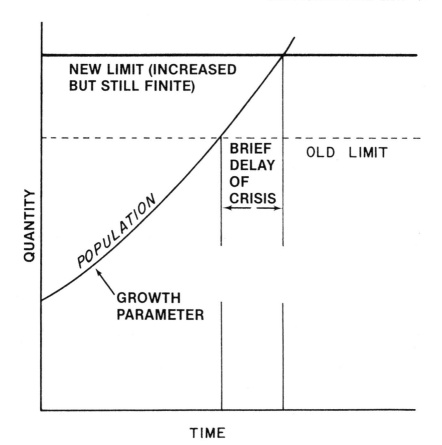

Figure 5. Brief delay of crisis.

in the growth rate take place to keep the system below the limit. For example, as the use of a particular metal grows toward the limit of its availability (i.e., less and less is available due to past use), the price of the metal will rise and the use will taper off with either the introduction of substitutes, or with the less important or inefficient uses being abandoned (Figure 8). The result of the operation of these natural social mechanisms is that growth will not continue to a catastrophic collision with a limit to growth, and thus, while some environmental controls to improve day-to-day living might be justified, there is no need for immediate, strict governmental curtailment of economic growth to avert catastrophe.

The issue of whether one believes in the prophecy of the "Limits to Growth" thesis or dismisses the thesis based on arguments such as those noted above is relevant to one's belief concerning the role of government with respect to environmental issues. Should government take no action at

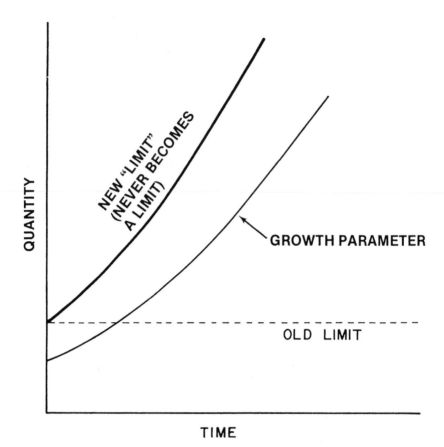

Figure 6.   Scenario of never reaching a crisis.

all on behalf of environmental protection; should it take mild action such as educating the public toward voluntary conservation of resources; should it take firm action such as imposing actual limits on the amounts of a pollutant in the air; or should it take drastic measures to stop industrial growth?

2.   The Need Today—A Status Report

The rapid growth of environmental law in the form of government regulation continues today. If governmental regulation were not succeeding in solving environmental problems, one might conclude that such regulation should be discontinued or its approach drastically altered. Also, if our environmental problems have been solved or are now being fully addressed by mechanisms other than governmentally imposed controls, then those

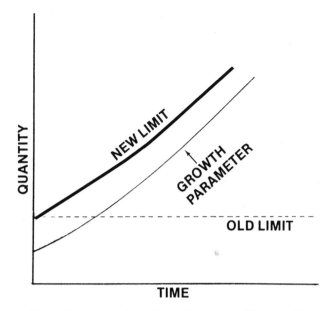

Figure 7.   Scenario of long delay in reaching a crisis.

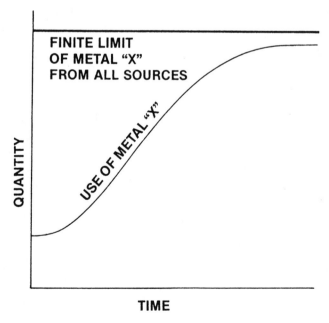

Figure 8.   Leveling off of growth as the finite limit of growth is approached.

controls should not continue. It is clear, however, that, while government controls have been quite successful, our environmental problems are not even close to being completely solved. The success, but not complete success, with respect to some old problems, coupled with the emergence of new environmental problems, indicate that the continued growth of environmental law by governmental regulation is probably necessary and certainly going to happen. Indeed, the issues debated today no longer focus on the question of whether to have government control, but rather on questions of what is the best type of control mechanism to use, at what level of government should control be exercised, and the time when new controls should become applicable.

Since both the successes and failures of environmental efforts by government seem to point in the direction of increased controls, let's consider examples of the successes of environmental law and examples of areas that need more attention. Some of the United States' greatest successes in environmental regulation have involved controlling toxic materials. Lead emissions are drastically lower due largely to a 78% reduction of lead used in gasoline between 1970 and 1985. Also, because of low demand for leaded gasoline due to vehicles needing unleaded gasoline so as not to ruin their catalytic converters, leaded gasoline is now totally unavailable in many areas of the United States. Polychlorinated biphenyl (PCB) releases are much lower due to a Congressional ban on their manufacture, and persistent organochloride pesticides like DDT and dieldrin have largely disappeared from use, with the result being sharp declines in the concentration levels of these substances in human tissues.[4]

Exposure to asbestos is also down substantially. Federal regulations exist with respect to asbestos in school buildings, asbestos emissions for buildings being demolished or renovated, and occupational exposure to asbestos. State and local governments are also setting asbestos exposure standards and, perhaps more significantly, the business community is reducing asbestos exposure even where not required to do so by law such as in new commercial buildings. This is due to the heightened awareness of the problems of asbestos and the desire of business to protect itself both from possible liability to those who may be injured and from having to redo some of its construction if government regulation of asbestos in commercial buildings does begin.[5]

The United States can also claim some success concerning air and water quality. Most of us know of a river or lake that was once too polluted for

4. *Earth '88: Changing Geographic Perspectives* (Washington, DC: National Geographic Society, 1988) pp. 276–279.

5. "Public Concern over Asbestos Still Present," *Resources*, Volume 10, No. 4 (Exton, PA: The Environmental Resources Management Group, Autumn, 1988) pp. 1, 4.

swimming but that is now considered safe. On the other hand, the number of hazardous waste spills in and around U.S. waters has increased significantly.[6] In considering our air, its quality has generally improved with steady reductions of emissions of particulate matter, sulphur dioxide, and carbon monoxide. The reductions for each of these pollutants was in the 15–30% range over a decade,[7] and the decreases have been achieved while the Gross National Product has increased by well over fifty per cent. Although particulate and sulfur oxide emissions have stabilized, carbon monoxide emissions have continued to decline.[8]

Our air pollution efforts have been relatively successful; however, many old air pollution problems still remain, and new problems have arisen. Despite our success in emission reduction for certain pollutants, over 100 American cities remain in non-compliance with federally mandated air quality standards. For example, smog caused by ozone pollution from automobile exhausts reaches extremely high, health-endangering levels in many cities during the summer months. Excessive ozone levels are also being found in rural areas where it is said to be causing crop losses amounting to billions of dollars. These effects are at least partly due to the number of miles driven having increased by more than 20% in the 1980's.[9]

The adverse effects of ozone and carbon monoxide air pollution from automobiles are problems that we have been aware of for many years. Other air related pollution problems that require government attention have only manifested themselves recently. Among these are acid rain and the depletion of the atmospheric ozone layer. The sources of acid rain are basically sulphur oxides and nitrogen oxides. Sulphur oxide emissions have decreased by about 15% in ten years, but still amount to about 20 million metric tons per year. Nitrogen oxides, also emitted at about 20 million metric tons per year, have shown no decline in total amount of emissions. There has been much discussion of acid rain in Congress, and many pieces of legislation have been introduced to control it. The costs of control are very high, and reaching an acceptable compromise about who should bear those costs stood in the way of enactment of meaningful legislation specifically addressed to con-

---

6. Council on Environmental Quality, *Environmental Quality 1986* (Washington, DC: 1988) Appendix C, Table 2–17b.

7. Ibid., Tables 3–16, 3–17, 3–18.

8. Council on Environmental Quality, *Environmental Quality 1991* (Washington, DC: 1992) Part II, Figures 13a, b, and e. These CEQ reports are issued annually and contain hundreds of pages of Tables and Figures showing environmental trends concerning topics such as energy, water and air quality, land use, and hazardous substances.

9. "The Planet Strikes Back!," *National Wildlife* (National Wildlife Federation, Feb.—March, 1989) p. 35.

trolling acid rain until 1990. The acid rain problem and the 1990 acid rain amendments to the Clean Air Act are discussed in detail in Chapter 3.

An air pollution problem even more recent than acid rain in terms of general recognition is depletion of the atmospheric ozone layer by chemicals called chlorofluorocarbons (CFCs) and halons. While ground level ozone is a harmful air pollutant, naturally occurring atmospheric ozone is necessary to prevent solar ultraviolet radiation from reaching the earth's surface. Adverse effects of ozone layer depletion almost certainly include an increased incidence of skin cancer and may include depression of the human immune system and a decrease in photosynthesis and crop yields.[10] The ozone depletion problem was first widely publicized in 1985. With amazing speed, by January 1, 1989, the Montreal Protocol on Substances That Deplete The Ozone Layer entered into force as 29 countries and the European Community had formally ratified the protocol.[11] The protocol required the halving of CFC emissions from their 1986 levels by 1998 and the freezing of the level of halon emissions at their 1986 levels starting in 1992. As discussed in Chapter 9, it is hoped that ozone layer destruction will peak by 2000, and the protective layer will begin to get thicker.

In addition to the pollution related problems discussed above that still require governmental control, other areas of environmental concern continue to need to be addressed by the legal system. With respect to waste, we have not solved problems like finding appropriate disposal sites for our huge volume of waste, reducing the amount of waste needing disposal by implementing widespread recycling or reuse approaches, and finding the funds to pay for the cleanup of existing hazardous waste sites. Population related issues have not been resolved. These include worldwide and especially third world population growth, immigration and its effects on an individual country, the impacts of population growth on rural areas, and, of course, the legality of abortion. Energy issues also continue to be hotly debated and are the subject of substantial government intervention.

The quantity of U.S. total domestic energy consumption appears to have stabilized,[12] but problems associated with the individual sources of energy remain. The burning of high sulfur coal and oil is a major contributor to acid rain. The transport of oil by the Alaskan pipeline has reportedly had much greater adverse effects on wildlife habitat and soil erosion than was

---

10. Shea, C.P., "Protecting the Ozone Layer," World Watch Institute, *State of the World 1989* (New York: Norton, 1989) p. 78.

11. *International Environment Reporter* (Washington, DC: Bureau of National Affairs, Inc., January 11, 1989) p. 3.

12. Council on Environmental Quality, *Environmental Quality 1986* (Washington, DC: 1988) Appendix C. Table 1–25.

predicted,[13] and tanker oil spills still create major environmental disasters even though controls have become stricter. Our state governments are as concerned as ever about whether to rely on nuclear power with its operating safety hazards and its radioactive waste disposal problems. A newly perceived energy problem is that the burning of fossil fuels and resulting carbon dioxide likely is a major source of the greenhouse effect which appears to be producing a global warming trend.

The examples noted in our brief status report on the environment indicate that government involvement in environmental control is certainly still necessary, but that, at least in the United States, significant progress has been made on environmental matters. Also, the vast majority of Americans are today highly sensitive to the existence of environmental issues and now believe that those issues are of major personal concern to them. This awareness is bound to lead to further improvement of environmental conditions in the United States. With regard to other parts of the world, the environmental status is not nearly as good, and the environmental prospects cannot now be viewed with the same optimism.

The third world, or the developing countries, are in a quite poor environmental state today and will need a great deal of help in order to achieve a sound environmental future. World population is growing by about 85 million people per year, and it is projected that 90% of the future population growth will occur in the developing countries. The source of 80% of all illness in the developing world is unsafe or inadequate water supplies and sanitation. With rare exception, all the cities with the worst air quality are in the developing countries.[14] The developing countries also face environmental problems not often considered in the industrialized world—food, clothing, and shelter. Although the 1972 Declaration of The United Nations Conference on The Human Environment called for the industrialized countries to make efforts to reduce the gap between themselves and the developing countries, that gap continues to exist and likely is widening.

The financial resources simply do not exist in the developing countries for them to solve their own environmental problems and provide decent living conditions for their people. The industrialized nations will have to bear the financial burden of improving environmental conditions throughout the world. International cooperation with respect to the global environment has been shown to be possible by the adoption of the Montreal Protocol concerning

13. "The Planet Strikes Back!," *National Wildlife* (National Wildlife Federation, Feb.—March, 1989) p.37.

14. *World Resources 1988–89*, A Report by The World Resources Institute and The International Institute for Environment and Development (New York: Basic Books, Inc., 1988) p. 171.

ozone depletion, and the problems of the developing countries should also be seen as global environmental problems. For example, unchecked population growth produces greater demands for cleared land which results in the burning of tropical rain forests, the greenhouse effect, and global climate changes. Even without addressing the question of whether it is morally right to allow a large part of the world to be environmentally poor, it is in the self-interest of the industrialized countries to have environmental conditions in the developing countries improve drastically. Throughout the world, as well as in the United States, there is certainly the need for a significant increase in environmental controls.

3. Legislative Perspectives

Having considered the issue of whether legislative environmental controls are needed, let's briefly note two contrasting points of view about how to regulate various types of activities affecting the environment. Consider the hypothetical "pure economist" vs. the hypothetical "pure ecologist." While both are concerned with the environment, the economist would tend to balance environmental concerns with the economic benefits to be derived from an activity and allow environmental harm when it is outweighed by the economic benefits. On the other hand, the ecologist's tendency is to allow activities only if they are not detrimental to the environment: activities which are detrimental to the environment should be banned regardless of their economic benefit.[15] Diagrammatically, the resulting legislative alternatives would be:

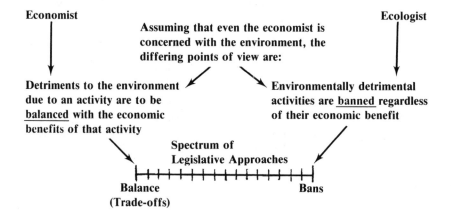

Economist

Ecologist

Assuming that even the economist is concerned with the environment, the differing points of view are:

Detriments to the environment due to an activity are to be balanced with the economic benefits of that activity

Environmentally detrimental activities are banned regardless of their economic benefit

Spectrum of Legislative Approaches

Balance (Trade-offs)

Bans

---

15. Heller, W., "Coming to Terms With Growth and the Environment," In *Energy, Economic Growth, and the Environment*, S.Schurr, Ed., 3:4–29 (1971).

There is, of course, a spectrum between the legislative poles of always balancing benefits and detriments (allowing trade-offs) and of always banning detrimental activity. The type and magnitude of a particular environmental problem are relevant to where on that spectrum our legislatures should place themselves. Is the environmental problem one of physical health or mostly one of aesthetics? Is a health problem one which has proven, drastic consequences for large numbers of people, or is the health problem speculative, relatively minor with respect to effects, or one involving very few people? Also quite relevant to where on the legislative spectrum a particular legislature will place itself is the degree of governmental control which is politically saleable. How many people favored a total shutdown of our automobile plants (with the resulting unemployment and economic decline) because the automakers could not meet the requirements of the Clean Air Act? Extensions of the Clean Air Act deadlines on automakers have been a trade-off clearly mandated by our political process. As we consider various pieces of environmental legislation, we will see that many are quite balance-oriented, but some provisions are on the "ban" side of the spectrum.

With the above introduction, we will leave for the reader's determination the question of whether and to what extent we need government-imposed environmental controls, and, if so, where on the balance/ban spectrum of legislative approaches our government should be on any particular environmental issue. Regardless of our individual viewpoints on what should be the degree of involvement between government and the environment, we do have a substantial body of environmental law in existence at the federal, state, and local levels, and it is to the question of what the law is that we now turn our attention. Let us then begin to consider what the law is by first looking at the sources of power for governmental regulation of the environment.

C. WHERE IT COMES FROM

The basic source of federal power with respect to the environment is found in Article I, Section 8 of the United States Constitution (the Commerce Clause) which vests in Congress the power "to regulate Commerce . . . among the several States . . . ." Historically, this granting to the federal government of the power to regulate interstate commerce (as contrasted to intrastate commerce) was based largely on the idea of preventing states from enacting laws which, although they might be beneficial to one state, would have a detrimental effect on the economic system of the new nation. Actions which had been taken by individual states, such as discriminating against goods produced in other states, resulted in adverse economic effects on other states and on the nation as a whole. These types of actions contributed significantly to the weakness the country experienced under the Articles of Confederation. The new Constitution sought to remedy that weakness by giving Congress the authority to regulate interstate commerce.

Although the words have not changed, the past 200 years have seen massive expansion of the scope of the Commerce Clause from what was likely its originally intended function. That expansion, in the nature of broad powers claimed by Congress, has been found by the courts to be within Congress' power under the Constitution, and today, Congress' power is said to include not only the regulation of interstate commerce, but also activities carried on wholly within one state but which have effects on interstate commerce. Clearly, a natural gas pipeline from one state to others is a matter of interstate commerce and therefore, environmental regulation with respect to the pipeline is within the federal power, but what about local rubbish disposal? Consider the following chain of events: the disposal of rubbish at a local disposal site might lead to runoffs after rains; such runoffs might pollute a lake; polluted lake waters have fewer sport fish in them; fewer sport fish means fewer fishermen; fewer fishermen buy less gasoline and fishing equipment; gasoline and fishing equipment are items produced and marketed in interstate commerce. Thus a rubbish disposal activity which is wholly within one state may have an effect on interstate commerce. Since Congress has been found to have the authority under the Commerce Clause to regulate activities which affect interstate commerce, Congress has the authority, if it chooses to use it, to regulate local rubbish disposal.

One might contend that the effect on interstate commerce due to what happens at one local dump in rural New England is quite small and that Congress' control does not extend to this small dump. The United States Supreme Court answered that argument in the context of a farmer who was growing wheat for consumption on his own farm, but in an amount in excess of his quota under federal legislation. The Court found that his excess production resulted in reduced demand for wheat in the marketplace and, while the farmer's "contribution to the demand for wheat may be trivial by itself . . . his contribution, taken together with that of many others similarly situated, is far from trivial."[16] The concept that Congress' power includes activities which affect interstate commerce, together with the finding that small effects may be regulated since they are large when viewed cumulatively, indicates that the courts have given us a very broad interpretation of Congress' power under the Commerce Clause. Just as the one small farmer was found to be under Congress' control, so could the one small dump in rural New England be subject to environmental regulation by the federal government

---

16. *Wickard v. Filburn*, 317 U.S. 111, 127 (1942).

pursuant to the power of Congress under the Commerce Clause of the United States Constitution. In fact, small rural dumps are subject to federal control under the Resource Conservation and Recovery Act, and, pursuant to that act, concerns about run-offs from landfills have led to the proposed requirement that landfills be lined to trap materials that might otherwise leach out of them and enter the groundwater.[17]

In addition to regulation at the federal level, there exists extensive environmental regulation at the state and local levels of government. The source of power for environmental regulation at these levels is the "police power," the power to protect the public health, public safety and the general welfare. The police power is inherent in the sovereign which is the state, and is also delegated by the states to the local governments that the states create. There are limits on the exercise of the state's police powers, such as the constitutional prohibitions against the taking of private property without just compensation discussed in Chapter 4. It would be fair to say, however, that the police power gives quite broad authority to state and local governments to regulate with respect to environmental matters.

D. HOW TO FIND THE LAW

The law on a given question is sometimes unclear. For example, the language in a statute may be subject to more than one reasonable interpretation, or there may be a conflict between two regulations which purport to control the same activity. In most situations, however, the law is quite clear if one can find it. Finding the law is largely a matter of understanding what the sources of the law are, being familiar with a few rather simple systems for gaining access to these sources, and going to a law library or other library which has basic legal materials. Table I is a shorthand version of the narrative description for finding the law which follows. Although this description may appear complex, if one proceeds a step at a time through the process while in the library, the complexity will rapidly disappear.

One major distinction to be made when considering the sources of law is that between the so-called common law and law by legislation. Law by legislation is law which has been enacted through the legislative process of any level of government. Congress' National Environmental Policy Act (NEPA), the Freshwater Wetlands Act of the State of New York, and the zoning ordinance of the Town of Barnard, Vermont are all examples of legislation. In contrast to legislation, the common law has often been referred

---

17. See Proposed Rules, 40 CFR § 258.40, in 53 Fed. Reg. 33410.

Table I.   Where to Look for the Law (Primary Sources)

Level of Government	Location of Legislative Law	Location of Administrative Law (Regulations)	Location of Common Law and Interpretations of Legislative and Administrative Law
Federal	United States Code United States Code Annotated United States Statutes at Large United States Code Service	Code of Federal Regulations Federal Register	[a]United States Reports (U.S.) Supreme Court Reports – Lawyers' Edition Supreme Court Reporter (S. Ct.) [b]Federal Reporter (F. or F.2d) [c]Federal Supplement (F.Supp.) Federal Administrative Agency decisions in publications such as the Public Utilities Reports.
State	(Name of State) Statutes	State Administrative Codes and State Administrative Regulations	[d]Regional Reporters State Reporters State Administrative Agency decisions in widely varying types of publications
Local	(Name of Municipality) Ordinances	Local Administrative Regulations	Local Administrative agency decisions in widely varying types of publications

[a]United States Supreme Court.
[b]U.S. Circuit Courts of Appeals.
[c]U.S. District Courts.
[d]Regional Reporters report cases from many states in the region.

to as judge-made law because courts have determined that the facts of a situation are such that they should provide a remedy even though there has been no legislative enactment. One example of common law action which is often used in environmental matters is the "nuisance" action. An activity of X which causes a substantial and unreasonable interference with Y's use and enjoyment of Y's land will constitute a common law nuisance, and a court will provide a remedy for Y even though no legislation prohibits X's activity or provides Y with a remedy. Both the common law and legislative law exist at the state and federal levels. In Chapter 3, using aircraft noise as an example, we will consider what happens when there is a conflict between state or local law and federal law. A less complicated situation exists where there is a conflict between legislation and the common law at the same level of government. In such a situation, the common law is overridden by the will of the legislative process.

Federal legislative law (also known as "statutory law") is enacted by the Congress. At the end of each session, all of the legislation enacted in that session is compiled and published in chronological order in the *United States Statutes at Large*. While these volumes have subject indexes, they are not cumulative, and it would therefore be necessary to search through many volumes to find all of the statutes relating to a given topic. The federal statutes have therefore been codified, which means that they are arranged in a subject-oriented manner under fifty broad topics called titles. The official codification, which is called the United States Code (U.S.C.), is revised every six years and is updated between revisions by annual hardbound supplements. Two major lawbook publishers, West Publishing Company and Lawyers' Cooperative Publishing Company, publish unofficial versions known as United States Code Annotated (U.S.C.A.) and United States Code Service (U.S.C.S.), respectively. Both of these sets are updated by the issuance of annual "pocket parts"—supplemental pamphlets which fit into pockets at the back of the hardbound volumes. U.S.C.A. and U.S.C.S. are more useful than the official codification because, in addition to the statutory language, they contain references to court decisions and other valuable research aids. If one wanted to find the provisions of NEPA, the National Environmental Policy Act, one might look in the "Popular Name Table" of the General Index of U.S.C.A. and find that NEPA is PL 91–190, Jan. 1, 1970, 83 Stat. 852 (Title 42, §§ 4321, 4331–4335, 4341–4347). NEPA is thus Public Law 91–190 which appears at volume 83 of the *United States Statutes at Large*, beginning on page 852. The provisions of NEPA also appear in Title 42 of the U.S.C., U.S.C.A. and U.S.C.S. in sections 4321, 4331–4335 and 4341–4347. Other access methods are possible depending on what you know and what you are seeking. For example, if the popular name were unknown, but the subject matter was known, one might look in the index of U.S.C.A. under "Environmental Policy" in order to find provisions concerning the subject matter. Once the above-mentioned books are picked up and inspected, finding federal statutory law is quite simple; however, care must be taken to be sure that the law you find is up to date. This is done by checking the supplement volume of U.S.C. or the "pocket part" updates which are found in the backs of the volumes of U.S.C.A. and U.S.C.S. In this way, amendments to NEPA since its original enactment in 1970 may be found.

State statutes may be found using similar tools in the state statute books which are published individually by each state and are once again readily obtainable in the libraries. Local legislative law is usually available at libraries in the local geographic area or through the local government unit itself.

When we come to finding the common law, the locating system is not much different from that used in finding legislative law. The basic structure and relationship of the federal and state court systems are shown in Figure 9. At both the federal and state level, court decisions are arranged and cited on a chronological basis by volume and page number in a "reporter" which contains the decisions of a particular court. United States Supreme Court decisions may be found in the United States Reports (U.S.), the Supreme Court Reporter (S.Ct.), or the Lawyers' edition of the Supreme Court Reports (Law. Ed.). Lower federal court decisions are found in the Federal Reporter (Fed. or F. and F.2d for the later second series of the Federal Reporter) if they are United States Circuit Court of Appeals cases and in the Federal Supplement (F.Supp.) if they are United States District Court cases. State court decisions appear in regional reporters such as the North Eastern Reporter (N.E.) and the Pacific Reporter (P.) as well as in official State Reporters such as the Vermont Reports. It should be noted that while legislation is enacted through the legislative process and the common law is made by courts without action by the legislature, courts become involved with legislation by virtue of their role as interpreters of legislation. Thus, the fourth column of Table I shows the location of both the court decisions involving the common law and those decisions which provide interpretations of legislative law. Court decisions which contribute to the body of common law and those which interpret legislative law are all reported together and are all cited in the same manner. As examples, the common law nuisance case of *Boomer v. Atlantic Cement Co.* is 257 N.E.2d 870, and *Calvert Cliffs Coordinating Committee v. Atomic Energy Commission*, a case which interprets NEPA, is 449 F.2d 1109. This means that the *Boomer* decision appears in volume 257 of the second series of the North Eastern Reporter and begins on page 870.

If one knows the citation of a case, finding the case is a one-step process. If one knows only the name of the case or if one does not know of a particular case but wishes to find cases about a given topic, the additional step of consulting a reference tool such as a digest or legal encyclopedia must be added. There is a *Federal Practice Digest* and there are other digests arranged

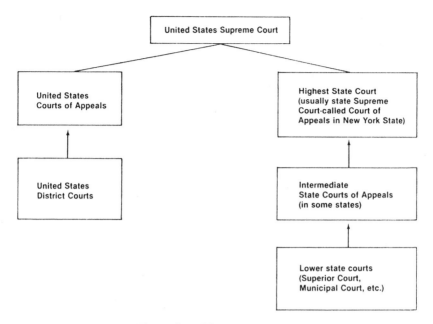

Figure 9. The court structure.

by region (the *Pacific Digest*), by state (the *Vermont Digest*), and chronologically (the *Decennial* and *General Digests*). These digests provide brief abstracts of cases, as well as case names and citations, under numerous subject matter headings. An example of a digest abstract is shown in Figure 10. In addition, the digests contain tables of cases listed alphabetically. Therefore, if one knows the name of a specific case but not its citation, the citation can be found in these alphabetical tables. Legal encyclopedias such as *American Jurisprudence 2d* and *Corpus Juris Secundum* can provide one with general discussions of many topics and case citations relevant to those topics. By using these reference tools and their various indices, cases which discuss the topic of one's interest may be located. Figure 11 shows an encyclopedia entry.

Just as we noted with respect to legislation, care must be taken when reading court decisions to be sure to determine whether those decisions are still "good law" or whether they have been overruled or narrowed in applicability by later cases. The analogue to checking the "pocket parts" and supplements in the statute books is to check the cases you have read in the volume of *Shepard's Citations* that applies to the court that wrote the decision. *Shepard's* is organized by listing cases by volume and by the page number on which they begin. Under each case citation, all other cases which have cited the case being checked are listed by their volume and page

⟨⟩25.10(6.5)   HEALTH & ENVIRONMENT   60 F P D 4th—378

For later cases see same Topic and Key Number in Pocket Part

mental Policy Act of 1969, § 2 et seq., 42 U.S.C.A. § 4321 et seq.
Friends of the Earth v. Hall, 693 F.Supp. 904.

Army Corps of Engineers' decision not to conduct further studies and not to prepare supplemental environmental impact statement concerning potential environmental impact from bioturbation before granting Navy dredge and fill permit was unreasonable in light of scientific study disclosing that magnitude of risks posed by new organisms was unknown. West's RCWA 90.58.010–90.58.930; Federal Water Pollution Control Act Amendments of 1972, §§ 401, 404, 404(q), 511(a), as amended, 33 U.S.C.A. §§ 1341, 1344, 1344(q), 1371(a); 33 U.S.C.A. § 407; 5 U.S.C.A. §§ 551 et seq., 706(2)(D).
Friends of the Earth v. Hall, 693 F.Supp. 904.

In developing supplemental environmental impact statement for dredge and fill operation, Army Corps of Engineers was required to completely disclose agency criticism of monitoring program and to take public comment on suffi-

ments and hearings, announced time extension in Federal Register and local papers, and adequately evaluated federal report and comments that report had generated when preferred route for expressway was selected. National Environmental Policy Act of 1969, § 102, 42 U.S.C.A. § 4332.
Coalition Against a Raised Expressway, Inc. v. Dole, 835 F.2d 803.

C.A.9 (Cal.) 1986. Environmental impact statements prepared in connection with proposed construction of road in national forest were inadequate by failing to sufficiently disclose impact of road construction on water quality or to describe what measures would be taken to mitigate adverse impacts on water quality. National Environmental Policy Act of 1969, § 2 et seq., 42 U.S.C.A. § 4321 et seq.
Northwest Indian Cemetery Protective Ass'n v. Peterson, 795 F.2d 688, certiorari granted Lyng v. Northwest Indian Cemetery Protective Association, 107 S.Ct. 1971, 481 U.S. 1036, 95 L.Ed.2d 812, reversed 108 S.Ct. 1319, 485 U.S. 439, 99 L.Ed.2d 534.

Figure 10.   Digest abstract sample.

§ 77   POLLUTION CONTROL   61A Am Jur 2d

§ 77. – Federal aid to highways.

Laws concerning federal aid in construction of highways[25] require full consideration of possible adverse environmental effects including air pollution and are required to be consistent with any approved plan for the implementation of any ambient air quality standard.[26] But highway construction cannot be nullified on the basis of inconsistency with such plans, where there is no approved implementation plan.[27]

Figure 11.   Encyclopedia entry.

numbers. Abbreviations are used to indicate whether the subsequent cases merely mention the case being checked, follow the case being checked as the controlling case (f), or whether the subsequent cases took other action such as reversing a lower court's decision when the case was appealed (r) or overruling the case in a subsequent case involving another situation (o). By "Shepardizing" the cases you read, you will be able to determine the current importance of that case as "the law" as well as find additional later cases which may discuss the topic in which you are interested. The *Shepard's* entries for the case abstract shown in Figure 10 (485 U.S. 439) are listed in the highlighted portion of Figure 12.

Vol. 485   UNITED STATES SUPREME COURT REPORTS

Mich	O'Connor	455NW44	– 360 –	s290Ark47	– 409 –	Cir. 1
443NW136	1st	Minn	(99LE380)	Ark	(99LE470)	909F2d'621
Minn	Cir. D.C.	460NW16	(108SC1184)	s716SW755	(108SC1261)	Cir. 2
450NW606	919F2d²151	Miss	s481US1036	cc748SW668	s484US813	852F2d'650
ND	919F2d¹152	552So2d824	s648FS1234	Cir. 2	58USLW	852F2d655
427NW309	f726FS²873	NY	s648FS1241	d898F2d¹327	[4628	688FS'960
NJ	742FS¹1194	532NYS2d	486US461	909F2d¹73	Cir. D.C.	e715FS1249
121NJ77	746FS¹196	[818	487US16	715FS1273	853F2d991	716FS758
577A2d1243	746FS¹216	Ore	487US²458	Cir. 8	Cir. 4	716FS763
NY	Cir. 1	306Ore187	58USLW	d743FS'681	852F2d782	720FS'330
558NYS2d	683FS²297	759P2d249	[4411	Cir. 9	Cir. 8	749FS'1263
[974	743FS²100	Tenn	Cir. D.C.	f878F2d265	745FS555	115BRW'412
Tex	Cir. 2	802SW212	d887F2d¹292	Ariz	Cir. 10	117BRW'780
798SW896	d686FS'80	755SW94	f887F2d²293	162Az593	880F2d1165	124BRW'445
805SW506	689FS²126	800SW307	j887F2d303	785P2d113	CIT	Cir. 4
	Cir. 4	Wash	746FS¹195	Ark	747FS739	f122BRW'684
– 312 –	907F2d¹444	111Wsh2d29	746FS²195	296Ark277	Calif	Cir. 5
(99LE333)	Cir. 6	759P2d369	Cir. 1	753SW866	762P2d455	c860F2d'1311
(108SC1157)	d896F2d¹199	Wis.	f916F2d²747	Colo		873F2d781
s479US1083	923F2d¹473	145Wis2d41	925F2d503	769P2d1059	– 415 –	f873F2d786
s798F2d1450	Cir. 8	152Wis2d513	743FS102	Ind	(99LE515)	f873F2d788
cc704FS5	723FS¹1352	426NW336	Cir. 2	531NE233	(108SC1306)	873F2d789
j486US483	726FS¹1191	449NW857	895F2d¹65	NH	Cir. 2	878F2d887
486US897	Cir. 9		905F2d¹635	131NH97	742FS¹803	f878F2d889
·487US479	847F2d¹512	– 340 –	915F2d¹63	550A2d112	Cir. 4	906F2d'1051
j487US495	914F2d²1228	(99LE357)	690FS¹1273	NY	750FS200	Cir. 7
j58USLW	Cir. 10	(108SC1173)	690FS²1273	561NYS2d	Cir. 6	854F2d207
[4444	f687FS¹543	s482US913	f733FS¹636	[973	847F2d¹1233	879F2d1546
58USLW	Cir. 11	s807F2d65	735FS1145	Pa	732FS871	f919F2d'1285
[4745	748FS²1525	f485US973	e735FS¹1146	125PaC454	Cir. 8	f919F2d1297
j58USLW		Cir. 4	Cir. 3	557A2d1163	879F2d400	724FS'620
[5020	O'Connor	f846F2d¹6	j845F2d1211		902F2d1351	108BRW'667
124FRD346	2nd	Cir. 5	725FS¹235	– 399 –	Cir. 9	Cir. 8
Cir. D.C.	Cir. D.C.	f844F2d226	Cir. 4	(99LE460)	872F2d929	743FS'660
d847F2d904	731FS¹1129	f844F2d¹228	926F2d²366	(108SC1255)	Cir. 10	Cir. 9
851F2d375	Cir. 2	Cir. 7	737FS¹953	s484US813	721FS¹268	e895F2d'587
852F2d1343	742FS¹1260	872F2d1024	Cir. 6	s802F2d860	Cir. 11	c913F2d'1424
Cir. 2	Cir. 6	Wis	Dk 6	s810F2d558	913F2d1571	756FS'1275
Dk 2	d896F2d¹199	157Wis2d8	90-1583	s609FS1360	Cir. 1	Cir. 10
90-7317	f730FS'85	458NW816	f854F2d¹827	f485US1018	252CaR458	f130FRD'452
j891F2d1031			922F2d341	f485US¹1018		Cir. 11
j903F2d166	Brennan	– 351 –	Cir. 7	486US209	– 439 –	105BRW'105
d915F2d63	Cir. 6	(99LE368)	847F2d²1220	486US291	(99LE534)	113BRW'727
753FS441	d896F2d¹199	(108SC1179)	Cir. 8	Cir. D.C.	(108SC1319)	124BRW'605
Cir. 3		s481US1047	753FS²800	895F2d¹769	s764F2d581	Cir. Fed.
747FS1527	_____	485US710	Cir. 10	f905F2d1567	Ore	d885F2d'861
Cir. 4		Cir. D.C.	d687FS¹543	Cir. 2	307Ore714	Ala
745FS327	Calif	907F2d1178	d687FS²543	795F2d688	763P2d149	540So2d62
Cir. 5	47C3d486	Cir. 2	Colo	s565FS586	SD	549So2d482
889F2d576	764P2d1067	867F2d¹752	758P2d1370	f58USLW	447NW516	571So2d1033
Cir. 7	253CaR690	Cir. 3	758P2d1386	[4436	Vt	Ariz
845F2d147	DC	859F2d¹2	Md	58USLW	577A2d261	159Az394
Cir. 8	573A2d1309	865F2d¹58	315Md287	[4441	Wash	767P2d1184
e897F2d924	581A2d351	Cir. 5	554A2d383	Cir. D.C.	57WApl32	Conn
j897F2d927	581A2d355	j901F2d62	PR	d850F2d733	112Wsh2d	212Ct638
728FS1419	585A2d1347	Cir. 6	1990JTS48	850F2d739	[372	563A2d299
Cir. 9	Fla	882F2d¹1080	f1990JTS48	Cir. 1	112Wsh2d	DC
898F2d1390	538So2d460	Cir. 7	Cir. 9	885F2d²944	[397	543A2d1365
908F2d421	Ga	f925F2d¹1067	– 386 –	Cir. 2	114Wsh2d	556A2d1085
f731FS419	260Ga671	684FS'1990	(99LE402)	847F2d¹1049	[363	562A2d136
754FS784	260Ga679	Cir. 10	(108SC1200)	914F2d355	114Wsh2d	Fla
Cir. 10	398SE549	16ClC¹82	s479US1083	689FS²129	[414	526So2d744
729FS1289	398SE555	DC	Cir. 9	728FS²963	114Wsh2d	526So2d745
Cir. 11	Md	585A2d156	853F2d638	Cir. 3	[891	531So2d1262
j867F2d1349	318Md447	586A2d694		919F2d195	787P2d574	531So2d1293
29MJ115	318Md473	Cir. 2	– 388 –	700FS¹1328	787P2d1364	531So2d1326
29MJ132	569A2d609	401SE715	(99LE450)	753FS1303	788P2d1071	534So2d736
	569A2d622	Mich	(108SC1201)	Cir. 5	792P2d156	537So2d500
First	Mich	435Mch561	s482US124	730FS¹749		549So2d1167
Cir. 2	434Mch47	435Mch570	s488US808	f350F2d1548	– 478 –	563So2d835
d686FS'80	434Mch433	460NW202	s490US1044	f350F2d'1549	(99LE565)	564So2d557
	455NW19	460NW206	CIT	Cir. Fed.	(108SC1340)	569So2d522
			714FS1227	917F2d1579	484US813	570So2d1126
		– 395 –	721FS¹309	CIT	Okla	Ga
		(99LE455)		714FS1227	733P2d396	400SE927
		(108SC1204)		721FS¹309		*Continued*
		s484US895				

542

Figure 12. Shepard's Citation entry example.

Having considered how to find the law as enacted through the legislative process and the common law as made by the courts, we should next consider a second major distinction in sources of law—the distinction between legislation and regulation. Legislation is the product of the legislative process, and it is binding unless it is violative of a constitutional provision. Regulations are usually the product of the administrative agencies, and they have the force of law if there is legislation which authorizes the creation of the regulation and the regulation is consistent with what the legislation mandates. Just as legislation exists at various levels of government, regulations can also be developed at the federal, state, and local levels. At the state and local levels there are different systems for publishing regulations depending on your location, and librarian assistance should be obtained. The system for finding federal regulations is easily described.

The permanent home of a federal regulation is in the Code of Federal Regulations (CFR). CFR is organized and cited by title and section numbers. Title 40 is Protection of Environment. Title 10 is Energy. 40 CFR § 39.100–39.150 sets forth the EPA's administrative implementation of the Federal Water Pollution Control Act with respect to loan guarantees for wastewater treatment works. CFR is completely revised once a year (one quarter of the titles are revised in each calendar quarter), and, prior to finding its way into a revision of CFR, a new federal rule or regulation will appear in the Federal Register (Fed. Reg.) which publishes activities of the federal agencies on a chronological basis. The Federal Register is published each business day, and the contents for the day are shown at the beginning of the issue. Cites to the Federal Register are by volume and page. For example, at 56 Fed. Reg. 6986, EPA established tolerance levels for the pesticide deltamethrin on tomatoes. This February 21, 1991, Federal Register publication amended 40 CFR part 180 to include § 180.435 which limits the residue on tomatoes to 0.2 parts per million of deltamethrin. Revisions of CFR which are published after February 21, 1991, will reflect this new tolerance level; however, the tolerance level contained in the Federal Register is effective even prior to its being incorporated into the next CFR revision. Administrative regulations may be interpreted by courts or by the agencies themselves. The various locations of interpretations of administrative law may be seen in column four of Table I.

Additional sources of information concerning environmental law include periodicals and looseleaf services. Most law schools publish law reviews either annually or more frequently. Articles and Notes in these periodicals usually provide in-depth analysis and commentary on various aspects of the law including environmental law. Some reviews have devoted themselves entirely to publication of articles relating to environmental matters. Law review articles are indexed in the *Index to Legal Periodicals* and in the *Current Law Index* and may be found by author or by subject matter. For keeping up-to-date on changes in the law, numerous looseleaf services which provide information on environmental topics can be consulted. A few illustrative examples might be the *Environment Reporter* from the Bureau of National Affairs (BNA), Federal Energy Guidelines from the Federal Energy Regulatory Commission, and the *Environmental Law Reporter* from the Environmental Law Institute (ELI). These contain material such as current developments, in addition to statutory and regulatory material.

In closing this section on how to find the law, we should note that most law libraries now have computerized research capabilities. Finding the law with the help of computers is a well-established approach to legal research today. The LEXIS and WESTLAW legal research systems, widely available at law libraries and other sites, allow users to obtain the full text of legal documents from numerous databases. These databases include, among others, federal and state statutes, regulations, and case law, periodicals such as law reviews, and some looseleaf services. The systems also have a specialized environmental law database. The number and extent of the databases for legal research are growing rapidly.

The databases may be accessed in a variety of ways depending on what you know and what you are trying to find. For example, if you are interested in a subject, asbestos, and you want to find information in a database about asbestos, you type "asbestos" as your key word after having selected the database in which you want to conduct your search. This could result in your getting a huge number of documents, so you would try to narrow your search. If your interest were federal regulations concerning asbestos removal from pipes, as opposed to the medical effects of exposure to asbestos or the removal of asbestos from the air in an industrial operation, you might use the federal regulations database, CFR, and type in the key words "asbestos, removal, pipes" requesting that the key words must appear in the same paragraph of a document or within 50 words of each other. This would narrow your asbestos search and reduce the number of documents obtained significantly. One document you would obtain is 29 CFR § 1910.1101, which requires that employees engaged in the removal of asbestos from pipes must be provided with appropriate respiratory equipment. Of course, if you knew you wanted 29 CFR § 1910.1101 without having to do a topic search, you would simply search by citation, typing in "29 CFR 1910.1101" and using the CFR database.

ADDITIONAL READINGS

Brown, L.R., *State of the World 1991* (New York: W.W. Norton, 1991).
Carson, Rachel L., *Silent Spring* (Boston: Houghton Mifflin, 1962).

Cohen, M.L., Berring, R.C. and Olson, K.C., *How to Find the Law* (St. Paul: West, 1989).

Council on Environmental Quality and Department of State, *The Global 2000 Report to the President* (Great Britain: Penguin Books, Ltd., 1982).

Introductory Guide to Westlaw Research (St. Paul: West, 1990).

Learning LEXIS/NEXIS, A Handbook for Modern Legal Research (Dayton: Mead Data Central, Inc., 1990).

Leopold, A., *A Sand County Almanac* (New York: Ballantine Books Inc., 1949).

Meadows, D.H., Meadows, D.L., and Randers, J., *Beyond the Limits* (Post Mills, VT: Chelsea Green Publishing, 1992).

Meadows, D.H., Meadows, D.L., Randers, J. and Behrens, W. W., III, *The Limits to Growth* (New York: Signet Publishers, 1972).

Odum, E.P., *Ecology and Our Endangered Life Support Systems* (Sunderland, MA: Sinauer Associates, 1989).

Stewart, Thomas A., "Using Market Forces to Save Nature," *Fortune* (January 14, 1991), p. 42.

Yandle, Bruce, *The Political Limits of Environmental Regulation* (Westport, CN: Quorum Books, 1989).

CHAPTER 2

NATIONAL ENVIRONMENTAL POLICY ACT (NEPA)

A. APPLICABILITY OF THE EIS REQUIREMENT—MAJOR FEDERAL ACTIONS SIGNIFICANTLY AFFECTING THE QUALITY OF THE HUMAN ENVIRONMENT

Although NEPA[1] contains provisions which create the Council on Environmental Quality (CEQ) and require an annual Environmental Quality Report from the President to Congress, the most well known, most litigated, most harmful or most beneficial (depending on one's point of view), but clearly the most important single aspect of NEPA is the environmental impact statement (EIS) requirement. In contrast to other federal statutes which we will consider later, this operative mechanism of NEPA is addressed primarily to agencies of the federal government—not individuals, not corporations, and not states. We will see that these other entities may be greatly affected by NEPA because of relationships which they may have with the federal government; however, it is only "all agencies of the Federal Government" that are directed to include as part of their "major Federal actions significantly affecting the quality of the human environment, a detailed statement by the responsible official on—(i) the environmental impact of the proposed action. . . ."[2] Since NEPA applies to "all agencies of the Federal Government," an EIS may be required not only for activities like the Department of Transportation's funding of highway construction, but also for the Comptroller of the Currency's chartering of a bank.

NEPA applies to all federal agencies; however, an EIS is not required every time an agency undertakes to do something. NEPA requires an EIS

---

1. 42 U.S.C.A. § 4321 et seq.; PL 91–190, 83 Stat. 852.

2. PL 91–190, § 102.

only for recommendations or reports on proposals for legislation and other "major Federal actions significantly affecting the quality of the human environment." The issues are which actions are "major" and which actions significantly affect the environment. Let's begin with the words "significantly affecting." Different federal courts in different parts of the country have used different interpretations of these words, but, beginning with the early NEPA court cases, the words have been interpreted broadly. For example, courts have decided that if a project "may cause a significant degradation"[3] or "could have a significant effect"[4] or "arguably will have an adverse environmental impact"[5] or has a "potentially significant adverse effect,"[6] an EIS is required. Today, the CEQ regulations describe "significantly" in terms of "context" and "intensity."[7] The significance of a proposed action may vary depending on its geographical context. For example, if a proposed action is site-specific, significance will likely depend on the effects in the local area as opposed to in the world as a whole. Intensity refers to severity or degree of impact on interests such as public health, unique geographic characteristics, and cultural resources. Consideration should be given to whether the impact of this proposed action taken together with other actions is cumulatively significant. Also, when impacts of a proposal may be both beneficial and adverse, a significant effect may exist, and thus an EIS will be necessary even if the agency believes that on balance the effect will be beneficial.

The word "major" has also been given a broad interpretation by the courts. Numerous different parameters, such as the amount of money to be spent, the geographical size of the area to be covered, and whether the project effects are long-term or short-term, have been used to decide if an action is major. The facts of a particular case are extremely important since they will determine the types of parameters which will be applied. The answer to the question of whether an action is a "major Federal action significantly affecting the quality of the human environment" will depend on which parameters are used. Perhaps the best way to see what are and what are not major actions with significant effects is to list and compare some cases. No case would be needed to decide if NEPA's EIS provision applied to the trans-Alaskan pipeline, but an EIS was also required in the following less clear situations:

---

3. *Save Our Ten Acres v. Kreger*, 472 F.2d 463, 467 (1973).

4. *Minnesota Public Interest Research Group v. Butz*, 498 F.2d 1314, 1320 (1974).

5. *SCRAP v. U.S.*, 346 F. Supp. 189, 201 (1972).

6. *Hanly v. Kleindienst*, 471 F.2d 823, 831 (1972).

7. 40 CFR § 1508.27.

1. adoption of Department of Transportation regulations to increase accessibility of the handicapped to mass transportation;[8]
2. a Department of Housing and Urban Development (HUD) loan of $3.5 million to construct a high-rise apartment building in an area containing no other high-rise buildings in Portland, Oregon;[9]
3. the Army Corps of Engineers' designation of a new waste dumping site in the waters of Western Long Island Sound;[10]
4. the trapping of red fox by the U.S. Fish and Wildlife Service in an effort to protect two endangered species of birds;[11]
5. participation of the United States in Mexican herbicide spraying of marijuana and poppy plants.[12]

In contrast, NEPA was found not to apply to:

1. an action by the Secretary of Transportation approving the crossing of an interstate highway by a huge strip-mining shovel;[13]
2. a HUD-insured loan of $3.7 million to construct a 272-unit apartment complex on 15 acres in Houston, Texas;[14]
3. the federal funding of a landfill containment project that was the result of a court order to remedy problems with the landfill;[15]
4. a decision by the U.S. Fish and Wildlife Service to enforce federal anti-baiting requirements governing the taking of migratory waterfowl;[16]
5. the use of aerial surveillance over federal lands for the detection of illegal marijuana.[17]

Let's compare the two HUD examples and analyze why the results with respect to the need for an EIS might have been different in the two cases. First, consider some possible explanations which are largely independent of the substance of the HUD cases. The two HUD cases were decided in different jurisdictions. Issues of interpretation of a statute like NEPA are usually decided by the Federal District Courts or the Federal Circuit Courts of Appeals. There are different courts in different areas of the country, and

---

8. *American Public Transit Association v. Goldschmidt*, 485 F. Supp. 811 (1980).

9. *Goose Hollow Foothills League v. Romney*, 334 F. Supp. 877 (1971).

10. *Town of Huntington v. Marsh*, 859 F.2d 1134 (1988).

11. *Animal Lovers Volunteers Association v. Cheney*, 795 F. Supp. 991 (1992).

12. *NORML v. Dept. of State*, 452 F. Supp. 1226 (1978).

13. *Citizens Organized to Protect the Environment v. Volpe*, 353 F. Supp. 520 (1972).

14. *Hiram Clarke Civic Club v. Lynn*, 476 F.2d 421 (1973).

15. *Miron v. Menominee County*, 795 F. Supp. 840 (1992).

16. *Calipatria Land Co. v. Lujan*, 793 F. Supp. 241 (1990).

17. *Carol Van Strum v. John C. Lawn*, 1991 U.S. Lexis 3719 (1991).

they often have different ideas on what the law is. Some, but not all, of these differences are resolved by the United States Supreme Court or by Congress. In the absence of a resolution of the conflict by one of these bodies, each lower court opinion is the law within the jurisdiction of that lower court even though the law may thus be different in different parts of the country. It is possible that if the two HUD cases had had identical rather than merely similar facts, the U.S. District Court in Oregon may still have interpreted the "major Federal action" test more broadly than the U.S. Fifth Circuit Court of Appeals in Texas, and an EIS could have been required in Oregon but not in Texas.

Another possible explanation of differing results in similar cases might be that the cases were decided at different times. The country's mood on environmental protection changes, and the mood of the courts also shifts with time. While the HUD cases do not represent time periods with great disparity in the nation's level of environmental concern, it would not be surprising to find an air pollution case with a given set of facts which was decided against industry in the early 1970s, a case with similar facts being decided in favor of industry in the energy shortage years of the 1980s, and similar facts again going against industry in the more air pollution conscious 1990s. A difference in time might also explain the opposite results in the two marijuana cases, but a more likely explanation is that one involved spraying and the other only observation.

Besides explanations based on different jurisdictions or different time periods, the results in the HUD cases can be reconciled because their facts are distinguishable. The dollar amounts in the two cases were nearly the same, but one was a HUD loan and thus involved dollars coming out of the federal treasury. The other case was a HUD-insured loan where the funds would come from private sources, and the only time money would leave the federal treasury would be if the borrower defaulted in repaying the loan. This second situation arguably involves less in the way of direct federal action and thus might not be a major federal action. Another factual explanation might be that the case in Oregon which required an EIS was dealing with a high-rise building in an area with no other high-rise buildings. Even though the Texas case which did not require an EIS was a proposal to build 272 units on 15 acres, the site was in Houston, which is a city that has many instances of inconsistent land uses and little in the way of land use controls. Which actions are major and require an EIS and which actions are not major is often an "I know it when I see it" situation; however, the courts have tended to resolve the doubtful cases in favor of requiring an EIS.

Let's next turn to another part of the "major Federal action . . ." test and consider the words "human environment." Clearly the human environment involves things such as air pollution, water pollution, and toxic chemicals in our food, but it was also interpreted in *Hanly v. Kleindienst* to include subjects such as housing, unemployment, and crime.[18] Thus, in considering the phrase "human environment," some courts gave a broad interpretation to the words used by Congress. That tendency was limited by the U.S. Supreme Court decision in *Metropolitan Edison Co. v. People Against Nuclear Energy*[19] where a residents' association challenged a decision by the Nuclear Regulatory Commission (NRC) to restart a reactor at Three Mile Island, site of the worst nuclear accident in the United States. The plaintiffs claimed that the NRC failed to take into account the psychological stress on local residents caused by reopening the plant and had thus not complied with NEPA. The Court said that, while effects on human health may include psychological health, NEPA is concerned primarily with the "physical environment." Therefore, the NRC did not need to consider the psychological effects of the existence of a risk before that risk had materialized. This decision led the 8th Circuit Court of Appeals to decide, in contrast to *Hanly,* that alleged effects of increasing crime and halting neighborhood development did not require EIS consideration because they were social changes rather physical impacts.[20] The effects on the human environment must be physical rather than socio-economic for an EIS to be required, and even physical effects must be related to humans. An agency action which might have a severe effect on something in nature might not be covered by NEPA unless a substantial link to humans and their needs can be shown.[21] Opinions my differ about whether the destruction of a unique habitat for a type of plant or fish is really a significant effect on the human environment, but we should recognize that, in NEPA, Congress' concern was not for the plant or the fish. While the plant or fish and its unique habitat may be protected under another statute such as the Endangered Species Act, if the habitat's destruction were not demonstrably connected to the human environment, NEPA might not apply, and an EIS might not be necessary.

Having discussed the words "major," "significantly affecting," and "human environment" in the EIS applicability test, let's consider the word "Federal" and note that, while NEPA is addressed to the federal agencies, courts have applied NEPA beyond situations of pure federal action to include

---

18. 471 F.2d 823 (1972).

19. 460 U.S. 766 (1983).

20. *Olmsted Citizens for a Better Community v. U.S.,* 793 F.2d 201 (1986).

21. Section 43.21C.030 of the Revised Code of Washington, Annotated. The Washington State Environmental Policy Act, which is nearly a carbon copy of NEPA with words like "Federal" changed to "State," does not contain the word "human" but says "major actions significantly affecting the quality of the environment."

activities of the private sector and of state and local governments. What are NEPA's effects on nonfederal entities? Certainly there are the economic costs of the EIS process, and those costs are borne by all segments of society. Also, the EIS process may result in a substantial delay before a private company receives a license or permit which it needs to conduct its business or before a state or local government receives a federal grant. A less obvious effect of NEPA on nonfederal entities arises when action which is largely that of private business becomes "federal" because the business has contact with the federal government and the private company is precluded from proceeding with its activity until a federal agency prepares its EIS. An example of this situation was a private developer of housing who had a HUD mortgage guarantee and interest grant. HUD could not provide its assistance until an EIS was filed, but the court also found the private developer could be enjoined from going forward with construction on his own property without HUD aid while HUD prepared its EIS. The court's theory for halting the private developer's action was that HUD's initial commitment to the developer made them "partners" in the undertaking, and, even though he was still only a potential recipient of HUD assistance, the developer had enough contact with HUD so that his action without HUD assistance could be stopped pending a HUD EIS.[22]

The developer in the above situation was seeking government assistance to build housing for low income people. A large number of low income housing developments have been opposed on environmental grounds. The question should be raised of whether plaintiffs in these cases may have sometimes had ulterior motives such as economic or racial discrimination rather than pure environmental protection motives. The further question should be raised of, if it became clear that the motive behind a NEPA complaint was to prevent the construction of housing that would allow poor or minority people to move into a previously all white, middle class community, should a court allow the lawsuit to go forward? On one hand, NEPA was not intended to be a tool of economic or racial discrimination in housing, and if a lawsuit ties up a low income housing development project, the project may become too costly, and it may be stopped. On the other hand, perhaps courts should not look to the motives behind a lawsuit but only consider its merits. If government is providing assistance for a low income housing project, maybe a court should give the same review for environmental compliance that it would give to a proposed highway or a proposed nuclear power plant. It is certainly possible that a plaintiff's motive behind bringing a NEPA action against a proposed nuclear facility is to delay the project

---

22. *Silva v. Romney*, 473 F.2d 287 (1973).

and make it so costly that it will be stopped even if, ultimately, it would have been in compliance with NEPA.

Turning to state and local government projects, we see that they, like the private housing project discussed above, can also become "federalized" and subject to NEPA. Where a state needed federal permits and discretionary approval prior to constructing a highway, the court found NEPA applicable because the federal agency had authority to exercise discretion over the outcome.[23] Yet not all state projects that have federal involvement become "federal actions" and trigger NEPA applicability. Where a state wanted to construct a light rail project and there was federal funding provided for preliminary engineering studies and a federal wetlands permit, the court said NEPA did not apply.[24] Its decision was based on findings that (1) the preliminary studies were not a commitment to further funding, (2) the federal agency had discretion only with respect to a minor part of the overall project as contrasted to the state highway case noted above, and (3) the relationship of the federal and state governments were not akin to a "partnership" such as in the HUD/private developer case discussed above. We may, therefore, conclude that not all situations of federal agency involvement will result in NEPA applicability, but, beyond some degree of federal participation, the private sector and nonfederal governmental bodies may have their activities impeded until the federal agency does its job under NEPA.

It should be noted that, although NEPA is directed at federal agencies, it has had a substantial carryover effect on state efforts at environmental regulation. Many states require environmental impact statements by state agencies when those state agencies undertake a state project that will significantly affect the quality of the environment. While the applicability and comprehensiveness of the state requirements vary among states, some states require at the state level just what is required by NEPA for a federal project.

In summary, if a proposal is for a major federal action significantly affecting the quality of the human environment, NEPA requires the responsible federal agency to prepare an environmental impact statement prior to commencing action under that proposal. Although NEPA requires an EIS from the *federal government* in situations of major *federal* action, the private sector and nonfederal governmental entities are very much affected by the EIS requirement. It should, however, be clearly understood that NEPA is not a statute which prohibits any specific activities by the federal government. What it does require is that environmental factors be taken into account in the decision-making process of whether or not to go forward with a project.

---

23. *Maryland Conservation Council v. Gilchrist,* 808 F.2d 1039 (1986).

24. *Macht v. Skinner,* 916 F.2d 13 (1990).

We will now look at how those factors are taken into account by considering questions involving the content of an EIS.

B.   CONTENT OF ENVIRONMENTAL IMPACT STATEMENTS

An EIS must consider the effect of a proposed action on the human environment. The EIS is a detailed report by the responsible official on:

1. the environmental impact of the proposed action;
2. any adverse environmental effects which cannot be avoided should the proposal be implemented;
3. alternatives to the proposed action;
4. the relationship between local short-term uses of man's environment and the maintenance and enhancement of long-term productivity; and
5. any irreversible and irretrievable commitments of resources which would be involved in the proposed action should it be implemented.[25]

To accomplish the above task, an EIS is supposed to clearly present the environmental impacts of the proposed action and the alternatives to the proposed action with the purpose of sharply defining the issues and providing a sound basis for the decision-maker to choose among the options.[26] Within the alternatives section, the EIS should explore *all reasonable* alternatives including the no action alternative and should identify the agency's preferred alternative. The EIS must describe the affected area concisely using summarized data indicating the impact. The environmental consequences must be scientifically examined in a comparative manner, and steps to mitigate adverse environmental effects as well as unavoidable adverse impacts should be discussed. The most important considerations are the direct and indirect effects caused by any proposed action or alternative. Such effects might include ecological, economic, historical, aesthetic, or social aspects. Indirect effects relate principally to population-induced changes and resultant uses of land, air, and water.

An environmental impact statement will evaluate the proposed action by considering the environmental consequences of the proposed action and alternatives to that proposed action. A cost-benefit analysis, which includes

---

25. PL 91–190, § 102(2)(c).

26. For a complete description of the Council on Environmental Quality guidelines for an EIS, see Appendix A. An example of the content of an EIS may be seen in Appendix B, which contains the Table of Contents and Summary sections of an actual EIS.

environmental costs and benefits as well as other costs and benefits, is used to provide a comprehensive evaluation of the desirability of following the proposed course of action. For example, if flood control could be accomplished to varying degrees depending on which one of five alternative dam configurations was selected, one would want to consider the initial construction cost of each configuration, the operation and maintenance cost for each, and the dollar amount of flood damage which each configuration would be expected to prevent. In addition, NEPA mandates that effects such as the destruction of wildlife and losses in commercial and recreational fishing for each alternative be made a part of the decision-making process. These costs must be put into the decision-making balance just as one would add the cost of cement. Also, some dam configurations might provide increased recreational opportunities such as boating. These benefits are a part of the decision-making process just as are the benefits of avoiding flood damage. NEPA asks that the federal decision-maker incorporate all the costs and all the benefits in his or her evaluation of a proposal, including those costs and benefits which are environmental in nature. Of course, not all elements of decision-making can be expressed in terms of dollars. What is the dollar cost of destroying 500 raccoons, 50 deer, or 10,000 starlings? What is the dollar benefit of saving 10 human lives every 50 years? Would saving those lives be worth an extra expenditure of $500, $500,000 or $500,000,000? An administrator's decision-making process, the evidence of which is the EIS, must consider these less quantifiable aspects of our environment as well as those which are more simply expressible in monetary terms.

Besides dealing with the questions of which parameters should be evaluated in the decision-making process and how these parameters should be evaluated, issues arise concerning the required scope of an environmental impact statement. If a federal agency is proposing a program to lease federal lands for energy production, is an EIS required for the leasing of each individual site, for each geographic leasing area, or only for the establishing of the overall leasing program with its rules and regulations? The Council on Environmental Quality has encouraged the use of overall "umbrella" statements for general programs. The Council believes that umbrella statements foster the desirable end of comprehensive planning and evaluation of long-term environmental goals and effects. The CEQ recognizes, however, that an overall program statement without a particularized statement on, for example, the leasing of site XYZ, may reduce or eliminate consideration of particular environmental problems of special significance at site XYZ. Thus, they have said that individualized statements should also be prepared, in addition to the overall program statement, when the individual actions will have significant impacts not adequately evaluated under the umbrella statement for the whole program. Repetitive discussion of issues that were considered in the general program statement is avoided by "tiering" of environmental impact statements. Tiering says that the EIS for the specific project only needs to summarize any issues which were already discussed in the overall program statement.[27]

A related issue with respect to the required coverage of an EIS is often referred to as "segmentation." Suppose that an agency's long-range planning contemplates a reasonable possibility of a 200-mile highway being constructed over the next 10 years, but current construction and funding is being proposed for only a 20-mile stretch. Should the entire 200-mile corridor be the subject of the EIS or just the 20 miles currently proposed? It would be extremely costly and time-consuming to do the EIS for the whole 200 miles, and if construction is never funded beyond the 20 miles, the EIS work on the rest is wasted. In addition, an EIS done today might be of questionable value with respect to work not to be undertaken for several years. It could thus be argued that the EIS should be limited in scope to the 20-mile segment currently under consideration. The danger of allowing this segmented approach to fulfilling the EIS requirement is that segmenting may undermine objective consideration of environmental issues by unfairly loading the EIS balance in favor of construction. In the diagram below, no significant en-

vironmental problems exist in proposed highway segments AB or CD, but a major environmental drawback to superhighway construction exists at point X. If the scope of today's EIS were limited to AB, no environmental problems are present to argue against construction. Once AB is built, the next likely segment to be undertaken by a dedicated superhighway builder is CD, and again no environmental problems present themselves to inhibit construction of CD. Concerning the construction of BC, an objective evaluation of segment BC by itself might result in a "no construction" decision because, on balance, the costs (including environmental costs) outweigh the benefits of construction; however, if that balance is struck with the added factor of already constructed superhighways AB and CD emptying onto winding country road BC and the resulting traffic problems which may now exist in BC because of AB and CD, a "yes construction" decision may be hard to avoid. The segmenting of the EIS into three parts has undermined the ability to fairly

---

27. 40 CFR §§ 1502.4, 1502.20, 1508.28.

consider the environmental detriment of a superhighway through point X. If an EIS for the whole route, ABCD, had been done prior to construction of the first segment, the problem at point X might have been considered important enough to mandate a different route such as AMND as shown below.

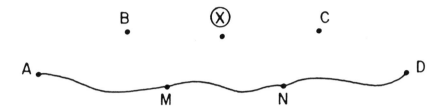

The courts have attempted to resolve the conflicting policies of, on one hand, not wanting to waste time and money on an over-encompassing EIS and, on the other hand, not wanting to allow the objectivity of the EIS balancing process to be jeopardized. The courts have said that if construction of one part of a potentially larger project has independent "local utility" and will thus not involve an irreversible or irretrievable commitment of government funds, the EIS may be limited in scope to that one part of the project.[28] If construction of that part alone would still be a sound decision even if no further action were taken beyond the part of the project currently being funded for construction, then the EIS does not need to go beyond the segment of what might someday become a larger project. In this way, the courts have tried to mitigate the argument of "now that we have AB and CD, we need BC to relieve the traffic problems those other segments have caused." AB and CD can only be built if they can stand as sound projects on their own without causing detriments which could only be overcome by constructing BC, regardless of the environmental costs of building BC.

C.   SUBSTANTIVE POLICIES, PROCEDURAL REQUIREMENTS, AND THE ROLE OF THE COURTS

NEPA's EIS requirement is a specific procedural step which federal agencies are directed to take. NEPA also makes some broad declarations, somewhat lacking in specificity, concerning the nation's environmental policy and goals and the federal government's responsibility for promoting and

---

28. *Conservation Society of So. Vt. v. Sec. of Transportation*, 531 F.2d 637, 640 (1976).

attaining them. The analysis of the distinction between NEPA's procedural requirements and its statements of substantive policy was presented in *Calvert Cliffs' Coordinating Committee v. Atomic Energy Commission*,[29] the leading court decision interpreting NEPA. The procedural/substantive distinction serves to define the role of the court system in the EIS process—a process which is directed at the administrative agencies.

The substantive policies and goals of NEPA are found in § 101 of the Act and are broadly worded declarations. They include Congress' desire to "promote the general welfare, to create and maintain conditions under which man and nature can exist in productive harmony . . ." and Congress' direction that the federal government act so that the nation may "fulfill the responsibilities of each generation as trustee of the environment for succeeding generations" and "assure for all Americans safe, healthful, productive, and aesthetically and culturally pleasing surroundings . . . ."[30] The court in *Calvert Cliffs'* noted that Congress required that these substantive goals and policies be pursued by the federal government using "all practicable means." In contrast, Congress directed that the procedural requirement of an EIS, found in § 102 of the Act, was to be followed "to the fullest extent possible." Based on this difference in the language used by Congress in the two sections of the Act, the court found that the substantive aspects of the Act were directives to the agencies which allowed for flexibility and agency discretion and thus provided only a very limited review role for the courts. With respect to the § 101 substantive aspects of NEPA, courts could only interfere with an agency decision when that decision was "arbitrary or clearly gave insufficient weight to environmental values." With respect to the § 102 procedural requirements, however, the court found that the language "to the fullest extent possible" was not highly flexible and that the language made the courts responsible to reverse agency decisions which were reached procedurally without the mandated consideration and balancing of environmental factors. Thus, if an agency failed to do an EIS where one was required, or did not do a legally sufficient EIS, or in some other way violated NEPA's relatively inflexible procedural directives to the federal agencies, the courts would reverse the agency's decision. Let's consider the issue of court review of agency decisions under NEPA today in two contexts: (1) where the agency has done an EIS but the agency's decision about a proposed project is alleged to be inconsistent with the § 101 substantive policies of NEPA and (2) where the agency has decided pursuant to § 102 that an EIS need not be done.

With respect to the court's role of reviewing an agency decision for

---

29. 449 F.2d 1109 (1971).

30. PL 91–190, § 101.

compliance with the § 101 policies, even the very limited review of checking to see if the result was arbitrary, as stated by the court in *Calvert Cliffs'*, has been placed in doubt. In the United States Supreme Court case of *Stryker's Bay Neighborhood Council v. Karlen*,[31] the majority opinion said that an agency's duties under NEPA are "essentially procedural," and "once an agency has made a decision subject to NEPA's procedural requirements, the only role for a court is to insure that the agency has considered the environmental consequences. . . ." In a footnote, the Court said that if the agency had acted arbitrarily, it *might* agree that plenary review was warranted. The use of the word "might" could be interpreted to be less than a full commitment by the Court to the position that arbitrary substantive decisions of agencies are to be set aside when the agency has complied with NEPA's procedures. Although later cases have not expressly said "no review with respect to § 101 policy compliance," they continue to focus on NEPA as a "process" statute and imply that, although the EIS process is almost certain to affect the environmental substance of an agency decision, there is probably no court review based on §101.[32] Thus, even the very limited judicial review pursuant to § 101 that was recognized in *Calvert Cliffs'* seems to have disappeared. There does, however, continue to be judicial review under § 102, and most of the controversies about the role of courts under NEPA have involved § 102. These cases consider the degree to which courts will review the procedural steps an agency has taken to comply with § 102's requirement that an agency must prepare an Environmental Impact Statement. They are the subject of our second inquiry about judicial review under NEPA.

Our second judicial review question is: to what extent will a court review on agency's decision, pursuant to § 102, to not do an EIS or to not supplement on existing EIS. As was discussed at the beginning of this chapter, NEPA requires agencies to prepare an EIS for any "major Federal action significantly affecting the quality of the human environment." When an agency is uncertain about whether its proposed action fits this statutory language, the Council on Environmental Quality has said the agency is to prepare an Environmental Assessment.[33] The function of an Environmental Assessment (EA) is to "provide sufficient evidence and analysis for determining whether to prepare an environmental impact statement or a finding of no significant impact."[34] If an agency's EA results in its issuing a Finding of No Significant Impact (FONSI), it does not prepare an EIS. When asked to review whether

---

31. 100 S. Ct. 497 (1980).

32. *Robertson v. Methow Valley Citizens Council*, 490 U.S. 332 (1989).

33. 40 CFR §§ 1501.3 and 1501.4.

34. 40 CFR § 1508.9.

the agency decision not to do an EIS was in compliance with NEPA, some Circuit Courts of Appeals used the "reasonableness" test—the court itself evaluates whether the agency reasonably concluded that the project would have no significant adverse environmental consequences.[35] Other Circuit Courts provided less in the way of judicial review—the agency decision not to do an EIS would be given deference and would only be set aside if the court found the decision was "arbitrary and capricious" rather than merely unreasonable when evaluated by the Court. This lesser role for courts of leaving the agency decision stand unless it is arbitrary and capricious was adopted by the U.S. Supreme Court in *Marsh v. Oregon Natural Resources Council* where the Army Corps of Engineers decided not do additional EIS work with respect to building the Elk Creek Dam to control water supply in Oregon's Rogue River Basin.[36]

Those who advocate more court watchdogging of agencies even after the *Marsh* case contend that the arbitrary and capricious standard from *Marsh* need not be applied to agency decisions not to do an EIS because Marsh involved an agency decision not to supplement an existing EIS rather than not to do one at all. In *Marsh*, an EIS had been done for the Elk Creek Dam, and the Corps decided not to do an additional supplementary EIS even though new and potentially relevant studies had been done. While this argument may convince some lower court judge to continue to ask if the agency decision was reasonable instead of only nonarbitrary, the language from *Marsh* makes that difficult because the Supreme Court stated in *Marsh* that "the decision whether to prepare a supplemental EIS is similar to the decision whether to prepare an EIS in the first instance. . . ."[37] Still, lower court judges in "first instance EIS" cases who do not want to be constrained by the limited judicial review standard of *Marsh* may accept the argument that the above quoted language from *Marsh* is not necessary to the decision of that case and is thus not part of the "holding" of the case. Since it is only "dictum" and not part of the "holding," it is not binding on lower courts. Regardless of whether one uses the reasonableness test or the arbitrary and capricious test as the standard for judicial review, it is clear that a court will not decide from scratch that on EIS is or is not required. It will only consider whether the agency decision is within the spectrum of either reasonableness or nonarbitrariness.

Our cases concerning judicial review lead to the conclusion that it is the federal agencies who are largely in charge of the NEPA process and that

---

35. *Save the Yaak Committee v. J.R. Block*, 840 F.2d 714, 717 (1988).

36. 490 U.S. 360 (1989).

37. Id. at 374.

NEPA is just that—a process. The substantive goals of NEPA are to be realized through a set of "action-forcing" procedures that require that agencies take a "hard look" at environmental consequences.[38] Although using the procedures (the EIS) will affect the agency's substantive decision, NEPA only prescribes a process—it does not mandate particular results, and it does not mean that environmental values cannot be sacrificed. Environmental values may be sacrificed under NEPA; all that NEPA requires is that environmental values be considered in the balance of the agency decision-making process. The substantive environmental concerns of § 101 are not exclusive goals of an agency, and those concerns may, on balance, lose out. That is allowed under the flexible language of § 101, but the environmental concerns must be given consideration—that is inflexible. Viewed with respect to the balance/ban legislative approaches we referred to in Chapter 1, NEPA is a balance statute—no activity is banned, but environmental values must be balanced with the economic benefits of a proposed agency action. The EIS is the mechanism for reporting on the balancing process, and it is the main procedural requirement of NEPA.

We have determined that the basic operative mechanism of NEPA is the EIS. Does this mechanism work? How does requiring a detailed statement of the environmental impact of a proposed action serve the purpose of fostering proper consideration for environmental values? First, the agency itself will have environmental concerns and information before it for the purpose of writing the EIS. This information will hopefully be considered by the agency, whereas prior to NEPA and the need to write an EIS, environmental information was often never even compiled. Second, the EIS requirement seeks to bring the public and other agencies, in addition to the agency proposing to act, into the picture by informing them of environmental consequences and giving them an opportunity to comment on them and possibly come up with alternatives to the proposed action. Third, if others outside the agency are able to see the agency's statement of the justification for its decision spelled out in the EIS, an informal pressure is placed on an agency to make a rational decision and to include environmental considerations in that decision. The theory is that better decisions are made when "someone is watching."

The above logic supports Congress' decision to use the EIS mechanism as the procedural tool to implement its substantive policies involving environmental protection; however, there are many who contend that the procedural requirement of an EIS has little or no positive effect on the environment and is just another "red tape/legal technicalities/bureaucratic

---

38. *Robertson v. Methow Valley Citizens Council*, 490 U.S. 332 (1989).

nightmare" standing in the way of those who seek to have government work to serve the interests of society. The basis of this position is that the preparation of an EIS is a time-consuming chore which adds large amounts of lead time and other economic costs to any project. Also, the EIS requirement allows a small number of people to tie up a project for long periods of time in a complex litigation process. These arguments might be made by people who would label themselves as being in favor of progress, economic growth, and development rather than being "environmentalists," but many "environmentalists" would join them in attacking the EIS process as undesirable. Some environmentalists claim that as agencies become accustomed to the EIS procedure and to what the courts require for compliance with that procedure, an agency can make any decision look reasonable on paper regardless of whether it is a good balance between the agency's program goals and NEPA's environmental goals. It is the opinion of these environmentalists that the only way for the § 101 substantive goals of NEPA to really be taken into account is for the courts, being independent bodies without any agency program goals, to be willing to take a close look at the substantive correctness of an agency decision rather than looking only at whether the § 102 procedures are followed. What is needed is for the courts to look more closely at whether an agency decision is right or wrong with respect to the environment rather than to only inquire whether the agency decision was "arbitrary or capricious." It is for you to determine whether you believe that the EIS is a sound mechanism for environmental protection or that the EIS severely handicaps agencies' efforts to work toward a better society or that the EIS can only work to attain NEPA's substantive environmental goals if the courts take a more active role in watchdogging agency actions which affect those goals. The status of the law is that the EIS requirement does exist, but, if the agency complies with the § 102 procedural steps, the courts will, at most, evaluate the substance of an agency decision to make sure it is not arbitrary with respect to its consideration of the environment.

Having now considered the basic structure of NEPA as established by Congress and as interpreted by the courts, let us digress and see how, in *Calvert Cliffs'*, the Atomic Energy Commission ran afoul of the EIS requirement. In this context, we should think about how a particular set of facts may be influential in shaping the interpretation that courts give to a statute. In *Calvert Cliffs'*, the AEC's procedure for licensing energy-producing facilities was challenged. The AEC made some quite reasonable arguments concerning how NEPA was supposed to be inapplicable to the fact situation in that case because another specific statute precluded NEPA's being applicable. Section 104 of NEPA says:

> Nothing in section 102 [the EIS requirement] . . . shall in any way
> affect the specific statutory obligations of any Federal agency . . . to

act, or refrain from acting contingent upon the recommendations or certifications of any other Federal or State agency.

Another statute, the Water Quality Improvement Act (WQIA), had resulted in water quality standards being set by other agencies, and the AEC said it could adopt those standards and did not need to address water quality in its EIS. The AEC, as further support for its position, cited a statement made by Senator Jackson, the sponsor of NEPA, which discussed the relationship between NEPA and the WQIA. Jackson said:

> The compromise worked out between the two bills provides that the licensing agency will not have to make a detailed statement on water quality if the state or other appropriate agency has made a certification pursuant to [WQIA].[39]

The court rejected AEC's position and found the AEC's EIS must consider water quality because, if it did so, AEC might decide to impose water quality standards that were stricter than those adopted under the other statute, the WQIA. The court interpreted § 104 to only allow on agency to exclude an issue from its EIS when its obligations under another statute were "mutually exclusive" with its obligations under NEPA to consider that issue. Considering and adopting stricter water quality standards under NEPA would not violate the minimum standards that had been set under the WQIA, and thus the obligations under the two statutes were not mutually exclusive. The AEC could not simply adopt the WQIA standards without discussing water quality in its EIS. Acceptance of AEC's reasonable and quite well-supported position might have narrowed NEPA's overall applicability and effect, but the AEC's reasonable arguments were rejected by the court. One can only speculate concerning whether that rejection (and perhaps a resulting broader interpretation of NEPA's scope) was in any way influenced by the following and possibly not-so-reasonable argument which the AEC made.

Under Section 102, copies of the EIS must "accompany" a proposal through the agency review process. The AEC adopted a literal definition of the word "accompany." With respect to some license application situations, the AEC had the EIS physically "accompany" the application, but the AEC rules precluded the EIS from being considered in the decision-making process of the licensing hearings. The court found that Congress did not intend by use of the word "accompany" to create a situation requiring physical proximity of the EIS without any requirement that it be considered by the decision-maker and that "the Commission's crabbed interpretation

---

39. 115 Cong. Rec. (Part 21) at 29053.

of NEPA makes a mockery of the Act."[40] The court was clearly outraged by the AEC's approach to its NEPA responsibilities. One may wish to consider what contribution, if any, has been made to the general proliferation of environmental controls and litigation by a few instances of agency or industry recalcitrance or lack of good faith in complying with existing environmental regulations. How much influence have the worst cases of lack of good faith had on the overall scheme of environmental controls?

D. REMEDIES

Having considered when NEPA requires an EIS, what is the content of an EIS, and how courts are involved with reviewing the manner in which agencies comply with both the procedural EIS requirement of NEPA and with NEPA's substantive policies, let's consider the question of remedies for noncompliance by a federal agency with NEPA's EIS requirement. The general remedy is an injunction to maintain the *status quo*—the court orders that the project be halted until a proper EIS is prepared; however, a *status quo* injunction is not granted in all situations of inadequate environmental impact statements. If a delay in continuing the project might result in safety or health hazards or heavy economic losses, and if the environmental harm is not very great, a court may refuse to hold the project in its *status quo* position. Instead, the court may issue a limited injunction which would prohibit certain activities (like site clearance) but allow other project activities to continue (like relocation of people from the site to be cleared). The likelihood of a *status quo* injunction with respect to the entire project would appear to be directly proportional to the seriousness of the environmental harm which the project threatens to create. Also, intentional noncompliance by an agency with NEPA may tend to induce a court to grant a broad injunction even though, in the absence of agency bad faith, the factual situation might have led the court to grant only a limited injunction. As one example of courts having to consider competing needs in deciding whether to issue an injunction because of agency noncompliance with NEPA, let's consider the interface between national security policy and environmental protection under NEPA.

In *Concerned About Trident v. Rumsfeld*,[41] the Navy was involved in the construction of a Trident Submarine Base at Bangor, Washington. The Defense Department claimed that NEPA cannot possibly apply to strategic

---

40. *Calvert Cliffs'* at 1117.

41. 555 F.2d 817 (1977).

military decisions and that there is a "national defense" exemption from NEPA. The court found that such a claim "flies in the face of the clear language of the statute" which requires that "all agencies of the Federal Government" prepare an EIS for "major Federal actions significantly affecting the quality of the human environment." There is no national defense exemption. When, however, in *Wisconsin v. Weinberger*, a court was asked to use the remedy of an injunction to stop the Defense Department's expansion of an extremely low frequency submarine communication system due to alleged violation of NEPA, an injunction was denied based on a balance of "the weight of the alleged NEPA violation against the harm the injunction would cause the Navy and to this country's defense."[42] Historically, an injunction is an "equitable remedy" which means that, even though there has been a violation of the law, courts have the discretion to balance the need for an injunction against the harm it might do. Yet, if a national defense activity is not enjoined when it is in violation of NEPA, do we not have a *de facto* national defense exemption which we were told does not exist under the clear language of NEPA? Although violations of NEPA have not always led to courts being willing to grant injunctions to stop agencies from proceeding until they have complied with NEPA, in most situations of NEPA violation, a *status quo* injunction stopping a project has been the appropriate remedy and has also been enough of a remedy to satisfy the courts that the project will not continue to violate NEPA permanently. Lurking in the background, however, is the possibility that the court will tell an agency that it has violated NEPA, and, since it should not have proceeded with its project, it must not only stop the project, but it must also undo what has been done. This remedy is rather severe and is thus reserved for extreme situations. Again, agency good faith would not be irrelevant to a court's determination of whether to apply this severe remedy.

Another remedy which some people have claimed is available under NEPA is the right of private citizens to bring suit when estimates or predictions made in an environmental impact statement are not adhered to or do not prove to be true once the project is approved and undertaken. Citizens have contended that these situations result in an "implied private right of action" under NEPA. Thus the owner of a bookstore sought an injunction and damages based on NEPA when the noise levels stated in the EIS for a rapid transit project were exceeded after the project was built and operating. The courts have found that Congress did not intend such a remedy to be available under NEPA and have dismissed lawsuits seeking to invoke such a remedy. The courts have said that if this private remedy were available, then decision-

---

42. 745 F.2d 412 (1984).

makers would receive and report distorted information which was "hedged" to ensure that information used as an estimate or prediction would in fact turn out to be true in practice. This would be inconsistent with the statutory purpose of NEPA which is to provide decision-makers with the best available information on which to base their decisions.[43] On the other hand, one may want to consider the argument that if representations made in the EIS as a basis for reaching the decision to proceed with a project are shown to not be coming true as the project is being implemented, the agency should have to reevaluate whether the project should continue based on the new information now available. Such reevaluation might result in a different decision on the project or modifications to the project which would provide greater consistency with the substantive policies that Congress asked be pursued using "all practicable means."[44]

E.   NEPA AND MULTI-MEDIA ENVIRONMENTAL PROTECTION

Although NEPA is limited in that it only applies to actions of the federal government, it is quite broad with respect to the environmental issues it covers. NEPA potentially encompasses all environmental issues including air pollution, water pollution, water allocation, land use, land pollution, resource conservation, species protection, and protection of our food supply from toxic materials. NEPA may thus be thought of as a "multi-media" environmental statute, and it stands in marked contrast to the bulk of our environmental legislation which has been enacted subsequent to NEPA. Those statutes each address a single medium or topic—the Clean Air Act, the Surface Mining Control and Reclamation Act, the Endangered Species Act, the Federal Environmental Pesticide Control Act. Since the existing pattern of environmental legislation is single medium oriented, much of the discussion of environmental law in this book focuses on one medium at a time. Let's, however, note a few examples of "multi-media environmental protection" approaches which have recently been proposed or begun and which may receive greater emphasis as environmental law continues to evolve. Our first two examples, an environmental amendment to the U.S. Constitution and a unified environmental protection statute to address cross-media pollutants, have been proposed, but they are longshots to become "environmental law" in the foreseeable future. Our third example involves the administrative

---

43. *Noe v. MARTA*, 644 F.2d 434 (1981).

44. PL 91–190, § 101.

level of environmental protection, and here multi-media mechanisms are now being used by EPA. Specifically, EPA is using the cluster approach to environmental management and operating multi-media enforcement activities.

1.   Constitutional Amendment

Many proposals to amend the U.S. Constitution to explicitly provide environmental protection have been advocated in recent years. Differences in approaches include the enumeration of popular rights as compared to a general statement of popular rights and a focus on the rights of nature rather than on the rights of people. The National Wildlife Federation proposal enumerates the popular rights:

> Each person has the right to clean air, pure water, productive soils, and to the conservation of the natural, scenic, historic, recreational, aesthetic, and economic values of America's natural resources. . . .

Other proposals consist of unenumerated statements such as: "Every person has the right to a clean, healthful environment. . . . " Still others look beyond protecting people and indeed view people as the threat. They would amend the Constitution to say: "The earth and all its life shall be treated considerately for they are vulnerable to human culture."[45] Those who argue in favor of an environmental amendment contend that we need to strengthen our commitment to environmental protection in order to compete with the human tendency toward growth and monetary profit. They also say that as long as our statutory scheme of environmental protection is based on anything less than an explicit constitutional mandate, it is too easy for courts and administrative agencies to neglect the statutory requirements.[46] Arguments opposing a constitutional amendment include not wanting to weaken the existing limits on government power, not wanting to undertake additional administrative costs and burdens, and not wanting to risk the possibilities of misinterpretation and misapplication of a new constitutional provision. A strong argument in opposition is the lack of a need. With all the environmental legislation in existence, it is claimed that there is sufficient power under the Commerce Clause of the Constitution for Congress to provide for

---

45. For a discussion of these and other amendment proposals, see *Environmental Amendment Circular No. 4*, The Comprehensive Environmental Amendment Project (Thornton, Colorado: June, 1991).

46. Caldwell, L., "A Constitutional Law for the Environment: 20 Years with NEPA Indicates the Need," *31 Environment 10* (Dec., 1989).

environmental protection. The issue, of course, is not whether Congress has the power. Instead, it is whether the people and nature have the right to environmental protection in the absence of action by Congress to provide that protection or as a limitation on Congress' power in the event Congress acts in a way that threatens environmental protection.

2. Unified Environmental Protection Act

The primary advantage claimed by proponents of a unified statute to protect the environment is definitional. It would be a unified or single law to deal with all environmental issues or at least with all forms of an environmental topic like pollution. The Conservation Foundation's study which led to a document titled "The Environmental Protection Act" discusses having one statute to replace the Clean Air Act, Clean Water Act, and seven other statutes which comprise the bulk of the activities of the Environmental Protection Agency. In this way, "[R]egulatory priorities, budget allocations, and research initiatives could be considered for the entire [proposed] Department of Environmental Protection (DEP) not just for one program at a time as is currently done."[47] Among the Conservation Foundation's stated reasons why a cross-media or integrated approach to pollution control would be beneficial are: (1) Successful control of pollutants such as heavy metals, organic chemicals, and sulfur and nitrogen oxides is unlikely if we focus on air or water or land one medium at a time. The single-medium focus tends to shift the pollution from one medium to another and to sometimes not recognize new problems such as acid rain from sulfur oxides or stratospheric ozone depletion from CFC releases. (2) The single-medium focus makes it impossible to set rational priorities among control approaches. (3) The cost of pollution control can be reduced by using an integrated approach while at the same time increasing the effectiveness of the control. Unified technology and unified administration, such as through the use of a single rather than a multiple permitting process, could provide this benefit.

While a more integrated approach to environmental protection probably makes good sense, it is not very likely that the massive existing statutory framework of single-media legislation will be dismantled anytime soon. However, incremental steps toward integration or multi-media environmental protection are now being taken by EPA with respect to both environmental management and environmental enforcement as discussed below.

---

47. From the "Rationale and Summary" introduction to the proposed "Environmental Protection Act," The Conservation Foundation, Washington, D.C.

3. The Cluster Approach to Environmental Management; Multi-media Enforcement

EPA's general organizational structure is single-media. Different parts of EPA deal with each medium—air, water, land. This has often resulted in industry being subjected to duplicative and sometimes conflicting regulations. It has also led to some issues "falling through the cracks" because each section of the regulatory process may leave the issue for another section to handle. In addition, the effort to mitigate adverse effects on one medium may create adverse effects on another medium. In the 1990s, EPA initiated its "cluster approach" and began applying it to the pulp and paper industry— one of the largest industries in term of the quantity of toxic chemicals it releases to the air, water, and land.

The pulp and paper industry releases are covered by many different statutes and were thus under the control of multiple program offices of EPA. To provide better integration of control, EPA established a cluster team to approach the problems holistically rather than from a program-by-program perspective. Thus air and water regulations for the pulp and paper industry would be developed jointly to seek the optimal combination of technologies to meet statutory requirements, avoid cross-media pollution transfers, and reduce industry compliance costs through coordination of action.[48] EPA has formed other clusters which focus on a specific economic sector like petroleum refineries, on a pollutant like lead (regardless of which medium the lead is affecting), on an environmental resource like ground water, or on other logical multi-media groupings of activities.[49] In order to be effective, the cluster approach will have to overcome institutional inertia in areas such as single media approaches to budgeting and setting statutory deadlines. It will also have to cope with power struggles among entrenched bureaucrats. Clusters do, however, have great potential to give us faster and better solutions for environmental problems—better in terms of both environmental protection and the costs of that protection. Indeed, at a time when there is growing interest in cooperative rather than confrontational environmental problem solving by industry, environmentalists, and government, the cluster approach's integration of environmental issues together with its single contact point between industry and the regulators seems to offer something for everyone.

Having a single contact point between the regulator and the industry that

---

48. Cleland-Hamnett, W. and Retzer, J., "Crossing Agency Boundaries," *The Environmental Forum* (March–April, 1993) p. 17.

49. Sandalow, D.B., "EPA Clusters: A New Approach for Environmental Management," *The 22nd Annual Conference on Environmental Law* (American Bar Association, Section on Natural Resources, Energy, and Environmental Law, 1993) Tab 14.

is being regulated is also the crux of EPA's "multi-media enforcement" program. As the term is often used, "multi-media enforcement" can involve coordinated enforcement activities which address air, water, and waste all in one inspection and enforcement process. It is also used to refer to enforcement activities involving more than one EPA or state organization. Multi-media inspection and enforcement seeks to identify facilities whose activities lend themselves to multi-media inspection and then to do a comprehensive inspection for air, water, and waste problems at those facilities.[50]

In identifying or targeting facilities for multi-media inspection, EPA considers factors such as the number of statutes under which the facility is regulated and whether the facility is subject to one or more EPA or state permits. A targeted facility may then be visited by a multi-media inspection team led by multi-media inspectors ("super-inspectors") all of whom have expertise in each major media—air, water, and waste. Violations that are found must be brought into compliance and penalties may be assessed, but, in addition, EPA's multi-media enforcement program includes the use of "innovative settlements." Innovative settlements may contain negotiated longer schedules for compliance for those facilities that agree to go beyond compliance and further reduce or eliminate discharges. A more innovative category of "innovative settlements" is "supplemental environmental projects" (SEP's). In addition to coming into compliance, the violating facility agrees to undertake a project such as community environmental education or implementation of a recycling program in the community. The SEP's may be multi-media in that they are not restricted to the subject area of the violations. The project is agreed to by the facility in exchange for a reduction in the penalties assessed for its environmental violations.

A multi-media enforcement action was taken at the Boeing Company facility in Philadelphia. Based on a multi-media inspection that showed violations of the Resource Conservation and Recovery Act (RCRA) and the Toxic Substances Control Act (TSCA), Boeing and EPA reached a settlement that, in addition to achieving compliance, resulted in $800,000 in civil penalties and a $350,000 payment to fund a seminar and the creation of plans to achieve chemical reduction by companies in Pennsylvania and Delaware. Although Boeing had some criticisms of the multi-media process, it concluded that "multi-media inspections appear to be an effective means of dealing with large facilities."[51]

---

50. Gaydosh, M., VandenBerg, C., and Greenwald, B., "Multi-Media Enforcement," *The 22nd Annual Conference on Environmental Law*, Ibid., Tab 16.

51. Waite, T., "Multi-Media Enforcement Actions: The Industry Perspective," *The 22nd Annual Conference on Environmental Law*, Ibid., Tab 17.

ADDITIONAL READINGS

Battle, J., *Environmental Law; Environmental Decisionmaking and NEPA* (Cincinnati, Ohio: Anderson Publishing, 1986).

Caldwell, L, *Science and the National Environmental Policy Act* (University, Alabama: Univ. of Alabama Press, 1982).

Environmental Law Institute, *NEPA Deskbook* (Washington, DC: Environmental Law Institute, 1989).

Gellhorn, E. and Levin, R., *Administrative Law and Process* (St. Paul, MN: West Publishing, 1990).

Orloff, N. and Brooks, G., *The National Environmental Policy Act* (Washington, DC: Bureau of National Affairs, Inc., 1980).

CHAPTER 3

POLLUTION

A. DEFINING THE PROBLEM

It is necessary, before we deal with specific pollution problems, to share some basic ideas on how the whole ecological system is put together so that we will better understand how pollution becomes a problem. In the simplest sense, all things are connected. You have heard that phrase before, but let us go a little further and see what this simple phrase can mean.

We will begin by examining how the connections in the ecosystem are put together, using Figure 1 as a reference point. While not all parts of all ecosystems look like those shown in Figure 1, the parts we will designate are quite common in most localities. In the figure, A represents the surface of the earth, where various human activities take place. These activities include manufacturing, mining, electrical generation, silviculture (logging), agriculture, fishing, and just plain living. In short, A represents the land and the activities we perform on the land. Designation B represents the air above the surface of the earth. For now we will consider only the lower part of the troposphere, the layer of air closest to the earth. Generally, this air moves from west to east in the North Temperate Zone where most people live and most industrial processes take place. This air can and does carry various materials such as gases, metals, and dust which originate from naturally occurring earth processes or from anthropogenic (man-made) sources. The distances these materials travel in the air and the form in which they return to earth will be discussed more thoroughly later. The letter C is used to represent a lake basin where water level is a function of E, the boundary between the saturated and unsaturated soil areas which will also be discussed later. The lake basin is like a teacup at the bottom of a funnel; it catches all the water that runs over the land and down the hill and additionally gets some water or exchanges some water with water in the areas designated F and G. So, material from land activities, A, can get washed into the lake

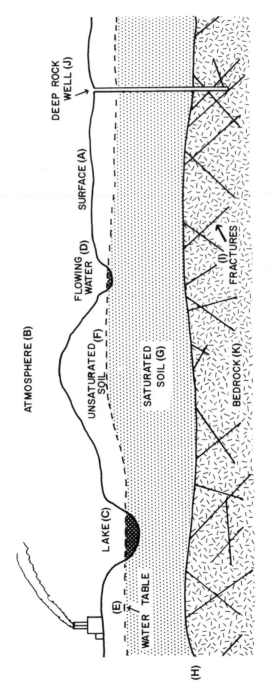

Figure 1.   A diagrammatic representation of how the ecosystem is put together.

basin C. Lakes are large bodies of water and, therefore, the total amount
of water in the lake takes a long time to be replaced, if ever. The letter
D designates a river or stream. This body of water is the kind that runs
downhill to a lake or some other larger body of water (sea, ocean). The
rivers and streams carry with them materials that have run off from the land,
fallen from the sky, and entered from F and G. These watercourses try to
fill the teacup through the funnel. Since the water in these bodies of water
is always moving, replacement of water in any defined space is very rapid
compared to replacement in C. The boundary between F and G is designated
as E, where E represents the area between the unsaturated soil material F
and the saturated soil material G. The distance below the soil surface (surface
of the earth) of E is variable both spatially and temporally, depending on
soil composition, the frequency and amplitude of rainfall (how often and
how much), temperature, and ground level land use patterns. In other words,
E is not fixed, but it moves as conditions change. Therefore, lake levels
vary and some streams dry up as E moves. Where E breaks the surface
of the earth, there is a body of water. In theory there is no real distinction
between area F and G other than the degree of water saturation. Both F
and G really contain ground water. The differences are mainly that in area
F there is unsaturated water flow (water flows downhill) while in area G
there is a saturated flow (water usually moves laterally, if at all). The rate
of flow in area F is very dependent on soil composition. The rate of flow
in area G is also a function of soil composition and of some type of water
drawdown (well) but is still very slow. As the movement of water in area
G is very slow, so too is the movement of chemicals, although these
movements are not necessarily the same. The letter H designates the boundary
between soil and bedrock, K, while the letter I designates fractures (holes)
in the bedrock that can accumulate water. When drained quickly, the area
I will usually refill quickly. It is into the bedrock that many wells are drilled,
but the depth and the composition of the deepest part of any well, J, is
a function of the geographic location of the well. The letter J is thus used
to designate a deep rock well, one that crosses fractures in bedrock. These
types of wells are drilled to a depth where recharge (water replacement)
after drawdown (water pumped out) is sufficient to accommodate the use
for which the well was drilled. Therefore, wells really get their water from
the surface after it has permeated through soil and reached a layer of saturation
(G) or an area of storage (I). Although subsurface conditions vary from one
geographic location to another, we can safely say that where water goes,
material that can be physically or chemically carried by water will be carried
by water as it passes around the ecosystem. The connectedness in the
ecosystem is then established as the flow of material, such as water, through
the parts of the ecosystem.

As a more specific example of connectedness than the generality of Figure

1, let us look at a simplified version of the nitrogen cycle. Nitrogen is a needed nutrient, an important part of all protein. What we are concerned with here is the structural forms of nitrogen in nature and the direction of flow from one nitrogen form to another. If we start with nitrogen as organic nitrogen (protein nitrogen) we can follow nitrogen around the connections of the nitrogen cycle (Figure 2). We see that organic nitrogen in plants or animals upon their death is eventually transformed into ammonium. Ammonium is changed into atmospheric nitrogen or nitrate or is taken up by plants and made into organic nitrogen in the plants. The shortest cycle is then organic nitrogen in plants converted to ammonium after plant death and then taken back up by other plants. If you follow some different pathways, the idea that materials (nitrogen here) go through cycles will become apparent. In fact, most materials we know about go around in cycles through processes that change their chemical makeup.

Having demonstrated the idea of how things are connected, we shall proceed to examine the concept of pollution and what kinds of pollution problems need solving. While we can relate to the whole ecosystem concept, society has broken the problem of pollution into two broad categories—water pollution and air pollution. Apparently, since in each category there is a transport of materials, and since in some geographic areas either air or water,

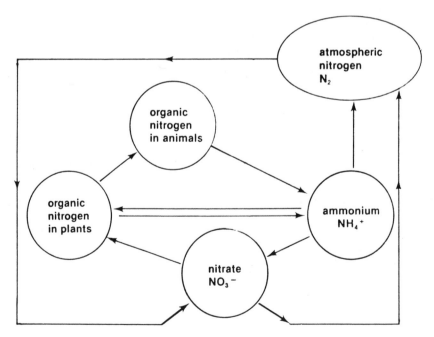

Figure 2. A simplified view of the nitrogen cycle.

but not necessarily both, were perceived to be of lower quality than the public health and welfare might tolerate, our legislatures elected to regulate them separately rather than collectively. While we may, in hindsight, criticize that decision, the fact remains that when society perceives a problem, it often tries to deal with that isolated problem. Therefore, to briefly outline the scope of the problem, we will consider water and air pollution separately after we examine the nature of pollution.

"Pollution" is defined by the federal government in one instance to mean "the man-made or man-induced alteration of the chemical, physical, biological, and radiological integrity of water."[1] A literal reading of this definition would make it appear that beneficial as well as detrimental effects are considered pollution. This definition seems to view people apart from nature with nature as the norm and anything done by people as being pollution. In point of fact, we will see that pollution control statues concern themselves largely with adverse effects on people and to a much lesser degree with adverse effects on nature. Another attempt to cope with the concept of pollution is to define "pollutant." The federal government has defined "air pollutant"[2] as including any physical, chemical, biological, or radioactive matter which enters the air. Again, this definition could encompass the effects of almost any event; however, we will see that in practice the application of this definition is not nearly so far-reaching.

1.   Water Pollution

Pollutants flow to common waters (usually surface water) by direct (point source) and indirect (nonpoint source) means. These respectively are the ones we know about and the ones we wish we knew more about. According to the Clean Water Act, a "point source" is a discernable, confined, and discrete conveyance from which pollutants may be discharged. Since every public and private facility that discharges any potential pollutant directly into waters of the United States is required to get a permit that describes discharge limitations for specific materials, we have presumably isolated and identified these point sources. Industrial point source uses of water include refining gasoline from crude oil (10 gal. water/gal. gasoline), making steel (35 gal. water/lb steel), refining synthetic fuel from coal (265 gal. water/gal. fuel),

---

1. 33 U.S.C. § 1251 et seq. at § 1362 (Clean Water Act).

2. 42 U.S.C. § 7401 et seq. at § 7602(g) (Clean Air Act).

and automobile manufacturing (100,000 gal. water/automobile).[3] What happens to this used water? A large portion of it is treated by various methods to remove identified pollutants, and it is then discharged into our watercourses. We either treat industrial wastewater separately or pretreat it before it flows to a municipal sewage treatment plant. Industrial treatment or pretreatment is used to recover metals such as silver and cadmium and to remove toxic chemicals such as carbon tetrachloride, trichloroethylene, and other organic as well as inorganic chemicals before discharge.

Municipal sewage treatment plants test for the presence of pollutants. Municipal plants test for biochemical oxygen demand (BOD), suspended solids (SS), total coliform (TC), fecal coliform (FC), phosphorous, nitrate, and pH.[4] The things we test for are good indicators of the level of pollution we wish to control. BOD is a measure of the oxygen demand of microorganisms in the water as they break down organic material. This demand for oxygen reduces the amount of oxygen available for fish and other water creatures. If the BOD is too high, the dissolved oxygen in the water will be too low to support fish such as trout, which require at least 5 parts per million of oxygen in water. SS is a measure of particles in the effluent discharge. If SS is high, aquatic life can be killed when breathing spaces are plugged. Also, sunlight is prevented from penetrating the water, resulting in plants dying and increasing the BOD as they decompose. TC and FC are monitored as indicators of human pollution in water and as a test for chlorination effectiveness in effluent from municipal treatment plants. Maximum levels are established to ensure no adverse effects from disease-causing bacteria. The measurement of phosphorous and nitrate was added in many places when it became apparent that these two nutrients could stimulate aquatic plant growth to such an extent that few other organisms could survive at the low dissolved oxygen (DO) level caused by plant decay. Therefore, through monitoring and a permit system, we have identified most point sources of possible water pollution and may eventually have all facilities operating as outlined in the Clean Water Act. The above briefly illustrates some of the problems with point source discharges into surface water.

The second major source of pollutants in our surface water and ground water is from nonpoint sources of pollution. Nonpoint sources include agriculture, construction, silviculture, urban runoff, mining, livestock operations, and home septic systems. The major pollutants from these sources are suspended solids from erosion and nutrients such as nitrogen and phosphorus. Each year, billions of tons of soil are eroded by water and wind.

---

3. Miller, G.T., Jr., *Living in the Environment* (Belmont, CA: Wadsworth Publishing Co., Inc., 1982).

4. 40 CFR Part 133.

About half of this eroded soil is deposited in watercourses. Fertilizer use by farmers is averaging about 20 million tons of primary nutrients (nitrogen, phosphorous, and potash) annually. Much of this eventually ends up in runoff to our waterways.[5] Construction is another significant contributor of sediment from erosion. One bared acre of land can contribute over 150 tons of sediment from erosion in one year. Silviculture may cause landslides, and certainly extensive erosion results from poor logging practices. Urban runoff (storm drains) carries metals and toxics as well as suspended solids into our watercourses. Mining operations—mainly strip mining for coal—have left over 400,000 acres of unreclaimed soil surface in Ohio alone. Water washing across this pyritic spoil turns acid before it enters watercourses. In Pennsylvania this has resulted in the destruction of many good trout streams. Another major source of water pollution potential is manure from livestock, both unconfined and those kept in feedlots. In addition, approximately 20 million homes are serviced by septic tanks, presumably with leach fields. Many of these are poorly maintained and serviced only when a noticeable problem develops, which is usually long after soil water has been contaminated. What all this means is that a lot of pollutants are not controlled because no point source can be identified.

When we consider nonpoint sources together with unlined sanitary landfills, secured landfills (hazardous waste), and other point sources where controls have not been fully effective, the entire problem becomes clearer. When water, polluted or not, comes in contact with any material it can physically or chemically carry, it will carry that material. Therefore, ground water as well as surface water has the potential to become polluted. Furthermore, it is next to impossible to completely clean ground water once it has become contaminated. There are many cities that have municipal wells contaminated with organic solvents, pesticides, and other hazardous wastes and their breakdown products (such as DDE from DDT).[6] Another problem with both surface water and ground water is that pollutants in the air can reach this water even if the water itself is far removed from the pollution source. We thus have a distinct connection between water pollution and air pollution.

2. Air Pollution

Air pollution is more difficult to deal with than water pollution. Water has organisms in it that can act to cleanse the watercourse, at least to a

---

5. Council on Environmental Quality, *Environmental Quality* (Washington, DC: U.S. Gov't. Printing Office, 1990).

6. Ground water pollution due to pesticide use is discussed in Chapter 6.

Table I.   National Ambient Air Quality Standards[7]

Pollutant	Averaging time	Primary standard levels, $\mu g/m^{3a}$	Secondary standard levels, $\mu g/m^{3a}$
Particulate matter	Annual (arithmetic mean)	50	50
	24 hr[b]	150	150
Sulfur oxides	Annual (arithmetic mean)	80 (0.03)	—
	24 hr[b]	365 (0.14)	—
	3 hr[b]	—	1300 (0.5)
Carbon monoxide	8 hr[b]	(9)	—
	1 hr[b]	(35)	—
Nitrogen dioxide	Annual (arithmetic mean)	100 (0.05)	100 (0.05)
Ozone	1 hr[b]	235 (0.12)	235 (0.12)
Lead	3 mo	1.5	1.5[a]

[a]Numbers in parentheses represent parts per million.
[b]Not to be exceeded more than once per year.

large degree. Air does not have these agents. It does not have an assimilative capacity like water. One way to view air pollution is to think of the atmosphere as a sewer in the sky. Like any sewer system, we dump material into the air and hope that the old saying "dilution is the solution to pollution" takes over. This is accomplished using tall smoke stacks, many of which occur upwind from areas currently complaining of acid rain problems. At one time, tall stacks were considered the answer to air pollution problems. What we did not adequately understand was that material placed into the air eventually gets washed out of the air when it rains and enters watercourses or soil. We also found out that a pollutant placed in the air could be chemically altered to produce a different pollutant before it is washed out of the air. An interesting example of this is the production in the atmosphere of sulfuric acid (H_2SO_4) from sulfur dioxide (SO_2). As more and more sources of pollutants were placed in production (we built more utility plants, more industrial facilities, and more motor vehicles with high compression engines), more pollutants were discharged into the atmosphere. Thus, the overall quantity of pollutants in the air increased, and eventually we began to no-

7. 40 CFR § 50.1 et seq.

Table II.   National Emissions Estimates, 1970–1987 (million metric tons per year)[9]

Year	TSP	SO_2	Nitrogen Oxides	Volatile organic compounds	CO
1970	18.5	28.3	18.1	27.5	97.8
1980	8.5	23.9	20.3	23.0	77.0
1981	8.0	23.5	20.3	21.6	74.4
1982	7.1	22.0	19.5	20.1	69.4
1983	7.1	21.5	19.1	20.9	71.3
1984	7.4	22.1	19.7	21.9	68.7
1985	7.0	21.6	19.7	20.3	64.6
1986	6.8	21.2	19.3	19.5	61.4
1987	7.0	20.4	19.5	19.6	61.4
Percentage change:					
1970–87	−62.2	−27.9	+7.7	−28.7	−37.2
1980–87	−17.6	−14.6	−3.9	−14.8	−20.3

tice them. The situation that led to this discovery is outlined in Figure 2 of Chapter 1.

Air pollutants for which we have established primary and secondary ambient air quality standards are shown in Table I. Primary standards are intended for protection of the public health; secondary standards are to protect the public welfare. Ambient air is the air around us as opposed to the air coming out of a specific source. A pollutant from a specific source is called an emission, and these are also limited by the federal government.[8] Probably the most familiar limits are for coal- and oil-fired electric generating plants on emissions of sulfur dioxide, nitrogen oxides, and particulate matter (TSP), but there are also emission limits for various air pollutants for incinerators, sulfuric acid plants, and petroleum refineries. In the United States we emit approximately 20 million metric tons of sulfur dioxide every year. On the bright side, this is a reduction from about 27 million metric tons emitted in 1977. Other emission limitations, notably those for cars, are also geared to reduce our air pollutant problems. Table II indicates the changes in emissions of pollutants over the years.

The pollutants referred to thus far in our discussion of air pollution certainly cause environmental problems; however, there are many other air pollutants that pose even greater types or magnitudes of danger. These are generally known as "hazardous air pollutants." The category of hazardous air pol-

8. 40 CFR Part 60.

9. Council on Environmental Quality, *Environmental Quality* (Washington, DC: U.S. Government Printing Office, 1990).

Table III. Sources of Some Hazardous Pollutants with
Established Emissions Standards[10]

Pollutant	Source
Asbestos	Asbestos mills, road surfacing with asbestos tailings, manufacturers of asbestos-containing products (fireproofing, etc.), demolition of old buildings, spray insulation
Beryllium	Extraction plants, ceramic manufacturers, foundries, incinerators, rocket motor manufacturing operations
Mercury	Ore processing, chlor-alkalai manufacturing, sludge dryers and incinerators
Vinyl chloride	Ethylene dichloride manufacturers, vinyl chloride manufacturers, polyvinyl chloride manufacturers

lutants includes substances such as asbestos, benzene, mercury, and inorganic arsenic and may be thought of as the types of air pollutants that are known to cause harms like cancer, nervous system disorders, mutations, or significant and widespread adverse effects on the nonhuman environment. Sources of some of our hazardous air pollutants are shown in Table III. Throughout the 1980's, there was a tremendous increase in public awareness and concern about the effects of hazardous air pollutants. Greater scientific evidence of harm was also presented. This led to Congress providing heavy emphasis on controlling hazardous air pollutants in the 1990 Clean Air Act. In addition, one type of air pollutant quickly rose from obscurity to the forefront of concern—those that deplete the earth's stratospheric ozone layer, the chlorofluorocarbons (CFCs), hydrochlorofluorcarbons (HCFCs) and halons. These gases have uses such as refrigerants, solvents, making plastic foam, aerosol spraying, and extinguishing fires; however, when they rise into the stratosphere, the CFCs release chlorine atoms and the halons release bromine atoms. These atoms combine with and break apart the ozone molecules, thus destroying the ozone layer that shields earth from damaging ultraviolet radiation.[11] Stratospheric ozone depletion, which would lead to huge increases in skin cancer and many other less well known or understood phenomena such as reduced crop yields, became another primary focus for Congress in the 1990 Clean Air Act.

The emergence of ozone layer depletion from being relatively unknown in the early 1980's to being a matter of critical international concern by the mid

---

10. Council on Environmental Quality, *Environmental Quality* (Washington, DC: U.S. Government Printing Office, 1980).

11. Nangle, O.E., "Stratospheric Ozone: United States Regulation of Chlorofluorocarbons," *Environmental Affairs*, Vol. 16:531 (1989).

to late 1980's is yet one more indication of how, unless we are vigilant, pollution can, with the large size of our population today, drastically change the environment. Pollution is a problem that results from a small population thinking that resources are limitless and that the byproducts of consumption can simply be discarded with immunity from any future detriment. This is like notions 1 and 2 presented in Figure 2 of Chapter 1. Then population grows, and the discarding of the by-products of consumption can no longer take place without accompanying detrimental effects. Pollution is a problem that will not disappear. We know that we will emit mercury to the air if we burn strip-mined coal from the western U.S. To completely remove this pollutant from emissions costs billions of dollars, but we will still have the mercury. Our former hazardous air pollutant is now a hazardous solid waste. What do we do with it? Who pays the cost of removal or disposal? How do you ask your neighbor (person next door, state, other country) to stop polluting your air and water, when you are using products that come from the production process that causes the pollution or are making similar pollutant contributions yourself? The number of pollution problems and the alternatives for dealing with those problems are perhaps limitless. The next sections will explore some of the mechanisms which have been put into effect to attempt to control pollution of one form or another.

B.   PRIVATE LAW REMEDIES—NUISANCE AND NEGLIGENCE, INJUNCTIONS AND DAMAGES

One method of analytically describing and evaluating the tools that the legal system uses for pollution control is to separate them into private pollution control mechanisms and public pollution control mechanisms. Private control mechanisms might include lawsuits instituted by individuals (or other entities, such as corporations or states) against a polluter where the lawsuit is based on a common law wrong such as negligence by the polluter or the polluter maintaining a nuisance. Remedies for these common law wrongs can be provided by the judicial system, even though no legislature has prohibited any specific actions or provided remedies for wrongful actions. By contrast, public pollution control is based on the enactment of legislation—federal or state statutes or local ordinances. This section will focus on private controls; the public mechanisms will be discussed subsequently.

1.   Nuisance

Consider this example: Assume that a cement plant is located near where you live, and it is discharging dirt and smoke into the air. You want to stop the pollution, so what might you do? You might hope for a statute or administrative regulation which would prohibit the pollution and bring with it a governmental enforcement scheme or at least provide you with the opportunity to bring a citizen's suit to enforce the prohibition. In the absence of such a statutory or administrative prohibition, you might initiate a private lawsuit against the cement company and ask the court for an injunction ordering the cement company to stop polluting and/or to order payment of damages for the harm they have done to you. Your case would be a tort case claiming "nuisance." This action basically claims that the cement company has a duty not to interfere with your peaceful enjoyment of your land, that it is so interfering, and that it is thus a nuisance. The common law (judge-made law from previous court cases) recognizes this tort of nuisance and allows judges to enjoin the action causing the nuisance and to provide compensation for harm. This private control mechanism also works on a deterrence principle—e.g., manufacturers who cause damage by polluting and are held liable for payment for that damage may be deterred from polluting.

This cement company situation is similar to the precedent setting New York case of *Boomer v. Atlantic Cement Company*.[12] In *Boomer*, the plaintiff's were successful in establishing that there was a nuisance. The question that was raised for the appeals court concerned the appropriate remedy to be given to the plaintiffs. The alternative remedies considered by the court were: (1) to issue an injunction prohibiting the cement company from maintaining the nuisance (stop polluting or close down) with a postponement of the injunction for eighteen months to allow the company an opportunity for technical advances to eliminate the nuisance, or (2) to in effect allow the company to continue operating as it had been on the condition that it pay permanent damages to the plaintiffs which would compensate them for the total existing and future economic loss to their property caused by the cement company.

In deciding between these two potential remedies, the court considered that the plaintiffs economic harm was relatively small compared to the consequences of an injunction. An injunction could have resulted in the closing of a $45,000,000 plant with over 300 employees. In addition to the magnitude of the economic harm to the company and the community, the court was influenced by the fact that the company was up to date in air pollution control technology and eighteen months would not result in meaningful technical advances. Furthermore, the court believed that the making of technical advances should be an industry responsibility rather than the responsibility of the defendant company. As for the deterrence of pol-

---

12. 309 N.Y.S. 2d 312, 257 N.E. 2d 870 (1970).

lution, the court believed that the risk of being required to pay permanent damages would be a sufficient incentive for research by cement plant owners for improved techniques to minimize pollution. The court thus opted for permanent compensatory damages. Plaintiffs would be paid off for past and future harm, but the pollution would be allowed to continue.

A dissenting opinion was filed in *Boomer*. The dissenting judge contended that by letting the cement company pollute if it paid damages, the court was licensing a continuing wrong. The company could do what the law said was wrong so long as it paid a fee. Perhaps the court could be accused of supporting or helping establish a societal norm of accepting polluted air because it had placed an official stamp of approval on pollution-causing activity so long as the polluter pays a price. Which result would you favor given the factual circumstances—stop the pollution or just make the company pay for the harm? Maybe if the cement company pays for 100% of the harm, then it is not really "polluting" since the benefits from the cement plant outweigh the detriments because there are no detriments due to the fact that those suffering have been fully compensated for their loss. Full compensation results in no harm, and, without harm, perhaps there can be no such thing as "pollution." Regardless of the reader's position, the difference between the philosophies of the majority of the New York high court and the dissenting judge should be carefully noted since it is basic to the continuing environmental debate—should an activity which does cause harm be stopped or can it continue if it pays its way? It can be argued that if the company can produce the cement, pay for the pollution damage, and still make a profit by asking and getting a high enough price for the cement to cover the damages it has to pay, then the utility to society of the cement outweighs the harm which its manufacture creates.

While the court in *Boomer* chose compensatory damages over enjoining the nuisance, other cases have resulted in the issuance of an injunction. It is possible that these different results are due to the fact that states vary with respect to what their body of common law contains; however, an attempt at explaining differing results based on factual differences rather than jurisdictional differences is worthwhile. First, we should note that *Boomer* may have been an example of "good guys or bad guys" law. What was in fact the proper remedy in *Boomer* may be said to be a close or at least reasonably debatable question. In close cases the court may tend to give the benefit of the doubt to a defendant with a good track record. Perhaps the result in *Boomer* might have been different if it had not been found that the most modern dust control devices available had been installed in the defendant's plant and that it was unlikely that the defendant itself could develop improvements in the near future. Second, we should consider what factual situations have led other courts, as opposed to the *Boomer* court, to enjoin the operation of facilities that were causing nuisances by polluting.

One case in which an injunction prohibiting the operation of a polluting facility was issued was *Spur Industries, Inc. v. Del E. Webb Development Co.*[13] That case involved a cattle feedlot which had been operating lawfully but became a nuisance when nearby land was developed for residential purposes (Del Webb's Sun City in Arizona). The odor and flies from the feedlot were at the least annoying and perhaps also unhealthy for the nearby residents. Del Webb's request for an injunction against Spur's operation was granted by the court. The court raised some factors which, if present in a given situation, may lead courts to be willing to grant an injunction. If a large number of people or an entire neighborhood is affected by the nuisance rather than a small number of persons, a court might be more likely to enjoin the nuisance instead of providing damages as a remedy. In *Spur*, the court also emphasized the type of injury, health rather than property damage, as a factor in its decision. A breeding ground for flies which are capable of transmitting disease had been declared dangerous to the public health by the Arizona legislature. Another factor possibly supporting the granting of the injunction may have been the harshness of the injury to the developer, Del Webb. Its parcels of land were difficult if not impossible to sell. Factors such as those discussed here have led courts to find that the nuisance is a "public nuisance" rather than a "private nuisance" and to be more willing to enjoin it. Yet a remedy based on a finding of "public nuisance" is still within the realm of private pollution control since it is a court-made remedy which does not need to be based on legislation.

In the *Spur Industries* case, Spur's operation of a feedlot was found to be a nuisance and, for the above reasons, the operation was enjoined; however, Spur did not come away from court as a total loser. The court recognized that at the time Spur established its feedlot there was no indication that a new city would spring up alongside it in what had been a rural, agricultural area. The court said that Spur was enjoined not because of any wrongdoing on its part but because of the court's regard for the rights of the public. The court also found that Del Webb was not blameless with respect to the problem. It had taken advantage of the lower land values and the availability of large tracts of rural land. The court thus required Del Webb to indemnify Spur Industries for damages to Spur occasioned by the injunction that required Spur to cease operation or move its feedlot.

The court itself noted that the result in *Spur* "may appear novel," and the court also carefully limited its decision to cases where a developer has, with foreseeability, necessitated the granting of an injunction against a lawful business by coming into a previously agricultural or industrial area.

---

13. 108 Ariz. 178, 494 P. 2d 700 (1972).

This novel decision raises some interesting questions. The court clearly finds that the polluting nuisance must be stopped, but it also acknowledges that when one who is engaged in lawful activity is stopped from continuing that activity because of changes in circumstances, consideration should be given to the idea of not requiring that the heretofore lawful enterprise also bear the economic losses brought about by the changed circumstances. If Bethlehem Steel has been operating in a lawful manner for years and the public decides that air pollution problems require stricter emission standards and hence installation of pollution control equipment by Bethlehem Steel, shouldn't the public compensate the company for its costs brought about by the public's new demands and not leave those costs to be borne by the shareholders or customers of the company? One response to this argument might be that, although Bethlehem Steel had been using the public's air in the past when the new emission standards were not in effect, that prior use does not give the company any interest which should be financially protected with respect to its continuing to use the air without meeting the new restrictions. An effort to reconcile this response with the *Spur Industries* case runs into problems. In the operation of its feedlot, Spur was not confining itself to its own land and the air above it. Odor and flies appeared on or above land owned by others. For a period of years no one complained, but when new needs of the public required that the odor and flies be halted, the court appears to have found that Spur's prior use was relevant to giving it an interest which was to be financially protected when its continued use of the surrounding air was inconsistent with the public interest.

A question related to the above discussion is: if Del Webb was simply asking that its land and property rights not be interfered with by others in a way which is prohibited by the common law of nuisance, then why should it have to pay to have that prohibited interference stopped? If Spur is the one causing the pollution, it would appear that Spur should bear the costs of stopping the pollution rather than the cost being placed on Del Webb, which was merely making sound business use of land which it owned. The "novel" *Spur Industries* case may be an example of the judicial system working at its best and taking the unusual approach of reaching a compromise solution to a problem which is the fault of no one and the costs of which are better shared than placed on one party. Yet, what would the court have done if many residents surrounding the feedlot had bought and built there individually rather than buying from a land developer? Would the court have required them to indemnify Spur for Spur's losses due to the injunction, or would the court have refused to issue an injunction? Should the result in the case have depended on the fact that Del Webb was a convenient corporate treasury which was both allowed and required to "buy an injunction"?

2. Other Private Law Mechanisms

In addition to nuisance actions, there are other legal mechanisms which are not based on pollution control statutes and which parties have sought to utilize for pollution control purposes or to obtain compensation for harms which may have come to them due to the conduct of a polluter. Since these private law mechanisms are applicable to fewer pollution situations and/or have met with less success than the tool of a nuisance suit, some but not all of them will be noted here, and our consideration of them will be relatively brief.

If your drinking water supply became polluted because of the unintentional but careless discharge of a toxic water pollutant, you might bring a negligence suit against the discharger of the pollutant and seek monetary compensation for the harm done. This suit is like a negligence suit brought against a driver who struck your car in the rear because he was following you too closely. Negligence suits may be contrasted to nuisance suits by noting that negligent conduct can generally be described as a "one-shot deal" rather than the continuing conduct and continuing harm which forms the basis of a nuisance suit. Thus monetary compensation for harm is the appropriate remedy, since there is not continuing wrongful conduct to enjoin. Although a negligence suit does not stop the polluting event from taking place (it has already happened), negligence suits can deter pollution in addition to providing compensation for pollution's harms. At least in theory, the potential liability of a polluter for his negligence will result in greater care being taken by people so as not to be negligent, causing a deterrence of negligent conduct and thus a reduction in pollution. The practical effect of this deterrence mechanism is dependent on factors such as the added costs to the potential polluter of greater care compared to the costs of paying for damages caused by negligent conduct. Furthermore, the utility of negligence suits as a pollution control tool is attenuated by factors such as the cost and bother for a victim to bring a lawsuit. The magnitude of the harm may not be worth the effort of the suit, or the victim's insurance may cover the loss. Chapter 6 contains additional discussion of the theory of negligence suits and the difficulties which a victim may face with respect to winning such a suit.

Some of the other approaches to private pollution control may be illustrated by the examples of suits based on the federal antitrust laws and provisions of the federal constitution. While these suits are not common law actions, they are discussed here as private pollution control because the statutes or constitutional provisions being invoked were not specifically directed at pollution problems.

One attempt to invoke the antitrust laws to combat pollution involved a suit wherein plaintiffs alleged that automobile manufacturers had conspired to eliminate competition among themselves with respect to the development, manufacture, and installation of automotive air pollution control devices.[14] The plaintiffs asked the court to find that there was such a conspiracy and that the conspiracy was a violation of the Clayton Act which prohibited conspiracies that restrained competition and to order the automobile companies to retrofit with effective air pollution control devices those automobiles which they had manufactured and sold to the public without such devices. The court found that while "the invitation to provide an innovative solution to it [smog] is tempting," the only purpose of the antitrust laws is to prohibit restraints on competition in order to guarantee a free marketplace in which an unsophisticated consumer can be assured of the best possible product for the least possible expense. Even assuming that there was a conspiracy, the court found that retrofitting automobiles with pollution control devices would not further the purpose of the antitrust laws and that the antitrust laws do not provide a remedy for pollution.

An attempt to bring provisions of the United States Constitution to bear directly on pollution problems without resorting to statutory or common law remedies was made in *Tanner v. Armco Steel Corp.*[15] Among other contentions, the plaintiffs claimed a right to a healthy and clean environment pursuant to the Ninth Amendment of the United States Constitution. The Ninth Amendment states: "The enumeration in the Constitution of certain rights, shall not be construed to deny or disparage others retained by the people." The court determined that this residual retention of rights by the people would not be interpreted to embody a legally assertable right to a healthful environment. While neither the antitrust approach to pollution control nor the attempt to use the Ninth Amendment was successful, they are noted here to raise the question of whether, if the facts of a case were compelling enough, and if resort to some nonenvironmental body of law were necessary to provide a remedy for a wrong, a court might accept an invitation to provide an innovative solution to an environmental problem.

Perhaps there may be better potential at the state level for success in bringing constitutional provisions to bear on the environment without resorting to statutory mechanisms. Some state constitutions have provisions which speak expressly of environmental concerns. For example, Article 1, Section 27 of the Pennsylvania Constitution states: "The people have a right to clean air, pure water, and to the preservation of the natural, scenic, historic and esthetic values of the environment. . . ." In an appropriate case, a court may be disposed to invoke such a state constitutional provision, in and of itself, as the basis for a remedy. Since these state constitutional provisions

---

14. *In re Multidistrict Vehicle Air Pollution*, 481 F. 2d 122 (1973), 367 F. Supp. 1298 (1973).

15. 340 F. Supp. 532 (1972).

deal specifically with the environment and are not a part of the common law, from the point of view of the organization of this chapter they are really a part of our next section—Public Pollution Control.

C. PUBLIC POLLUTION CONTROL—STATUTES AND REGULATIONS: FEDERAL, STATE, AND LOCAL

As an introduction to our discussion of pollution control mechanisms which are established through legislation, we should note that the legislation addresses various subject areas such as pollution of the air and water and pollution by noise, heat, and even light. These subject areas are often interconnected, yet legislative enactments have usually separated them and treated them individually. While for purposes of analysis, this section will also tend to treat these subjects individually, we should not completely forget their interrelationships. In addition, the reader should be aware that some issues that will be discussed here in one context, such as air pollution, are relevant to other pollution subject areas such as water or noise. The discussion of similar issues will not be repeated for different subject areas; however, the reader is encouraged to consider how an issue raised under water pollution might apply to air pollution.

1. Air Pollution—Control Mechanisms, Economic Costs of Control, Prevention of Significant Deterioration of Air Quality, Emission Reduction vs Dispersion Techniques, Stratospheric Ozone Protection

The main tools for air pollution control are created by the Clean Air Act.[16] The Clean Air Act vests the EPA Administrator (the head of the federal Environmental Protection Agency) with information gathering, research, and planning functions, but of more significance to us are the direct operative control mechanisms that the statute establishes. The act segregates automobiles and aircraft as "moving sources" of air pollution and requires administrative promulgation and enforcement of emission standards for these sources. While moving sources are certainly of great importance, our discussion will emphasize the parts of the statute that establish quality standards

---

16. 42 U.S.C. § 7401 et seq.

for the air around us (ambient air quality standards) and emission limitations for nonmoving or "stationary" sources.[17]

Leaving the moving sources and postponing acid rain control until our next section, we can think of the Clean Air Act as having three focuses: (1) the medium (air), (2) the sources of pollution, and (3) the pollutants. With respect to the medium, the act provides for establishment of and compliance with ambient air quality standards for various pollutants. This mechanism states that regardless of where the pollutants come from, there may only be certain levels of them present in the air. With respect to sources of pollution, the act says that regardless of whether the air around us is clean or dirty, there is no justification for allowing stationary sources of pollution (like factories or power plants) to emit higher levels of pollutants than necessary so long as we take into account available control technology and the cost of such technology. Thus emission standards are established for stationary sources. With respect to the focus on the pollutants themselves, Congress decided that some air pollutants are so hazardous that especially strict emission limitations, and perhaps prohibitions, are necessary. Also, production of the specific chemicals that destroy the stratospheric ozone layer is to be halted regardless of cost or availability of substitute products. Let's consider the "pollutant" focus of the Clean Air Act (CAA) first.

Under the 1970 CAA, Congress defined a "hazardous air pollutant" as one which may "reasonably be anticipated to result in an increase in mortality or an increase in serous irreversible, or incapacitating reversible, illness" and directed EPA to set emission standards for these pollutants to provide "an ample margin of safety to protect the public health."[18] No mention was made of the costs which might be incurred in achieving this strict standard, although EPA was specifically directed to take costs of emission reduction into account in setting emission standards for "nonhazardous" air pollutants in other parts of the CAA. One could thus conclude that the sole factor of relevance in setting emission standards for hazardous air pollutants was health, and cost could not be considered. EPA contended that Congress did not intend to preclude the use of cost as a factor, and, in *Natural Resources Defense Council v. EPA*,[19] the court found that, while Congress was primarily concerned with health in the hazardous air pollutants part of the statute, the history of the legislation did not indicate an intent by Congress to preclude

---

17. Reducing air pollution from automobiles by encouraging the use of alternative fuels is discussed in Chapter 7.

18. 42 U.S.C. § 7412 prior to 1990 amendment.

19. 824 F.2d 1146 (D.C. Cir. 1987).

EPA from using cost as a factor in setting hazardous air pollutant emission standards.

Even with cost as a legally allowable factor, EPA was presented with a statutory quandary. Emission standards were required to provide an ample margin of safety to protect the public health, but most hazardous air pollutants are potential carcinogens with no known threshold below which emission levels would be considered "safe." Yet if EPA were to set emission levels at zero, the effect on industry and the economy would be significant. As a result, between 1970 and 1990, EPA had listed only eight hazardous air pollutants and set emission standards for only seven of them.[20]

In the 1990 amendments to the CAA, Congress, dissatisfied with EPA's slowness in listing and limiting hazardous air pollutant emissions, took the unusual step of specifically listing 189 hazardous air pollutants.[21] Such a specific task is usually left to an agency and its expertise. Congress did, however, continue to leave the setting of the emission standards in the hands of EPA, but it provided a new framework for doing so. EPA is directed to promulgate emission standards that require the maximum degree of emission reduction achievable for new and existing sources of hazardous air pollutants. While the statute now explicitly says EPA is to take the cost of emission reduction into consideration, the emission standard for a new source of pollution cannot be less stringent than the emission control that is achieved in practice by the best controlled similar source. Analogously, emission standards for existing sources may not be less stringent than the average of the few best performing existing sources. If costs allow, the standards may be stricter, but the best in the industry is now Congress' benchmark for hazardous emissions. In addition, within eight years of the setting of the "best in the industry" type standards noted above, even stricter emission standards will be set if needed to provide an ample margin of safety to protect the public health or to prevent an "adverse environmental effect." "Adverse environmental effect" is defined to include significant and widespread adverse effects on wildlife, aquatic life, or other natural resources. Thus the scope of hazardous air pollution control has broadened from being solely directed at protecting human health in 1970 to include protection of the nonhuman environment from significant and widespread harm in the 2000's.

The "pollutant" focus of the CAA is also manifested in the sections of the 1990 amendments that control by name those pollutants that contribute to the destruction of the stratospheric ozone layer. The pollutants are the

---

20. Marchant, G. and Danzeisen, D., "'Acceptable' Risk for Hazardous Air Pollutants," 13 *Harv. Envtl. L. Rev.* 535 (1989).

21. 42 U.S.C. § 7412(b).

chlorofluorocarbons (CFCs) and halons. The adverse effects resulting from use of these chemicals, including increases in skin cancer, and the worldwide concern about ozone layer depletion that led to the treaty known as the Montreal Protocol are noted in Chapter 1. The 1990 Clean Air Act restricted United States production and consumption of CFCs and halons by providing for a phasing out of these chemicals by the year 2000. In each year from 1991 through 2000, decreasing percentages of production levels from a baseline year (1986 or 1989 depending on the chemical) were allowed.[22] While Congress apparently thought this phaseout schedule would probably be sufficient to address the ozone depletion problem, it authorized an acceleration of the phaseout if scientific information showed that a more stringent schedule was necessary to protect human health or the environment.[23] In response to new scientific data showing major ozone depletion likelihood in highly populated northern hemisphere areas including the U.S., the President accelerated the phaseout by ordering that CFC and halon production halt entirely by the end of 1995.[24]

Having outlined the "pollutant" focus of the Clean Air Act (the approach used to control hazardous air pollutants), let's next consider the control mechanism that focuses on the "medium" (the air)—the ambient air quality standards. Congress has said that the quality of our air should be protected and enhanced to promote the public health and welfare. The Administrator is thus directed to study the effects of pollutants having negative impacts on the public health and welfare and to establish national primary and secondary ambient air quality standards based on that study. The national primary ambient air quality standards are those the attainment and maintenance of which, allowing an adequate margin of safety, are requisite to protect the "public health." The national secondary ambient air quality standards are those the attainment and maintenance of which are requisite to protect the "public welfare" from known or anticipated adverse effects. Effects on welfare are said to include, but not be limited to, effects on items such as soils, water, crops, animals, climate, property, economic values, and personal comfort. The list is very broad, but even if one could think of something adversely affected that is not on the list, the "but is not limited to" clause would allow its inclusion.

The setting of the ambient air quality standards is done at the federal level, but the implementation of the federally set standards is placed in the

---

22. 42 U.S.C. § 7671 and § 7671c. The less harmful "hydrochlorofluorocarbons" are phased out on a different schedule (see 42 U.S.C. § 7671d).

23. 42 U.S.C. § 7671e.

24. *Weekly Compilation of Presidential Documents* (Washington, DC: Office of the Federal Register, Feb. 17, 1992) p.249.

hands of the states. The attainment or implementation phase of the ambient air quality standards mechanism is a good illustration of the fact that many environmental statutes are political compromises between those who favor state control and those who favor federal control, either because of differing beliefs about which level of government can best perform a task or about which level should be in control of local geographic areas. The air quality standards are set by the federal government, but each state has the opportunity to implement the standards and to choose its own methods of doing so. Thus one state may choose to implement the standards by being more restrictive with respect to automobiles, while another may choose instead to emphasize limiting industrial growth. The states submit their state implementation plans (SIPs) to EPA, which may approve or disapprove a plan or any portion thereof depending on whether it meets requirements listed in the statute. Those requirements include items such as having monitoring and enforcement programs, showing the capability of attaining the air quality standards within the time frames set by the statute, and containing provisions to prohibit any stationary source within the state from emitting pollutants which will prevent another state from attaining the ambient air quality standards. If a state does not adopt an approvable state implementation plan, then EPA is authorized to establish an implementation plan for the state and to impose it. Federal courts have ordered EPA to promulgate federal implementation plans (FIPs) in the absence of appropriately approved state implementation plans[25] and have found that EPA may pay for the cost of creating the FIP by using funds which might otherwise have gone to the state under a grant program provided in the Clean Air Act.[26]

The last operative mechanism of the Clean Air Act that we will consider focuses on the "sources" of pollution. We have noted that the act uses separate approaches for dealing with moving vs. stationary sources and we will here discuss the stationary source standards. As we said earlier, the stationary source standards mechanism of the act is based on the premise that stationary sources of pollution like oil refineries, power plants, and cement plants should only be allowed to emit levels of pollutants that they cannot prevent with available control technology. Even if the ambient air meets the federal standards, stationary sources should control their emissions. The main thrust of the stationary source emission standards is on new stationary sources. Although existing stationary sources may become subject to emission limitations, standards of performance for existing stationary sources may be less restrictive than for new sources and may take into account

25. *Delaney v. Environmental Protection Agency*, 898 F. 2d 687 (1990).

26. *Illinois Environmental Protection Agency v. United States Environmental Protection Agency*, 947 F. 2d 283 (1991).

the remaining useful life of the existing source. Perhaps the justification for treating existing sources differently from new sources can be analogized to the court's requirement in the *Spur Industries* case (Section B) that the preexisting polluter be indemnified for its losses when it was ordered to stop its polluting activity.

With the above explanation of the operative mechanisms of the Clean Air Act as a base, let's next look at some of the issues of policy and interpretation which have arisen concerning this statute, how those issues were handled in the courts, and how subsequent amendments to the statute addressed questions which were raised in some of the court cases.

One issue that has been raised in connection with the stationary source standards required under Section 111 is whether it is unfair discrimination to have different stationary source standards for different industries—e.g., one set of standards for cement plants and less strict standards for power plants. One way of supporting the position that different standards create unfair discrimination is to argue that if the level of emission control is based on the available technology, then those industries that developed technology voluntarily prior to the statutory requirements would be punished for their good faith efforts in the past. They are saddled with a higher standard because the technology is available to them, while those industries that were the "bad guys" and never developed control technology willingly are rewarded with looser standards since technology is not available to them. When this issue was presented in court, the court's response was that Congress intended to clean up the air in whatever ways the available technology would allow, and that no uniformity of standards for all industries was required.[27] Furthermore, it can be said that comparisons between industries should not matter since, as long as the standard is the same for all competitors within one industry, none are disadvantaged. The only time that comparisons between industries should be relevant is when the industries produce substitute or alternative products. In those situations, failure to at least take the inter-industry competitiveness into account would be a failure to take into account the economic costs of achieving the Section 111 standards, and the words of Section 111 require that when EPA sets emission reduction standards, there must be a "taking into account the cost of achieving such reduction." The need for interindustry comparisons in such competitive situations was recognized by the court in the case noted above.

With respect to the Section 109 ambient air quality standards, an issue that has generated longstanding and widespread debate is known as the question of "prevention of significant deterioration." This issue was litigated

---

27. *Portland Cement Association v. Ruckelshaus*, 486 F. 2d 375 (1973).

in the courts and was subsequently addressed by Congress in amendments to the Clean Air Act. The issue is whether air that is cleaner than the secondary ambient air quality standard (the stricter standard) should be allowed to be degraded to the level of the secondary standard or should this cleaner than secondary standard air be kept at or near its existing level of cleanliness.

In favor of allowing the air quality to deteriorate to the secondary level is the argument that having air that is cleaner than the secondary standard serves no purpose. The secondary standard is the level of air quality that is requisite to protect the public welfare from any known or anticipated adverse effects. That is a broad protection in and of itself but is further broadened by the Clean Air Act's definition of welfare as including but not being limited to effects on "soils, water, crops, vegetation, manmade materials, animals, wildlife, weather, visibility, and climate, damage to and deterioration of property, and hazards to transportation, as well as effects on economic values and on personal comfort and well-being."[28] These listed parameters appear to include everything imaginable, but the definition is made even broader by the words that say welfare includes but is not limited to even this comprehensive list. The argument thus says that the secondary standard protects everything and there is no reason to preserve air that is cleaner than the secondary standard if allowing deterioration will serve some function such as enabling more industry to locate in an area and bring with it jobs and a potentially better standard of living. Unindustrialized sectors of the country would argue that it is unfair to require them to keep their air cleaner than the all-inclusive secondary standard even if that is not their wish. To do so would impose on them the risk of losing out on industry, jobs, and a better standard of living. They would contend that just because they did not industrialize before the enactment of the Clean Air Act as other parts of the country did, they should not forever be precluded from industrializing.[29] Also, they should not be required to forever be America's "clean air paradise" dependent on tourism revenues from those who live in more economically prosperous locations.

In favor of requiring that air that is cleaner than the secondary standard be kept substantially at the cleaner level is the argument that the secondary standard, while it appears to provide 100% protection, is really the product of both factual and political compromises. Factually, different scientific experts will disagree on what numerical standard of air quality is necessary to protect the public welfare. The secondary standard is likely to be a

---

28. 42 U.S.C.S. § 7602(h).

29. This position is also taken on a global basis by the less developed nations who argue that any internationally set environmental standards should be not as strict and/or not applicable as soon for the less developed countries.

compromise between those who are very worried about the adverse effects of air pollution and those who are less concerned. From the political perspective, people will disagree about matters such as what are the "known or anticipated adverse effects" which the secondary standard is required to protect against. This political disagreement among those involved in the decision-making process of setting the secondary standard may well result in a compromise on the numerical level that is set as the standard. Those who favor not allowing air that is cleaner than the secondary standard to be degraded down to the secondary standard say that since the standard is a product of compromise, society is better off to err on the side of caution and keep clean air at its existing level of cleanliness.

The issue of prevention of significant deterioration of air that is cleaner than the secondary standard was presented to the courts in *Sierra Club v. Ruckelshaus*.[30] The United States District Court looked at one of the stated purposes of the Clean Air Act which is to "protect and enhance the quality of the Nation's air resources" and concluded that the words "protect and enhance" evidenced Congress' intent to improve air quality and prevent deterioration rather than allowing deterioration. The court further noted that Congress had used the words protect and enhance in earlier air pollution legislation and that those words had been administratively interpreted as not allowing significant deterioration. Congress then used the same words in the Clean Air Act, and thus the court said it must have intended that the same interpretation be adopted. Also of importance to the court was the legislative history of the Clean Air Act. The court cited a Senate Report, uncontradicted by the House, that said that air that was cleaner than the air quality goals should be maintained in its cleaner condition. The District Court's conclusion was that the EPA Administrator could not approve a state implementation plan that allowed areas with air quality cleaner than the secondary standard to have their air be degraded down to that standard. To do so would be contrary to Congress' policy of protecting the quality of the air. The District Court thus seemed to have resolved the deterioration issue in a straightforward way relying on the intent of Congress as manifested by its words, its actions, and the statute's legislative history. This "straightforward" decision was taken to the United States Supreme Court, which, one year later, voted 4 to 4 on the issue.[31] Procedurally, an equally divided Supreme Court vote serves to affirm the lower court decision, but the 4 to 4 split underlines the legal and political division that existed on the issue. In an effort to remove the issue from the arena of statutory interpretation by the courts and to resolve

---

30. 344 F. Supp. 253 (1972).

31. 412 U.S. 541 (1973).

it as a political matter to be decided by the people's representatives, Congress addressed the deterioration question in the 1977 amendments to the Clean Air Act.

In the amendments, Congress specifically required that state implementation plans must prevent "significant deterioration" of air quality in areas where the air is cleaner than the ambient air quality standards. Congress then went on to define what it meant by "significant deterioration." Its definitional mechanism is noteworthy because of its contrast to the usual relationship of statutes to administrative regulations. Usually Congress will leave the detailed numbers of an environmental standard to be established by the agency in its administrative regulations. This is what it has done with respect to setting the ambient air quality standards themselves. In the amendments, however, Congress itself established the numbers which would define when deterioration of air quality is significant deterioration and unacceptable. For example, in class I areas (large national parks and wilderness areas) the maximum allowable increase in particulate matter is 5 $\mu g/m^3$ measured as an annual geometric mean. Class II areas (most of our land mass) are allowed 19 $\mu g/m^3$ as an increase, and class III areas (where the most intensive development will be allowed) can have a maximum allowable increase of 37 $\mu g/m^3$. It should be emphasized that these increases are for areas where the air quality is cleaner than the ambient air quality standards. These allowable increases do not mean that the ambient air quality standards can be exceeded.

Another air pollution issue which demonstrates the interrelationship between Congress and EPA is the use of economic incentives to achieve air pollution targets. Congress has often used economic incentives to foster environmental goals, and some examples that are related to energy production and use are discussed in Chapter 7. In the air pollution area, EPA took a leadership role by providing for "marketable emission reduction credits." If a company reduces its emissions to a greater extent than required by the law, the surplus reduction in emissions becomes a credit which can be sold under EPA's Emission Trading Policy.[32] Polluters are thus given an incentive to make cost effective emission reductions beyond those that are mandated. Cost effectiveness occurs when you can sell your emission reduction credits for a higher price than it cost you to make the extra emission reductions. Those industries who buy the credits will be ones that cannot control their emissions at as low a cost as the industries who are selling credits.

One criticism that can be made of the trading in emission credits is that the total amount of emissions is not reduced. EPA does, however, discount

---

32. 47 Fed. Reg. 15076.

the emission credits, and a 100 ton surplus reduction may only be worth 80 tons to the purchaser of the credit. Another way that the overall amount of emissions may be reduced with marketable credits is that a company may choose to return the credits to the government rather than selling them. It may make that choice because of a combination of factors including a belief that reducing emissions is environmentally responsible business behavior and the positive public image that can be created by publicity about returning rather than selling emission credits. It should also be noted that, since marketable emission reduction credits have values of millions of dollars, significant tax deductions can be taken based on the value of the credits that are given to the government.[33]

Another criticism that is made of marketable emission credits is that when new technology allows emission reductions beyond the mandated level, that technology should be required to be used by all rather than letting some industries not use the technology and instead buy credits from others. This argument is bolstered by the language of the Clean Air Act that says new stationary sources of pollution must use "the best system of emission reduction which . . . has been adequately demonstrated."[34] Yet, in the 1990 Clean Air Act, Congress apparently approved of EPA's market incentive approach by legislatively authorizing the transfer of the SO_2 allowances which Congress was enacting to control acid rain.[35] The acid deposition controls of the 1990 Act are discussed in the next section.

2. Acid Rain—A Hybrid Form of Pollution

Acidic metal-containing precipitation (acid rain or acid deposition) is a hybrid form of pollution. It is really a water pollution problem downwind from emissions of air pollution. Sulfur oxides and nitrogen oxides are produced from stationary and mobile point sources when fossil fuels are burned. Acid rain results when these sulfur oxides and nitrogen oxides form sulfuric and nitric acid and fall to earth as rain. In addition, acid rain often contains heavy metals such as cadmium, lead, and zinc. The damage done by acid rain includes possible respiratory disease in humans, loss of profits from farming, accelerated building deterioration, and numerous negative impacts on our lakes, rivers, and forests. For example, the increased acidity can kill all the fish and other life forms in lakes and, in ways not fully understood

---

33. "Hutchinson No Longer Holds Its Nose," *New York Times* (Feb 3, 1991) p.D1.

34. 42 U.S.C. § 7411(a)(1).

35. 42 U.S.C. § 7151b(b).

but being studied extensively, the combination of acidity and metals in the soil reduces growth or kills some species of trees.[36] At the ecosystem level, this may result in altered species composition and succession because resistant species may be favored while sensitive species decline. In our discussion of acid rain, we will first consider some historical aspects of the phenomenon. We will then examine why past approaches to regulation were seemingly inadequate and how the long-awaited Congressional action that specifically focuses on acid rain is designed to solve the problem.

Acid rain is, as far as we can determine, a phenomenon of recent origin. After World War II, the people of the United States indicated dissatisfaction with the particulate emissions from industrial facilities that burned fossil fuels. Precipitators were installed at the facilities to remove most of the particulates (soot), and, while this provided a solution to one problem, it created another. Particulates had acted to neutralize sulfur dioxide emissions and essentially prevent the formation of atmospheric sulfuric acid that might eventually fall to earth. At the same time, we built a lot of tall smokestacks to help remedy the local pollution situation by dispersing the pollutants over a wide area, an undertaking that likely contributed to the regional problem we faced later. Around 1950, the automobile industry introduced the high compression engine and with it a combustion product of much greater magnitude than previously experienced, nitrogen oxides. Thus, in our effort to be more efficient in one case (automobiles) and less polluting in another case (precipitators and tall stacks), we allowed two oxides into the air. In the atmosphere, these oxides can be transported long distances and can be chemically altered to form sulfuric and nitric acids, the components of acid rain.

For many years there was not sufficient evidence to convince everyone that acid rain was indeed causing the harm that was being attributed to it. Today, research and debate have shifted to the severity of the effects of acid rain, and the question of causation is an increasingly settled one. Few scientists or politicians currently doubt the serious threats acid rain poses to the public and the environment; however, the significant economic costs and political fallout from efforts to control acid rain stood in the way of Congress and EPA directly attacking the acid rain problem until 1990. Prior to 1990, the Clean Air Act recognized what turned out to be the main sources of acid rain—sulfur oxides and nitrogen oxides. It set both emission limits and ambient air quality standards for these oxides, but the emission restrictions and ambient standards were designed to insure that the public

---

36. Smith, W.H., "Air Pollution and Forest Damage," *Chemical and Engineering News* (Nov. 11, 1991) p.30.

health and welfare were protected locally, without regard for the impact of the emissions on other regions through acid rain. The problem of acid rain was finally specifically addressed by Congress in the 1990 Clean Air Act.

The 1990 Clean Air Act amendments retain the original scheme for controlling acid rain but add an entirely new subchapter titled Acid Deposition Control.[37] The new provisions focus on the major source of acid rain causing pollutants, power plants that burn fossil fuel. These power plants, which are usually steam generating electric utilities, produce 80% of the sulfur dioxide and 33% of the nitrogen oxides emitted nationally. The goal of the amendments is to reduce the annual emissions of sulfur dioxide, SO_2, by 10 million tons and nitrogen oxides, NO_x, by 2 million tons from the 1980 levels.[38] The approach taken by Congress with respect to acid rain is another example of the unusual but becoming more common scenario of Congress acting with a degree of specificity normally left by it to the administrative agencies such as EPA. Perhaps this is an indication of legislative frustration with EPA, or legislative concern about having waited a long time to control acid rain and not wanting to have more time spent in the administrative agency process, or legislative awareness about foreign affairs and the deteriorating goodwill between the U.S. and Canada over the issue of U.S. caused acid rain in Canada. For whatever reason(s), Congress listed by name 111 power plants, sometimes called the "big dirties," and the individual generators at those plants and provided numerical "allowances" for each in tons of SO_2 which may be emitted annually. Part of Table A from 42 U.S.C. §7651c(e) is shown in Figure 3. These allowances are Phase I of the control program, with applicability as of January 1, 1995. Phase II, applicable January 1, 2000, reduces the Phase I allowance allocations and also applies to smaller, cleaner plants. In Phase II, a national "cap" on SO_2 emissions from power plants will limit their aggregate annual emissions to 8.9 million tons.[39] While a plant must have one allowance for each ton of SO_2 to be emitted each year, as discussed in our last section, SO_2 allowances are transferable. With respect to NO_x emissions, Congress was more traditional. It directed EPA to establish regulations which would reduce annual power plant NO_x emissions by a total of approximately 2 million tons, but left to EPA's expertise the setting of the emission standards based on emission rates achievable with low NO_x burners.

---

37. 42 U.S.C. §§ 7651–7651o.

38. 42 U.S.C. § 7651(b).

39. 42 U.S.C. § 7651b(a).

TABLE A.—AFFECTED SOURCES AND UNITS IN PHASE I AND THEIR
SULFUR DIOXIDE ALLOWANCES (TONS)

State	Plant Name	Generator	Phase I Allowances
Alabama	Colbert	1	13,570
		2	15,310
		3	15,400
		4	15,410
		5	37,180
	E.C. Gaston	1	18,100
		2	18,540
		3	18,310
		4	19,280
		5	59,840
Florida	Big Bend	1	28,410
		2	27,100
		3	26,740
	Crist	6	19,200
		7	31,680
Georgia	Bowen	1	56,320
		2	54,770
		3	71,750
		4	71,740
	Hammond	1	8,780
		2	9,220
		3	8,910
		4	37,640
	J. McDonough	1	19,910
		2	20,600
	Wansley	1	70,770
		2	65,430
	Yates	1	7,210
		2	7,040

Figure 3. Part of the list of power plants and their SO_2 allowances.[40]

3. Water Pollution—Control Mechanisms, Federal Jurisdiction, Thermal Pollution

We have just concluded a detailed analysis of the Clean Air Act's mechanisms for air pollution control and some of the issues raised by those mechanisms which needed court interpretation or Congressional clarification. Rather than going through a similar discussion concerning water pollution and being quite repetitive at times, we will instead briefly make comparisons between the Clean Air Act and the Clean Water Act.[41] We will then discuss two issues in the context of water pollution which could arise in an air pollution context just as issues similar to those we discussed in our air pollution section could arise with respect to water pollution. These will be

---

40. 42 U.S.C. § 7651c(e).

41. 33 U.S.C.S. § 1251 et seq.

the extent of federal authority and thermal pollution. Finally, we will explore Congress' solution to the problem of preventing and responding to oil spills.

The Clean Air Act's approach of addressing the medium being polluted, the sources of pollution, and the nature of the pollutants themselves is also utilized in the Clean Water Act. Thus the ambient air quality standards (the medium focus) have their counterparts in the use of water quality standards and state implementation plans under the Clean Water Act. The counterpart of the stationary source standards for air pollution can be said to be the effluent limitations for point sources. The Clean Water Act also singles out toxic water pollutants for special control efforts following the Clean Air Act pattern of providing a separate control mechanism for hazardous air pollutants.

Although similar in the above ways, the two statutes are significantly different in terms of the emphasis placed on the various control mechanisms. While the Clean Air Act made substantial use of the ambient air quality standards with state implementation plans to achieve them, the Clean Water Act leans very strongly toward pollution control by limiting the discharge of effluents from their sources. For different types of pollutants, different levels of technology originally were required to be used by specified dates to limit the amount of discharge of each type of pollutant. As examples, for "conventional" pollutants such as those classified as biochemical oxygen demanding (BOD) and suspended solids, effluent limitations initially required application of the "best conventional pollutant control technology" (BCT) by July 1, 1984. For "toxic" pollutants, effluent limitations required the use of the "best available technology" (BAT) economically achievable by July 1, 1984. BAT may be a higher level of technology than the BCT level. A lower level of technology, "best practicable control technology" (BPT) governed the effluent limitations for earlier years. There have been delays in meeting established deadlines, and, eventually, Congress was forced to amend the statute to provide for compliance with the required technologies by March 31, 1989.[42] Perhaps needless to say, delays in implementation continue. Discharges of effluents are allowed only if they are in compliance with the effluent limitations, and only by obtaining a permit to discharge within those limits. Permits are issued federally or by states if the state has an EPA-approved plan with limitations at least as strict as those of EPA. An example of some of the conditions which may be imposed on a discharger may be seen in Appendix D, which shows a portion of a Discharge Permit form used by the State of Vermont. A basic overall goal of the above mechanisms and of the entire Clean Water Act originally was the elimination

---

42. 33 U.S.C.S. § 1311(b).

of all discharges of pollutants into navigable waters by 1985. Today, one suspects that Congress' goal is water pollution control in accordance with the statute as soon as practicable.

With the above description of some of the federal methods used to control water pollution, and acknowledging that other significant control mechanisms have been omitted from our discussion (such as the massive federal grants made to finance municipal treatment works), let's consider in a water pollution context the issue of the extent of the federal government's power to deal with pollution matters. For this, we look at *United States vs. Holland*,[43] a case that, early in the history of federal water pollution control efforts, tested the authority of the federal government. The *Holland* case involved defendants who admitted that they were discharging pollutants into man-made mosquito canals and wetlands without a permit which the government said was required under the Water Pollution Control Act Amendments (now referred to as the Clean Water Act). The defendants claimed that they did not need a permit because they were discharging into waters which were not within the federal jurisdiction. Their argument had two distinct parts. One part was that Congress never intended that its statute be applicable to waters which were not navigable waters and, secondly, that even if Congress did want to assert jurisdiction or control over the waters at the point where defendants were discharging, it did not have the Constitutional authority to do so.

To answer the question of whether Congress intended to control the waters into which the defendants were discharging, the court looked at the statutory language that Congress had used which said that the statute applied to "navigable waters." The court went on, however, to say that what was meant by "navigable waters" was not necessarily what it would mean in the technical sense or in average usage but rather what Congress intended it to mean. In the statute itself, Congress had defined "navigable waters" to be "waters of the United States," and the legislative history of the statute from the House and Senate clearly indicated that Congress intended that the statute apply to "all waters of the United States." The court thus found that Congress had intended to control the waters into which the defendants were discharging even though they were wholly unsuited for navigation and even though the statute said it applied to "navigable waters." Thus an important lesson concerning the reading of statutes is that the words used do not necessarily mean what they appear to mean. At least in situations where a term is used in the statute and specifically defined in that statute, the term's meaning may not be its ordinary language meaning. Rather, the

---

43. 373 F. Supp. 665 (1974).

term will mean what the statutory definition says it will mean. In the Clean Water Act, "navigable waters" means "waters of the United States" and the legislative history adds the gloss of "all waters of the United States."

The second issue for our consideration in *Holland*, that of whether Congress has the constitutional authority to regulate pollution of non-navigable canals and wetlands, has more far-reaching implications and an interesting history that bears on the answer. As we noted in Chapter 1, Congress' power to regulate concerning environmental matters comes from the Commerce Clause of the United States Constitution, which gives Congress the power "to regulate Commerce . . . among the several States . . . ." We also noted that the scope of the Commerce Clause power has been interpreted to include the power for Congress to act with respect to matters which have an effect on interstate commerce. The court in *Holland* said that it is beyond question that water pollution has a serious effect on interstate commerce, and Congress can thus regulate activities which cause pollution such as the dredging and filling in which the defendants were engaged. The court used the "effect on interstate commerce" approach to find that the pollution causing activities at the defendant's site would have serious effects on interstate commerce. If it had not been able to use the "effect" approach, one can speculate that the court may well have taken another step in the historical expansion of Congress' power with respect to bodies of water. That expansion was detailed by the court as follows.

The court noted that since much of 19th century commerce was carried out on the water, Congress' power "to regulate Commerce" had early been held to necessarily include the power over navigation.[44] If you are to effectively regulate navigation, you must have the power to keep navigable waters open and free, and Congress was found to have that power also.[45] Subsequent steps in the expansion of Congress' authority included the authority to regulate waters over which commerce is or *may be* carried on with other states;[46] waters capable of commercial use, not merely those in actual use;[47] waters with a history of commercial use;[48] and waterways which could be made navigable by reasonable improvements.[49] Few bodies of water could escape from the Congressional power under these expanded interpretations of what the Commerce Clause supposedly authorized Congress

44. *Gibbons v. Ogden*, 22 U.S. 1 (1824).

45. *Gilman v. Philadelphia*, 70 U.S. 713 (1865).

46. *The Daniel Ball*, 77 U.S. 557 (1870).

47. *The Montello*, 87 U.S. 430 (1874).

48. *Economy Light and Power v. United States*, 256 U.S. 113 (1921).

49. *United States v. Appalachian Electric Power Co.*, 311 U.S. 377 (1940).

to control. If mosquito canals and wetlands could escape, and if the "effect on interstate commerce" approach were not available to bring them within Congress' jurisdiction, it would not be difficult to imagine the court taking the next step and further expanding its interpretation of the Commerce Clause to include those bodies of water also. The question to be left for the reader is whether, in light of the above described scope of Congress' power under the Commerce Clause, there is any body of water (or land, or air, or mineral or . . .) over which Congress does not have the Constitutional power to act? Can Congress control what you do with a temporary puddle that forms in your backyard or basement after a rainstorm? Is it likely that the people who drafted the United States Constitution would have approved of such power being in the hands of the federal government?

As a second topic that raises air as well as water pollution implications, let's consider thermal pollution. Thermal pollution could be an air pollution problem as well as a water pollution problem, as anyone who has stood in heavy traffic on city pavement on a hot summer day can verify. Today's most significant thermal pollution problems are, however, water-related, and the Clean Water Act provides for thermal pollution control for bodies of water. Thermal pollution problems result from the fact that even minor changes in water temperatures can affect the reproduction, migration, and metabolism of cold-blooded heat-sensitive aquatic animals. Heat also causes adverse effects on aquatic plants, and the death of a body of water could result due to heat-caused oxygen depletion.

A major cause of thermal pollution is the electric utility industry. Other sources include steel mills and pulp processing plants. In order to control thermal pollution problems, Congress has included "heat" within the definition of "pollutant" under the Clean Water Act, and thus water quality control measures like effluent limitations are to include thermal discharge standards. While Congress has recognized thermal pollution as a problem, it has also recognized that the characteristics of heat make its effects more temporary and localized than many other pollutants. With this in mind, the Clean Water Act provides that thermal discharges should not be subject to any limits more stringent than necessary to assure the protection and propagation of a balanced, indigenous population of shellfish, fish, and wildlife in and on the relevant body of water. Some examples of mechanisms which have been used to control thermal pollution are allowing only limited rises in the temperature of a plant's outlet water over its inlet water, holding down the size of the water's "mixing zone" to prevent the formation of migratory barriers, and keeping the dissolved oxygen level sufficient to support local species.

Although heat is generally viewed as a pollutant of water and the law has sought to regulate it in at least a limited way, thermal discharges may have a positive side. Projects are underway which will explore the commercial possibilities of aquafarming of species like freshwater shrimp and rainbow trout using the heat from cooling water discharged by operations such as power plants. A pollutant could therefore become something from which a benefit could be derived and perhaps the better the control of the pollutant, the greater the enhancement of the benefit. That would be a highly desirable result for other pollutants as well as for heat.

As a final topic in our water pollution section, let's review Congress' approach to preventing and responding to oil tanker spills. Motivated by a rash of oil spills during the late 1980's, especially the *Exxon Valdez* catastrophe, Congress realized that the federal scheme for controlling oil pollution was inadequate. The *Valdez* incident was especially dramatic. 240,000 barrels (10 million gallons) of oil were spilled, eventually covering 3000 square miles of the pristine Prince William Sound area in Alaska, with cleanup costs surpassing $2 billion. At the time, the Comprehensive Environmental Response, Compensation, and Liability Act (CERCLA)[50] provided guidance for responding to releases of hazardous wastes *except* for oil. Instead, the Clean Water Act addressed the prevention of and response to oil spills;[51] however, the maximum liability levels contained in the Clean Water Act were much too low for spills the size of *Valdez*, and the Act had no controls with respect to vessel personnel or construction standards. In addition, the fund authorized by the Act for cleanup costs incurred by the government was woefully small, containing only $7 million. Yet another problem was that private parties were not given any federal remedy for recovering damages. They had to resort to state law remedies in actions separate from federal ones brought under the Clean Water Act.

In response to the inadequacies of the then existing federal oil pollution control scheme, Congress enacted the Oil Pollution Act of 1990.[52] The new statute presents a comprehensive effort to prevent oil tanker spills and, in the event a spill occurs, to make cleanup more effective and place greater financial liability on the responsible party. This increased liability potential will, hopefully, also serve as an incentive for the prevention of spills. Let's consider three significant aspects of the Oil Pollution Act—the liability provisions, the enhancement of federal cleanup capabilities, and personnel and construction standards to aid in preventing spills.[53]

The statute contains a liability system that covers oil spills in navigable

---

50. 42 U.S.C. § 9601 et seq., generally known as the Superfund Act.

51. 33 U.S.C. § 1321.

52. 104 Stat. 484, 33 U.S.C. § 2701 et seq.

53. Randle, R.V., "The Oil Pollution Act of 1990; Its Provisions, Intent, and Effects," 21 *Envt'l. L. Rep.* (Envt'l. L. Inst., March, 1991) p. 10,119.

waters, in the 200 mile coastal zone, and along the nation's shorelines. The liability limits are increased from the $150 per gross ton of the vessel amount under the Clean Water Act to $1200 per ton under the Oil Pollution Act. Responsible parties may be held liable for harm above this much higher limit if the release of oil is due to gross negligence, willful misconduct, or a violation of federal operating regulations. In these situations, the statute provides for unlimited liability. In addition, the Oil Pollution Act does not preempt state law remedies, and thus responsible parties may be liable under state law for amounts even higher than the increased federal limits.

With respect to federal cleanup activity, an Oil Spill Liability Trust Fund of $1 billion was created. This fund is designed to pay for cleanups in situations such as insolvency of the responsible party or harm in excess of that party's liability limitation. It is, however, from the Oil Pollution Act's personnel and construction standards that the greatest increase in potential for environmental protection can be derived. Standards have been significantly tightened for personnel staffing, training, and licensing, with special emphasis on preventing alcohol and drug-related problems. Beyond demanding greater competence and integrity of the people running the tanker, the structural integrity of the tanker itself has been increased. Construction standards now require that all new tankers have double hulls to reduce spill possibilities, and, by 2010, all existing single-hulled vessels will be phased out. At the time of their enactment, these construction standards set the United States apart from other nations in the international shipping community. If other countries decide not to follow the U.S. lead, many oil shipping companies could simply boycott U.S. ports. Congress apparently thought that this would not happen, or, if it did, the negative effects were worth the added environmental protection to be gained. The double hull requirement raises the importance of international solutions for environmental problems of international significance, but also suggests that if international agreement is not forthcoming, perhaps an individual nation needs to lead the way where technology is available to protect the environment.

4. Noise Pollution—Control Mechanisms for Aircraft Noise and Nonaircraft Noise, Federal Preemption

We will conclude our discussion of public pollution control by considering what some people believe will soon become a major issue in the area of pollution control—noise pollution. While air pollution and water pollution problems have been coming under control to a large extent, noise pollution problems may be moving in the opposite direction. Some studies have indicated that the "ambient noise level" in urban communities is doubling every ten years and, should that pattern continue unchecked, noise could have direct lethal effects within thirty years. But without going to the extreme of noise being lethal in and of itself, noise is thought to be a possible contributing factor to diseases such as heart disease, arthritis, and diabetes, and to have adverse effects on unborn children. Some research has also indicated a possible relationship between noise levels and the human body's ability to handle toxic materials. Huge numbers of toxic substances are in common use in industry and business, and there is some indication that the body's intake of substances such as toxic ozone from copying machines may be increased under the stress of high noise level.

Besides the above "possible problems," there are the well documented hearing loss problems which are derivative of noise and the plain fact that noise is often unpleasant regardless of whether it is unhealthy. Job-related hearing loss affects many, and excess noise in the workplace is said to have the potential of harming 16 million American workers. Regulations established pursuant to the federal Occupational Safety and Health Act (OSHA)[54] have sought to limit the permissible exposure of workers to noise. The question is not so much whether there should be permissible levels established, but rather what those levels should be. While prevention of overexposure to noise may be a sound goal, achieving noise control means accepting the costs inherent in control. The usual related questions are present. Is noise reduction to be achieved while taking into account the costs of achieving the reduction, or are the evils of noise sufficient in some circumstances to require reduction regardless of cost? Also, from a factual point of view, what is the noise level above which a certain type of harm will occur? As with most factual questions, opinions concerning the answer are often widely divergent. Our emphasis in the noise control area will be to consider the mechanisms for noise control established by or pursuant to the Federal Noise Control Act[55] and then to discuss the question of whether state and local control of one type of noise, aircraft noise, is allowable or prohibited.

Just as we saw that there are mechanisms in the Clean Water Act that closely parallel those in the Clean Air Act, so too are there parallels between the Noise Control Act and the Clean Air Act. The Noise Control Act directs the EPA Administrator to establish levels of environmental noise the attainment and maintenance of which are requisite to protect the public health and welfare. This control mechanism (which might be called "ambient noise levels") could be thought of as analogous to the ambient air quality standards

54. 29 U.S.C. § 651 et seq.

55. 42 U.S.C.S. § 4901 et seq.

under the Clean Air Act since it seeks to address the medium which is polluted without regard to the source of the pollutant. A critical difference exists, however, with respect to the utilization of those "ambient" standards or levels. The ambient air quality standards were required to be implemented by state implementation plans or by an EPA plan in the absence of an acceptable state plan. On the other hand, while the environmental noise levels are published for information and possible use in connection with other parts of the Noise Control Act or by other agencies or levels of government, there is no mandatory implementation of the noise levels which were found to be requisite to protect the public health and welfare.

A second parallel between the noise statute and the air statute is that both provide control mechanisms which focus on the source of pollution. The Clean Air Act has its stationary source standards, and various sections of the Noise Control Act are directed at major sources of noise such as products distributed in commerce (e.g. construction equipment, motors, engines), railroads, and motor carriers. For products distributed in commerce to which the act is applicable, the Administrator is directed to publish noise emission standards. These standards are to protect the public health and welfare, and they are to take into account the magnitude and conditions of use of the products. Thus motors used for short periods of time in unenclosed spaces may be subjected to a less strict standard than those used continuously and in enclosed areas. The manufacturer of each applicable product is to warrant to the ultimate purchaser and subsequent purchasers that the product conforms to its noise emission standard at the time of sale. In addition, enforcement of the noise emission standards may take place through citizen suits, and willful or knowing violation of the emission standard regulations may result in criminal penalties. The noise emission standards are to be promulgated as a result of a balancing by the Administrator similar to the balancing which leads to new stationary source emission standards under the Clean Air Act. The noise emission limitations are to be set with a goal of protecting the public health and welfare by attaining the degree of noise reduction achievable by the best available technology but also by taking into account the cost of compliance.

Striving to achieve noise reduction through the use of the best available technology while recognizing economic reality and thus taking into account the cost of compliance is also the methodology of the sections of the act pertaining to railroad noise and motor carrier noise. Appendix C illustrates the typical statutory and administrative relationship for environmental matters, in this case regulating motor carrier noise. The statute imposes the duty on the Administrator to regulate motor carrier noise and provides general standards such as "best available technology," "taking into account the cost of compliance," and "assure appropriate consideration for safety." The Administrator must abide by the statutory direction and guidance; however, there is a substantial amount of administrative discretion allowed in the setting of the standards. The detailed standards, such as how much noise, at what speed, and measured how far from the vehicle, are contained in the administrative regulations. The reader is encouraged to study Appendix C not necessarily for its substantive content but to become acquainted with the relationship between statutes and regulations.

In addition to the mandatory control mechanism that applies to certain noise-emitting products (the noise emission limitations), a control mechanism of consumer education is also provided by the act. Products which emit noise capable of adversely affecting the public health or welfare, or which are sold on the basis of effectiveness in reducing noise, are required to give notice to the prospective user by labeling the product with information on the level of noise the product emits or its effectiveness in reducing noise. Thus even without mandatory controls, purchasers should be able to factor noise levels into their decision-making process regarding which of competing products should be purchased.

Another nonmandatory approach to noise control which Congress has utilized in the Noise Control Act is to encourage development of "low-noise-emission" products. A low-noise-emission product is one which emits noise in amounts significantly below the levels specified by the noise emission standards discussed earlier. Such products are eligible to be certified as low-noise-emission products. That certification may have provided a competitive advantage in the marketplace sufficient to encourage the development of low-noise-emission products; however, Congress has made the incentive even greater. The statute requires that the federal government purchase a certified low-noise-emission product in preference to other products of its type so long as its retail price is no more than 125% of the least expensive product for which it is a substitute. A producer that develops a low-noise-emission product will thus have preferred access to a very large volume buyer. Congress established this incentive mechanism with a hoped for result of quieter products which, once the products have been developed, will become available for purchase by the general public as well as by the government.

Given the legislative mandate of the Noise Control Act, EPA promulgated regulations providing for the certification of low-noise-emission products and the identification of products as suitable substitutes for federal procurement.[56] The Office of Air, Noise & Radiation of EPA established noise emission criteria for a number of federally procured products such as motorcycles, trucks, and air compressors. Despite the hope of Congress and the efforts

---

56. 40 CFR § 203.1 et seq.

of the EPA, no applications for low-noise-emission certification have ever been received.[57] Apparently, industry never found the financial incentives of the program attractive enough to apply for low-noise-emission status. Interestingly, the Air Force purchases thousands of portable air compressors for starting their jets and incorporates into the procurement specifications noise emission standards that meet low-noise-emission criteria. Though certification would appear to permit manufacturers to make a greater profit by charging a premium for their products, no low-noise-emission certifications have ever been pursued. The EPA office which administered the Noise Control Act was renamed the Office of Air and Radiation due to a lack of activity regarding the statute. Most of the attention focusing on low-noise-emission product procurement is now found at state and local levels with "buy-quiet" programs being implemented by cities including New York, Chicago, and Salt Lake City.

An area of federal noise control which has seen greater federal regulation than the subject areas covered in our above discussion of the Noise Control Act is that of aircraft noise. Under the Federal Aviation Act,[58] the Federal Aviation Administration has had the authority to provide for control and abatement of aircraft noise and sonic boom. Our inquiry in the area of aircraft noise will consider whether, given the large federal role, there is also a nonfederal (state/local) role in aircraft noise regulation. Our starting point will be the United States Supreme Court case of *Burbank v. Lockheed Air Terminal.*[59]

In the *Burbank* case, the City of Burbank had enacted an ordinance which made it unlawful for jet aircraft to take off from the Hollywood-Burbank Airport during certain hours (11 p.m.–7 a.m.). The validity of the ordinance was challenged based on the Supremacy Clause of the United States Constitution. The Supremacy Clause, found in Article VI, says that the "Constitution, and the Laws of the United States . . . shall be the supreme Law of the Land; . . . anything in the Constitution or Laws of any State to the Contrary notwithstanding." Two theories which might possibly invalidate a state or local law are derived from the Supremacy Clause. The first is conflict—where state or local law and federal law address the same subject matter and are structured such that they cannot stand side by side. If, for example, state law required an aircraft to have blue lights and federal law said no lights other than red lights are allowed, one could not possibly comply

---

57. Telephone interview with the former Director of the Noise Regulatory Program in EPA's Office of Air, Noise and Radiation.

58. 49 U.S.C.A. § 1431.

59. 411 U.S. 624 (1973).

with both state and federal law. There is a conflict, and the state law is invalid pursuant to the Supremacy Clause. The Supreme Court did not address the conflict theory in *Burbank* but based its decision on the second theory derived from the Supremacy Clause—federal preemption.

If federal law set a 95 decibel (dB) maximum noise level for aircraft, and local law set a 90 dB maximum level, there would be no conflict since one could comply with both laws. Operation at 90 dB or anything less would satisfy both laws. The preemption theory says that even though both laws could stand side by side since they create no direct conflict, if Congress intended to fully take over or "preempt" the field of regulation of certain subject matter, then the nonfederal law concerning that subject matter is invalid. Sometimes Congress will expressly indicate in its legislation that it is preempting a field of control. No express preemption existed with respect to aircraft noise control; however, the Supreme Court found that Congress' intent to preempt the field of control was evidenced by the pervasive nature of the scheme of federal regulation of aircraft noise. The Court said that the pervasive control authority vested by Congress in federal agencies left no room for local curfews or other local controls. The Court further pointed out that if local ordinances such as Burbank's were allowed and other localities followed suit, the federal government's flexibility in controlling air traffic would be severely limited with potential problems such as increased air traffic congestion resulting in decreased safety and possibly increased noise levels. The Burbank ordinance was thus invalidated as having been preempted.

After the *Burbank* case, the Concorde aircraft arrived on the scene, and the New York Port Authority sought to prevent its flight into New York due to noise (*British Airways v. Port Authority*).[60] Was that then a clear case of federal preemption and the Port Authority could not act? The answer is that the federal preemption finding in *Burbank* did not apply to the Port Authority because the *Burbank* case involved an ordinance of a government unit (a city), and the Supreme Court specifically stated in *Burbank* that it was not addressing the issue of the power of a proprietor of an airport to regulate aircraft noise. Although the Port Authority was a government unit, it was also the proprietor of the airport, whereas the City of Burbank was not the proprietor. The Second Circuit Court of Appeals decided that, as the proprietor of the airport, the Port Authority was fully within its power to regulate aircraft noise. The reasoning behind what might appear to be a strange distinction (allowing regulation by a proprietor but invalidating regulation by a local government) was: (1) that Congress never intended

---

60. 558 F.2d 75 (1977).

to preempt aircraft noise control by proprietors—this statement of "intent" came from the legislative history in the form of House and Senate Reports, and (2) that proprietors of airports are liable for harm to others which may result from noise of aircraft using the proprietor's facility. Thus the proprietor must have the right to protect against this liability by restricting the use of its airport. The "proprietor" exception to the *Burbank* preemption rule resulted in the Port Authority having the power to regulate aircraft noise.

Two notes in closing: First, if the Port Authority was found to have the power to regulate noise, and since it clearly wanted to limit access by the Concorde, why did the Concorde avoid being controlled? The answer is that while proprietors may regulate their airports, such regulation must be reasonable and nondiscriminatory. The Port Authority never found a way to exclude the Concorde in a reasonable and nondiscriminatory manner, and it did not want to exclude other aircraft as well. Second, the viability of the position that airport proprietors are liable for aircraft noise was reinforced in *Greater Westchester Homeowners Association v. City of Los Angeles.*[61] The California Supreme Court in fact expanded the proprietor's liability in that nuisance case to include not only the traditional liability for property damage but also liability for injury to the person. Although public law with respect to pollution has relegated private law to a secondary status, the *Greater Westchester* case indicates that private law remedies in the pollution area continue to be available and even adaptable to current needs.

D.   SPECIALIZED ENVIRONMENTAL MEDIATION AND DISPUTE RESOLUTION

We have previously discussed two ways we use to resolve environmental disputes. The first was private law remedies (the adversarial process) which creates the feeling of a winner and a loser. The second way was through the legislative process that, because of the large number of interests to which it must respond, often results in a cumbersome mechanism that tries to serve everyone responsibly while clearly considering economics as the overriding variable.[62] Although the former appears an acceptable means of dispute resolution in situations such as automobile accidents, falling ceilings in theaters, manure odor from beef feedlots, and even smokestack emissions

---

61. 603 P.2d 1329 (1979).

62. Wolin, S.S., "The New Public Philosophy," *Democracy*, 1(4):23–36 (1981).

from a single industrial site, this process was not really designed to address large-scale environmental issues. These issues do not need a winner and a loser, nor a court that fashions contorted legal remedies. These issues may need resolution in a forum that addresses the central issue and seeks a resolution acceptable to everyone involved. The legislative approach also has its shortcomings with respect to resolving environmental disputes because the economic position is often viewed as paramount. Legislative resolution may come, but only if there is an economically sound, which usually means cheap, solution. Alternative dispute resolution approaches are now often used with respect to environmental issues.

One suggested method of resolving environmental disputes is the process of mediation. This process attempts to bring together all parties involved in a dispute to try to reach a solution that is legally supportable by and fundamentally acceptable to all parties. This type of undertaking requires trust among all parties, truthfulness and openness, and a commitment to abiding by the result of the collective process. Professional mediators will often be needed in such instances. Central to the idea of using mediation is the necessity of compromise and an issue that is capable of resolution by compromise. What mediation also provides is a less costly means of "solving" a problem. What mediation does not provide is a winner, nor does this process necessarily create a binding result. There is always still the recourse to the courts or, theoretically, the legislative arena where new law could greatly alter the result which the parties have reached through mediation. The use of environmental mediation and negotiation has grown dramatically in recent years.[63]

Another approach to the resolution of environmental issues might be the use of courts or judges with specialized expertise. A science court[64] could be used for making factual scientific determinations, and an environmental law judge could be appointed to bring environmental expertise to bear on resolving environmental issues.[65] Perhaps the breadth and depth of the effects of the results of complex environmental disputes warrants placing the decisionmaking in the hands of people who specialize in environmental matters.

---

63. Miller, J.G. and Colosi, T.R., *Fundamentals of Negotiation: A Guide for Environmental Professionals* (Washington, DC: Environmental Law Institute, 1989). For a detailed discussion of negotiated settlements as a government agency enforcement tool, see Novick, S.M., *Law of Environmental Protection* (New York: Clark Boardman Company, 1991) § 8.03.

64. Kantrowitz, A., "The Science Court Experiment: An Interim Report," *Science* (1976) 193:653–56.

65. An environmental law judge position has been established in the Vermont court system. 4 V.S.A. § 1001.

ADDITIONAL READINGS

Cross, F.B., *Legal Responses to Indoor Air Pollution* (Westport, CT: Quorum Books, 1990).

Godish, T., *Air Quality* (Chelsea, MI: Lewis Publishers, 1991).

Harrison, R., *Pollution: Causes, Effects and Control*, 2nd ed. (Cambridge, England: The Royal Society of Chemistry, 1990).

Kormondy, E.J., *International Handbook of Pollution Control* (New York: Greenwood Press, 1989).

National Research Council, *Rethinking the Ozone Problem in Urban and Regional Air Pollution* (Washington, DC: National Academy Press, 1992).

Patrick, R., *Surface Water Quality: Have the Laws Been Successful?* (Princeton, NJ: Princeton Univ. Press, 1992).

Raufer, R. and Feldman, S., *Acid Rain and Emissions Trading* (Totowa, NJ: Rowman and Littlefield, 1987).

CHAPTER 4

LAND USE

A.   CONTROL VS. NONCONTROL

1.   What Is Land?

On the surface land could be measured in terms of area, but land is really three-dimensional. Scientifically, land is a mixture of particles of various sizes. Larger particles are called gravel, and what is usually called soil consists of sand, silt and clay. These are differentiated by size (Table I). The greater amount of sand in a soil, the more porous the soil, and therefore water and other liquids will move through it faster. Conversely, as the amount of clay increases, the less porous the soil and the more slowly liquids move through it. This is the reason that ponds and some landfills and waste disposal sites are often lined with clay. The belief is that "pure" clay is so impermeable that leakage is not a problem. Soils are classified throughout the world based on the above properties as well as other characteristics such as depth prior to reaching bedrock, water holding capacity, organic matter content, color, iron content and aluminum content. An example of one very large-scale classification of soil is given in Figure 1.

In addition to the makeup of the soil itself, other important properties

**Table I.   Sizes of Soil Particles as Currently Used
by the United States Soil Conservation Service**

Soil Particle	Diameter (mm)
Sand	2.0–0.02
Silt	0.02–0.005
Clay	≤0.005

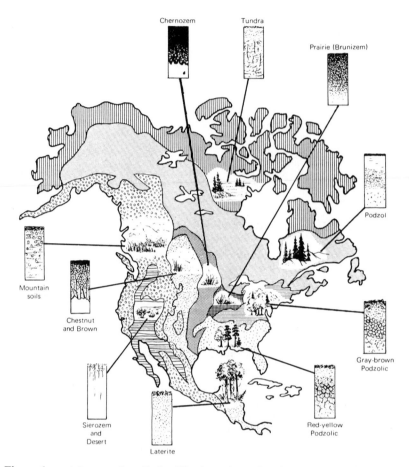

Figure 1.   A large-scale soil classification scheme for North America. The system considers soil in great groups.[1]

are latitude, altitude, slope of the land and the amount and seasonal distribution of rainfall. These factors are important not only in classification of soil but also in the use of land.

2.   Land Classification

Various methods have been used to classify land, resulting in numerous maps with definitions of land classifications based on the current uses of

---

1. Smith, R. L., *Ecology and Field Biology* (2nd ed.) (New York: Harper & Row Publishers, Inc., 1974).

the land, the potential uses of the land or simply the soil types grouped together into general use categories that may describe both the current and potential uses. These maps and classifications are usually prepared by or for some governmental agency for use in assessing, allocating or controlling land use patterns.

Let us look at two examples of land classification: one by the Fish and Wildlife Service of the United States Department of the Interior, and the other, the ongoing effort of the Soil Conservation Service of the United States Department of Agriculture. In 1974, the Fish and Wildlife Service assigned its Biological Services Office the task of making an inventory of the wetlands of the United States. To accomplish this task, the office decided to first define the limits of wetland as a natural ecosystem with the eventual objective of inventory, evaluation and management of such areas. Realizing that no definition adopted by them could withstand scrutiny in all cases, the drafters decided on the following definition:

> Wetlands are lands transitional between terrestrial and aquatic systems where the water table is usually at or near the surface or the land is covered by shallow water. For purposes of this classification wetlands must have one or more of the following three attributes: (1) at least periodically, the land supports predominantly hydrophytes, (2) the substrate is predominantly undrained hydric soil, and (3) the substrate is nonsoil and is saturated with water or covered by shallow water at some time during the growing season of each year.[2]

Hydrophytes are plants that either tolerate or enjoy being extremely wet. Hydric soils have their pores totally filled with water during at least part of a typical year. Most commonly, one considers bogs, marshes, swamps or rocky shores as wetlands. The above definition and its characterization eventually led the Fish and Wildlife Service to identify the systems shown in Figure 2 as either wetlands or deepwater (permanently flooded) habitats. What is classified as a wetland is of major land use significance since local, state and federal restrictions often prevent wetlands from being used as building sites.

The Soil Conservation Service has classified the soil of most counties in most states. While the process is continually being updated as better mapping information is required or as new information or techniques become available, and thus the information may be presented in different formats,

---

2. Department of the Interior, *Classification of Wetlands and Deepwater Habitats of the United States* (Washington, DC: U.S. Government Printing Office, 1979).

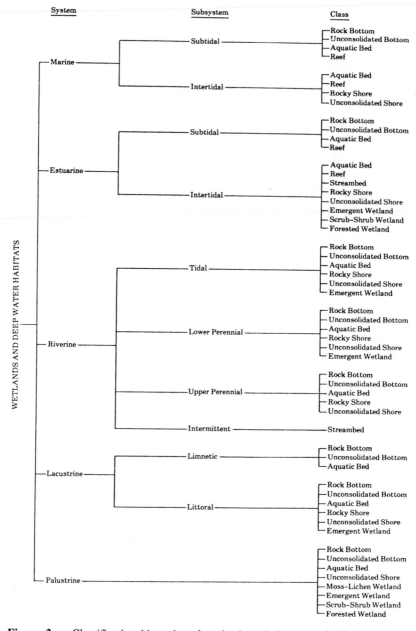

Figure 2. Classification hierarchy of wetlands and deepwater habitats, showing systems, subsystems and classes. The Palustrine System does not include deepwater habitats.[3]

3. Ibid.

the classifications all attempt to evaluate the soil in a particular location with respect to possible uses for that soil. An example of a soil evaluation is given in Figure 3. Though these soils are in different parts of the United States and were evaluated at different times, one can see that the same basic considerations are included in each report.

3. The Uses of Land

The major uses of land in the United States and the approximate numbers of acres allocated to each use are indicated in Table II. As one can see from the table, the amount of special use (developed) land use has significantly increased, while the acres of forest land have decreased. Let us take a closer look at each of the land uses and examine not only the uses but some consequences of the uses.

Cropland is a resource used to produce not only much of the food consumed either directly or secondarily in the United States, but also as a food resource for other parts of the world. Currently, the United States contains in excess of 400 million acres of agricultural land. Reportedly, each year about 3 million of these acres are converted to development while an additional 2 million acres become nonproductive after isolation by development. Conversion and isolation are but two mechanisms by which cropland is lost. Two other mechanisms are erosion and loss of fertility. Current estimates indicate that about 3 million acres of cropland are lost annually to erosion. Loss of fertility is a rather newly recognized form of cropland conversion. Since the discovery of the Haber process, it has been possible to make synthetic fertilizer containing nitrogen at a low cost. Having an inexpensive source of fertilizer made from various synthetic chemicals has allowed farmers to dispense with green manuring or animal manure as a source of nutrients for crops. These synthetic chemicals have proven both effective and reliable for farmers in terms of dependable production. However, the application of these chemicals also enhances the breakdown of organic matter in soil and consequently alters soil structure, making the soil more susceptible to flooding and water erosion as well as wind erosion. Additionally, the soil's binding ability for nutrients and water is decreased. Thus, the fertility of the soil itself is being lost, and much agricultural soil has become merely a holdfast for crops while they are fed nutrients so that they may produce. Eventually, all of the above mechanisms could deplete our cropland resource, and our overall amount of cropland would be going down greatly even today but for the fact that forest land is being converted to cropland.

Specialized land (see Table II) includes the many different land uses that we often refer to as developed land. Although this category of land use appears relatively small in terms of acres, the use of land for these purposes

ENGINEERING INTERPRETATIONS

Somewhat poorly drained soils with loamy surface layer over sandy clay loam or clay loam. Calcareous, stratified gravel and sand at a depth ranging from 24 to 42 inches. Outwash plains and moraines. Water table fluctuates between 2 and 10 feet.

ESTIMATED PHYSICAL AND CHEMICAL PROPERTIES

General Soil Profile	Classification			% of material passing sieve			Permeability		Available water capacity in./in.	Soil reaction pH	Shrink-swell potential
	USDA Texture	Unified	AASHO	No. 4 4.7 mm.	No. 10 2.0 mm.	No. 200 0.074 mm.	Inches per hour	Minutes per inch			
12"	Sandy loam	SM	A-2 or A-4	95-100	25-45	25-45	2.5-5.0	12-24	0.14	5.5-7.0	Low
24" 36"	Sandy clay, loam and clay loam	SC or CL	A-6	95-100	85-95	35-65	0.8-2.5	24-62	0.16	5.5-6.5	Moderate to high
48" 60"	Stratified gravel and sand	GP or SP	A-1	40-80	35-70	0-5	over 10	less than 6	0.02	7.5-8.0 calcareous	Low

SUITABILITY OF SOIL AS RESOURCE MATERIAL

RESOURCE MATERIAL	SUITABILITY
Topsoil	Fair for sandy loam, good for loam - medium content of organic matter, gravel and cobble on surface in some areas, seasonal high water table.
Sand	Good - stratified sand and gravel, excess wetness hinders excavation.

Gravel	Good - stratified sand and gravel, excess wetness hinders excavation.
Borrow for highway fills	Fair to poor in upper 24 to 42 inches.- moderate volume change, fair to poor bearing capacity. Good in sand and gravel - low volume change, good subgrade material.
Impermeable material for dams and levees	Good in upper 24 to 42 inches - fair workability and compaction. Not suitable in sand and gravel - rapid permeability, subject to piping.

FACTORS AFFECTING USE

USE	FACTORS
Highway construction	Seasonal high water table. Wet conditions may exist and hinder construction. Substratum has fair to good bearing capacity.
Winter grading	High moisture content may exist and hinder operations.
Foundations for low buildings	Seasonal high water table, fair to good bearing capacity, low volume change on wetting or drying, low compressibility, high shear strength.
Pond reservoir areas	Medium seepage rate in subsoil, seal blanket required when porous sand and gravel substratum is exposed.
Dams, dikes, and levees	Upper 24 to 42 inches has fair to good stability and compaction properties, slow seepage rate; substratum has fair stability and compaction properties, rapid seepage rate.
Septic tank disposal field	Seasonal high water table, rapid percolation of effluent may pollute shallow water supplies. Need on-site investigation.
Sanitary land fill	Seasonal high water table, upper 24 to 42 inches has fair compaction and workability, fair to poor bearing capacity, slow seepage rate. Sand and gravel has good workability, good bearing capacity, and rapid seepage rate.
Artificial drainage	Drainage usually needed. Seasonal high water table. Moderate permeability above 36 inches, rapid below. Special blinding required for tile.
Irrigation	Medium to low water holding capacity, rapid water intake rate, moderate depth to sand and gravel.
Corrosion hazard	Metal conduits: Moderate Concrete conduits: Low

UNITED STATES DEPARTMENT OF AGRICULTURE   National Cooperative Soil Survey - USA
SOIL CONSERVATION SERVICE in cooperation with
MICHIGAN AGRICULTURAL EXPERIMENT STATION

DEGREE OF LIMITATION OF SOIL FOR VARIOUS USES [1]

URBAN USE

USE	LIMITATION AND QUALIFICATION
Residential development with public sewer	Moderate - seasonal high water table; wet depressions in some areas; fair to good bearing capacity; material flows when wet; low volume change; driveways and streets subject to cracking and frost heave; wet basements are a problem during wet periods.
Residential development without public sewer	Moderate - seasonal high water table; wet depressions in some areas; fair to good bearing capacity; material flows when wet; low volume change; driveways and streets subject to cracking and frost heave; wet basements are a problem during wet periods; severe limitations for septic tank filter fields because of wet conditions; filter fields are saturated during wet periods.
Buildings for light industrial and commercial use	Moderate - seasonal high water table; wet depressions in some areas; fair to good bearing capacity; low volume change; construction difficult during wet periods; filling and grading required in many areas.
Highways and streets	Moderate - seasonal high water table; wet depressions in some areas; fills required in wet areas; construction difficult during wet periods; fair to good bearing capacity; low volume change; moderate frost heave problem.

RECREATION

USE	LIMITATION AND QUALIFICATION
Cottages and utility buildings	Moderate - seasonal high water table; wet depressions in some areas; fair to good bearing capacity; low volume change; dries out slowly in spring and after rain.
Intensive camp sites	Moderate - seasonal high water table; wet depressions in some areas; fair to poor bearing capacity for vehicles and foot traffic when wet; dries out slowly in spring and after rain; soft and muddy when wet; good strength for tent stakes.
Picnic areas	Moderate - seasonal high water table; wet depressions in some areas; soft and muddy when wet; dries out slowly in spring and after rain; fair to poor bearing capacity for foot traffic when wet; turf easily maintained.
Intensive play areas	Moderate - seasonal high water table; wet depressions in some areas; soft and muddy when wet; fair to poor bearing capacity for foot traffic when wet; dries out slowly in spring and after rain; turf easily maintained.

Paths and trails	Moderate - seasonal high water table; wet depressions in some areas; surface layer muddy and soft when wet; dries out slowly in spring and after rain; fair to poor bearing capacity for foot traffic when wet.
Golf fairways	Moderate - seasonal high water table; wet depressions in some areas; dries out slowly in spring and after rain; fair to poor bearing capacity for foot traffic and motorized carts; turf easily maintained.

AGRICULTURE AND OTHER VEGETATION

USE	LIMITATION AND QUALIFICATION
Land capability class and soil management group	Class II. Class III in northern zone if undrained. If not drainable, soil is Class V, VI, or VII, depending on degree of wetness. Group 3b.
Farm crops	Slight - seasonal high water table; artificial drainage required for optimum crop yields; sandy material below 18 to 42 inches is unstable when wet and caves in readily; wet depressions in some areas; wide crop adaptability; fair to poor bearing capacity for farm machinery during wet periods; moderate to severe limitations if drainage cannot be obtained.
Trees	Severe - low to medium production for both hardwoods and conifers; seasonal high water table limits root development; severe windthrow hazard; drainage required before planting.
Lawns and shrubs	Moderate - seasonal high water table; water-tolerant shrubs required in undrained areas; dries out slowly in spring and after rain; difficult to establish lawns during wet periods.

1/ The soil is evaluated only to a depth of 5 feet or less. Soils are rated on the basis of four classes of soil limitations: Slight - relatively free of limitations or limitations are easily overcome; Moderate - limitations need to be recognized, but can be overcome with good management and careful design; Severe - limitations are severe enough to make use questionable; Very Severe - extreme measures are needed to overcome the limitations and usage generally is unsound or not practical.

Figure 3. Sample soil interpretation sheet for Matherton soil in Michigan.

Table II.   Major Uses of Land in the United States, 1959–1987 (in millions of acres).[4]

Year	Cropland (includes idle & pasture that could be cropland)	Pasture and Range	Forest Land (excluding special uses like state parks)	Special Use-developed (urban, road, rural parks, etc.)	Other (wetland, tundra, etc.)	Total (in millions of acres)
1959	458	633	745	142	293	2271
1964	444	640	732	173	277	2266
1969	472	604	723	174	291	2264
1974	465	598	718	182	301	2264
1978	471	587	703	203	301	2265
1982	469	597	655	320	224	2265
1987	464	591	648	335	227	2265

Note: Much of the large increase in special use land and decrease in other uses between 1978 and 1982 as shown above is due to definitional changes in classifying land in Alaska by the Department of Agriculture.

is expanding very rapidly as population increases and as the demands of society for these land uses increases. While this phenomenon in and of itself may give little cause for alarm, it is the type of land selected for use under this category that is troublesome. It is easier to develop land that is flat. Croplands are therefore prime targets. Wetlands are also flat and inexpensive, and many people like to live near water. Consequently there are pressures to develop wetlands. Wetlands are reservoirs for water, breeding grounds for various forms of wildlife and feeding areas for other kinds of wildlife. Viewing the choice of what land to develop from another perspective, even though people want to live in a given location, that does not mean that such a place can support them in terms of needed resources. Witness the migrations to the sunbelt areas of the Southwest. While the climate is hospitable in many ways, the demands for water have all but eliminated any sustained supply and have necessitated the proposal of various large-scale engineering masterpieces to transport water to these water-impoverished areas. This type of solution, even if technically and economically feasible, masks the problem, and may be only a short-term solution.

Forest land is a major land use category in the United States (see Table II). About 38% of all forest land was government-owned in 1982, with 32% being owned by the federal government. Management of such lands has received various forms of attention over the years, but many people believe that a comprehensive approach to the management of forest land is yet to

---

4. "Major Land Use Database" (Economic Research Service, U.S. Dept. of Agriculture).

come. Maximum growth-sustained yield was and is one concept that forest management has championed. This concept emphasizes harvesting trees at a time that achieves maximum productivity of the forest rather than allowing trees to reach their mature growth size (see Figure 4). While this approach would keep forests actively growing, it does not allow for old age stands useful for wildlife habitat as well as aesthetics and soil rejuvenation. It could also eventually lead to the management of forests totally for commercial production, with the selection of only fast growing, highly marketable tree species for cultivation. This could eliminate tree species considered unprofitable and consequently the gene pool of such species. Once this extinction occurs, the species cannot be retrieved. Perhaps the most alarming point to note about forest land is that it decreased in amount by 13% between 1959 and 1987. The question is what role, if any, should government play in preventing the conversion of cropland to developed land and forest land to cropland.

Grassland, pasture and range also constitute a major portion of the land use of the United States. Much of this land is federally owned and leased to ranchers, or is privately owned by ranchers. As with cropland, the owner/

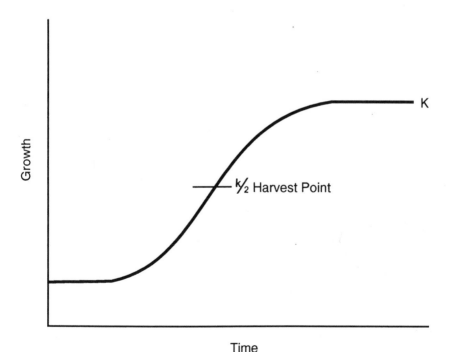

Figure 4. Harvest point of trees in relation to growth, where K equals the maximum size a tree would reach.

investor is interested in maximum dollar return. This situation has led to a drastic deterioration of our rangelands through over-grazing. A recent survey of our national rangelands indicates that there have been too many animals allowed to feed on much of the vegetation, with the result that the better grazing plants have been all but eliminated while the less useful plant species are proliferating. Until grazing was introduced into many desert areas, cacti were not the dominant form of vegetation. While overuse of an area may only lead to a shift in the kind of plants located there, the shift may be to a variety of plants that are less palatable to grazers and ultimately reduce the utility of the land for grazing.

Marshes, deserts and tundra also deserve consideration as natural resources. Humans have and continue to use these areas without an understanding of their role in nature. These areas are not simply there to be developed; they are areas that support various gene pools of plant and animal species that may be very necessary for the continued functioning of the ecosystem even though we may not today fully understand their utility.

4.   The Need to Control

The above discussion of land and its uses has focused largely on land use problems related to topics like agriculture, forestry and wildlife. There are many additional land use problems that are of greatest significance in heavily populated areas. One example of these problems might be the question of whether retail stores should be located in numerous small clusters within residential areas or kept out of residential areas and instead grouped into one huge shopping center area. Another example is whether a 25-acre suburban housing development should have 25 one-acre building lots or 25 houses clustered on 10 acres with 15 acres of common open space. Sections B, C, and D of this chapter will concentrate on land use control mechanisms that most often come into play when pressures are created by population growth in a specific location. Section E will then emphasize agriculture, forestry and wildlife when it addresses controls on federally owned lands. As a further introduction to our sections on control mechanisms, we note that when considering the need for land use controls in any context, one could contend that control is necessary only when things get "out of hand." When is the point at which things are "out of hand" is an issue upon which reasonable people could differ. Also, most people are of the opinion that land use issues should be resolved before they become major problems rather than later. Thus we will see that many of our "control" mechanisms will really be land use "planning" mechanisms that try to prevent problems rather than remedy them.

B.   PRIVATE AND QUASI-PRIVATE LAND USE PLANNING AND CONTROL

In Chapter 3 we discussed the doctrine of "nuisance" that prevented landowner X from using his land in a way that would interfere with the peaceful enjoyment by landowner Y of landowner Y's land. The common law of nuisance thus exists as a minimum degree of restriction that society has placed on what one can do with his land. It is also the minimum level of protection that a landowner has available against those who interfere with his use of his land. This level of control is imposed by society, but it is still a "private" mechanism since it merely gives victims the opportunity to seek a remedy if they so choose. Beyond this private control mechanism created by society, there are private planning and control mechanisms which can be created by individuals themselves. These privately created control mechanisms are called easements and restrictive covenants.

If one is the owner of an easement, it can be said that he holds an interest in someone else's land. If your rural neighbor has a good water source on his property and you want to use it to supply your pond, you might purchase the right to use that water source and to go on his land to lay and repair pipe to bring the water to your land. Your neighbor would convey this right to you by deeding you an easement on his land for the stated purposes. The benefit of that easement would pass to subsequent owners of your land unless the easement were created for the personal benefit of the holder ("easement in gross") rather than to benefit the land owned by the holder of the easement ("easement appurtenant to the land"). Most easements are created by voluntary transactions between the parties, but easements can sometimes come into existence in other ways. For example, if you were to use your neighbor's water source for a long enough period of time (often fixed by statute), with his knowledge but without his consent, and adverse to his interests, you may acquire a "prescriptive easement" to use the source.

Restrictive covenants, unlike easements, do not give one landowner the ability to make active use of another landowner's land. Rather, a restrictive covenant will give to A an interest that allows A to restrict how B will use B's land. These restrictions by covenant go beyond limits that would be imposed by the nuisance doctrine and beyond public controls such as zoning. Thus if A owned fifteen adjoining lots that were zoned to allow either single-family or multifamily residential housing, A might sell one lot to B, and others to other buyers, with restrictive covenants that the lots be used only for single-family housing. In general, if the parties who agree to a restrictive covenant intend that the restrictive covenant shall bind subsequent owners, it can be written to do so, i.e., to "run with the land."

While restrictive covenants are generally enforceable and are well accepted as private land use planning tools, we should note some circumstances where the law has precluded their use. The clearest situation in which restrictive covenants may not be used is where the covenant would lead to the exclusion from housing on the basis of race. *Shelley v. Kraemer,*[5] a United States Supreme Court case decided in 1948, held that racially restrictive covenants could not be enforced by courts because to do so would violate the equal protection clause of the Fourteenth Amendment to the United States Constitution. The equal protection clause makes it unconstitutional for a *state* to "deny to any person within its jurisdiction the equal protection of the laws." In *Shelley,* the court decided that for a state to use its court system to enforce covenants that provide restrictions based on race would be *state action* denying persons equal protection of the laws.

The prohibition on the use of racial restrictions with respect to housing and some of its related facilities has gone far beyond *Shelley v. Kraemer. Shelley* prohibited state action to enforce a racially restrictive covenant. What about situations where there is no state action, but a completely private land use restriction mechanism operates in a racially discriminatory manner? In *Sullivan v. Little Hunting Park, Inc.,*[6] a corporation had been formed to operate recreational facilities for the residents of a subdivision. A homeowner could have a share in the corporation that entitled him to use the facilities, and that share could be assigned to a tenant but only with the approval of the corporation's board of directors. The board refused to approve an assignment to a Negro tenant, and the court held that the tenant had a right to the assignment. Even though no state action was involved, a statute that had been enacted by Congress, the Civil Rights Act of 1866,[7] prohibited private individuals from discriminating in housing on the basis of race. The Civil Rights Act of 1866 states: "All citizens of the United States shall have the same right . . . as is enjoyed by white citizens . . . to . . . purchase, lease, sell . . . real . . . property." The Court had earlier held that Congress had the constitutional power to prohibit private as well as public racial discrimination with respect to the sale and rental of property, and that Congress' words in the statute meant just what they said: all racial discrimination, both private and public, in the sale or rental of property is prohibited.[8]

A somewhat less clear situation in which restrictive covenants are limited in their validity involves the law's long adhered to policy against "restraints on alienation." This policy is based on the belief that restrictions on the

---

5. 334 U.S. 1 (1948).

6. 396 U.S. 229 (1969).

7. 42 U.S.C.A. §§ 1981, 1982

8. *Jones v. Alfred H. Mayer Co.,* 392 U.S. 409 (1968).

ability to transfer one's interest in land inhibits economic and commercial development. Thus a covenant that kept a property owner from selling his land except to members of a designated property owners association was unenforceable.[9] There are, however, policies that compete with that of free alienability of property. One such policy is freedom of contract—courts enforcing the terms of an arrangement into which the parties have voluntarily entered. Some courts have adopted the position that covenants that restrict the alienation of property are invalid only if they are unreasonable. Possible factors bearing on the reasonableness of the restriction might be how long it lasts or whether it is absolute in that it makes no provisions for hardship situations. Thus a covenant prohibiting a condominium owner from leasing his unit was found reasonable and therefore valid since provisions were made for hardship situations and the duration of the restriction was not necessarily forever.[10]

But for the possible need to resort to the courts to enforce them, restrictive covenants and easements are wholly private land use planning tools. Let us next look at a quasi-private mechanism. We call this quasi-private because, although it is not mandatory and is utilized on the initiative of private parties, government has created the mechanism for use by the private parties. The mechanism seeks to keep land from being built upon by providing an income tax incentive to the owner to act in ways which will keep the land perpetually undeveloped.

Assume that Ms. Rich is in the 50% tax bracket for federal income tax purposes. For every dollar of taxable income she receives above the upper limit of the next lowest tax bracket, she pays fifty cents of that dollar as income tax. Ms. Rich owns a large and valuable piece of real estate in a rural area. Adjacent to that real estate is a parcel owned by someone else. That parcel is about to be subdivided into 100 lots with a house to be put on each lot. Ms. Rich does not like this subdivision from an environmental point of view and, possibly, because she also believes it will reduce the value of her real estate holding. The owner of the 100 lots is willing to sell them all together for $500,000 which is their value as land for a housing development. What action can Ms. Rich take to prevent the sub-division and what will it cost her?

First, she could just buy the adjacent parcel for $500,000 and keep it from being developed. She will have protected the environment (and her other property) from the development at a cost to her of $500,000 minus whatever comparatively small income she can obtain from the property in its un-

---

9. *Mountain Springs Association v. Wilson*, 196 A.2d 270 (1963).

10. *Seagate Condominium Association v. Duffy*, 330 So.2d 484 (1976).

developed state. Let us see if we can help Ms. Rich preserve the undeveloped land by making it less costly for her to do so. Under Section 170 of the Internal Revenue Code, Congress has provided that individuals may deduct from their income the amount of a "charitable" contribution that they make to a qualifying "charitable" organization. A "charitable" organization is much more broadly defined than merely those that give help to the poor. An organization whose purpose is to keep land from being developed may qualify under Section 170, with the result that gifts that are made to it are tax deductible. These organizations are usually called "land trusts." Ms. Rich can buy the proposed development for $500,000 and donate the land to the land trust. The land trust will then sell the land for a lesser amount, but with restrictions that allow it to be used only for such activities as agriculture or forestry. Ms. Rich takes the value of her donation to the land trust, $500,000, as a tax deduction, and she removes the adverse effects of the development at a cost to her of $250,000 rather than $500,000. This is because on $500,000 of her very high income she would have paid income tax of $250,000. By giving the $500,000 to the land trust and taking a deduction, she saves having to pay $250,000 in income tax. Of the $500,000 she gave to the land trust, only $250,000 is a net out-of-pocket cost to her—the other $250,000 is money that she has just chosen to send to the land trust instead of to the United States Treasury. Ms. Rich has now accomplished her objective at a cost to her of $250,000 rather than $500,000. Can we do still better for her?

Instead of having Ms. Rich give all 100 lots to the land trust after she buys them, let us have her keep ten of them. Since she paid $500,000 for the whole parcel and is donating 90 out of 100 lots, her tax deductible charitable contribution is 90/100ths of $500,000 or $450,000. Being in the 50% tax bracket means she saves paying taxes on $450,000 at the 50% rate. She thus saves $225,000 in taxes. She has spent $500,000, saved $225,000 in taxes, and is therefore out-of-pocket $275,000—but she still owns ten building lots for which she paid $5000 apiece. These ten lots are now surrounded by 90 lots that the land trust has perpetually restricted from development, and, since these ten building lots will be *forever* surrounded by open space instead of by 90 houses, their value is greatly increased over the $5000 that was paid for each of them. Ms. Rich sells these prime building lots for $35,000 each and receives $350,000. On this sale she has made a profit of $300,000 (paid $5000 each and sold them for $35,000 each). Assuming that she kept them for more than one year after she bought them, her profit would be taxed as a capital gain, which means she would pay tax on only 40% of the gain, pursuant to Section 1202 of the Internal Revenue Code. She would be taxed on 40% of her profit of $300,000. She is thus taxed on $120,000. Being in the 50% tax bracket means she will pay a tax of $60,000 on her profit. She has taken in $350,000 on the lots she sold and pays a tax of $60,000, leaving her with $290,000 on the sale. Her donation of $450,000 to the land trust left her out-of-pocket $275,000 as we saw above. The donation and the sale taken together have left her with a minus $275,000 and a plus $290,000 for a net gain of $15,000. The 100-lot subdivision that threatened the environment and Ms. Rich's other real estate has been reduced to ten prime building lots, the cost to Ms. Rich has been nothing, and in fact she has $15,000 in the bank to pay her legal fees for all the transactions.[11]

The reader may want to question the justification for Congress allowing and even encouraging the above actions by Ms. Rich. On one hand, Congress' environmental and land use objectives of preserving agricultural and forest land are furthered, and the rich are the ones with the capital and the risk taking ability that can help Congress achieve its land use objectives. Also, the charitable contribution deduction is an incentive for wealthy landowners to keep land they already own from being developed. On the other hand, it can be argued that the United States Treasury (all taxpayers) is subsidizing Ms. Rich's achieving her objective of protecting the value of her real estate. Furthermore, even if we look only at the environmental objective that Ms. Rich may have and not at her property value objective, should Ms. Rich's environmental desires be heavily subsidized by the treasury when someone named Ms. Poor will not be subsidized to anywhere near the same level to accomplish those things that she believes are environmentally important? That is because the lower the donor's tax bracket, the less is the percentage of the donation that actually is provided by the treasury instead of by the donor. A $1 donation by someone in the 50% bracket is really 50 cents of her money and 50 cents of money that does not get sent by her to the treasury. A $1 donation by someone in the 20% bracket is 80 cents of her money and 20 cents of money that she does not have to send to the treasury. Is then the proper perspective from which to view the above-described tax mechanism: (1) "should more government money be spent on the environmental goals of the rich than on those of the poor?" or (2) "should government accomplish its environmental objectives by encouraging the use

---

11. The numerical results in this example depend on the tax rates in existence. Section 1202 of the Internal Revenue Code, discussed in the text, was in effect when land trusts began to play a significant role in preserving farm and forestry land from development. Section 1202 was then repealed by Congress. The financial costs to Ms. Rich of these transactions would therefore be somewhat greater without the special treatment for capital gains under Section 1202. Lower taxation of capital gains has, however, been the law for decades, and any period without it is likely to be relatively brief. Regardless of the current status of capital gain taxation and the financial help it would provide for a "Ms. Rich" in trying to achieve her environmental and/or personal goals, the Section 170 charitable contribution deduction greatly reduces the costs for a "Ms. Rich" to achieve those goals.

of privately initiated voluntary methods wherever possible?'' Congress has decided to use the charitable contribution deduction incentive to help protect farm and forestry land from development, and the system appears to be working. The land trust approach is perhaps most justified when preserving large amounts of land from development is coupled with providing affordable housing on part of that land or on other land. Land trusts have begun to view assisting in the construction of reasonably priced housing as a very significant part of their mission.

C. PUBLIC PLANNING AND CONTROL AND THE "TAKING CLAUSE" LIMITATION ON CONTROL

While the federal government exercises some control over how privately owned land is used, most public planning and control of privately owned land is done by local governments under authority given to them by the states. The degree to which states get directly involved in land use control varies from state to state. Some states do very little. Vermont, however, has a Land Use Development Law[12] that mandates, in addition to local requirements, a state permit for developments which might have significant environmental impact. We will focus on local land use controls and then look at the extent to which the "taking clauses" of the United States and state constitutions limit public control of land use.

1. Local Control

The dominant local land use planning and control mechanism is zoning. There are numerous different forms of zoning controls and numerous purposes for enacting them. The most well known type of zoning is "use zoning." Use zoning categorizes different activities which people may seek to undertake on land and prescribes which activities can be conducted on which parcels of land within the local government's jurisdiction. For example, a suburban city may have its land allocated for five types of "uses" and thus call its use zones R-1, R-2, R-3, C-1, and C-2. R-1 could be single-family residential, R-2 could be two-, three-, or four-family residential buildings, and R-3 could be apartment buildings of 5 or more units. C-1 areas might be for light commercial operations providing consumer goods and services on a retail basis, while C-2 might be for heavy commercial operations

---

12. 10 V.S.A. § 6001 et seq.

conducted at the wholesale level. Some of the possible purposes for seg-
regating these uses to different areas might include keeping heavy traffic
out of places where people live, protecting property values by assuring people
that a movie theater will not be built next door to their ranch house, or
facilitating the efficient provision of city services like trash collection or
police protection.

The uses designated for a given zone may be "permitted uses," which
are activities that are allowed in that zone as a matter of right, or "conditional
uses," which may be allowed in the zone if the user meets certain conditions.
These conditions may either be stated in the zoning ordinance itself, or the
ordinance may authorize a local body such as a Zoning Board of Adjustment
to impose conditions in a discretionary manner. Our C-1 zone described above
could provide that all uses allowed in it are permitted uses unless the use
will involve more than 30 people being on the premises at any one time.
If more than 30 people will be there, the use may be conditioned on the
landowner providing a specified number of off-street parking spaces.

In addition to the distinction between permitted and conditional uses, we
should note the distinction between two other terms, exclusive zones and
cumulative zones. If a zone is established as an exclusive zone, only the
activities specified for that zone may take place there. If a zoning scheme
provides for cumulative zoning, then, in addition to the activities specified
for a particular zone, any "higher" (i.e., less intensive) use may also take
place in that zone. Thus under cumulative zoning, a light commercial zone
could be used for residential use but not for "lower" (i.e., more intensive)
heavy commercial activities. Exclusive zoning can be said to have the
advantage of better serving the health and safety protection purpose of zoning
by ensuring that people cannot choose to live in a heavy traffic commercial
area or in an industrial area with high air pollution. Also, if residential uses
are allowed in an area zoned for industry, industries that want to locate there
may be deterred from doing so because they could be subject to liability
as a nuisance to the residential landowners. Cumulative zoning, however,
has the advantage of flexibility and diversity. Perhaps people should be able
to choose to live in a commercial area if rents are lower there, if it is simply
more convenient for them, or if they like living in an area where non-
residential activity is happening. Depending on the character and planning
objectives of a city, it may choose to have some of its zones be cumulative
and some exclusive.

Many other types of zoning ordinances exist besides use zones. Maximum
height limitations may be provided for purposes such as added fire safety,
aesthetics, or to ensure adequate availability of light. Distances may be
established as a required "setback" of a building from a street for reasons
such as planning for possible future widening of streets or to provide greater
visibility at street corners. Communities may establish agricultural zones to

preserve the character of the community by protecting it from invasion by intensive development. Regardless of the type of zoning that a local government may want to enact, it must get its authority to impose its zoning scheme from the state, since local governments are the creations of the state.

The zoning power is a part of the state's police power—the power to protect the public health, public safety, and general welfare. Usually, the states have delegated the zoning power to local governments, with the most common mechanism for the delegation being zoning "enabling acts" which enable or permit local governments to zone but do not require them to do so. Whether the zoning power was a valid part of the state's police power was questioned in the 1926 case of *Village of Euclid, Ohio v. Ambler Realty Co.*[13] A landowner contended that a use and a height and minimum area requirements zoning scheme that restricted his use of his land and thereby reduced its market value was not a valid exercise of the state's police power. The United States Supreme Court found that a comprehensive zoning ordinance bears a rational relationship to the public health and safety and is therefore a valid exercise of the police power. *Euclid* thus clearly established the validity of comprehensive zoning, but that is not to say that all attempts at zoning are necessarily valid. One type of zoning where the trend has been in the direction of invalidity is exclusionary zoning.

Exclusionary zoning was the subject of a New Jersey case, *Southern Burlington County N.A.A.C.P. v. Township of Mount Laurel.*[14] The Township of Mount Laurel had a zoning ordinance that provided for varying minimum lot sizes, widths, and dwelling unit sizes for each of its residential zones. There was very little available land in the zones with the least restrictive requirements. Most of the available residentially zoned land required a minimum lot size of about one-half acre. Although the New Jersey Supreme Court noted that Mount Laurel's requirements were not as restrictive as those in many similar municipalities, it said that a developing municipality may not, by a system of land use regulations, make it physically or economically impossible to provide low and moderate income housing in the municipality and thereby exclude people from living within its confines because of the limited extent of their income and resources. The result of such a system would be presumptively contrary to the general welfare and therefore outside the scope of the zoning power.

Two other factors that tend to attenuate harsh results which may otherwise flow from the exercise of the zoning power should be mentioned briefly. These are variance and nonconforming use provisions often contained in local

---

13. 272 U.S. 365 (1926).

14. 336 A.2d 713 (1975).

zoning ordinances. A variance will allow someone to put his land into use in a way which is not allowable under the zoning ordinance as it applies to his land. The purpose of having a variance procedure is to account for special situations involving the property itself, rather than its owner, which in fairness or good sense should result in the property not being required to be used in compliance with the zoning laws. This might include situations where a lot is so small that to enforce compliance with minimum lot size requirements would preclude putting a building on the lot and make it useless. Another example might be where a restaurant will be located near ample public parking facilities. A variance from zoning requirements for off-street parking for restaurants would appear to be in order. As a matter of practice, zoning variances are often given where the legal criteria for a variance have not been met. In the absence of significant adverse effects on neighboring property or on the public, a variance is often issued even though the property has nothing in the way of physical characteristics that make it different from other property that is zoned in the same way.

Nonconforming use provisions also attempt to mitigate possible hardships by allowing a use to continue in violation of the applicable zoning ordinance if it lawfully existed prior to the adoption of that zoning. The nonconforming use provisions do reduce hardship to the landowner, yet, if the use has been made unlawful for the public benefit and would not be allowed had it not already been there, is not that public benefit being partly sacrificed by allowing the nonconforming use to be there just because it was there before the zoning enactment? Might not a better remedy for any unfairness to the owner be to compensate the owner for losses due to his having to give up his nonconforming use?

Besides zoning, local governments have other land use control mechanisms available to them. State statutes often authorize local governments to require local approval of subdivisions of land. In exchange for providing this local approval, local governments have sometimes sought ''exactions'' from developers who want to subdivide. For example, if a developer wants to subdivide her land for residential use, the local government may require that she dedicate land to the community for park or recreational purposes. Such exactions have been found valid for reasons such as, using the above example, an influx of new residents brought in by the subdivision will increase the need for park and recreational facilities. The subdivision will also make the developer's land more valuable. Part of her gain can be required to be used to provide for the local needs she will be creating.[15] The subdivision approval

---

15. *Associated Home Builders v. Walnut Creek*, 484 P.2d 606 (1971).

mechanism has also been used to regulate the rate of growth of a community by restricting the number of subdivision permits that will be issued within a given period of time. A discussion of this approach is presented in Section B of Chapter 8.

The source of power for the local land use planning and control mechanisms discussed above is the police power. Another source of power to control land use is the eminent domain power, which is the power of government to take private property for public use. Rather than being an explicitly stated power, the eminent domain power is an inherent power of the sovereign—either the federal government or the state government and its authorized offspring, the local governments. Acknowledgment of the existence of the eminent domain power comes by way of limitations on that power that are expressed in the United States Constitution and in various forms in state constitutions. The "taking clause" of the Fifth Amendment to the United States Constitution reads: "nor shall private property be taken for public use, without just compensation." Thus the taking of private property by government is acceptable so long as it is taken for a public use and just compensation is paid to the owner. If a local government wanted to establish a park, it could "take" or condemn private property and use it for a park. Similarly, if a local government wanted certain land to be used only for agriculture, it might, instead of zoning it for agricultural use only, "take" or condemn the land and resell it with restrictions that it be used only for agriculture. The key difference between accomplishing these local government objectives by using the eminent domain power, as opposed to the police powers of zoning or subdivision exactions discussed above, is that when government is acting under the eminent domain power, it must pay "just compensation." While in many instances government will voluntarily act under its eminent domain power to handle a land use situation, since regulation under the police powers does not require payment of compensation to the landowner, there is a strong inclination for government to "regulate" rather than to "take." Landowners who have found themselves subjected to uncompensated regulation often have contended that government has gone beyond the scope of its police power authority and either does not have the power to do what it seeks to do at all or, if it can act, it can do so only under the eminent domain power and with the payment of just compensation. Suits brought by private landowners alleging that an attempt to "regulate" is really a "taking" and that just compensation should be paid, are called "inverse condemnation actions."[16]

---

16. *Fulton County v. Wallace*, 393 S.E.2d 241 (1990).

2. The "Taking Clause" Limitations on Public Control

In this section we will consider two issues involving the taking clause. First, if it is conceded that government can act as it wants to act and that its action is for the public benefit, when does that action exceed its police powers and amount to a taking requiring the payment of just compensation? In other words, what distinguishes an eminent domain "taking" from a police power "regulation?" Second, if government is admittedly seeking to act under the eminent domain power and willing to pay compensation for its taking of private property, what will qualify as a "public use" to bring its action within the confines of those words and thus within the scope of the eminent domain power?

In trying to define the line between a police power regulation and an eminent domain taking, a realistic beginning point is the United States Supreme Court's opinion in *Goldblatt v. Town of Hempstead*.[17] The Court acknowledged that the line is a fuzzy one: "There is no set formula to determine where regulation ends and taking begins." Instead, a court will engage in an *ad hoc*, fact-oriented inquiry to examine several potentially significant factors relating to the taking question.[18] Let us then look at some of the factors that have been used by courts to determine whether a government action is a compensable taking or a noncompensable regulation.

Goldblatt concerned a town ordinance that placed restrictions on mining excavations. Those restrictions included fencing requirements, prohibitions on further excavation below the water table, and filling any existing excavations below that level. The landowner had operated a gravel pit on his property for many years and contended that the ordinance was not regulatory but completely prohibitory and confiscated his property without compensation. The Court said that, although a beneficial use of the property had been prohibited, that does not mean that the ordinance is beyond the scope of the police power and thus a taking. The owner was not disturbed with respect to his control or use of his property for other purposes, and his right to dispose of his property was not restricted. Besides factors of control, disposability, and use, the *Goldblatt* opinion also referred to how onerous the government action might be in terms of decreasing the value of the property. A comparison of property values before and after the government action was said to be relevant but by no means conclusive.

This type of analysis, or balancing test, in which the court weighs several factors including effects on property values, has repeatedly been used in

---

17. 369 U.S. 590 (1962).

18. *Keystone Bituminous Coal Assn. v. DeBenedictis*, 480 U.S. 470 (1987).

"taking" cases. In addition to examining the character of the government action and the nature of the different rights of property ownership that are restricted or retained, courts will weigh the extent of the economic impact and the degree of interference with the owner's reasonable investment-backed expectations that the governmental action is imposing. These factors formed the basis for the United States Supreme Court's decision in *Lucas v. South Carolina Coastal Council.*[19] Lucas had purchased two beachfront lots intending to build houses. After his purchase, but before construction, the state enacted the Beachfront Management Act designed to preserve South Carolina's beaches from erosion. Under the provisions of the Act, construction on the Lucas lots was prohibited. Lucas's property was rendered valueless, and Lucas claimed a taking requiring compensation. The Court stated that: "Where the State seeks to sustain regulation that deprives land of all economically beneficial use, we think it may resist compensation only if . . . the proscribed use interests were not part of his title to begin with." Thus only if common law principles of nuisance and property law would have prevented construction, can construction be prohibited without compensation. If these principles had prohibited construction, his title to the land would not have included a right to construct on it. The Court further noted that such principles rarely support prohibition of the "essential use" of land. It appears that, while historically ingrained aspects of the public interest like nuisance may be used to prohibit construction without paying compensation, areas of the public interest that have become of concern more recently, such as beach erosion and wetlands preservation, may only be protected if government is willing to pay private landowners for losses—at least if those losses are the total value of the land.

Although many cases, including *Lucas,* have focused on the extent of the loss of property value and use, other courts and writers have used factors in addition to or instead of the degree of diminution in value of the property or remaining uses for the property. Actual physical use by the government or the public may be a taking, whereas prohibiting uses by the owner may not be a taking. A United States Supreme Court opinion held that "a permanent physical occupation authorized by government is a taking without regard to the public interests that it may serve." A New York statute that required landlords to allow installation of cable television facilities on rental properties was a permanent physical occupation and was thus a taking for which just compensation was required.[20] Another analytical possibility is a sliding scale approach to the taking/regulation distinction. This may be used

---

19. 112 S. Ct. 2886 (1992).

20. *Loretto v. Teleprompter Manhattan CATV Corp.*, 458 U.S. 419 (1982).

to say that the higher the type or degree of public interest, the greater the infringement on property rights that should be allowed without there being a taking. For example, action X should be a taking if government does X for historic preservation purposes, but the same action X should not be a taking if done to protect the more important interest of the public health. The *Lucas* case contains language that appears to be related to this sliding scale approach.

Three additional elements that are important when determining when the payment of just compensation is required may be found by referring to a group of United States Supreme Court opinions from 1987. First, there may be a land use regulation that prohibits a landowner from causing a nuisance to her neighbors, and that regulation may also protect the landowner from her neighbors imposing a nuisance on her. This "reciprocity of advantage," by simultaneously restricting a landowner's use of her land and conferring a benefit to the landowner, may persuade a court that no taking has occurred.[21] Second, if a government regulation is not sufficiently related to the public purpose it purportedly is designed to further, a court may determine that the regulation is an improper exercise of police power and amounts to a taking. For example, if a privately owned ocean front lot was between two public beaches, a municipality could attempt to condition a building permit for the private lot on the landowners' granting the public an easement to pass from one public beach to the other across their lot, and to base its requirement on a desire to protect the public's ability to see the beach. The restriction requiring public access *along* the beach is not related to the public's "visual access" to the beach *across* the property. The easement would not improve the public's view. Therefore, the landowners must be compensated for a "taking" if the easement is required. The attempted "regulation" is not sufficiently related to the public purpose.[22] Finally, the Court's third recently stated element leading to requiring payment of just compensation is the notion of a "temporary taking." When an attempted regulation is determined by a court to be a taking, the government may repeal the regulation or amend the regulation to permissible standards for non-compensable regulations. Nevertheless, even if the municipality repeals or modifies the regulation, payment of just compensation may be required for that period of time that the taking was in effect.[23]

Regardless of the factors that have been used by individual courts to draw the taking/regulation line, it is fair to say that the result has been that

---

21. *Keystone Bituminous Coal Assn. v. DeBenedictis*, 480 U.S. 470 (1987).

22. *Nollan v. California Coastal Commission*, 483 U.S. 825 (1987).

23. *First English Evangelical Church of Glendale v. Los Angeles County*, 482 U.S. 304 (1987).

government can go a long way in restricting private property rights and reducing private property values by those restrictions without needing to pay compensation. At the extreme are cases like the California case in which the California Supreme Court found that the application of a local zoning ordinance did not result in a taking requiring compensation even though the trial court had determined that the ordinance precluded the landowner from making any economic use of his property.[24] To the extent that Americans believe that they are secure from their government acting in ways that reduce their property value from $200,000 to $100,000 without paying compensation, that feeling of security is a myth. Yet there is a limit. Beyond some ill-defined point, government action that adversely affects private property will be a taking and constitutionally require the payment of just compensation.

One might want to consider the wisdom of allowing government to act in ways that substantially reduce individual property values without compensating the owners for the loss. Would it not be better to say that when government acts for the public benefit, all citizens should pay the price for that benefit rather than having the cost fall on one property owner or a small group of property owners who stand to bear the cost because of fortuitous circumstances? Thus, perhaps all government action that results in a substantial loss in property value should be compensated, and the question of whether there has been a "taking" or a "regulation" should not be relevant. Furthermore, should compensation be limited to losses related to land use? For example, if a company has been operating lawfully for 20 years and even been encouraged to expand its operation by federal income tax incentives, should new pollution laws enacted for the public benefit be allowed to put this company out of business without compensating its shareholders? Are there compensation systems for land or other property value losses that might be workable and yet be fairer than the taking/regulation distinction is to those whose economic interests may be injured by action taken by the government for the public benefit? If one looks for them, one will find many possibilities;[25] however, requiring government to pay for property value losses brought about by environmental regulations would present a significant challenge to our nation's principal environmental laws. That challenge has recently manifested itself in the form of increasingly successful lawsuits against the U.S. Government in the United States Claims Court. When the government is ordered to pay millions of dollars to mining companies and

---

24. *Consolidated Rock Products v. City of Los Angeles*, 370 P.2d 342 (1962).

25. Hagman, D., and Miczynski, D., *Windfalls for Wipeouts* (Chicago: American Society of Planning Officials, 1978); Epstein, R.A. *Takings, Private Property and the Power of Eminent Domain* (Cambridge, MA: Harvard University Press, 1985).

developers for restricting their activities which would have destroyed wetlands or created water pollution, basic environmental protection laws may become too expensive to enforce.[26] Indeed, the willingness of the United States Supreme Court in the *Lucas* case described above to require that government pay compensation when it acts to protect parts of the public interest, such as beachfronts, wetlands, and endangered species, that are not historically imbedded in the common law, may be a big step in putting some environmental protection measures out of the realm of budgetary possibility. This will be especially true if the Court goes one step beyond its *Lucas* decision and requires compensation for property owners who would have very substantial but not total economic loss of their land.

Our last topic in this section concerns the reasons for which government can take private property even if it will pay just compensation for it. The taking clause says: "nor shall private property be taken for pubic use, without just compensation." There is thus a recognition that while the inherent eminent domain power allows a taking for public use, there cannot be a taking by government for private use even if just compensation is paid. The issue is what is meant by the words "public use." Is it a public use and thus an allowable exercise of the eminent domain power for a municipality to condemn private property, paying compensation to the owners who do not voluntarily want to sell it, and then transfer that property to another private owner like the General Motors Corporation? Quite clearly, if a municipality were to condemn private land for a park to be used by the public, that would be a taking for public use. Our General Motors question would appear to be a taking for private use and thus not within the eminent domain power. But let us add some additional facts. If the municipality were the City of Detroit, and General Motors were going to use the property to build a new plant, thereby promoting industry and commerce and adding badly needed jobs and taxes to the economic base of the city and the state, do we now have a "public use?" A narrow interpretation of the words "public use" would still result in our answer being no. The use is a private use—use by General Motors. The courts have not, however, given the words "public use" a narrow interpretation. Public use has been held to include serving public purposes or providing public benefits, and so long as the public interests are dominant, the fact that private interests will also benefit from the condemnation does not mean that the condemnation is outside the scope of the eminent domain power. In the General Motors example, the Michigan Supreme Court said:

---

26. "Environment Laws Face a Stiff Test From Landowners," *New York Times* (Jan. 20, 1992) p. 1.

> The power of eminent domain is to be used in this instance primarily
> to accomplish the essential purposes of alleviating unemployment and
> revitalizing the economic base of the community. The benefit to a private
> interest is merely incidental.[27]

Public takings in which private property is condemned and transferred
to new, private owners were also approved by the United States Supreme
Court in *Hawaii Housing Authority v. Midkiff*.[28] In *Hawaii*, the state legislature found that, because 47% of the state's land was owned by 72 private
landowners and the federal and state governments owned another 49%,
concentrated land ownership skewed the real estate market, inflated land
prices, and injured public tranquility and welfare. The legislature, in response
to the land oligopoly, provided for the condemnation of residential tracts
and the transfer of ownership to existing tenants. The tenants also were
provided with state assistance in financing the land purchases. The Supreme
Court held that the "public use" requirement does not mean that the government must possess and use the property during a taking. The Court found
that, despite incidental private benefits incurred by the purchasing tenants,
the dominant public interest of reducing the concentration of land ownership
statewide demonstrated that the land reforms were constitutional exercises
of the state's eminent domain power.

When we discussed the line between what is a police power regulation
and what is an eminent domain taking, we concluded that government can
go quite far in restricting property use and still be on the regulation side
of the line. To conclude our discussion of the limits on public control of
land use, we should also note that if government is acting either under its
eminent domain power or its police power, it has a substantial amount of
latitude with respect to what it chooses to call a public purpose or public
benefit. In *Berman v. Parker*, the United States Supreme Court decided that
aesthetics is a valid public purpose. The Court said: "It is within the power
of the legislature to determine that the community should be beautiful as
well as healthy, ..."[29] Thus there are legal limits on public control of
land use, but the legal limits are not very limiting. Perhaps the more significant limits are political.

D. THE PUBLIC TRUST DOCTRINE

In addition to police power regulations and eminent domain takings, a
third doctrine provides some restrictions on private ownership and use of

---

27. *Poletown Neighborhood Council v. City of Detroit*, 304 N.W.2d 455 (1981).

28. 467 U.S. 229 (1984).

29. 348 U.S. 26 (1954).

land. Originating in English law, the public trust doctrine held that title in the land under the sea belonged to the public but was managed in trust for the public by the king. Although the king, or today the state, can convey this land to private owners, the state cannot convey or "alienate" the land free of public trust obligations or rights of use by the public such as for navigation or fishing. The legislature may thus convey public trust lands to private parties, but some public rights in the land will continue to exist, and grants of property subject to the public trust doctrine may even be revoked. In *Illinois Central Railroad v. Illinois*, the United States Supreme Court allowed Illinois to revoke its grant to the railroad of title to an area of the bed of Lake Michigan bordering Chicago. The Court found that the conveyance violated the public trust with respect to public rights in navigable waters. The court said:

> The state can no more abdicate its trust over property in which the whole people are interested . . . than it can abdicate its police powers in the administration of government and the preservation of the peace.[30]

As the public trust doctrine has evolved, its applicability and operation have expanded and become more defined. Let's first consider what types of land or natural resources, although privately held, may be subject to public rights, and what public rights or benefits may exist with regard to that land. We will then discuss the scope of the limitations or "encumbrances" that these rights place on the private ownership of land.

Traditionally, the king's trust responsibilities extended to lands under the sea for use by the public in navigation, commerce, and fishing. Subsequently, the public trust doctrine has been extended to include other navigable waters such as lakes and rivers, and also tidelands and wetlands. For example, when the state of Mississippi began issuing oil and gas leases on land underlying a bayou and streams which were several miles from the Gulf of Mexico and non-navigable, the state's ownership of the land was contested by private parties claiming ownership. The United States Supreme Court held that Mississippi's public trust rights extended not only to lands under navigable waters, but also to those under tidal waters because of public interests including geographical, chemical, and environmental qualities of non-navigable tidal waters.[31]

Although the concept of an inalienable public trust originally was used to protect public rights concerning navigation, commerce, and fishing, the public trust doctrine approach manifests itself today in numerous other

---

30. 146 U.S. 387 (1892).

31. *Phillips Petroleum v. Mississippi*, 484 U.S. 469 (1988).

conflicts ranging from the regulation of grazing land in national forests[32] to the protection of and recovery for damages to natural resources. Where on oil spill destroyed 30,000 birds, a court held that the government had a right and duty to protect the public interest in preserving wildlife resources.[33] Legislatively, Congress has provided, in the Superfund Act (CER-CLA), that government "shall act on behalf of the public as trustee of such natural resources to recover for . . . damages."[34] Natural resources are defined as "land, fish, wildlife . . . ground water . . . and other such resources belonging to, managed by, held in trust by . . . the United States . . . State or local governments . . . ."[35] The types of lands and natural resources which may carry with them rights of the public as a whole appear to be expanding. Pursuant to the public trust doctrine, land that is in the hands of a private landowner, may still be subject to the public's rights in that land or in natural resources related to it.

Once we determine that a parcel of land is covered by the public trust doctrine, we must next examine what constraints the public trust doctrine places on the interests of the private landowner. The scope of the encumbrances that the public trust doctrine may establish on the ownership of applicable lands can extend to restrictions on the use, development, and alienability of the land, and can lead to the modification or revocation of ownership interests. The legislature, as trustee, has the discretion to impair public uses of trust lands, but it also has an affirmative obligation to consider public interests and to minimize harms done to those trust interests. For example, where water rights to a lake have been granted to a municipality, the legislature retains an obligation of continued supervision and a power to revoke or modify the conveyed water rights.[36] Thus, the municipality acquires the water rights subject to the trust and can assert no vested right which would do harm to the public's interests such as by draining a lake beyond certain levels. Also, development of lands adjacent to trust lands may be restricted to a greater extent than other lands. State courts have determined that, because lands adjacent to navigable lakes, streams, or oceans have a special relationship to public trust lands, to permit the development of these adjacent lands would degrade or deteriorate public trust lands and would contravene the intent of the doctrine.[37] Therefore, more restrictive

---

32. *Light v. United States*, 220 U.S. 523 (1911).

33. *In re Steuart Transportation Co.*, 495 F. Supp. 38 (1980).

34. 42 U.S.C. § 9607(f).

35. 42 U.S.C. § 9601 (16).

36. *National Audubon Society v. Superior Court of Alpine Cty.*, 658 P.2d 709 (1983).

37. *Graham v. Estuary Properties, Inc.*, 399 So.2d 1374 (1981).

land use regulations may be imposed on lands adjacent to trust lands than on other lands without exceeding the police power authority and creating a compensable taking.

Perhaps the most restrictive public trust constraint on private land ownership would involve a prohibition on sale of the land or on converting it to other than its present use. Assume that local government condemns some private land for a public purpose and pays just compensation to the owners. It then transfers the land to another private owner to achieve that public purpose. What if the new private owner discontinues its initial public interest use—can it put the property to another use or sell it? This issue could arise with respect to the city of Detroit/General Motors situation discussed in Section C above. Since, in that example, no trust land is involved, General Motors may be allowed to subsequently use the land for other purposes or to sell it. The situation could be different, however, for a private landowner who was granted public trust land upon which to build a wharf for navigation and commercial uses. If the owner later wants to develop the property into a hotel or apartment building, courts may require that the changed use be consistent with the public trust. The Massachusetts Supreme Judicial Court has stated that public trust land "can be granted by the State only to fulfill a public purpose, and the rights of the grantee to that land are ended when that purpose is extinguished."[38]

Another example involving changing use and ownership of public trust land concerns federal military installations. Assume that the federal government purchases public trust lands from the state for use as a naval base. If the Navy subsequently ceases operation of its base, may it sell the land to another private owner, or does the public trust doctrine require that the land revert back to the state? Federal courts in California and Massachusetts, both of which confronted questions similar to this, reached opposite results. The Massachusetts court decided that federal condemnation did not extinguish the public trust; instead, the federal government assumed the trustee responsibilities.[39] In effect, the public trust is administered jointly by the federal and state governments, and the public trust requirements persist. Conversely, the California court focused on the supremacy of federal law over state law.[40] That court decided that federal condemnation of the land extinguished the state's public trust because the federal power of eminent domain is supreme over the state duty of public trust. Therefore, the federal government was free to convey the land, after ceasing its naval base operations, to a private

38. *Boston Waterfront Dev. Corp. v. Commonwealth*, 393 N.E. 2d 356 (1979).

39. *United States v. 1.58 Acres of Land*, 523 F. Supp. 120 (1981).

40. *United States v. 11.037 Acres of Land*, 685 F. Supp. 214 (1988).

concern. Today, the federal government is contemplating closing several
military facilities. Whether a federal public trust obligation in this context
will be recognized remains to be seen. Though the public trust doctrine has
recently received considerable support both academically and judicially, the
doctrine often remains rather vague and obscure in its definition and application.

As a possible further expansion of the public trust doctrine, one may
speculate about whether, in the future, the act of taking land by government
through the eminent domain process might be found, by itself, to have made
land that is not otherwise public trust land into public trust land. Such a
result could be supported by arguing that, since the eminent domain process
can only be used for the public interest, once it is so used, the public acquires
permanent rights in the land that has been obtained under that process. This
would be a significant expansion of the public trust approach. With a growing
number of environmentally concerned plaintiffs embracing the public trust
doctrine for protecting land and other environmental interests, it is not clear
whether the courts will continue to expand the scope of a state's public trust
rights and duties, or whether the doctrine, even as it currently stands, will
be found to be too restrictive of private interests in the ownership and use
of land.

E. USE OF FEDERALLY OWNED LANDS

Over 700 million acres of land are owned by the federal government.
Additional acreage is controlled though the federal government holding
various interests in land that do not amount to an ownership interest. Currently
the use or control of use of these lands includes 75 million acres under
the National Park System, 84 million acres for Wildlife Refuge and Ranges,
190 million acres in National Forests, 340 million acres managed by the
Bureau of Land Management (mostly for grazing), and over 80 million acres
of Wilderness. Two of these uses of federal land will be discussed here.
Use of federal land for energy production is discussed in Chapter 7.

1. Wildlife Habitat

Prior to 1966, the wildlife refuges run by the federal government were
administered as many separate administrative units and by different federal
agencies. With the passage of the National Wildlife Refuge System Administration Act of 1966,[41] these units were consolidated into the National

---

41. 16 U.S.C.A. § 668dd.

Wildlife Refuge System. Under this statute the Refuge System is to be administered by the Secretary of the Interior to

> permit the use of any area within the System for any purpose, including but not limited to hunting, fishing, public recreation and accommodations, and access whenever he determines that such uses are compatible with the major purposes for which such areas were established. . . .

This statutory standard for administration adopts the management concept of "dominant use" as opposed to "single use" of the land in the Refuge System. Wildlife is the dominant use, but it is not the single use to which the land can be put since other uses compatible with wildlife are allowed. The dominant use management approach appears to provide for a more efficient use of land; however, it also raises the issue of when are other uses compatible and when are they not compatible. With the pressures that are often applied to use land for economic yields such as recreation or grazing, use as wildlife habitat is subject to being compromised in ways that could not happen under single use management. In enacting the dominant use approach, Congress has decided that the administrative tool of requiring "compatibility" of other uses with wildlife is sufficient protection, and that to go beyond the compatibility level to protect wildlife would be an unwarranted waste of land resources.

The protection of wildlife as the dominant use for Wildlife Refuge land has been called into question by the federal appeals court case of *Schwenke v. Secretary of the Interior*.[42] In *Schwenke*, which originated in Montana, the Department of Interior argued that grazing was permitted on the Charles M. Russell Wildlife Refuge only to the extent it was compatible with wildlife values. Reductions in the existing grazing levels were proposed by the Department because of evidence of overgrazing and destruction of wildlife habitat. Cattle ranchers contended, however, that grazing on the Russell Range should be administered under the Taylor Grazing Act[43] rather than the Wildlife Refuge Act, and that management of the refuge ought to give equal priority to livestock and wildlife. Though the cattle ranchers won at trial, the government prevailed on appeal, and the appellate court determined that the refuge land must be administered under the Refuge Administration Act. The court held that, given the goals of maintaining specific numbers of various wildlife species including antelope and sharptail grouse, a limited priority in favor of wildlife existed. Only when the designated wildlife populations have been achieved, can wildlife and livestock grazing have equal

---

42. 720 F.2d 571 (1983).

43. 43 U.S.C.A. § 315.

priority in access to the resources of the range. Thus, not only is wildlife the dominant use under the Refuge Administration Act itself, but also it may be dominant over other uses established by other federal laws such as the Taylor Grazing Act.

2. Forest Land

A combination of the Forest Reserve Act of 1891,[44] authorizing national forests, and the Organic Act of 1897,[45] which limited the purposes for which national forests could be established, resulted in the designation of national forests (1) for the protection of the forest, (2) for securing favorable waterflows, or (3) to furnish a supply of timber. While these were the only purposes allowed by law as the basis to establish a national forest, once a national forest was established, the practice was to manage it for other purposes also, such as for grazing and recreation. In the Multiple Use-Sustained Yield Act of 1960,[46] Congress addressed itself to the question of what in fact were to be the allowable uses for national forest land. The statute declared that, in addition to the previously authorized purposes for establishing national forests, the national forests were to be administered as well as established "for outdoor recreation, range, timber, watershed, and wildlife and fish purposes." The Secretary of Agriculture was instructed "to develop and administer the renewable surface resources of the national forests for multiple use and sustained yield of the several products and services obtained therefrom." The multiple use approach to forest land management was thus codified by Congress with the five above-quoted purposes being the allowable multiple uses.

The Multiple Use-Sustained Yield Act gives us an example of how Congress often provides guidance to an administering agency but still leaves much in the way of how the statute will work in the control of the agency and, in part, in the hands of the courts that will interpret Congress's intent in its statute. The statute requires management for a sustained yield of products and services and defines sustained yield in terms of striving for perpetual output. In defining multiple use, the statute speaks of managing the resources in the combination that best meets the needs of the American people, while recognizing that some of the land may be used for less than all of its resources. The combination of uses selected for each piece of forest is to take into account competing uses by considering the relative value of

---

44. 26 Stat. 1103.

45. 30 Stat. 34.

46. 16 U.S.C.A. §§ 528–531.

the various resources, but the use pattern is to be "not necessarily the combination of uses that will give the greatest dollar return or the greatest unit output." Perpetual output management; a combination of uses; not necessarily maximizing dollar return or unit output—these are reasonably clear boundaries set by Congress within which the agency must work, but the statute also says that in administering the national forests, "due consideration shall be given to the relative values of the various resources in particular areas." What is "due consideration?" This question is not clearly answered by Congress since the statute just says "due consideration." It has been argued that due consideration means equal consideration of the various competing uses, and that a use plan that is formulated by giving anything less than equal consideration to any potential use is invalid. The courts have, however, taken the position that "due consideration" means merely "some consideration," and that "the decision as to the proper mix of uses within any particular area is left to the sound discretion" of the administrative agency.[47] The courts have thus adopted an interpretation of the statute that, even with the boundaries discussed above within which the agency must work, allows substantial agency discretion in the actual determination of what uses will be emphasized for our national forest land.

One use of our nation's forests that is expressly provided for in the Multiple Use-Sustained Yield Act is timber harvesting. The U.S. Forest Service, the agency administering the national forests, created a two stage process for making timber available for private sale.[48] First, a forest planning process, much like a comprehensive zoning plan, determines which lands are suitable for harvesting and what the allowable sale quantities are from each forest considering environmental, economic, and other pertinent factors. The planning process is followed by the sale and harvest implementation process in which potential buyers competitively bid for the rights to harvest the timber. The Act mandates, however, that forests shall be used for uses in addition to timber sales, including the protection of wildlife. The Forest Service, therefore, must reconcile the inherent tension that exists between these competing uses. A combination of agency regulations and federal statutes, each aimed at protecting wildlife and the environment, in effect serves to constrain the harvest of timber throughout the national forest system.[49] Let's consider some examples.

The Forest Service has established broad wildlife management regulations

47. *Sierra Club v. Hardin*, 325 F. Supp. 99 (1971).

48. Lundquist, T., "Providing the Timber Supply from National Forest Lands," *Natural Resources & Environment* (American Bar Association, Winter, 1991) p. 6.

49. Rutzik, M., "Wildlife Constraints on Timber Harvesting," *Natural Resources & Environment*, (American Bar Association, Winter, 1991), p. 10.

requiring that viable populations of wildlife be maintained in national forests by insuring that adequate supporting habitats exist and are well distributed.[50] An example of how the regulation works is found in the case of the northern spotted owl. A Forest Service committee of biologists has proposed to permanently dedicate 5.3 million acres of forest to habitat conservation areas in which no harvesting or other conflicting uses would be allowed. In effect, this proposal, made pursuant to the regulations, would make protection of the spotted owl the dominant use in these areas, perhaps consistent with or perhaps contrary to the approach of multiple uses. Besides agency regulations, federal statutes also constrain the harvest of timber in national forests. The National Environmental Policy Act[51] has caused significant impacts on the quantities of timber harvested. NEPA requires that the Forest Service, with considerable public involvement, prepare an environmental impact statement (EIS) to examine the consequences of proposed tree harvests. In addition, NEPA may permit environmental interest groups to contest timber sales based on potential inadequacies in the EIS. A second federal statute constraining timber harvests, the Endangered Species Act,[52] requires that virtually all other federal laws yield to its mandate. Section 1536 of this act provides that Forest Service activities must not jeopardize species of wildlife identified as endangered or threatened. This limitation is implemented for each proposed timber sale through interagency consultations with the U.S. Fish and Wildlife Service. The consultations are designed to determine whether such species will be jeopardized by the proposed activity.[53] As a result, efforts to protect wildlife including the red cockaded woodpecker in the southeast, the caribou in Maine, the grey wolf in Minnesota and Idaho, and the Mexican spotted owl in the southwest, have limited the harvest of timber on federal lands.

Both Congress and the federal agencies must constantly deal with the issue of how to appropriately resolve the need to protect wildlife and other environmental interests in the face of continuing pressure for increasing timber harvests on federal forest land. Whether or not to allow clearcutting practices in the national forests or even any logging in the nation's old-growth forests involves many factors. Among them are: thoughts about the near total destruction of the existing environment on a huge amount of acreage; the effects of replanting a monoculture of trees; aesthetics; the probability of unemployment and major changes in lifestyle for loggers and their families;

---

50. 36 CFR § 219.19.

51. 42 U.S.C. § 4321 et seq.

52. 16 U.S.C. § 1531 et seq.

53. 50 CFR § 402.01 et seq.

The missing ecosystem

Photographs by Michael J. Firestone

and how possible increases in the cost of building materials might affect the ability of people to afford decent housing. These interests may not always be reconcilable.[54]

ADDITIONAL READINGS

Hill, G.R., *Regulatory Taking: The Limits of Land Use Controls* (Chicago: American Bar Association, 1990).

Mantell, M.A. et al., *Creating Successful Communities* and *Resource Guide for Creating Successful Communities* (Washington, DC: Island Press, 1990).

Simon, D.J., *Our Common Lands: Defending the National Parks* (Washington, DC: Island Press, 1988).

Slade, D.C. et al., *Putting The Public Trust Doctrine To Work* (Connecticut Dept. of Environmental Protection, 1990).

Williams, N., *American Planning Law* (New York: Clark Boardman Callaghan, Multivolume Treatise with annual supplements).

---

54. Problem: What should be done if the following alleged facts are and continue to be true? 1. The bark of the slow growing pacific yew tree is the only approved source of taxol, a drug that is highly effective in treating ovarian and breast cancer. 2. In years to come, the need for taxol will far exceed the supply. 3. Much of the yew supply grows on land that is home for the northern spotted owl, a threatened species. See "Trees That Yield Drug For Cancer Are Wasted," *New York Times* (Jan. 29, 1992) p. 1.

CHAPTER 5

SOLID WASTE AND RESOURCE RECOVERY

A. THE SCOPE OF THE SOLID WASTE PROBLEM

"Gee whiz mom, my bicycle finally fell apart, and now I need a new one. What should I do with this junker?" "Put it out in front son, and the garbageman will take it away," she said. And take it away he did, just like that garbage has been taken away for decades and just like that waste disposal company you hire takes your garbage away. But, as we observed in Chapter 1, you cannot always take it away and put it someplace else. So, where do we put it? "It" is really a collection of stuff we assume we do not have a use for anymore and is defined by our federal government under the general heading of solid waste. According to federal statute, we define "solid waste" as;

> . . . any garbage, refuse, sludge from a waste treatment plant, water supply treatment plant, or air pollution control facility and other discarded material, including solid, liquid, semisolid, or contained gaseous material resulting from industrial, commercial, mining, and agricultural operations, and from community activities, but does not include solid or dissolved material in domestic sewage, or solid or dissolved materials in irrigation return flows or industrial discharges which are point sources subject to permits under section 402 of the Federal Water Pollution Control Act, as amended, or source, special nuclear or by-product material as defined by the Atomic Energy Act of 1954, as amended.[1]

As shown in Table I, in 1990 we discarded 167 million tons of municipal solid waste, about 1340 pounds per person, or 3.67 pounds per person per day. That is a lot of solid waste, and our annual total and per capita solid

---

1. 42 U.S.C.S. § 6903.

Table I.   Municipal Solid Waste Generation and Recovery, 1960–1990.[2]

Year	Gross discards Per capita (pounds per day)	Gross discards Total (million tons)	Materials recovery Per capita (pounds per day)	Materials recovery Total (million tons)	Energy recovery (million tons)	Net discards (million tons)
1960	2.65	87.5	0.18	5.8	0	81.7
1965	2.88	102.3	0.17	6.2	0.2	95.9
1970	3.22	120.5	0.21	8.0	0.4	112.1
1975	3.18	125.3	0.23	9.1	0.7	115.5
1980	3.43	142.6	0.32	13.4	2.7	126.5
1985	3.49	152.5	0.35	15.3	7.6	129.7
1990	3.67	167.4	0.40	18.4	13.3	135.7

Source: U.S. Environmental Protection Agency, Office of Solid Waste and Emergency Response. Characterization of municipal solid waste in the United States, 1960 to 2000. Prepared by Franklin Associates, Prairie Village, KS.

Notes: Data for 1990 are projections.

waste production continues to increase. The makeup of our municipal waste stream is shown in Figure 1.

On the bright side, our recovery of materials is increasing, and our increased use of waste burning to produce energy is dramatic (see Table I). Over 130 municipal waste-to-energy plants are in operation, and the projections are that by 2010, waste-to-energy plants will produce seven times the amount of power currently generated from such sources.[3] While an improvement with respect to waste disposal and waste use, one might question the overall environmental soundness of the waste to energy process. Combustion of waste, in addition to causing air pollution, leaves a residue—ash. This ash may have high concentrations of heavy metals which, without extremely careful handling, could have severe environmental impacts such as leaching into and contaminating ground water.

To further complicate this issue, we must add the fact that hazardous waste is a "species" of solid waste. A hazardous waste is generally identified by the federal government as a solid waste (remember the above definition of solid waste) that may cause or significantly contribute to increased mortality or illness or threaten human health or the environment when improperly handled *and* can be measured using a standard test or easily detected by

2. Council on Environmental Quality, *Environmental Quality* (Washington, DC: U.S. Government Printing Office, 1990) p. 492.

3. Council on Environmental Quality, *Environmental Quality* (Washington, DC: U.S. Government Printing Office, 1991) p. 114.

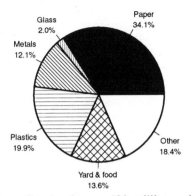

Glass
2.0%

Paper
34.1%

Metals
12.1%

Plastics
19.9%

Other
18.4%

Yard & food
13.6%

Note: Total volume= 400 million cubic
yards. Total weight= 179.6 million tons.
Source: See Part II, Table 87; U.S.
Environmental Protection Agency; Office
of Solid Waste and Emergency Response,
*Characterization of Municipal Solid Waste
in the United States,* (Washington, DC:
EPA, 1990).

Figure 1. Material Discards in the 1988 Municipal Waste Stream, by volume.[4]

generators of hazardous waste.[5] Most hazardous waste is further characterized
as a solid waste that is ignitable, corrosive, or reactive. In the United States,
over 200,000 producers generate over 230 million tons of hazardous waste
annually. Industries that generate hazardous waste include makers of cos-
metics, petroleum products, leather, and plastics. While we keep track of
what hazardous wastes these industries are putting where, hazardous wastes
generated in our homes when we discard materials like drain cleaners,
solvents, and garden pesticides are generally unregulated. We usually cope
with industry generated hazardous waste by incineration, chemical or biological detoxification, or landfills.

Incineration of hazardous waste raises similar, but perhaps greater, problems of air pollution and water pollution than the ash problem noted above
with respect to solid waste. Chemical detoxification involves mixing a hazardous waste or wastes with some other chemical to create a relatively
harmless solid waste. Biological detoxification is the use of microbes to break
down organic contaminates. These methods may hold promise, but today's
most common method of dealing with hazardous waste is putting it in
landfills. Storing hazardous wastes in landfills until methods are developed
to render them nonhazardous or, hopefully, to make use of them causes

---

4. Ibid., p. 110.

5. 40 CFR § 261.0 et seq.

significant concern that, in the meantime, landfill leakage will result in the poisoning of our drinking water. When considering hazardous waste, even more than with respect to nonhazardous solid waste, there is no good answer. Yet, during the 1980s, progress was made under the Resource Conservation and Recovery Act (RCRA)[6] in controlling the widespread disposal of hazardous waste to unknown locations and at least reducing its potential for contamination of land and water. Efforts were also made under the Superfund Act[7] to remedy the hazardous waste contamination that had occurred in earlier years. Little progress took place, however, in reducing the volume of ordinary, nonhazardous solid waste or in finding appropriate disposal sites or other approaches for dealing with that solid waste. What to do with solid waste is now at or near the top of the list of concerns of local governments.

No area of the United States is immune from the pressing environmental and economic problems of solid waste disposal. New England towns with populations of a few hundred people are faced with having to close their landfills pursuant to state laws that require plastic-lined landfills in order to protect ground water against the leachate from waste. These lined landfills are very expensive, and small towns are exploring ways to join together to provide environmentally sound landfill sites at costs that are within their financial capabilities. Urban areas have been faced with the issue of where to put their trash for many years, but the magnitude of today's concern can be highlighted by noting the extremes which are being considered for coping with the urban solid waste problem. Cities on the west coast of the United States have discussed sending millions of tons of trash by boat to the Marshall Islands and paying the Republic of the Marshall Islands $56 million annually for the right to dispose of trash there. Other issues aside, the fact that shipping trash across 4,000 miles of ocean may be a financially viable solution compared to the available alternatives demonstrates the degree of our solid waste problem. In addition, our hazardous waste efforts, especially those for the cleanup of contaminated sites under Superfund, have been widely criticized for falling far short of what it was hoped they would achieve.

The environmental problems of waste are numerous. Waste disposal is related to air pollution (smell and the pollutants created by the burning process), water pollution (runoffs from dump sites), and the aesthetic pollution of disposal sites. Improper disposal can also result in disease transmitted by rats and birds. In addition, the whole approach of disposal results in the loss of resources that have a potential for future use. Whether it be by incineration or by the mixing of wastes in a landfill, future use is precluded.

---

6. 42 U.S.C. § 6901 et seq.

7. 42 U.S.C. § 9601 et seq.

We next look at how the problems associated with waste disposal are addressed by the legal system and what the law is doing to provide alternatives to disposal.

B. MECHANISMS FOR CONTROLLING WASTE DISPOSAL—LOCAL, STATE, NATIONAL, AND INTERNATIONAL

The two interrelated facets of the solid waste problem are, as noted in Section A, collection and disposal of solid waste and the fact that waste "disposal" results in the depletion of natural resources. Both the disposal and resource depletion aspects of the problem have received substantial consideration at all levels of government—local, state, national, and international. This section will consider regulatory mechanisms which are addressed to disposal. Mechanisms addressed to the resource depletion problem will be discussed in Section C.

1. Nonhazardous Wastes

Collection and disposal of solid waste was a local government function until the 1960s. There was little federal involvement other than studies and advice. The mechanisms which regulated disposal were local health laws, other local ordinances such as zoning to restrict where a dump could be located, and private lawsuits. If you were bothered by a disposal activity, your recourse was to bring a nuisance action against those private parties who were interfering with your use of your property or against the local government that ran or planned a dump near your property.[8] Your remedy might take the form of receiving money damages to compensate you for the harm you suffered, a court-issued injunction to prevent the harmful conduct from continuing, or the imposition of a wide variety of conditions which the disposing party must adhere to in order to be allowed to continue the disposal activity. Examples of such conditions might be time periods when burning is prohibited or requiring treatment of certain types of waste prior to disposal. While a wide array of private law remedies was available, they were generally only available with respect to harm inflicted on real estate. Also, the remedies tended to come into play after a harm had been

8. See Chapter 3 for a discussion of nuisance actions and remedies.

done rather that as a preventative measure against harm, and those harmed had to go through the process of a lawsuit to attempt to obtain a remedy. Local legislative efforts to control waste disposal encountered enforcement problems and a lack of technology to provide a sound disposal system. Perhaps of greater significance with respect to local efforts was the lack of funds to effectively deal with waste disposal. The costs are high and, since there was little political glamour involved with promising a strong waste disposal program, waste disposal never got proper local funding.

In the 1960s and early 1970s, the federal government entered the picture. The first federal statutes had minimal federal involvement such as providing states with technical assistance and funding for research and demonstration projects. These statutes were the wedge that opened the door to serious federal regulation of solid waste disposal. They helped set the stage for public and Congressional acceptance of federal control over what had been historically a local matter.

In the Resource Conservation and Recovery Act of 1976, RCRA,[9] Congress undertook to impose a broad federal scheme for regulating solid waste disposal. That statute, with amendments, is the heart of waste disposal law today. It seeks to control the disposal of solid wastes by providing financial incentives for the adoption of state or regional plans which will comply with federally established requirements. In addition to dealing with "general" solid wastes through the use of an incentive approach, the statute also established a mandatory regulatory system for the management of "hazardous" wastes.

With respect to nonhazardous solid wastes, if a state adopts a solid waste plan which is approved by the federal government (EPA), then the state qualifies for federal financial and technical assistance involving many facets of the development and implementation of the state plan. In order for a state plan to be approved, it must meet federally established requirements for approval which include a prohibition on the establishment of new open dumps and a phasing out of existing open dumps. Approved plans must also provide that disposal be in sanitary landfills, through resource conservation and recovery methods, or by other environmentally sound methods. In order for a disposal site to be a "sanitary landfill," there must be "no reasonable probability of adverse effects on health or the environment from disposal of solid waste at such facility."[10] One requirement for a site to be a new sanitary landfill is that it be lined with a material such as heavy plastic and

9. 42 U.S.C. § 6901 et seq.
10. 42 U.S.C. § 6944(a).

have a leachate collection system. Widely debated questions about the liner/ leachate collection requirement include: will plastic liners really work in the long run, and how will we pay for the high cost of liners and collectors?

A point of contrast between the Resource Conservation and Recovery Act and both the Clean Air Act and the Clean Water Act is that, while the latter two statutes provide that in the absence of an approved state implementation plan EPA will impose a federally prepared plan on the state, no such federal imposition takes place with respect to soled waste. The only sanction in the event of state noncompliance with the federal requirements for state plan approval is the state's ineligibility to receive federal financial and technical assistance. Why then, without compulsion, do the states go along with the federal objectives and requirements? The answer is twofold: money and money. First, the offer of a significant amount of federal money is hard for a state to pass up. Federal money provides jobs and other elements of economic well being. Furthermore, state administrations which pass up "free" federal dollars usually take a sound beating in the press for doing so. Being efficient in bringing federal money to the state is good politics for state officials. Perhaps a more substantive money argument for states accepting the federal solid waste disposal requirements is an awareness that, sooner or later, the waste disposal problems will have to be faced. States may feel that they might as well address the problem while the federal government is picking up a good share of the bill rather than wait to address the problem after other states have gotten federal assistance and the federal program is no longer available to help.

Although there is now substantial federal prodding and federal assistance, nonhazardous solid waste management is still largely a matter of state control. One step which some states took to attempt to reduce the magnitude of their solid waste problem was to prohibit the disposal within the state of waste which originated or had been collected outside of the state. New Jersey had such a prohibition, and the validity of the New Jersey law was challenged repeatedly in the courts until a final decision was reached by the United States Supreme Court.

The first attempts to have the out-of-state prohibition declared invalid were made in the New Jersey state court system in a case called *City of Philadelphia v. New Jersey*.[11] The major grounds on which invalidity was alleged were (1) that the enactment of solid waste disposal legislation by the federal government preempted the field of solid waste disposal regulation and thus

11. 68 N.J. 451 and 73 N.J. 562.

the state law was invalid under the Supremacy Clause of the United States Constitution, and (2) that the New Jersey statute was invalid because it violated the Commerce Clause of the United States Constitution by unjustifiably discriminating against articles of commerce coming from outside of the state. Let's consider the preemption and Commerce Clause issues one at a time.

The Supremacy Clause, contained in Article VI of the United States Constitution, says that the "Constitution, and the Laws of the United States . . . shall be the supreme Law of the Land; . . . any Thing in the Constitution or Laws of any State to the Contrary notwithstanding." It is thus clear that the state laws which are in direct conflict with the federal law are invalid. The Supremacy Clause has, however, been given broader scope by the courts. If it is found that Congress intended to *exclusively* control or "preempt" the field of regulation of certain subject matter, then state laws which seek to regulate the same subject matter are invalid even though they do not directly conflict with the federal law. Whether Congress has intended to preempt a field of regulation is often analyzed in terms of how pervasive is the scheme of federal regulation which Congress has created and whether Congress has indicated in that legislation that it is willing to accept additional, nonconflicting state legislation.

In the New Jersey Supreme Court cases decided both before and after the federal Resource Conservation and Recovery Act was enacted, the New Jersey Court found that Congress' statutes, rather than evidencing a hostility to state regulation, affirmatively encouraged state action with respect to the disposal of solid waste. Thus there was no Congressional intent to preempt the field of regulation, and the state law prohibiting out-of-state waste was not invalid under the Supremacy Clause. When *City of Philadelphia v. New Jersey* found its way to the United States Supreme Court, the United States Supreme Court agreed with the New Jersey Supreme Court on the issue of preemption.[12]

The New Jersey Supreme Court had also determined that the out-of-state prohibition did not violate the Commerce Clause of the United States Constitution. The Commerce Clause, contained in Article I, Section 8 of the Constitution, gives Congress the power "To regulate Commerce . . . among the several States. . . ." The courts have interpreted this constitutional grant of power to Congress to preclude states from enacting laws which discriminate against articles of commerce coming from outside the state unless there is some reason, apart from their origin, to treat them differently. This

12. 437 U.S. 617 (1978).

interpretation is consistent with the policy of preventing a state from engaging in protectionism by treating out-of-state commerce in a less favorable way than it treats its own commerce. That policy was much on the minds of the drafters of the Constitution who were well aware that many of the economic woes of the country under the Articles of Confederation were a result of states practicing protectionism.

The New Jersey Supreme Court had found that the out-of-state prohibition advanced vital health and environmental objectives with no economic discrimination against and with little burden upon interstate commerce. The United States Supreme Court reversed that judgement. It decided that solid waste is an item of commerce and is thus under the protection of the Commerce Clause. Even if an object of interstate trade is valueless, it is not outside the scope of the Commerce Clause. Furthermore, unlike diseased cattle, there are no dangers inherent in the movement of solid waste from one state to another which would justify a prohibition against its crossing a state line. The Court found that while it was true that some items of commerce may be validly subjected to state regulation, such regulation cannot take place where the purpose is basically protectionism. Although New Jersey may have an interest in conserving its remaining landfill space, it may not attempt to isolate itself from a problem common to many states by erecting a barrier against interstate movement of an item of commerce such as solid waste. The New Jersey statute prohibiting disposal of out-of-state waste in New Jersey was unconstitutional, and, while Congress has given the states a large role to play under the Resource Conservation and Recovery Act, states may not seek to limit their solid waste problems by prohibiting the entry of out-of-state waste.

If a state cannot limit the entry of out-of-state waste, and if the volume of its own waste is growing rapidly, and if its existing landfills are full and/or a threat to ground water, what can the state do? After doing all that can be done to minimize the creation of solid waste and to recycle or reuse what would otherwise be solid waste, the problem of disposing of the remainder becomes unavoidable. Incineration results in air pollution and the need to dispose of the ash that may contain substances that have become especially hazardous due to concentration by the process of incineration. There is great resistance to locating an incinerator or ash disposal site anywhere. So what are the choices? Let's consider two possibilities that are currently being explored and the issues they raise: (1) export and (2) high-tech lined landfills.

Given the lack of willing sites in the United States, proposals for disposing of American solid waste in foreign nations have been presented. These proposals, such as the one for a site in the Marshall Islands noted in Section A above, raise many interesting issues. While most of the discussion about and opposition to international transport of waste for disposal has focused on hazardous waste,[13] the Marshall Islands proposal involves nontoxic trash from west coast cities. The Marshall Islands were part of the Trust Territory of the Pacific Islands administered by the United States under United Nations auspices after World War II. In 1986, the Republic of the Marshall Islands became an independent nation. It is a Third World country and also has virtually no economic base. It is almost wholly dependent on funds from the United States which come from rent for a missile testing facility and foreign aid under a compact that was part of the independence process. The prospect of receiving $56 million annually as a nonhazardous waste disposal site is enticing to a Third World nation with a population of about 45,000 and an extremely high rate of population growth; however, the money received is not the only advantage that might be derived from being a disposal site.

The Marshall Islands consist of narrow coral atolls that barely rise above the high tide mark. Land is very scarce, and a solid waste landfill placed in a lagoon of an atoll means more usable land. In addition, the existing land is very close to sea level, and a landfill brings the possibility of raising the elevation, something that sounds very attractive to people concerned about rising sea levels due to global warming. Another advantage that must be acknowledged is that waste disposal is an industry that will provide jobs and perhaps the beginning of an independent economic base. The waste disposal industry might also provide, as a "by-product," the means for establishing other industries on the Marshall Islands because the boats that bring the waste may be available to transport freight to the United States at a reasonable price since they would otherwise be returning empty. The availability of cheap transport could make the isolated Marshalls competitive as an exporter. All of these advantages led the government of the Marshall Islands to tentatively endorse the waste disposal proposal. There are, however, numerous disadvantages that should be very carefully considered prior to any nation agreeing to accept waste from another nation for disposal.

Although waste may be of the "nonhazardous" type, it does bring with it the likelihood of significant adverse effects on the ecology of an area. This is especially true of an ecologically fragile coral reef which is used as a source of food for the local people and which may also have the potential to be developed for export of reef products and for tourism. Also, even nonhazardous waste can easily cause pollution of drinking water, and that is one of the main reasons for opposition to sites in the United States. Besides the environmental problems that nonhazardous waste might cause in the

---

13. "Halt to Transboundary Waste Shipment Sought by Caribbean Environmentalists," *International Environment Reporter* (Washington, DC: Bureau of National Affairs, Inc., Feb. 14, 1990) pp. 45–46.

Marshalls, how can they be sure that they are not going to get hazardous waste? Can a tiny, unsophisticated, Third World nation adequately monitor the waste it receives to be sure it is "nonhazardous," or can it trust those bringing the waste to do this monitoring for them?

The environmental disadvantages of being a waste disposal site might be outweighed by economic advantages, but there are also economic disadvantages that should be considered in the decisionmaking process. Already noted above is the potential physical damage to the economic resource of the coral reef, yet, even if there were no real physical damage or contamination from waste disposal in the Marshalls, the establishment of the waste industry might work to psychologically preempt other business and industry. Tourism certainly would not benefit by the image of the islands as waste disposal areas, and fish, even if not actually contaminated, would be shunned due to having been caught in suspect waters. Consider the economic desirability of real estate in the United States that is located near "the dump" or on the "Dump Road."

The temptation for a Third World nation to provide a waste disposal site in exchange for large amounts of money and the hope of other related benefits is quite understandable and may or may not be the right decision. Assuming that a Third World country decided that it would accept solid waste from the United States, should the United States allow its waste to be exported, or should it enact a statute prohibiting the export? On one hand, not to allow such commerce might be viewed as an undue interference by the U.S. with the right of another sovereign country to decide for itself what is best for it. On the other hand, can sending waste to an impoverished, Third World country in exchange for money be anything short of exploitation of the developing nations by the industrialized nations? Similar arguments have been raised concerning the export of unregistered pesticides from the United States, but, not without opposition both within the U.S. and in the international community, the U.S. does allow unregistered pesticides to be exported.[14] An export decision may have to be made by Congress with respect to solid waste, and, regardless of what it decides about nonhazardous solid waste, a further question is what should be allowed or prohibited when the issue is the export of hazardous waste or even nuclear waste?[15]

At the other end of the spectrum from the large cities with grandiose plans for massive waste disposal projects are the small American towns that, until recently, simply had some vacant land and used bulldozers to cover what

14. See Chapter 6.

15. In 1989, the Marshall Islands did offer to be a storage site for high-level nuclear waste from the U.S. That offer was withdrawn, but there are those in the Marshall Islands government who continue to favor the idea.

was trucked into their "sanitary landfills." These towns are today having to confront the question of how to better handle their solid waste. The vacant land and the bulldozer do not protect the ground water from contamination, incineration problems have been discussed above, and plastic-lined landfills are extremely expensive. Although there is some doubt about the environmental effectiveness of lined landfills, federal and state law now requires that new municipal solid waste landfills be lined.[16]

Historically, waste disposal in rural and suburban towns was handled by each town separately or by some towns contracting to have others dispose of their waste for them. Today, largely due to the high costs of disposal and waste reduction facilities, smaller governmental units are exploring forming independent, multitown entities for waste management and affiliating with them.[17] These affiliation efforts have raised the fundamental issue of whether representation on and decisionmaking power within a multitown waste control district should be based on the population of the member towns. While population is the norm for representation in the United States, smaller towns are concerned about being outvoted by those with greater population and are especially concerned about being "elected" by the other towns to be the "host" town for a multitown dump. This brings with it the tension-filled issues of whether to empower the multitown district to acquire land by the forced sale eminent domain process and whether a small town without much business or industry will be selected as the disposal site for waste from larger towns that generate what is perceived as much riskier types of waste.

Site selection for a landfill is, without doubt, the waste disposal issue that creates the highest level of emotional involvement among the general public and most infringes on smaller communities' traditional notions of "wanting to control our own destiny." The NIMBY (not in my back yard) syndrome is very strong. The costs of disposal are also, however, in the forefront of the voters' thoughts when they are asked to decide whether their town will join in forming a multitown waste district. Much of the impetus behind affiliation of smaller units is to achieve economies of scale—one larger facility being more economical than several smaller facilities for handling the same volume of trash or for sorting and marketing recyclable materials. The opposing view is that large facilities will lean in the direction of high cost, high technology solutions which would be less economical and less

---

16. 40 CFR § 258.40, effective 1992, see 53 Fed. Reg. 33410, 33381 (August 30, 1988); 10 Vermont Statutes Annotated § 6605(d).

17. States are encouraging the formation of multitown waste districts by providing funding for planning and organization. See, for example, Vermont Public Act No. 78, 1987 Session, § 5.

environmentally sound than a greater number of smaller alternative approaches such as waste stream reduction through consumer education and curbside recycling by individual households.

If landfills are all required to be lined, a strong argument can be made in favor of the economies of scale because the costs of constructing either a lined landfill or an incinerator are enormous. The district must be able to pay the cost, and that usually entails financing the construction through the borrowing or "bonding" process and paying off the lenders over a period of time such as the expected useful life of the facility. In order for a lender to be willing to finance landfill or incinerator construction, the lender wants to be assured that the loan will be repaid. This requires that the facility take in a predetermined amount of revenue each year to cover the loan payments for the year as well as the operating expenses. A waste facility generally derives its revenues by charging "tipping fees" based on the amount of trash that someone brings to it. If tipping fees are to be reasonable and still provide enough revenue to repay the loan, at least a certain minimum amount of trash must come to the facility. This minimum is based on the annual volume that the facility was built to handle and the facility's lifespan and loan repayment period.

If less trash arrives than was predicted in planning for what size facility to build, one alternative to produce the needed revenue is to charge a higher rate to those who are bringing the trash. This approach worries the users of the facility because it exposes them to higher charges for what they do bring. It also worries the lenders because, with higher charges, the trash might go elsewhere and endanger the repayment of the loan. Alternatively, the district could require that all its members bring all their trash to the facility, but an overall reduction of the amount of trash generated within the district could still lead to higher tipping fees than people are willing to pay and a possible default in loan repayment. This need for at least a minimum amount of trash to feed the facility, or an amount of revenue equivalent to what would have been collected if that amount of trash had been brought in, has led to lenders requiring, and some district members advocating, "put or pay" clauses in agreements among the member communities of a multitown district.[18]

"Put or Pay" clauses obligate a member community to "put" at least a certain amount of trash in the facility and be charged the tipping fee or to "pay" the full tipping fee as though it had put in the trash. This assures

18. Authorization for "put or pay" clauses typically appear in the organizational charter of a district. See, for example, Article I, § 5h and Article IV, § 2c of *Agreement for the Formation of the Greater Upper Valley Solid Waste Management District*, January 4, 1990, available from the Two Rivers-Ottauquechee Regional Commission, Woodstock, Vermont 05091.

that there will be revenue for paying the lenders without having to raise the tipping fee for those whose trash arrives at the facility. It also, however, removes a significant incentive for individuals and communities to undertake very important environmental efforts like reducing the amount of waste generated or recycling wastes. These efforts are sound for purposes of both conserving resources and lowering environmental risks from waste disposal, but communities are told that if there is waste reduction and a community does not "put," it will still have to "pay."

A possible solution to the "put or pay" dilemma begins by assuming that it is unlikely that there will be a widespread shortage of solid waste in the foreseeable future even if use reduction and recycling efforts are highly successful. The district facility to be built would be designed for an estimated volume of trash taking into account realistic or even optimistic projected success at waste reduction in the district. Each member community would be allowed to "put" in its quota or "pay" as though it were putting it in, or, alternatively, to put in less than its quota and get trash from outside the district to be brought to the facility to make up for the reduced revenue from that member community. The facility gets the revenue, the lenders are secure, the community that reduced waste and its citizens save money on tipping fees, and the environment benefits from waste reduction. This solution is hampered, however, by a widespread aversion to trash generated outside the local area. Perhaps this aversion is a phobia, or perhaps it is justified by a diminished ability to monitor the quality of non-local trash and the greater risks it might present. There is also a sense of not wanting to use the local land resource for disposal of non-local waste. For these reasons, communities may agree to prohibit out of district waste from being brought to the district's facility. The legality of such a prohibition is questionable in light of *City of Philadelphia v. New Jersey*,[19] in which the United States Supreme Court held that a state could not prohibit out of state trash from entering the state because trash is an item of commerce, and its ability to move across state lines is protected by the Commerce Clause of the U.S. Constitution. It may be argued, however, that *City of Philadelphia* does not preclude a waste district and its members from refusing to take waste from outside the district. *City of Philadelphia* involved a willing private recipient of waste in New Jersey and a willing sender of waste, Philadelphia. The State of New Jersey acted to unconstitutionally interfere with their voluntary transaction involving commerce. If, however, a waste district and its members agree that they will not be willing recipients of non-member trash, perhaps their agreement and prohibition is valid.

---

19. 437 U.S. 617, discussed earlier in this section.

Assuming a waste district can and does agree not to take out of district trash, it may have little choice but to require its members to "put or pay" and accept the negative impacts on waste stream reduction efforts. A better approach might be to allow a member community to substitute out of district trash for its own so long as the incoming trash is "subject to at least as stringent standards, conditions and controls as solid waste generated within the district."[20] Flexibility with respect to disposal issues like accepting non-local trash and site selection, coupled with massive efforts at waste stream reduction, are necessary immediately if we are to cope with the critical nature of the solid waste problem that exists today in all geographic areas of the United States.

2. Hazardous Wastes

A primary focus of the Resource Conservation and Recovery Act (RCRA) is how to manage those wastes which, because of their hazardous nature, raise problems that might not be raised by non-hazardous wastes and are so significant in character that they must be controlled by a stricter regulatory approach than that used for nonhazardous wastes. We will begin by looking at RCRA's system for preventing harm from hazardous wastes and then consider the Superfund legislation which addresses issues that arise in cases where RCRA did not prevent harm.

Hazardous waste, as defined in the statute, is waste which because of its quantity, concentration, or its physical, chemical, or infectious characteristics may significantly contribute to an increase in mortality or serious illness or may, when improperly managed, pose a substantial hazard to human health or the environment. Thus, while a pesticide could be a hazardous waste, and a chemical substance under the Toxic Substances Control Act could be a hazardous waste, the definition of hazardous waste under RCRA is much broader and can also include many other types of wastes. Among the factors which EPA and the states use to determine whether a material is hazardous are toxicity, corrosivity, flammability, and potential for bioaccumulation. Examples of what are hazardous wastes are industrial wastes containing heavy metals, infectious hospital wastes, waste oils like crankcase oil, and waste paint.

The two main operative mechanisms used by RCRA for controlling hazardous wastes are the "manifest system" and the requirement of permits

---

20. *Agreement for the Formation of the Greater Upper Valley Solid Waste Management District,* Article I, § 7b, (see fn. 18).

for the treatment, storage, or disposal of hazardous wastes.[21] RCRA focuses on the disposal stage in the life of a hazardous substance; however, its methodology for ensuring proper disposal is to provide a tracking of the substance through its entire life or what is commonly referred to as from "cradle to grave." This tracking approach is the manifest system. In addition, those who handle the hazardous waste at various stages after it has been created will have to have a permit and/or conform to federal standards in order to be allowed to handle the substance. By knowing who has the hazardous waste at every point in time and by controlling who can have the waste and making those who have it be responsible for what they do with it, Congress hopes that improper and hence environmentally unsound disposal will be avoided.

The tracking process begins with the generator of a hazardous waste. If you generate something which falls within the statutory definition of "hazardous waste," unless you are exempted, you are part of the manifest system for tracking the material's location at any time. You must initiate the manifest process by completing the "Generator Completes" section of the Hazardous Waste Manifest and Shipping Paper, a sample of which is shown in Figure 2. The manifest has multiple copies. The original stays with the waste from the point of generation until it reaches the hazardous waste facility where the waste will be disposed of, treated, or stored. Other copies are kept by those who come into contact with the waste during its journey to the hazardous waste facility, and copies are also sent to the state where generation took place and the state of destination. The idea is to keep track of who has the hazardous waste, with the intent that it ultimately end up in a proper hazardous waste facility for treatment, storage, or disposal.

One important exemption from the manifest system should be noted because, to some extent, it cuts back on the protection which the system was designed to provide. That exemption is for "small generators" of hazardous wastes. Under federal regulations, one is not required to comply with the manifest system if one generates less than 1000 kg per month of hazardous waste that is to be reclaimed at a recycling facility.[22] Also, if one generates less than 100 kg per month of hazardous waste and does not accumulate over 1000 kg or generates less than 1 kg per month of acutely hazardous waste and does not accumulate 1 kg, that generator is exempt from the manifest system.[23] While it is clear that many small, and thus exempt, generators of hazardous wastes can, in the aggregate, have very

---

21. 42 U.S.C.A. § 6921 et seq.

22. 40 CFR § 262.20.

23. 40 CFR § 261.5.

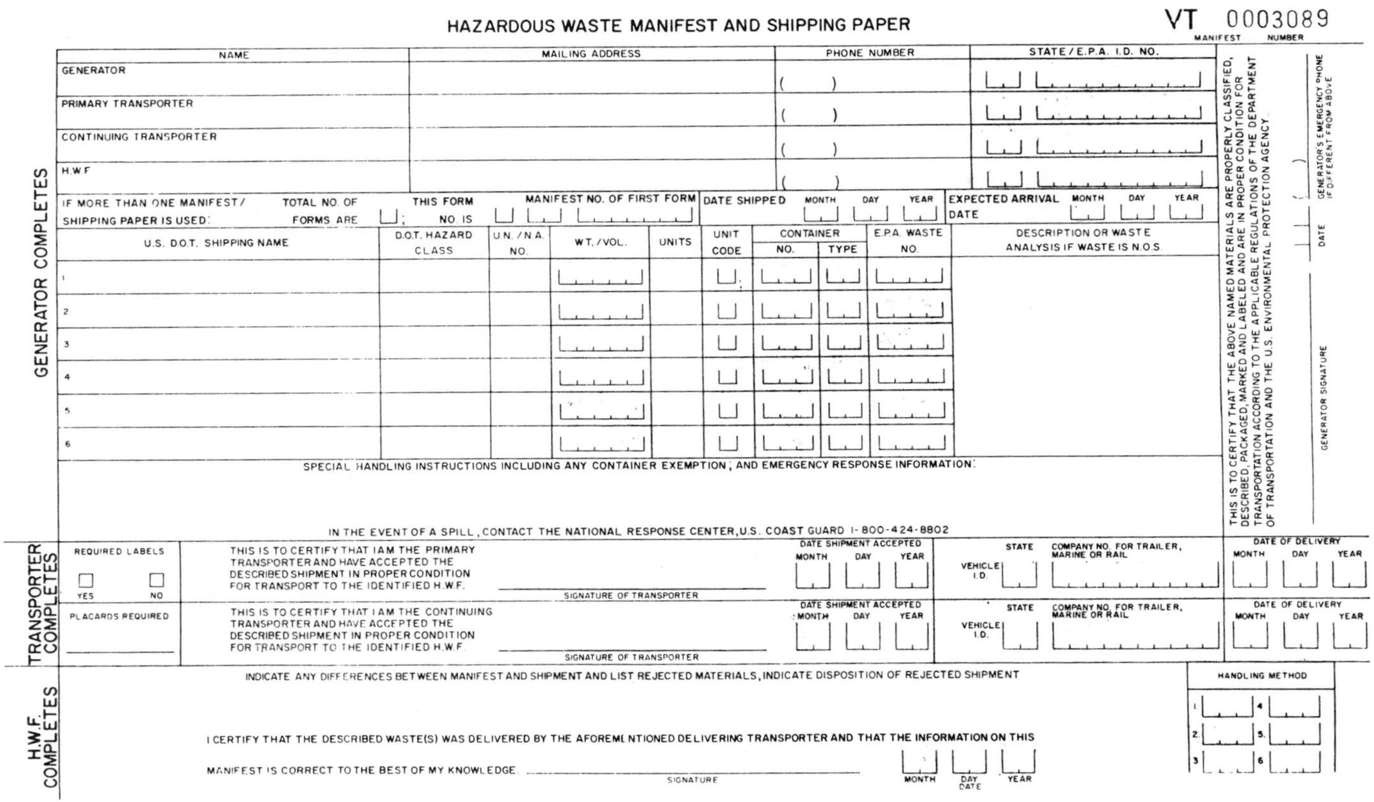

HAZARDOUS WASTE MANIFEST AND SHIPPING PAPER

VT 0003089
MANIFEST NUMBER

GENERATOR COMPLETES

	NAME	MAILING ADDRESS	PHONE NUMBER	STATE / E.P.A. I.D. NO.
GENERATOR			( )	
PRIMARY TRANSPORTER			( )	
CONTINUING TRANSPORTER			( )	
H.W.F.			( )	

IF MORE THAN ONE MANIFEST / SHIPPING PAPER IS USED: TOTAL NO. OF FORMS ARE ___; THIS FORM NO. IS ___ MANIFEST NO. OF FIRST FORM ___ DATE SHIPPED MONTH DAY YEAR EXPECTED ARRIVAL DATE MONTH DAY YEAR

	U.S. D.O.T. SHIPPING NAME	D.O.T. HAZARD CLASS	U.N. / N.A. NO.	WT. / VOL.	UNITS	UNIT CODE	CONTAINER NO.	CONTAINER TYPE	E.P.A. WASTE NO.	DESCRIPTION OR WASTE ANALYSIS IF WASTE IS N.O.S.
1										
2										
3										
4										
5										
6										

SPECIAL HANDLING INSTRUCTIONS INCLUDING ANY CONTAINER EXEMPTION; AND EMERGENCY RESPONSE INFORMATION:

IN THE EVENT OF A SPILL, CONTACT THE NATIONAL RESPONSE CENTER, U.S. COAST GUARD 1-800-424-8802

THIS IS TO CERTIFY THAT THE ABOVE NAMED MATERIALS ARE PROPERLY CLASSIFIED, DESCRIBED, PACKAGED, MARKED AND LABELED AND ARE IN PROPER CONDITION FOR TRANSPORTATION ACCORDING TO THE APPLICABLE REGULATIONS OF THE DEPARTMENT OF TRANSPORTATION AND THE U.S. ENVIRONMENTAL PROTECTION AGENCY.

GENERATOR SIGNATURE DATE GENERATOR'S EMERGENCY PHONE IF DIFFERENT FROM ABOVE ( )

TRANSPORTER COMPLETES

REQUIRED LABELS YES NO

THIS IS TO CERTIFY THAT I AM THE PRIMARY TRANSPORTER AND HAVE ACCEPTED THE DESCRIBED SHIPMENT IN PROPER CONDITION FOR TRANSPORT TO THE IDENTIFIED H.W.F.

SIGNATURE OF TRANSPORTER

DATE SHIPMENT ACCEPTED MONTH DAY YEAR VEHICLE I.D. STATE COMPANY NO. FOR TRAILER, MARINE OR RAIL DATE OF DELIVERY MONTH DAY YEAR

PLACARDS REQUIRED

THIS IS TO CERTIFY THAT I AM THE CONTINUING TRANSPORTER AND HAVE ACCEPTED THE DESCRIBED SHIPMENT IN PROPER CONDITION FOR TRANSPORT TO THE IDENTIFIED H.W.F.

SIGNATURE OF TRANSPORTER

DATE SHIPMENT ACCEPTED MONTH DAY YEAR VEHICLE I.D. STATE COMPANY NO. FOR TRAILER, MARINE OR RAIL DATE OF DELIVERY MONTH DAY YEAR

H.W.F. COMPLETES

INDICATE ANY DIFFERENCES BETWEEN MANIFEST AND SHIPMENT AND LIST REJECTED MATERIALS, INDICATE DISPOSITION OF REJECTED SHIPMENT

HANDLING METHOD 1. 2. 3. 4. 5. 6.

I CERTIFY THAT THE DESCRIBED WASTE(S) WAS DELIVERED BY THE AFOREMENTIONED DELIVERING TRANSPORTER AND THAT THE INFORMATION ON THIS MANIFEST IS CORRECT TO THE BEST OF MY KNOWLEDGE.

SIGNATURE MONTH DAY YEAR DATE

Figure 2. Sample hazardous waste manifest and shipping paper.

significant effects on the environment, the federal government has decided that to require small generators to be part of the manifest system would be placing an excessive administrative burden on them which would not be justified by the potential for harm which they may cause. This is the balance that the federal government has made; however, states, if they choose, can tighten up on the exemption for small generators and impose additional regulations on them. State control which is stricter than federal control is specifically allowed by RCRA with respect to hazardous wastes.

The complementary mechanism to the manifest which tracks the hazardous waste to its ultimate location is RCRA's requirement that the ultimate location be one which has a permit evidencing that it meets specific standards with respect to such matters as recordkeeping, satisfactory treatment, storage, or disposal methods, contingency plans for minimizing unanticipated damage, proper personnel, and financial responsibility. Unless the applicable standards are met, the facility will not receive a permit and, unless the facility has a permit, a generator of hazardous waste may not send the waste to the facility. Violations of the federal control mechanisms which we have discussed can subject the violator to sanctions including EPA compliance orders and criminal penalties of large fines and imprisonment.

As mentioned above, Congress' goal is to have hazardous waste find its way to a "proper" facility. A practical problem which bears on the fulfillment of that goal is the availability of "proper" facilities. Realistically, no one wants a hazardous waste facility in his or her backyard even if it is financially responsible and has contingency plans for unanticipated damage due to the activities of the facility. State and local governments or the federal government will have to work out an approach which will result in an adequate number of proper facilities being sited. Also, these sites must be located where their use by generators is not prohibitive in cost. Even with stiff penalties for violations, the effectiveness of RCRA's hazardous waste provisions may well be diluted if it is economically prohibitive for a generator to send its waste to a proper facility.

The specific hazardous waste control mechanisms of the Resource Conservation and Recovery Act are designed to prevent hazardous waste problems. RCRA's preventative efforts have not always worked, and, in addition, hazardous wastes that were disposed of prior to RCRA have resulted in numerous dangerous situations. The remedial provisions of the Superfund Act[24] held out great promise for cleaning up hazardous waste sites by providing for federal financing of cleanups[25] and ultimately imposing the

---

24. Comprehensive Environmental Response, Compensation, and Liability Act, 94 Stat. 2767.
25. 42 U.S.C. § 9611.

costs of cleanup on those responsible for the problem.[26] The Superfund process, first enacted in 1980 and later amended by the Superfund Amendments and Reauthorization Act (SARA),[27] has, however, been widely criticized as operating too slowly, being financially inefficient, and providing an inadequate finished product at the cleanup sites.

EPA has a "priority list" of approximately 1200 of the most hazardous sites. The list is certain to grow substantially, yet even of those now listed, only 58 have been completely cleaned up.[28] Also, the $8.5 billion federal fund will likely be exhausted by the cleanup of only 300–400 sites. This has been attributed to various combinations of knowing underappropriation by Congress, bad cost estimates, and inefficient management of expenditures by EPA. EPA has also been criticized for making substantively incorrect choices of how to technically do a cleanup. For example, a site in Uniontown, Ohio, that contains vinyl chloride, benzene, toluene, and numerous other toxic substances is to be capped by EPA with a clay dome to prevent the entry of water. Already contaminated water in the site will be pumped out and treated to remove the dangerous water from the ground water system. Local residents say that this is not the correct approach and that, unless EPA excavates and removes the toxic materials themselves, it is not adequately cleaning up the source of cancer and birth defects.[29]

Scientifically, there are many different possible solutions for hazardous waste cleanup problems, and it cannot be expected that there will often be full agreement on what is the appropriate response even if cost were not a factor. Cost is, however, a very significant factor, and Superfund seeks to make those who caused the contamination liable for its cleanup wherever possible. Sometimes the responsible party no longer exists, and government cannot pass the cost of cleanup on to it, but, assuming the business enterprise that caused the problem does exist, the question has been raised of whether that business should be liable for the cleanup costs. The argument is made that if the business had been negligent in not acting as a reasonable business would have done at the time it dumped its waste, then it should be liable. If, however, the business was acting legally and also in accordance with the generally accepted business practices of the time, then it should not now be held liable for the high cleanup costs. This retroactive liability puts a business at a serious competitive disadvantage that is unfair because, at the

---

26. 42 U.S.C § 9607.

27. 100 Stat. 1613.

28. "Cleanup of Waste Site Criticized by Residents," *New York Times* (January 15, 1990) p. A13.

29. Ibid.

time of the action for which it is now being held liable, it was not doing anything then known to be wrong.

One possible result of accepting this argument is that government, meaning all taxpayers, must pay the cost of cleanup. Another possibility, suggested by the insurance industry, is to establish a trust fund with money collected from assessing a small additional amount on commercial and industrial insurance premiums. It is claimed that an assessment of 2% of current premiums would provide $40 billion over a decade and would enable cleanup of all the high priority waste sites. This approach would spread the costs of cleanup broadly throughout the business community rather than having all the costs fall on a few businesses or on the taxpayers.[30] It would also allow less money to be spent negotiating and litigating about who should pay for the cleanup and instead spend the money on the cleanup itself.[31]

Regardless of whether the funds come from those who caused the hazard, from all the taxpayers, or from a broad spectrum of business enterprises, it is clear that a huge amount of new money will be necessary from some source if we are to make serious inroads into cleaning up our hazardous waste sites. Some of the entities that have been looked to as sources of funds for cleanups include insurance companies, lenders like banks, and state and local governments. Insurance companies collected premiums to provide general liability insurance for property owners. If a property owner is liable under the Superfund Act, isn't it the responsibility of the insurance company to pay for the cleanup, especially if the insured is not financially capable of doing so? The insurance companies argue, however, that it is unfair for them to pay for this liability based on policies that were written and rates that were paid without any knowledge of the extensive liability scheme of the Superfund Act.

Banks that become involved with borrowers or property subject to Superfund have also been seen as sources of cleanup funds. Banks that become the owners of hazardous sites when they foreclose on a mortgage or that exercise control over their borrowers may be liable for cleanup costs. In *U.S. v. Fleet Factors Corp.*,[32] the court said that a bank's "capacity to influence" the day to day management of hazardous waste may make it liable under Superfund. The banks, as have the insurance companies, also raise the issue of fairness. They contend that, as lenders, they have done

---

30. American International Group (AIG), "Why It's Vital to All Americans to Create a National Environmental Trust Fund . . . and To Do So Now," *The New Yorker* (November 20, 1989) pp. 20–21.

31. AIG, "Isn't it Time to Stop Wasting Millions and Start Cleaning Up America's Waste Sites?" *The Atlantic* (July, 1992) pp. 56–57.

32. 901 F.2d 1550 (1990).

nothing to warrant liability and are only being found liable because they have "deep pockets." EPA has attempted to provide some protection for lenders,[33] and, in turn, its rules have been challenged as unfair by the Chemical Manufacturers Association because special protection is being provided for lenders that is not provided for others.[34]

State governments are another source of funds for hazardous site cleanup which have claimed they should be immune from liability. Congress and the U.S. Supreme Court have, however, found that a state government that has been the cause of a hazardous waste incident is liable. In *Pennsylvania v. Union Gas Co.,*[35] Pennsylvania was doing flood control excavation when its workers struck a large coal tar deposit. The coal tar began to seep into a creek, and EPA, having determined that the coal tar was a hazardous substance, declared the site to be the nation's first emergency Superfund site. Pennsylvania and the federal government cleaned up the area, and the United States sued Union Gas, pursuant to the Superfund Act, for the costs of the cleanup because Union Gas had deposited the coal tar in the ground when Union Gas owned the property. Union Gas sued Pennsylvania claiming that the state was responsible for at least a part of the costs because, at the time of the coal tar release, the state was an "owner or operator" of the site and because its flood control work had negligently caused the release of the hazardous substance into the creek. Pennsylvania defended the suit by contending that it was immune from liability under earlier Court decisions involving the Eleventh Amendment to the U.S. Constitution in which the states were granted sovereign immunity from suits for money damages brought in federal courts. The Court ruled against Pennsylvania, holding that such immunity does not apply if Congress has specifically provided for liability in the exercise of Congress' power under the Commerce Clause to the U.S. Constitution. Congress had clearly and specifically provided for liability of the states in SARA when it said that a state "shall be subject to the provisions of this chapter in the same manner and to the same extent, both procedurally and substantially, as any nongovernmental entity, including liability. . . ."[36] State treasuries are thus apparently fair game under Superfund if the state is the cause of a hazardous waste problem. The concern of the states about potential liability is indicated by the fact that seventeen states joined Pennsylvania at oral argument to the Supreme Court and maintained

---

33. 57 Fed. Reg. 18343 et seq. (April 29, 1992).

34. Judy, M.L., "Superfund Issues Summary," *The Superfund Project at the Vermont Law School Environmental Law Center* (1992).

35. 109 S.Ct. 2273 (1989).

36. 42 U.S.C. § 9601(20)(D).

that their treasuries would be improperly burdened if they were not immune from liability.[37] Congress' position is that the sites should be cleaned up and that the cause of the hazard, be it a private sector entity or a state government, should be responsible for the cleanup costs.

C.   RECYCLING, REUSE, AND CONSERVATION

As we have seen, there are many control mechanisms that affect the disposal of waste materials. In addition, there are mechanisms that encourage the recycling, reuse, and conservation of those materials. Let's consider alternatives to the "dump it or burn it" philosophy.

The most popular alternative strategy for dealing with the solid waste dilemma is recycling. This method encompasses everything from glass bottles and beer cans to sludge application on forests and crops—the recycling method depending on the resource in question. The two basic approaches to solid waste recycling are the centralized approach using high technology (Figure 3) and the decentralized approach using low technology (Figure 4). Centralization involves collecting all the solid waste from an area such as a large city and bringing this material to a central location where separating and sorting takes place. There are several claimed advantages to this system. The weight and volume of materials needing a landfill will be drastically reduced while, at the same time, a municipality can use revenues gathered from resource separation (iron, aluminum, glass) to pay for the operation of the program. The biodegradable remainder could be burned to heat water and get steam to make electricity or heat for municipal offices or, using a more efficient energy recycling strategy, the biodegradable portion could be properly digested under low-oxygen conditions. Using this process, methane gas is produced and burned to heat water and provide heat or electricity. If properly executed, the above plan could reduce the tax burden on residents of the municipality participating in such a program; however, the initial cost of such a facility is high, and the amount of organic waste needed on a continuous basis for the energy recovery portion of such an undertaking is very high.

The other strategy for recycling municipal solid waste is source separation (Figure 4). The object of this alternative is to convince consumers that it is to their advantage to separate paper, glass, metals, plastics, and organic material before collection. Once this separation is complete, a municipality could either collect the resource or attempt to get the consumer to deliver

---

37. "Supreme Court Solidifies Trend Holding States Liable under CERCLA," *Natural Resources & Environment* (American Bar Association, Winter, 1990) p. 35.

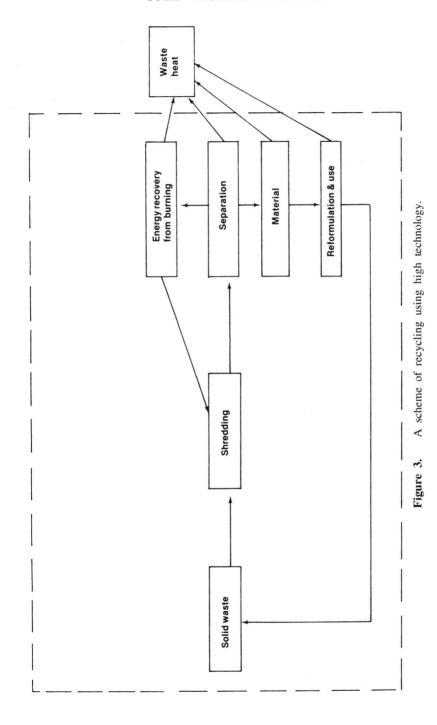

Figure 3. A scheme of recycling using high technology.

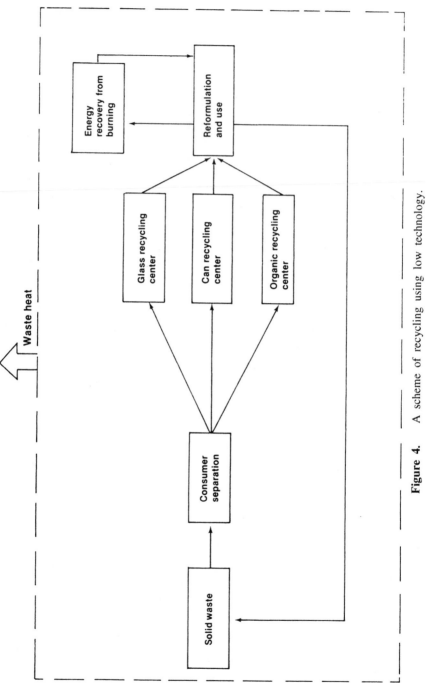

Figure 4.   A scheme of recycling using low technology.

the resource to a recycling center. The center then sells the resource and uses revenues to keep the center operating. This type of system usually is operated by volunteers or governmentally subsidized employees because most centers cannot support themselves. In order to sell a recovered resource to a potential reformulator, it is usually necessary to provide continuity of supply. Since this decentralized system relies on many people to keep the flow of resources constant, there are often problems. Volunteer efforts may be sporadic, and changing consumer patterns and seasons of the year can make continuity of supply difficult. Of greatest significance, this type of recycling requires interested consumers who are willing to take the time to sort out the stuff. On the positive side, this type of operation requires little initial investment. In the long run, no single alternative will likely provide the solution to the problem of recycling consumer solid waste. A combination of the approaches, using each where it is most appropriate, is serving as a basis to increase our recycling efforts. Of course, the most certain way to make recycling successful is to have new technology and new personal habits result in recycling being economically as well as environmentally sound. Those with waste need to find it financially rewarding to recycle rather than dispose, and those who are buying need to find recycled materials that are competitive in quality and price.

Up to now our recycling discussion has considered mainly domestic solid waste, not municipal solid waste such as sewage sludge or industrial solid waste such as fly ash. While a complete discussion of each of these would be informative, we will focus on the sludge issue. Sewage sludge is usually the product of a municipal sewage treatment plant. These sewage treatment plants may receive sewage from domestic sources, industrial sources, and storm runoff, and thus the potential for recycling is problematical because of possible metal content. Recent advances in removing metals from industrial sewage at the industrial site may, however, eliminate the problem-causing metal content of these sludges. In addition, if we assume that municipal sludge which is domestic in origin has a greatly reduced probability of having toxic content, then possibilities for sludge use are worth considering. Since this material contains many nutrients crucial to the maximal productivity of crop plants, sludge can be used for fertilizer on crops. Using sludge for fertilizer means we are returning to the soil an array of nutrients that we got from the soil, and we are truly recycling to get new proteins, fats, and carbo-hydrates.

Although recycling is more in vogue today, there are other non- disposal strategies for dealing with solid waste, and reuse is one of them. Reuse is the concept of "do not throw it away but use it again." If that glass bottle is empty, why not fill it again with the same stuff? This could lead to selling all possible consumer products in containers that can be used over and over again. While this notion seems to give us some advantage in reducing material consumption, there are several problems. One is convincing the consumer to buy the contained product, use the product, clean the container if circumstances so require, and bring the container back to the retailer for a refill. Sounds easy, the cooperative food stores do it and it works—sometimes. Also, what about products of limited life? How much bulk storage can a retail refill station accommodate and continue to make a profit without having to increase the cost of the product to the consumer? The reuse idea is a good one, but the mechanics still need to be refined. There are also related issues which cannot be ignored such as what to do about workers and businesses who used to make the containers we would no longer need if reuse were mandated.

Probably the least formally exercised approach to the solid waste dilemma is the alternative of conservation. Conservation can be viewed in many forms. Although we may consider conservation to mean only no use or limited use of a resource such as newspaper or packaging material, there are other ways of conserving. Buying products, such as cars, that have long life expectancies and operate efficiently conserves in two different ways. Conservation is a disadvantage to those businesses that depend on the principle of planned obsolescence, and, until very recently, the concept of unlimited resources allowed planned obsolescence to be a producer's managerial strategy. With increasing awareness of global resource limitations, conservation, coupled with resource recovery and reuse, appear to be forming a viable matrix for better utilization of resources.

Let's next consider some examples of how Congress has acted to encourage recycling, reuse, and conservation of materials. Subchapter V of the Resource Conservation and Recovery Act[38] assigns certain duties to the Secretary of Commerce which are designed to encourage resource recovery. The Secretary is given the responsibility of stimulating the development of markets for recovered materials by identifying existing or potential markets and identifying economic and technical barriers to the use of recovered materials as well as encouraging the development of new uses for recovered materials. It would appear that the taking of such steps should lead to a reduction in the amount of waste which will have to be dealt with by disposal and also should result in a reduction in the amount of virgin materials which would be used in the absence of those steps. Consistent with these goals, the Secretary is directed to promote resource recovery technology by evaluating its commercial feasibility, publishing the results of the evaluation, and assisting those interested in making a choice of a recovery system. The Secretary is further charged with initiating the process of developing spec-

---

38. 42 U.S.C.A. § 6951 et seq.

ifications for secondary materials. If reliable specifications are available for secondary materials, it is hoped that users will be more likely to avail themselves of such materials because they will be confident about how the materials will function.

A summarizing phrase for the above-described federal mechanisms relating to stimulating resource recovery might be "information dissemination." A more direct approach to resource recovery is contained in that part of RCRA which addresses itself to federal procurement policy.[39] Under RCRA, federal procuring agencies are required to purchase items composed of the highest percentage of recovered materials practicable consistent with maintaining a satisfactory level of competition. Unless such items are not reasonably available, fail to meet quality standards, or are unreasonably priced, their procurement is mandated if it is consistent with administrative guidelines prepared to achieve Congress' objectives. This "taking the lead" approach can spur the use of recovered materials in various ways including providing a substantial demand for a product and thus encouraging someone to become a supplier. In turn, that supplier may very well attempt to find other buyers for the product that it is now producing in order to satisfy its large customer, the federal government. Also, having large amounts of items made from recovered materials in general use throughout the country may serve to reduce psychological barriers to the use of secondary materials. Thus, with respect to resource recovery, Congress sought to achieve its goals using relatively noncoercive mechanisms—information dissemination and the use of the federal purchasing power.

How have these approaches worked? Not well at all. The federal procurement policy has had little practical impact, and the duties assigned to the Secretary of Commerce, such as to develop specifications for secondary materials, have simply not been done. While some industry organizations have published specifications for secondary materials, the Secretary of Commerce did not. Congress named the centerpiece of its solid waste and resource recovery effort the Resource Conservation and Recovery Act (RCRA), but that is clearly a misnomer. Although RCRA does occasionally address conservation such as by requiring an "energy and materials conservation" component in state plans,[40] RCRA is primarily and almost exclusively a disposal statute. Resource conservation and recovery has grown extensively in recent years, but this has been because local governments, faced with dwindling disposal sites, have mandated recycling. The real boom in resource conservation and recovery will likely be the result of the free enterprise

---

39. 42 U.S.C.A. § 6962.

40. 42 U.S.C. § 6943(c).

system as many resources become more limited in supply and recovery technology makes recovery economically profitable. In many situations, products such as gypsum wallboard and poultry bedding made from recycled materials are performing functions better and as cheaply or cheaper than the products they are replacing.[41] Ultimately, resource conservation and recovery will probably turn out to be plain good business.

ADDITIONAL READINGS

Cooke, S., Davis, C., and Gentry, B., *The Law of Hazardous Waste* (New York: Matthew Bender & Co., 1987 with 1992 Supp.).

Environment Reporter—State Solid Waste-Land Use (Washington, DC: Bureau of National Affairs).

Garbage—The Practical Journal for the Environment (Gloucester, MA: Dovetail Publishers).

Resource Recycling (Portland, OR: Resource Recycling Inc.).

Rodgers, W., *Environmental Law—Hazardous Waste and Substances* (St. Paul, MN: West Publishing, 1992).

Stensvaag, J., *Hazardous Waste Law and Practice* (New York: John Wiley & Sons, 1989 with 1992 Supp.).

---

41. "Recyclers Find New Users for Newsprint," *Environment Today* (Oct., 1992).

CHAPTER 6

PESTICIDES AND TOXIC SUBSTANCES

A. WHERE DO THEY COME FROM AND WHY DO WE NEED THEM?

While pesticides are considered to be toxic substances, there are other toxic substances which are not pesticides. The regulatory scheme is different for pesticides than for other toxic substances, so let's begin by considering them separately with respect to their origins and uses.

1. Pesticides

A pesticide can be defined as a chemical agent that can be used to cause the death of, or the regulation of, nonhuman organisms that people consider detrimental. Thus, the intended target species of pesticides are the insects, plants, fungi, rodents, mites, and any other organisms that negatively affect humans. These effects are usually in the form of reduced crop yields, disease infestation, general nuisance situations (flies, mosquitos), or real estate destruction (termites, powder post beetles, nematodes).

To illustrate the extent of pesticide development, let's take a look at the history of three forms of pesticides: herbicides, fungicides, and insecticides. Herbicides (chemicals to control plant growth, usually resulting in death) were first noted in modern times around the turn of the century with the use of arsenic compounds as soil sterilants. Arsenic compounds work by degrading cell membranes and thereby disrupting normal cell metabolism, resulting in death of the organism. About the end of World War II, the first organic herbicides (phenoxy herbicides), 2, 4-D and 2, 4, 5-T, and silvex were developed. These three herbicides act like plant auxins (growth stimulators) and virtually cause the plant to grow itself to death. The two latter compounds are commonly known to contain dioxin, sometimes known as agent orange. Later, in the 1950s and 1960s, urea base nonselective soil sterilants were developed. These act by inhibiting the photosynthetic process. Durion and linuron are examples. Still later came the desiccant herbicides diquat and paraquat which disrupt plant membranes and cause the plant to dry up. Continued efforts to produce more effective and more specific herbicides led to the carbamate and phenolic herbicides which also disrupt membranes.

Fungicides (chemicals that destroy fungi) were first used in modern times in France in the 1850s, with the use of lime-sulfur on ornamental plants. Later, Bordeau mixture, mainly copper sulfate, was used to protect the French grapes. In the early 1900s, mercurial fungicides were developed to protect seeds. Some of these are still used today. Organic fungicides (PCP) were developed in the World War II time period. These fungicides alter enzyme action in cells and thus kill the fungus. The fungicide business really came of age with the appearance of captan, a foliar (leaf) spray, in 1951 and systemic fungicides in 1966. The systemic fungicides are carried in the transport vessels throughout the plants, giving a more certain effect. These fungicides inhibit chemical reactions and eventually leave cells unable to breathe.

By far the most researched pesticides are the insecticides. In fact, it has only been recently that entomology has returned from the near total devotion to insecticide pursuits to more traditional areas of endeavor. The first insecticides (1860s) were arsenic compounds which are stomach poisons that eventually cause muscle paralysis and death to organisms that eat it. In the 1880s came the cyanide insecticides and a natural insecticide, rotenone (still used today). In 1939, the most widely recognized insecticide ever developed, organic DDT, was placed on the market. DDT is a long-term, highly effective, broad-spectrum insecticide that causes repetitive nerve discharges and eventually kills the insect. The cyclodiene insecticides (chlordane, dieldrin, aldrin) were developed about 1945 and are all neurotoxins operating on the junction between sensory and motor neurons, causing a malfunction which results in death. The organophosphorus insecticides, parathion and malathion, came along later. These cause muscles to keep tensing and never relax, eventually causing death. Recently the carbamate insecticides such as Sevin have been developed which operate much the same as the organophosphorus ones. More recently the juvenile hormone insecticides, which disrupt metamorphosis, and the chitin synthesis inhibitors, which make exoskeleton formation difficult, have been developed to combat insects. Some interesting notes are that most of our insecticides were developed around World War II, are organic in nature, and have spawned an industry of multinational proportions. Over $7 billion worth of pesticides are sold in the U.S. annually.[1]

The fact that we have pesticides has resulted in the widespread belief that we need pesticides, and, ironically, the availability of pesticides has led to

---

1. Environmental Protection Agency, *Pesticide Industry Sales and Usage: 1989 Market Estimates* (Washington, DC: 1991) p. 2.

the need to constantly create new pesticides. A look at how we raise our food crops should illustrate this situation.

Our crop raising efforts are primarily concentrated in a few families of plants, the grasses (corn, sorghum, barley, oats, rice, wheat), the nightshades (tomatoes, potatoes, peppers), and the legume family (beans, peas, peanuts). Also, we have found it to be more economical to plant large areas in a single crop (monoculture) so we can easily plant, cultivate, fertilize, protect, and harvest the crops; however, this allows pests that prey on a particular crop to thrive because we have provided a concentrated food source. We make these crops even more susceptible to pest attack by selecting genetic strains that maximize food output at the expense of producing defense mechanisms. Therefore, the crops we have created through genetic selection require protection from various pests and necessitate the use of pesticides so we get abundant food and the farmer makes a reasonable profit. Estimates of crop losses from discontinued use of pesticides vary widely—from 10% to 50% depending largely on effectiveness of alternative methods of control.[2] Since pests themselves have a varied genetic make-up within the pest species population, some individuals of the species population will be resistant to the pesticide, and we therefore help or "select" in favor of these individuals when we apply the pesticide. These resistant members of the species population breed, and eventually a pest species population will be present that resists the previously effective pesticide to such an extent that the pesticide is considered useless and a new one is needed.

Although pesticides create many evils and also create the above described dependency on pesticides, there certainly are sound arguments favoring their use. One example of our need for pesticides is the economic need. If one assumes that pests destroy 10% of a crop and this reduces profit by an amount X, and if the use of pesticides will cost less than 100% of X, then pesticides would probably be used to increase profits and yields (see Table I). As can be seen, it is generally more profitable in terms of food yield and money to use a pesticide, and thus most people are satisfied that there is a real need for pesticides.

2. Toxic Substances

In the broadest sense, a toxic substance can be defined as any chemical or mixture which could, under proper circumstances, do harm to health or the environment. Therefore, a toxic substance could be any chemical or

2. Day, C., "Integrated Pest Management: Towards a Greening of American Pesticide Policy," *Temple Environmental Law and Technology Journal* (Fall, 1989) p. 93.

Table I.   Hypothetical Relationship Between Use and No
Use of Pesticides on Profit from Raising Silage Corn

	Pesticide	No Pesticide
Yield/acre	25 tons	22 tons
Selling price/ton	$ 20	$ 20
Total price	$500	$440
Cost pesticide/acre	$ 5	0
Profit/acre	$495	$440

mixture that is manufactured, distributed, and eventually discarded. Congress has, through its findings at the outset of the Toxic Substances Control Act, implicitly defined a toxic substance as any chemical or mixture whose manufacture, processing, distribution, use or disposal may present unreasonable risk of injury to health or environment.[3] The Council on Environmental Quality then further defined the situation by identifying classes of toxic substances, some of which are shown in Table II.

Toxic substances include almost everything we use in modern manufacturing. After the proliferation of organic chemicals following World War II, we became a society dependent upon these for our way of life. We need motor oil, plastics, paint, pesticides, film, and car batteries. Because of the way we live, the occurrence of toxic substances in our environment is inevitable. This is not to say that our lifestyle is totally wrong, nor is this to say that such products ought not to be used. What the reader should have is an awareness of the scope of the toxic substances situation such that the following sections will seem more realistic. Toxic substances are with us. Our problem is to ensure that the least amount of damage to health and environment occurs during the process of making, using, and disposing of these chemicals and mixtures.

B.   WHY DO WE NEED TO REGULATE THEM?

Let's first consider some statistics about pesticides and toxic substances. The current annual pesticide usage level in the U.S. is approximately 1.1 billion pounds of *active* ingredients. This is almost 5 pounds of active poisons

---

3. 15 U.S.C.A. § 2601 et seq.

Table II.   Examples of Toxic Pollutants by Classes[4]

Pollutant	Characteristics	Sources
PESTICIDES Generally chlorinated hydrocarbons	Readily assimilated by aquatic animals, fat-soluble, concentrated through the food chain (biomagnified) persistent in soil sediments	Direct application to farm- and forest-lands, runoff from lawns and gardens, urban runoff, discharge in industrial wastewater
POLYCHLORINATED BIPHENYLS (PCB) Used in electric capacitors and transformers, paints, plastics, insecticides, other industrial products	Readily assimilated by aquatic animals, fat-soluble, subject to biomagnification, persistent, chemically similar to the chlorinated hydrocarbons	Municipal and industrial waste discharges disposed of in dumps and landfills
METALS Antinomy, arsenic, beryllium, cadmium, copper, lead, mercury, nickel, selenium silver, thallium and zinc	Not biodegradeable, persistent in sediments, toxic in solution, subject to bio-magnification	Industrial discharges, mining activity, urban runoff, erosion of metal-rich soil, certain agricultural uses (e.g., mercury as a fungicide)
OTHER INORGANICS Asbestos and cyanide	Asbestos: May cause cancer when inhaled, aquatic toxicity not well understood Cyanide: Variably persistent, inhibits oxygen metabolism	Asbestos: Manufacture and use as a retardant, roofing material, brake lining, etc.; runoff from mining Cyanide: Wide variety of industrial uses
HALOGENATED ALIPHATICS Used in fire extinguishers, refrigerants, propellants, pesticides, solvents for oils and greases and in dry cleaning	Largest single class of "priority toxics," can cause damage to central nervous system and liver, not very persistent	Produced by chlorination of water, vaporization during use

4. Council on Environmental Quality. *Environmental Quality, Ninth Annual Report* (Washington, DC: U.S. Government Printing Office, 1978).

for each member of our population.[5] Farm pesticide use is in the 500 million pounds per year range—about 2 pounds of active poison per person being used to grow crops.[6] The number of pesticide products registered with EPA is approximately 21,000, and there are 17,000 dealer-distributors of pesticides, 40,000 commercial pest control firms, and over 1.2 million certified applicators[7] who have access to our most dangerous pesticides, the ones we will later be referring to as "restricted use pesticides." With respect to non-pesticide toxic substances, the numbers are also staggering. Leaving aside releases on land and into surface water, approximately 2.2 billion pounds of toxics are released into the air annually.[8] The huge variety of pesticides and other toxic substances, the vast quantities of them in use, and the large number of people with access to them is alarming. Adding to these concerns are the uses to which we put these materials and the potential effects to which those uses can lead. We normally use pesticides to increase crop yield, to control weed growth on rights of way, and to kill disease-carrying or annoying pests. While all of this use creates an environment seemingly pleasant to live in, there are other biological effects of pesticide application besides market considerations. These effects force us to consider regulation.

Pesticide application in agriculture is viewed today as a necessity. Because we have genetically selected for strains of crop plants that maximize the yield of usable product, we have removed the plant's natural defenses against most pests. Therefore, we protect these crops by applying large quantities of pesticides to them, based on the assumption that if we did not, marketable yields would be drastically reduced, possibly causing pockets of starvation and definitely causing reduced profits. The reason we produce so many different pesticides is because target species become resistant to a pesticide after long-term exposure. What happens in this instance is that some individuals of the target species are not killed by a particular pesticide application. These individuals breed and produce many offspring that are resistant to that particular pesticide. Then, we either use more of the particular pesticide per unit area, hoping that quantity will kill, or we shift to another pesticide and use it until the same resistance is evidenced.[9] Agriculture and disease and annoyance prevention are the main reasons we use pesticides.

---

5. EPA, *Pesticide Industry Sales and Usage: 1989 Market Estimates* (Washington, DC: 1991) p. 2.

6. Council on Environmental Quality, *Environmental Quality 1991* (Washington, DC: 1991) p. 4.

7. EPA, *Market Estimates*, id.

8. EPA, *1990 Toxics Release Inventory Public Data Release* (Washington, DC: May 27, 1992).

9. Johnson, J.M. and Ware, G.W., "The Problem of Resistance to Pesticides," *Pesticide Litigation Manual*, 1992 ed. (Deerfield, IL: Clark Boardman Callaghan, 1991) p. 15–1.

The reasons we need to regulate pesticides are scattered among several concerns which we will consider now.

One case usually made for regulation of pesticides deals with the notion of United States industry wanting to make a profit by selling products without any care as to the effects of those products on non-target species, including humans. While industry might argue that all their pesticides are properly labelled, many unregistered and banned pesticides as well as regulated pesticides are currently sold outside this country. These unregistered pesticides have usually not been tested according to United States standards. Interestingly, it has been shown that many of the crops sprayed with these pesticides are crops raised by foreign agriculture for export to the United States. So, in some instances we are getting imported food that contains levels of registered or unregistered pesticide residue far above those allowed by United States law.[10] It appears in this case we need to regulate to protect us from us.

Other concerns of those stressing regulation deal mainly with biological effects on nontarget species and long-term effects of pesticide application. We know that when pesticides are applied, species other than the target species are killed. In many instances, the other species are predators on the target species (natural controls) or economically useful species such as honeybees.[11] Persistence of pesticides is also a concern. Ideally, a pesticide should eliminate a target species and dissipate into a harmless end product. However, many of the first pesticides, DDT in particular, did not degrade for a long period of time and consequently were consumed along with any crop to which they were applied.

Two very significant environmental concerns with respect to pesticides are the biological effects of pesticide degradation products and the phenomenon of biological magnification. Probably the most publicized pesticide degradation product is DDE, a decay product of DDT. DDE has been implicated in the decline of many carnivorous bird species such as the brown pelican and the peregrine falcon because DDE affects the shell gland in these birds to such a degree that the egg shells of chicks are so fragile the mother crushes them during incubation. Therefore, many people believe we should know of these decay products ahead of time and should regulate pesticides accordingly. A major concern only recently receiving widespread attention is biological magnification. What this means is that organisms higher on the food chain concentrate the most pesticide in their systems, sometimes to levels detrimental to their health. Let's illustrate this. Suppose that or-

---

10. Wolterding, M., "The Poisoning of Central America," *The Sierra Club Bull.* 66:63–67 (1981).

11. Johnson and Ware, id. p. 17–1.

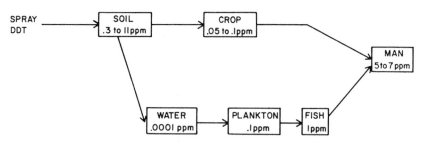

Figure 1.   Simple example of biological magnification of pesticide residue through a food chain.[12]

ganism A contains 1 part X. If a fish ate 100 of these organisms, the fish could theoretically contain 100 parts X. If you ate two of these fish you could contain 200 parts X. This is called biological magnification. If 150 parts X causes death to humans, you could eat only one and one-half fish until your body metabolized the pesticide. If your body never metabolized the pesticide, then you would have to stop eating fish. Consider the problem with DDT as outlined in Figure 1. If a person ate a lot of highly contaminated fish and very little mildly contaminated crops, there would be a rapid accumulation of a high level of DDT.

Suffice it to say that many similar arguments could be advanced concerning toxic substances other than pesticides. With other toxic substances, an additional concern is human health in terms of cancer-causing agents. While agent orange is a pesticide, benzene, naphthalene, and other possible carcinogens are not. The need to regulate all toxic substances is apparent when one considers not only the volume of potential industrial production, but also the preservation of human health. While one might consider industry to be at fault in the production of such chemicals and mixtures, industry is satisfying a demand of the human populace for food, less disease, and a better quality of life. Furthermore, industry's responsibility is not only to produce a useful product, but also to make money for stockholders who have invested in the production process. While industry may be said to be at fault, perhaps the fault is really that of the public as consumer and the public as investor.

On the bright side, there appears to be a trend of declining use of pesticides in American agriculture. The peak use of agricultural pesticides in the United States occurred in 1982 with 880 million pounds being applied, but since

---

12. Edwards, C.A., *Persistent Pesticides in the Environment* (Cleveland: CRC Press, 1974). Woodwell, G.M. et al., "DDT in the Biosphere: Where Does it Go?" *Science* (1971) pp. 174:1101–1107.

then the use of pesticides has been gradually decreasing as food consumers and farmers have become more concerned about the health problems caused by pesticides, especially the increased risk of cancer. In California, which provides the greatest percentage of our domestically produced fruits and vegetables, the number of organic farms recently doubled within one year.

In addition to organic farming, which has not yet resulted in prices low enough for the average consumer to afford, non-organic farms are using pesticides to a much lesser degree. Instead of making regular applications of pesticides, many farmers are now applying them only when and where there is a clear need. Also, the need for pesticides is being reduced by alternative control mechanisms such as the release from airplanes of beneficial insects that are bred and sold for controlling harmful insects. Consumer demand is the driving force behind the reduction in pesticide use, and consumers are being courted by sellers who are in fierce competition for customers. Supermarkets have begun providing information to customers about whether or not pesticide residues remain on the fruits and vegetables that they are selling. This information is being obtained from independent testing laboratories hired by the supermarkets themselves to assist them in knowing from whom to buy their produce and in informing customers about the pesticide content of what is being sold.[13]

Perhaps if advances in alternative pesticide controls continue, and if consumers require farmers to use less pesticides, the need for extensive government regulation of pesticides may also decrease. Pesticides do continue, however, to be in widespread use and to pose increasingly troublesome environmental problems such as leaching into ground water. Other toxic substances also continue to cause severe environmental problems; therefore, it appears likely that extensive regulation of pesticides and toxic substances will remain with us into the foreseeable future.

C. HOW WE REGULATE THEM

Having considered the benefits which society derives from pesticides and other toxic substances as well as the harms that such products might create, we next turn to how we try to keep the benefits while reducing or eliminating the harms. How far we should go in controlling our use of pesticides and toxic substances is a question to be left for the reader's own determination. The question that will be addressed here is how far the law has gone in establishing control mechanisms. We will first focus on control through the

---

13. "America Tackles the Pesticide Crisis," *New York Times Magazine, Part 2* (October 8, 1989) p. 22.

private law control mechanism of a lawsuit where someone (a plaintiff) will be asking a court for relief without the request for relief being based on any action of a legislative body. Relief will thus be based on the "common law" or judge-made law. We will then examine public law control mechanisms in the form of legislation directed at pesticide use and at the manufacturing of toxic substances.

1. Private Controls—Negligence Actions, Nuisance Actions, and Inverse Condemnation

Our primary example of a private control mechanism will be where a plaintiff seeks a remedy for harm caused to the plaintiff by someone's (the defendant's) improper use of a pesticide. The plaintiff's lawsuit will likely be a negligence action since injuries caused in pesticide cases are usually one-time occurrences such as aerial spraying of pesticides in high winds or failure to stop spraying when the defendant's airplane has flown over the plaintiff's land. A brief description of the theory of negligence is that: (1) society has established a duty of care, e.g., do not spray in a high wind, (2) the defendant has breached or acted inconsistently with that duty (sprayed in a high wind), (3) the defendant's breach of its duty brought harm to the plaintiff of a type which was foreseeable, and (4) the defendant had no justifiable excuse for its conduct. If the plaintiff is successful in establishing these elements of negligence by the defendant, the court will award plaintiff money damages to compensate for the harm that has been suffered. The defendants in negligence suits involving pesticides are usually applicators of pesticide or the person or company for whom the applicator is working, but other defendants might be manufacturers of pesticides. Manufacturers might be responsible for breaches of duties of care such as failing to warn the user of possible harms to the health of the user or of harms which would occur to species other than those which were intended to be adversely affected by the pesticide.

While the theory of negligence is available to an inured party with respect to improper pesticide use situations, there are hurdles to be crossed before that theory leads to an actual remedy. The hurdle of establishing "causation" (number 3 above) is especially difficult in some pesticide cases because the plaintiff must show that the defendant's actions are connected to the resultant injury to the plaintiff. There are substantial problems in proving such a connection when the injury is delayed in manifesting itself or if the injury could have resulted from other causes in addition to or instead of the defendant's actions. If the lifespan of dairy cattle that were subjected to negligent crop-spraying activity is reduced by three years, that effect will likely not make itself known until a time in the future when demonstrating the cause of the reduced lifespan is difficult. Similarly, if a beekeeper's bees die over the winter, it may be difficult to determine whether they died due to negligent pesticide spraying the previous spring or due to climatic conditions or due to a combination of both. Although not all cases present problems of proof such as those noted here, many of them do. Situations where the cause of harm is in doubt can result in a worthy plaintiff being left without a remedy, but can also result in a defendant being found responsible and liable for a harm which the plaintiff has suffered but which the defendant did not cause.

In addition to negligence suits, private lawsuits based on the theory of nuisance, discussed in Chapter 3, have been used to obtain relief from environmental harm, especially where the harm is of a continuing nature rather than a one-time occurrence. Many of these cases have concerned harm due to toxic substances. Historically, the usual subject matter of nuisance suits was someone interfering with your use and enjoyment of your land. Today, toxic substance personal injury in the form of discomfort, annoyance, irritation, and anguish, as well as injury to property, can be compensated in a nuisance action. In *Wilson v. Key Tronic Corp.*,[14] where the defendant private company had disposed of a cleaning byproduct containing an extremely hazardous waste in a landfill, and the waste had leached into the plaintiff landowners' well water, the landowners were compensated not only for the loss in the market value of their real estate, but also for mental anguish caused by the threat and actual ingestion of contaminated water. They also were given compensation for the inconvenience of having to haul water and for the disruption of ordinary activities of family life.

In *Wilson*, Spokane County, as well as the private defendant, was also found liable for the harm to the landowners. The county's liability was based on the theory of "inverse condemnation." The Washington Constitution provides that: "No private property shall be taken or damaged for public or private use without just compensation having been first made. . . ." Where a governmental entity with eminent domain power acts in a planned way that results in property being "taken or damaged," even though the entity did not intend that the property be "taken or damaged," the property has been "inversely condemned."[15] The county operated the landfill and had asked that the chemical waste be dumped in it rather than at another site. This planned action by the county amounted to an inverse condemnation,

---

14. 40 Wash. App. 802, 701 P.2d 518 (1985).

15. The eminent domain power and taking or condemnation are discussed in Chapter 4, Section C.2.

triggering the landowners' right to compensation for damages under the Washington Constitution.

Through use of private lawsuits, the common law seeks to provide help for those harmed by pesticides or other toxic substances and to deter people from acting in ways that cause harm. Deterrence will hopefully result from one's knowing that causing harm will mean you will have to pay damages. While the common law mechanisms have proven somewhat helpful, they have been criticized as inadequate deterrents due to the ability of parties to pass on to their customers the costs of paying damages or to insure themselves against liability. In addition, compensatory damages come after the harm has been inflicted. They are remedial rather than preventative. For these reasons, it has been felt that additional protective mechanisms are needed to prevent harm from happening rather than to merely compensate for harm after the fact, and to prevent harm in a more certain way than through the deterrence mechanism of the possibility of a judgment for damages. To answer this need, public controls in the form of statutes were enacted, but private lawsuits continue to be an important tool for relieving those who have suffered from toxic activities. State courts appear to be quite interested in having private lawsuits compensate those who have not been protected by statutory preventative mechanisms. For example, one's reasonable fear of contracting cancer due to exposure to asbestos has been recognized as an allowable factor in assessing damages from exposure.[16] The scope of protection offered by private lawsuits to victims of toxic materials is increasing.

2.   Public Controls—Pesticide Control Act, Food, Drug, and Cosmetic Act, Toxic Substances Control Act

a.   Pesticide Control

The major tool for public control of pesticides is the registration system established in the Federal Insecticide, Fungicide, and Rodenticide Act (FIFRA).[17] Under FIFRA, a pesticide may not be sold unless it is registered with EPA, and who may use a registered pesticide depends on the type of registration it receives.

FIFRA defines what is a pesticide very broadly. Substances intended to prevent, destroy, repel, or mitigate any "pest" (a term also very broadly defined) or to be used as a plant regulator, defoliant, or desiccant are all

---

16. *Sorenson v. Raymark Industries, Inc.*, 51 Wash. App. 954, 756 P.2d 740 (1988).

17. 7 U.S.C.A. §§ 136 to 136y.

pesticides. The prerequisites for approval of the registration of a pesticide by EPA (and thus to its qualifying to be lawfully sold) are that the pesticide composition is such that it will do what it is claimed that it will do, that its labeling complies with the law, that "it will perform its intended function without unreasonable adverse effects on the environment," and "when used in accordance with widespread and commonly recognized practice it will not generally cause unreasonable adverse effects on the environment." If these criteria are met without any need for limiting who can use the pesticide and without any need to place restrictions on its use, then the pesticide will qualify to be registered as a "general use" pesticide. If, however, unreasonable adverse effects on the environment may generally result unless restrictions on who may use the pesticide or other restrictions on its use are imposed, the pesticide may still be registered, but it will be as a "restricted use" pesticide. If the pesticide cannot satisfy the criteria even with restrictions placed on its use, its registration will be denied.

In those situations where a pesticide has been classified as a restricted use pesticide, unreasonable adverse environmental effects are sought to be avoided by restricting who may use the pesticide or placing other restrictions on its use. Pesticides which the EPA Administrator has classified as "restricted use" because they present a hazard to persons due to the pesticides' acute dermal or inhalation toxicity may only be applied by or under direct supervision of a "certified applicator." If the pesticide has been classified as "restricted use" because it may cause unreasonable adverse effects on the environment other than the toxity to humans mentioned above, then application is allowed by or under the supervision of a certified applicator or subject to whatever other restrictions on use EPA may impose by administrative regulation.[18]

From the above description of the registration system and the fact that the most dangerous pesticides are restricted to use by certified applicators, we can see that a key mechanism of public control and protection with respect to pesticides is the process by which applicators are certified. Applicators may be certified either by federal certification or by state certification under a state plan approved by EPA. In either situation, Congress has established that the standard for qualifying for certification is that the applicator be "competent." The factors which affect competency are determined administratively by EPA and include topics like safety, equipment use, and application techniques. For "commercial applicators," those who are in the business of applying pesticides for others, competency with respect to these

---

18. 7 U.S.C.A. § 136a(d).

topics is determined by written examinations and performance testing;[19] however, FIFRA exempts "private applicators" from being required by the federal government to take any examination to establish competency in the use of the restricted use pesticide. A "private applicator" is one who uses the restricted use pesticide on property owned or rented by the applicator or the applicator's employer or on property of another person if done without compensation other than trading of personal services between producers of agricultural commodities. Under an approved state plan, a "private applicator" can certify himself by merely completing a certification form. While EPA can require a private applicator to affirm that he has completed a training program, EPA may not require that a private applicator be examined to establish competency.

The above-described self-certification provision, which was added by amendment in 1975, recognizes that farmers working on their own land or that of their neighbors in an agricultural services exchange will likely be very careful in their use of pesticides and are also probably quite knowledgeable concerning pesticide use. Congress has thus been satisfied that such people need not pass examinations to determine their competency. It is true that farmers have strong motivations to use pesticides properly. In addition to the protection of their own health and land and the health and land of their neighbors (items which will likely be of importance to them even without the possibility of sanctions), they are also motivated to be careful by the possibility of lawsuits against them if they are not careful. It is also true that examinations would be bothersome to many farmers. Yet the same or similar motivations for care are present for commercial applicators and have been present for many years, and still Congress found that these motivations need supplementation in the form of a system which restricts the use of our most dangerous pesticides to those we are sure are competent to use them. Farmers (and agribusiness) are large users of pesticides, and, if Congress was concerned enough about the environmental hazards of pesticide use to create the "restricted use" classification, one may want to question the wisdom of allowing such large users of "restricted use" pesticides to use them without a real check on their competency. The words of the statute allow a large agribusiness corporation to have its employees apply restricted use pesticides on the corporation's land without those employees being examined as to their competence. While the corporation may be motivated to make sure its employees are competent in order to protect itself against lawsuits, if the threat of lawsuits had successfully controlled the problems associated with pesticide use, FIFRA would not have been needed. Some

19. 40 CRF § 171.4(a).

states have closed the "private applicators" loophole by providing, as a matter of state law, that users of restricted use pesticides, private applicators as well as commercial applicators, may be given a competency examination.[20] The following is a question which appeared on a state examination for commercial applicators:

> Q: If a 100-gallon sprayer sprays 5 acres per tankful and the spray recommendations call for 2 pounds actual per acre, how many pounds of 50WP pesticide must be added to the sprayer?
>
> A: 50WP means 50% active; to get 2 pounds actual, you need 4 pounds of product. The sprayer treats 5 acres per load and you want 2 pounds actual per acre, so you add 4 pounds of product for each acre treated or 20 pounds of product.

One further protection which is provided by the FIFRA scheme should be noted, and that is the set of mechanisms for ending registration and thus ending the sale of a pesticide. First, registration is automatically cancelled after a five-year period unless the registrant takes affirmative action to continue the registration. This automatic cancellation provision should then result in an automatic review of the pesticide's acceptability under the established criteria for registration. Second, cancellation or a change in classification from general use to restricted use may take place if the EPA Administrator determines that the registration criteria (labeling, performance, unreasonable adverse effects on the environment) are not currently being met. In order to protect the registrant against unjustified cancellation or classification changes, procedural requirements for notice and hearings are a part of the cancellation process, and thus the time for the "cancellation" process is measured in months or years. If, however, the Administrator determines that quicker action is needed to prevent an "imminent hazard" during the time required for cancellation proceedings, a third mechanism may be triggered—an order of "suspension" of the registration may be issued. The suspension order process still carries with it the procedural safeguards of notice and hearing for the registrant, but the timing of the procedures is much shorter—days and weeks, rather than months and years. An imminent hazard can be an imminent hazard to human health or a situation which will likely result in unreasonable adverse effects on the environment during the time required for cancellation proceedings or will involve an unreasonable hazard to the survival of a species declared endangered or threatened under the Endangered Species Act. Finally, if the Administrator determines that an "emergency" situation exists, the suspension or stopping

---

20. Vermont Regulations for Control of Pesticides, IX.

of sales and use of the pesticide may be made effective immediately and prior to any notice or hearing for the registrant.

In addition to FIFRA, Congress has sought to protect the public health from problems associated with pesticide use by enacting provisions of the Food, Drug, and Cosmetic Act to limit pesticide residues on food.[21] If an amount of residue in excess of a federally established "tolerance level" is present in or on the food, that food is considered "adulterated." Introducing adulterated food into interstate commerce is a criminal offense, and the food is also subject to seizure. "Tolerance levels" are the maximum amounts of residue consistent with protecting the public health, and they vary for each pesticide and for each food on which that pesticide is used. For example, the tolerance level for the insecticide malathion is eight parts per million on apricots and one part per million on sweet potatoes.[22] The tolerance level for the fungicide 2, 6-dichloro-4-nitroaniline is 20 parts per million on apricots and 10 parts per million sweet potatoes.[23]

The above-described system of legislative and administrative control of pesticides has been in place, largely unchanged, since the 1970s. The 1988 amendments to FIFRA made some significant changes in the federal legislation but did not address what many people think is the key issue of pesticide protection—contamination of ground water. The amendments do address the previously existing indemnification procedures for banned pesticides, and they also require that pesticide manufacturers assume part of the burden of paying for EPA assessment of the environmental effects of pesticide ingredients and the costs of storage and disposal of banned pesticides. In addition, a time limit of about nine years is placed on EPA to complete its review of the environmental effects of approximately 600 active pesticide ingredients. Although nine years is a lengthy period, that limit reduces the time for EPA to finish the review by about 75% from the projected time of completion had EPA continued at its prior pace of doing the work.

The changes in the indemnification requirements for banned pesticides are probably the most significant aspect of the 1988 amendments. Under pre-1988 federal pesticide legislation, EPA could only suspend or cancel the registration of a pesticide if it paid financial compensation to the manufacturer or other owner of the banned pesticide for their existing stock. EPA had spent about $20 million for indemnifications over the years, but the heavy

---

21. 21 U.S.C.A. §§ 346, 346(a), 348.

22. 40 CFR § 180.111.

23. 40 CFR § 180.200.

cost of indemnification that came along with a pesticide ban was felt to be a major disincentive for EPA to take a suspension or cancellation action. It was also thought that the taxpayers should not be the ones to bear the loss if a registered pesticide was subsequently found to be unsafe and had to be banned. The 1988 amendments preclude EPA from paying indemnification to a manufacturer for a banned pesticide unless a specific line item appropriation for payment is made by Congress.[24] If, however, the owner of the banned pesticide is an end user, such as a farmer, and that owner cannot be reimbursed by the manufacturer, then indemnification from EPA is available.

Since EPA will not be paying manufacturers for existing stocks of banned pesticides, that lack of indemnification raises the question of what will happen to the existing stocks of pesticides in the hands of the unindemnified manufacturers. Although notices of EPA's cancellation or suspension of a pesticide registration must be given to foreign governments, federal pesticide legislation specifically and affirmatively allows unregistered pesticides intended solely for export to be sold to foreign purchasers.[25] It would appear that existing stocks of banned pesticides, as well as newly manufactured supplies of unregistered pesticides manufactured in the United States but intended for export, can be sold in other countries. An additional incentive for export sale is that manufacturers, rather than EPA, now bear the cost of disposal of a banned pesticide.

The exporting of pesticides from the U.S. that have been deemed unsafe for use in the U.S. is troublesome. First, some of the unregistered pesticides likely do end up in the American food supply. The United States imports about 25% of its fruit and 6% of its vegetables. Although inspection for harmful pesticide residues takes place pursuant to the Food, Drug, and Cosmetic Act, a Government Accounting Office Report says that less than 1% of the imports are actually inspected.[26] Even assuming, however, that the unsafe pesticide never finds its way to the United States, the wisdom of allowing its export has been questioned. It has been argued that it is immoral for the United States to allow its manufacturers to sell pesticides for use in other countries when those pesticides are not safe enough for use by Americans. Unregistered pesticides are often sold to developing nations whose governments lack the expertise or the resources to properly regulate them or to appropriately train the people who will use them. Annual

---

24. 7 U.S.C. § 136m.

25. 7 U.S.C. § 136o.

26. "Third world grows addicted to pesticides," *Christian Science Monitor* (July 21, 1987) p. 3.

pesticide poisonings are said to be at least 1 million per year with upwards of 11,000 deaths each year worldwide.[27] In the face of these facts, are profits from the export of unsafe pesticides warranted?

On the other hand, the arguments in favor of allowing the export of unregistered pesticides cannot be viewed as wholly unreasonable. Other sovereign nations should have the right to choose for themselves whether the benefits from the use of a given pesticide outweigh the detriments. So long as a foreign government has been told that a pesticide it is importing is not allowed in the United States, it is claimed that it would be paternalistic for us to interfere further with that sovereign nation's decision. In addition, the needs of other countries, especially the developing countries, are far different than ours. They have a greater need for food for consumption and for the help that increased food production gives their economies. The harm associated with lower productivity from not using a pesticide may outweigh the harm attributable to increased health risks. While the U.S. may be able to afford to reduce agricultural productivity, other nations may not be so fortunate. Are long term risks of possible cancer relevant in societies with short term problems of malnutrition and starvation, when those problems can be mitigated by the use of a potentially carcinogenic pesticide? Yet another argument in favor of allowing the export of unregistered pesticides is that if another country wants this product, it will obtain it even if it is not sent from the United States. Production facilities can be set up in many other countries, and they will not even be subject to safeguards such as the strict hazardous waste disposal and employee protection provisions contained in American law. The use of the unregistered pesticide would continue, with additional risks being created that would not be present if the pesticide were manufactured in the United States.

The battle over whether to allow the export of unregistered pesticides has been fought in the Executive Branch of government as well as in the Congress. Pursuant to the President's asserted power over the conduct of foreign policy, President Carter issued an Executive Order that could, under certain circumstances, have resulted in prohibitions on the export of unregistered pesticides even though export is allowed by Congressional legislation.[28] President Reagan revoked that Executive Order with his own Executive Order about one month later.[29] The export of unregistered pesticides from the United States is legal today, but the disagreement continues. Legislation has been repeatedly introduced in Congress to prohibit the export

---

27. Ibid.

28. Executive Order 12264 of January 15, 1981, 46 Fed. Register 4659.

29. Executive Order 12290 of February 17, 1981, 46 Fed. Register 12943.

of unregistered pesticides.[30] In addition, it is now possible that the export of harmful chemicals may prove disadvantageous enough to American manufacturers to inhibit them from exporting. After a number of unsuccessful efforts, allegedly injured plaintiffs have convinced the Texas Supreme Court to allow lawsuits to be brought in Texas for personal injury that took place in foreign nations due to American manufactured pesticides that had been exported.[31]

The recent amendments to our pesticide legislation made progress in environmental protection by removing the indemnification deterrent from the pesticide banning process and by accelerating the pace of pesticide ingredient review. The legislation failed, however, with respect to addressing the issue of protecting ground water from contamination by pesticides. This has been a major pesticide issue in recent years and, once again, no consensus on what to do about it emerged from Congress. Various ground water contamination control mechanisms have been considered. One illustrative example was the proposed, but not enacted, Ground Water Safety Act.[32] The approach advocated by the Act was to determine, in the registration or registration process, whether a pesticide has the potential to leach into ground water. If it did, the registrant would be required to develop management practices which, if followed by the applicators, would prevent leaching to the maximum extent practicable. These practices might include recommendations to users about the time and frequency for use and the method of application. Also at the time of registration or reregistration or if a pesticide has been detected at certain water supply points, EPA would establish a health based ground water residue guidance level (GRGL) for that pesticide. If ground water monitoring, which would be required under the Act, indicated that pesticide residue had reached 25% of the GRGL, EPA would notify the public and the registrant and take steps to amend the registration to further restrict the use of the pesticide. The scope of such amendments could include limiting the purposes, locations, and rate of use. If 50% of the GRGL were reached, states would have to establish site specific plans to insure that the GRGL would not be exceeded. Failure of a state to take appropriate action would, under the proposed statute, result in EPA prohibiting the use of the pesticide in the vicinity of the underground drinking water source.

It is quite likely that federal legislation to control ground water contamination by pesticides will be enacted in the not too distant future; however, some states are not waiting. They are using "action limits" that are similar

---

30. S. 2227, 101st Congress, 1st Session.

31. *Dow Chemical Company v. Castro Alfaro*, 1990 WL 33528 (Tex.) [WL is Westlaw citation].

32. H.R. 3174, 100th Congress, 1st Session.

to the GRGL's in an effort to prevent contamination. For example, Wisconsin law requires that the Wisconsin Department of Natural Resources monitor and sample ground water. It must also establish "enforcement standards" and "preventative action limits" with respect to ground water contamination.[33] The enforcement standard for a substance is the maximum allowable concentration of that substance in ground water, and, if it is exceeded, the department *must* require that the owner or operator of the activity take corrective actions to bring the contamination level below the enforcement standard. In addition, if contamination of ground water reaches a preventative action limit, which is a percentage of the enforcement standard, then the department *may* require corrective action, but it must at least be given notice by the owner or operator of the activity that this preventative level of concern has been reached and that the department should consider greater vigilance in monitoring the ground water quality.[34]

The concern over ground water contamination from pesticides has been largely driven by agricultural pesticide use. There is, however, some concern that ground water contamination could result from nonagricultural pesticide use on golf courses or lawns. In addition, health issues have been raised related to simply coming into personal physical contact with pesticides that have been applied in landscaping situations. States have begun greater regulation of non-agricultural pesticide use by requiring landscaping companies to post conspicuous signs warning that they have recently applied pesticides on areas including not only golf courses and public athletic fields, but also on the lawns and landscape plants of single or multi-family residences.[35] Golf courses are also being required to get permits prior to applying pesticides, with those permits being conditioned on the applicant establishing buffer strips to protect surface waters and environmentally sensitive areas and doing periodic sampling and analysis of ground and surface water. Additionally, the proposed golf course must be built in accordance with the construction plans presented in its pesticide permit application.[36] The states, rather than the federal government, appear to be taking the lead today in expanding public control of pesticide use.

b.   Toxic Substances

Many substances which would certainly qualify as being "toxic" are regulated under laws other than the Toxic Substances Control Act

---

33. Wisconsin Statutes Annotated, §§ 160.07, 160.09, 160.15, and 160.27.

34. Wisconsin Administrative Code, §§ NR 140.24 and 140.26.

35. Vermont Regulations for Control of Pesticides, § IV.8, Vermont Department of Agriculture.

36. Id. § IV.9.

(TSCA).[37] We discussed above legislation which is directed at pesticides. Examples of other legislation controlling "toxics" are the Clean Air Act which regulates hazardous air pollutants, the Atomic Energy Act which regulates nuclear materials, and the Resource Conservation and Recovery Act which establishes controls on hazardous waste disposal. In enacting TSCA, Congress focused on newly developed chemical substances and took the position that chemical substances were being developed and introduced into the marketplace in such volume and with such a high degree of potential harm that they should be the subject of a particularized regulatory framework.

The basic operative mechanism of TSCA is that new chemical substances may not be manufactured unless a notice of intention to manufacture is filed with EPA at least 90 days before manufacture. The manufacturer must submit information such as the test data which it has on health and environmental effects, estimated volume of manufacture, and methods of manufacture and disposal of the substance. The thrust of the legislation is to provide EPA with the opportunity to review risks to health or the environment in advance of the manufacture of the chemical substance rather than leaving such review until sometime after the substance has been manufactured when harm may already have occurred. If EPA does not take action within the 90 days to prohibit or restrict manufacture of the substance, manufacturing may commence unless EPA, for good cause, extends the review period for up to 90 additional days. If EPA concludes that the new substance presents or will present an unreasonable risk of injury to health or the environment, it may prohibit or limit the manufacture of the chemical. Action to temporarily prohibit the manufacture of the chemical may be taken where EPA finds that it needs additional information in order to evaluate the potential effects of the new chemical.

EPA also has regulatory power with respect to existing chemical substances. If there is a finding of unreasonable risk to health or the environment, EPA may invoke remedies which range from labeling requirements and notifying purchasers of risks to prohibitions on manufacture and distribution of the product.

Although TSCA likely does provide an increased level of protection for the public, our TSCA discussion should not end without expressly noting some potential costs of that protection. Obviously, there are the administrative costs of establishing, implementing, and enforcing the regulatory scheme. Less obvious costs might be the disincentives on the chemical industry to provide new products. This could result in society not having the benefit

---

37. 15 U.S.C.A. § 2601 et seq.

of valuable and safe new chemical products. One rather direct potential disincentive may be that companies which have choices to make concerning whether to invest in new product development or to use their capital in other ways will be deterred from developing new chemicals because the cost and the time needed to get a new product on the market may be substantially increased. A less direct disincentive may lie in the fact that going through the TSCA process of information disclosure can result in a company's competitors acquiring the company's trade secret concerning its new product. Since the trade secret may represent a substantial share of the worth of the new product, the risk of losing trade secrets may dilute the profit potential of developing new chemicals and thus shift companies away from chemical product development. While TSCA does seek to protect the confidentiality of information submitted to EPA, not all information submitted will remain confidential, either because of exceptions to confidentiality allowed by the statute or merely through inadvertence by agency employees. There is thus a price for TSCA's protection, but Congress has determined that the health and environmental protection provided by TSCA are worth the decrease, if any, in new chemical development and availability to the American public.

In addition to federal statutes designed to protect against toxic substances, states are also heavily committed to the control of toxic substances through state legislation. Public concern about toxic substances in California was so high that, by a ballot initiative known as Proposition 65, California voters overwhelmingly adopted the Safe Drinking Water and Toxic Enforcement Act.[38] This initiative contains two major provisions: (1) The Discharge Prohibition and (2) The Warning Requirement.

The discharge provision generally prohibits any person in the course of business from knowingly discharging a chemical into water or land if it will probably pass into a source of drinking water and if the chemical is known to the state to be cancer causing or to have reproductive toxicity. There are exceptions from the discharge provision for entities employing fewer than 10 people and for insignificant discharges. However, for a discharge to be "insignificant" means that the drinking water contamination level would result in no significant risk of cancer assuming lifetime exposure at that level and no observable effect with respect to reproductive toxicity assuming lifetime exposure at 1000 times that level. The discharge provision also raises the question of which chemicals should be listed as "known to the State" to be the causes of cancer or reproductive toxicity. The list is promulgated by a Scientific Advisory Panel established by the Governor, and there was,

---

38. California Health and Safety Code, §§ 25249.5–25249.13.

at least initially, substantial disagreement about which chemicals should be on the list. Most of the chemicals sought to be included by environmental groups have now been added to the list. The comprehensive nature of that list, along with the very narrow scope of the insignificant discharge exemption, indicates that Californians are now quite committed to preventing toxic discharges.

The warning requirement of California's Proposition 65 generally prohibits any person in the course of business from knowingly exposing any individual to a cancer causing or reproductive toxicity chemical without giving the individual clear and reasonable warning. The warnings contemplated include labeling on consumer products, mailed notices to water customers, and news media notices.[39] California uses the mechanism of protection by notification in other ways as well. For example, certain owners, tenants, property managers, and contractors are required to warn employees of the presence of asbestos in buildings.[40] Also, the presence of asbestos was added to the list of conditions which must be disclosed to a buyer of residential property of four units or less by a seller who knows of its existence.[41] A buyer is now entitled to be aware of asbestos, formaldehyde, radon gas, and other environmental hazards that pertain to residential property. This will help assure that the buyer is getting a fair deal, and may also result in the cleanup of environmental hazards if buyers refuse to purchase contaminated property or if lending institutions refuse to provide financing for those properties. The issue should be raised, however, of whether the costs of a cleanup that may be needed to satisfy a bank that its loan is secured by sound collateral and that it will not someday become subject to liability for cleanup costs are justified by the environmental health risks that are present on a property. It may be that vast amounts of money will be spent to remove materials that pose only an extremely small risk to human health, but are perceived as a risk to the health of a loan when viewed from the perspective of the conservative banking industry.

ADDITIONAL READINGS

Carson, R.L., *Silent Spring* (Boston: Houghton Mifflin, 1962).
Lave, L.B. and Upton, A.C., *Toxic Chemicals, Health, and the Environment* (Baltimore: John Hopkins University Press, 1987).

---

39. For additional information on Proposition 65, see "Overview of Proposition 65" (American Bar Association Business and Corporations Section, December 7, 1988).

40. California Health and Safety Code, § 25915.

41. Disclosure Form, California Civil Code, § 1102.6.

Rodgers, W.H., *Environmental Law—Pesticides and Toxic Substances* (St. Paul, MN: West Publishing, 1988, 1992).

Searcy, M.T., *A Guide to Toxic Torts* (New York: Matthew Bender & Co., 1993).

Stever, D.W., *Law of Chemical Regulation and Hazardous Waste* (Deerfield, IL: Clark Boardman Callaghan, 1992).

CHAPTER 7

ENERGY

A. AN ENERGY PERSPECTIVE—KNOWN FORMS OF USABLE ENERGY

Energy may be considered the lifeblood of the ecosystem. Energy can neither be created nor destroyed, but it can change state such as by burning wood and releasing its energy for heat. These changes of state can be spontaneous or externally generated by the addition of a little "startup" energy. We use trapped energy to do work such as turning turbines for electricity, moving cars, moving trains, and heating homes. The gross energy consumption of the United States over time is shown in Figure 1, with the 1990 level of energy consumption being 81.4 QBtus or "quads." One quad is equal to 1,000,000,000,000,000 British thermal units. A British thermal unit (Btu) is the amount of energy required to raise the temperature of one pound of water by one degree Fahrenheit, and therefore, each American consumes enough energy in a year to raise the temperature of about 327 million pounds of water one degree Fahrenheit. Expressed in different terms, the 1990 level of energy consumption was equivalent to 13 tons of coal or 2400 gal of oil per year for each person in the United States. Two important energy questions that involve the environment are: from where does all this consumable energy come, and how long can it last?

Our energy needs are supplied by two very broad categories of energy resources—nonrenewable energy and renewable energy. Nonrenewable energy is viewed as a resource base that is depletable on a time scale measured in generations. Renewable energy is an energy supply that is always there and is not considered finite (exhaustible). Examples of nonrenewable energy resources are fossil fuels, nuclear fuels, and geothermal energy from pockets of heat, while renewable energy supplies are thought of as including solar energy, water power, ocean tides, wind, plant biomass, and geothermal energy from heat deep in the earth. Now, let us take a closer look at these energy sources in terms of their relationship to our needs.

U.S. energy consumption, by end-use sector.

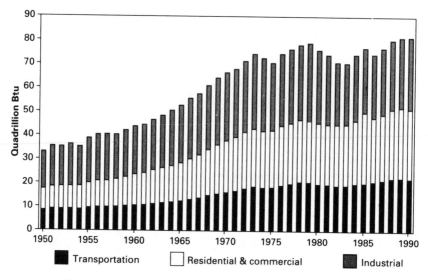

Figure 1.   U.S. gross energy consumption (1950–1990).[1]

As shown by our domestic production and imports of energy graphs in Figure 2, fossil fuels provide the largest portion, over 90%, of our energy needs, followed by nuclear power at 6% and hydropower at 3%. Fossil fuels include petroleum, natural gas, coal, oil shale, and tar sands, as well as derived fuels like gasoline and kerosene. The other nonrenewable energy sources currently contribute little toward meeting our energy demands. The main problem with nonrenewable energy resources is just what the category name implies, the sources are nonrenewable. Once used up, they are gone.

In contrast to the concept of nonrenewable energy sources is that of renewable ones. Those renewable sources most mentioned and successfully utilized today include hydropower, wind energy, and solar energy. The main concerns with our current nonrenewable energy sources are the cost per unit of energy (solar and wind), the dependability of the source (wind and hydro), and the amount of space devoted to the source conversion (solar, tides, and biomass). While the renewable energy sources offer the clear advantage of not running out, two additional problems with their use must be considered.

1. Council on Environmental Quality, *Environmental Quality 1991* (Washington, DC: 1992) p. 72.

U.S. energy production, by source, 1950-1990.

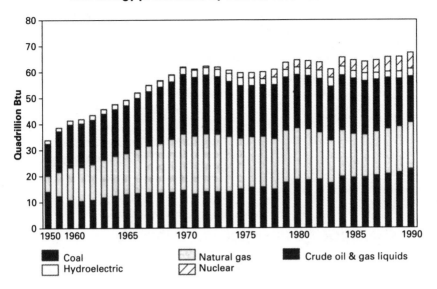

Net U.S. imports of energy, 1950-1990.

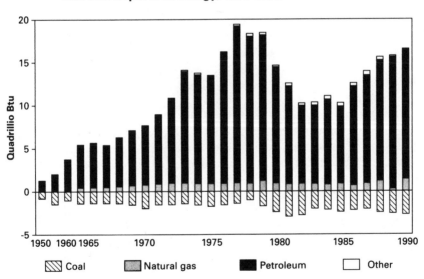

Figure 2. Domestic energy production and imports of energy (1950–1990).[2]

2. Ibid., p. 237.

First, as we begin to run out of some of our nonrenewable energy sources, the implementation of any strategy to replace one energy source by another or group of others often requires a long lead time and long-term planning. We may not be able to accomplish a minimally disruptive transition if we wait too long to make a serious beginning. Second, our long-term planning must allow for a balance that considers not only our energy needs, but also costs to the environment. For example, commitments to hydroelectric power have had in the past, and will have in the future, the potential for interfering with fishing as both a food resource and a recreation resource. Achieving a balanced approach in energy planning may be difficult and certainly requires ample lead time for thoughtful consideration.

B. THE NEED FOR ENERGY DEVELOPMENT AND CONTROL OF DEVELOPMENT AND USE

The American public has been acutely concerned about energy issues since the 1970s when supplies of oil became unreliable and prices of energy increased drastically and almost instantaneously. The concern of the 1970s focused largely on issues of the available supply of energy, while public sensitivity today appears to be oriented more toward the environmental pollution problems that are created by energy consumption. Both in the United States and worldwide, there is great concern that the burning of fossil fuels, with its carbon dioxide emissions, is causing global warming. Also, the use of high sulphur coal is giving us our now well-known acid rain problems. In much of the world, however, today's most important energy issue remains the supply of energy.

The primary source of energy for nearly half the world's population is wood. Since consumption rates in many areas now exceed sustainable yields, fuelwood in these areas is no longer a renewable resource. Fuelwood is usually obtained locally and on a noncommercial basis in developing countries. If this source of nonpurchased energy becomes unavailable, the poverty of these countries will make providing a substitute form of energy extremely difficult.[3]

In the United States today, the availability of supplies of energy is not generally perceived to be as critical an issue as it was in the 1970s. Although our total energy consumption continues to increase, significant progress has been made in terms of the per capita amount of energy we consume. Our efficiency also appears to have improved as shown by our energy con-

---

3. *World Resources 1988–89*, A Report by the World Resources Institute and The International Institute for Environment and Development (New York: Basic Books, 1988) p. 111.

sumption per unit of gross national product being reduced by 25% since 1973.[4] The lessening of our concern with availability due to the progress we have made in energy consumption can be seen in the abandoning of some energy conservation measures that used to be part of the law. For example, the national maximum speed limit of 55 mph,[5] originally established to conserve fuel, has now been raised to 65 mph. The question of what the appropriate speed limit should be is now considered to be more one of highway safety than of fuel conservation. Another example of our diminished concern for energy conservation is the tax credit provisions for residential energy conservation expenditures. This tax incentive to conserve energy became law in 1977 but terminated at the end of 1985.[6] The overall wisdom of the public's and the government's relative complacency about the availability of energy has been doubted by many people, and, concern for the availability of energy is once again in evidence in legislation. The Energy Policy Act of 1992[7] contains many provisions addressed to issues of energy availability. For example, mandatory efficiency standards for products such as lighting, electric motors, and heating equipment are provided for by the Act. Six years earlier, similar requirements in proposed legislation were vetoed by President Reagan.

Our success in making energy availability into at least a non-crisis issue has not been mirrored fully in our attempts to control the harms caused by the process of obtaining energy. The well-publicized environmental disaster in Alaska from the *Exxon Valdez* tanker oil spill clearly demonstrates our environmental vulnerability to accidents that will inevitably happen due to human error or due to events beyond human control, even where we have a substantial set of laws designed to avert environmental harm. American law has a Ports and Waterways Safety Program to provide supervision by the Coast Guard of vessel and port operators in order to protect cargo, life, property, and the marine environment.[8] Part of this program requires the Coast Guard to assure that the people operating vessels are competent and that vessels will be operated so as to insure safe navigation.[9] More specifically, federal law provided: "The Secretary of the Department in which the Coast Guard is operating is hereby directed to establish a vessel traffic

4. "The Planet Strikes Back!," *National Wildlife* (Natural Wildlife Federation, Feb.-March, 1989) p. 37.

5. 23 U.S.C.S. § 154.

6. Internal Revenue Code, § 23.

7. Public Law 102–486, 106 Stat. 2776.

8. 33 U.S.C. § 1221 et seq.

9. 33 U.S.C. § 1228.

control system for Prince William Sound and Valdez, Alaska. . . ."[10] Yet the *Exxon Valdez* oil spill happened, bringing with it not only "environmentalist" oriented harms such as very substantial wildlife damage, but also severe economic harm to the $130 million per year fishing industry.[11] Less dramatic failures to prevent harm from energy obtaining activities include the fact that while the environmental impact statement about the development of Alaska's Prudhoe Bay oil field predicted the destruction of 6,000 acres of wildlife habitat, 11,000 acres have been destroyed. There has, however, been some progress in the effort to reduce environmental damage from energy producing activities. One example concerns the strip mining of coal.

Pursuant to the federal Surface Mining Control and Reclamation Act,[12] areas where coal is to be surface mined can only be mined if a permit is obtained, and, in order for a permit to be issued, there must be a reclamation plan that will restore the mined land to usable condition. Under the original statute, however, the reclamation plan requirement did not apply to surface mining operations affecting two acres or less. This was seen as a relief provision for small operators who could not afford reclamation and whom Congress did not want to put out of business. Abuse of the relief provision occurred when large coal companies began hiring small contractors to mine their coal, and had each small contractor mine a plot with less than two acres of surface area. Another avoidance technique was for a mine operator to mine a number of sites along a coal seam, skipping a few feet between each two acre site. Due to these and other practices, the reclamation of surface mined land was not taking place.[13] After unsuccessful efforts by the Department of the Interior to administratively correct abuses of the two-acre exemption, Congress amended the Surface Mining Control and Reclamation Act to repeal the two-acre exemption and thus carry forward the land protection policy that was intended to be implemented through the reclamation plan requirement.[14]

Regardless of whether we are talking about obtaining oil and coal as discussed above or getting our energy from nuclear power, natural gas, or renewable energy sources, environmental problems are presented. An example of an oil source problem besides the hazards of transporting oil in ships involves

---

10. 87 Stat. 589.

11. "Drilling in Arctic Wildlife Refuge Becomes Casualty of Alaskan Oil Spill," *International Environment Reporter* (Washington, DC: Bureau of National Affairs, Inc., April 12, 1989) pp. 196–199.

12. 30 U.S.C.S. § 1201 et seq.

13. House Report No. 100–59 to accompany H.R. 1963, April 27, 1987.

14. Public Law 100–34, § 201.

the drilling process. Oil deposits are usually associated with salt water deposits where drilling is done on land, and adequate removal of this salt water must take place so that plants in the area are not destroyed and ground water is not contaminated. If we consider natural gas as an energy source, the environmental concerns center mainly on the extent of pipelines necessary to transport the natural gas in a liquified form and the probabilities and consequences of pipeline breakage. Perhaps the biggest problem, however, with both natural gas and oil is that they are nonrenewable and supplies are dwindling rapidly. On the other hand, we have an abundant supply of coal in the United States—enough for hundreds of years—yet numerous health and other environmental factors must be evaluated with respect to the use of coal.

Coal—be it anthracite, bituminous, subbituminous, or lignite—is either deep mined or strip mined. Deep mining creates more human health problems than strip mining (gases in mine shafts, collapse of shafts, black lung disease). Strip mining, on the other hand, destroys land surfaces that are either not reclaimed or reclaimed slowly. The process of reclaiming strip mine spoil requires water, a resource in very short supply in the western areas where much coal is available for strip mining. This western land area is also used for ranching to raise the meat we demand for our tables, and it takes a lot of land to raise one head of cattle. We thus have a conflict between the energy resource of coal and the food resource of cattle. Accommodating the need for both of these resources requires that we return the land from which coal was removed to its former use as quickly as possible so that our food supply will not suffer. While this task would be considered relatively easy in Pennsylvania or Ohio, the strip mining sites in places like Wyoming are not so easily reclaimed. Even if the topsoil is put back in place, and even if the whole topography is restored, it takes a long time to establish the integrated ecosystem that is destroyed by strip mining. In the west, the lack of large quantities of water makes the process of land reclamation after strip mining of coal a long-term project.

Other environmental concerns relating to coal are the sulfur content of coal and its association with acid rain as well as the metal content of coal (mercury) which could eventually contribute to human health problems. Coal mined in the eastern United States is mostly bituminous coal that has a high enough sulfur content so that its use is a major contributing factor to acid rain. This problem can be resolved using current technology, but the cost is significant, and there is disagreement about the extent of the benefits that will result from incurring these costs.[15] Western coal is subbituminous coal and contains virtually no sulfur. Therefore, this coal would not contribute

---

15. The Acid Rain section of Chapter 3 discusses how the Clean Air Act is now attempting to control acid deposition.

to the acid rain situation in terms of sulfuric acid. However, western coal contains larger quantities of heavy metals than does eastern coal. Some of these metals, mercury in particular, are considered harmful to humans and can accumulate in biological systems. For example, bacteria can use mercury and thus allow it to enter the food chain. For a price, technology can resolve this problem by removal of the metals. This then leads to the question of what to do with the waste substances that we have removed. Lastly, and by no means of least significance in deciding on which type of coal to use under which circumstances, is the fact that eastern coal has a cost per ton of about half that of western coal and a heat content per unit weight of about twice that of western coal. Our domestic coal supply clearly offers us great potential, but it just as clearly leaves us with major environmental questions that cannot be ignored.

Our other nonrenewable energy resources are subject to criticisms similar to those for oil, coal, and natural gas. Geothermal energy is localized, advanced technology is needed to utilize it, and it is not transportable unless it is converted to electricity. Nuclear fission power, while atmospherically considered safer than other more conventional forms of energy, has other problems. Construction cost and time for construction, reliability of the plant, possibilities of meltdown and consequent water contamination by radioactive substances, and the problem of radioactive waste all detract from the appeal of a nuclear energy society. Nuclear fusion and breeder reactors are not yet at the stage of development where they could contribute to the energy resource pool; however, if these types of energy sources are eventually utilized, the potential environmental harms are of such a magnitude that serious consideration about the use of these types of energy is mandated. Not only could there be large-scale contamination of water and air by radioactivity, but also the storage of the radioactive wastes, which will include the buildings themselves, must be undertaken. In essence, there is a necessity to eventually store the whole facility, as even the nuts and bolts will be contaminated.

With all of the problems involving supply and use of nonrenewable sources of energy, it is unfortunate that one cannot immediately say that renewable energy resources are the answer. These too have technological as well as environmental problems. Renewable energy resources such as solar and wind are used to make electricity which must be stored. Large capital costs plus slowly developing technology of utilization of these resources makes these energy pathways currently very costly compared to the nonrenewable sources. Besides costs, these alternatives have their own environmental constraints. Solar energy requires space as well as long daylight periods free of cloud cover. These problems appear to be easy enough to resolve—build in the southwestern desert and transport the electricity around the country. Leaving aside the substantial questions of technological and economic feasibility of such a scheme, there are still potential environmental problems. If sunlight is intercepted on a very large scale by collectors, what will warm the earth beneath these collectors? Will the very large-scale placement of such facilities change weather patterns, induce warmer or cooler global climate, or generate some other environmental problem the nature of which is currently unknown? Wind energy generators require space and substantial amounts of wind. Again, geographic location and transport of electricity as well as lack of cost-effective technology currently present problems. Even if these are resolved, the idea of a windmill everywhere raises aesthetic questions. Biomass for energy also requires space as well as energy inputs to plant and harvest the biomass and time to grow the biomass. Once the biomass is generated it must be transported to a facility and prepared for energy production. This energy pathway also removes land from some other use and will eventually conflict with other land use practices. Hydroelectric power, while inexpensive once it is in place, is dependent on weather and must also deal with environmental problems such as dams which are impediments to fish migration.

From the above discussion it is clear that there are ample opportunities for us to obtain our needed energy, but it is also clear that none of our choices is free of environmental problems. A balance must be struck which will provide our needed supply of energy while leaving us with the quality of life that we find desirable. Inherent in such a balance is the giving up or compromising on some environmental concerns in order to obtain our needed energy. Also inherent in the balance is the fact that energy should not be provided at the minimum possible cost regardless of the effects on the environment. If the adverse effects on the environment are to be kept within reason, we must accept some controls on how we obtain our energy supply. We must also seek to conserve energy to the maximum degree consistent with our desired standard of living so that we do not need to supply ourselves with more energy than we really need and thus do more harm to our environment than is necessary. In the next section we will investigate some of the mechanisms that government uses to stimulate our supply of energy and some of the controls that have been imposed on obtaining that supply in order to protect the environment. The last section of this chapter will consider approaches to encouraging conservation of our energy supply.

C.   STIMULATING ENERGY SUPPLY

The question of what to do about our appetite for energy is often cast in terms of two opposing camps—those who argue for the production of more energy and those who argue for conservation of energy. While the arguments for conservation vs. the arguments for more production may, if simply stated, indicate a total polarization of points of view, that is not an accurate picture. Very few people who believe in greater production as the way to resolve our energy problems also believe that conservation is unnecessary. They are in favor of conservation, but their frame of reference is one of accepting that our country's well-being requires continued economic and thus industrial growth. Such growth is largely dependent on more energy being available, and, although some of that energy may be made available by conservation, the magnitude of the need is such that production increases will have to supply the bulk of it. The production orientation also favors satisfying some of our needs by developing alternative energy sources, but it also contends that our supply from our basic current sources of energy (oil, coal, gas) can and should be increased.

The frame of reference of those who lean heavily toward the conservation philosophy often incorporates a challenge to the need for or desirability of continued growth. Ever-increasing growth creates many of the other environmental problems discussed elsewhere in this book as well as depleting our current sources of energy. Most proponents of energy conservation would not, however, take the position that all economic and industrial growth should stop immediately or that alternative sources of energy should not be developed and utilized. For most Americans the proper course is somewhat between the extremes, and the question is one of emphasis—emphasis on production coupled with attempts at and hopes of conservation, or emphasis on conservation, with implementation of production increases from our current sources of energy only as a last resort for our economic well-being. Numerous efforts have been made by government to encourage both production and conservation, but we cannot answer the question of what to do about our energy appetite by merely saying that we should maximize both production and conservation at the highest levels we can technologically achieve. We must also consider the factors that compete with the policies of encouraging production and conservation.

If government is to encourage production, it must be willing to accept the accompanying financial costs, such as the decrease in tax revenues that might result from tax incentives created to encourage energy production. Encouraging production can also bring with it costs such as interference with land used for food production. Other environmental costs of encouraging energy production include water pollution from offshore drilling and aesthetic pollution from strip mining or windmills. A policy of encouraging conservation also has costs associated with it. Tax credits for those who install energy-saving equipment or materials decrease tax revenues. Furthermore, conservation of energy can create environmental costs. Small fuel-efficient automobiles (or motorcycles) may be more hazardous than larger, less fuel-efficient models, and highway safety must certainly be considered an environmental cost. The question thus comes back to one of emphasis, and government has attempted to pursue the parallel paths of encouraging both production and conservation.

One approach to encouraging production has been to focus on the price of energy. The amount of an energy resource that will be produced is greatly influenced by the price that it will sell for in the marketplace. An early use of this approach was in the Energy Policy and Conservation Act of 1975,[16] where Congress sought to encourage increased production of petroleum by allowing "new" oil to be sold at a price that was not kept artificially low by government price controls. "Old" crude oil remained subject to price controls. "Old" oil was defined as that amount which was produced from a property at a level equal to or less than the amount of oil produced from the property during an earlier time period. There was thus incentive for producers to raise their volume of production from a property since this increased volume (the "new" oil) could be sold at a price substantially higher than the government controlled price for "old" oil. Another price-related production enhancement step was taken in the Federal Energy Administration Act Amendments of 1976,[17] which exempted oil produced by "stripper wells" from price controls. "Stripper wells" are those whose production does not exceed 10 barrels per day and are often seen as the backyard oil wells in areas like Los Angeles. The above price decontrol steps were taken specifically to spur production of crude oil. All crude oil and refined petroleum products are now decontrolled with respect to price pursuant to Executive Order No. 12287[18] and in response to the belief of many people that oil prices should be allowed to seek their market levels in order to achieve the best mix of conservation along with optimizing levels of supply.

A price incentive mechanism has also been used by Congress to encourage renewable alternative energy sources, electric power production by "small power producers," and the increased efficiency of "cogeneration." The statute that seeks to achieve these goals is the Public Utility Regulatory Policies Act (PURPA),[19] under which the federal government regulates electric power suppliers. Governmental regulation of electric power suppliers and natural gas suppliers was in effect for many years prior to the time when government began to articulate concerns for environmental issues such as the volume of use of a natural resource. For example, in 1952, when the Federal Power Commission, the predecessor of today's Federal Energy Regulatory Commission, was asked to approve a rate structure for pricing

---

16. 89 Stat. 871 at 941.

17. 90 Stat. 1125 at 1132.

18. 46 Fed. Reg. 9909, Jan. 28, 1981.

19. 92 Stat. 3117.

natural gas, its determination of which of two alternative proposed rate structures to approve was based on its wanting to "achieve a reasonably equitable result" with respect to the prices that different types of natural gas customers would pay for the gas they used.[20] The decision was predicated on economic fairness to customers and not on the environmental issues of how much gas would be used and how efficient that use would be. While the decision was not necessarily intended to affect environmental issues, it incidentally would be likely to do so because the cost of gas to customers will influence the amount of gas they use. Today, instead of having incidental effects on the environment, public utility laws like PURPA are intentionally designed to address environmental questions such as from what sources we should obtain our energy.

PURPA was enacted by Congress to encourage small power production facilities and cogeneration facilities. A "cogeneration facility" has higher efficiency than traditional electric power producers since, as defined by the statute, it produces both electric energy and steam or some other form of useful energy such as heat. A "small power production" facility has a production capacity not exceeding 80 megawatts and produces electricity from biomass, waste, geothermal resources, or renewable resources such as wind, water, or solar energy.[21] "Congress believed that increased use of these sources of energy would reduce the demand for traditional fossil fuels."[22] The mechanism that Congress used to encourage these facilities was to direct FERC, the Federal Energy Regulatory Commission, to prescribe rules requiring that traditional electric utilities buy electricity from the co-generators and small producers. The purchase price could not be greater than what it would have cost the traditional utility to generate the purchased power itself or to purchase the power elsewhere. This is often called the "full avoided cost."[23] FERC acted by (1) requiring the utilities to make the interconnections that would be necessary to accomplish the sale and (2) requiring that the utilities actually buy from the small generators and co-generators at the "full avoided cost," the maximum price that the statute allowed.[24] The utilities challenged these regulations imposed by FERC, contending that the price the utilities should pay for the power they had

---

20. *Atlantic Seaboard Corp.*, 11 F.P.C. 43, 94 P.U.R.N.S. 235 (Federal Power Commission, 1952).

21. 16 U.S.C. § 796(18)(A) and (17)(A).

22. *FERC v. Mississippi*, 456 U.S. 742, 750 (1982).

23. PURPA § 210(a) and (b), 92 Stat. 3144, 16 U.S.C. § 824a-3(a) and (b).

24. 18 CFR § 292.303 and 292.304(b)(2).

to purchase under PURPA should be set at less than full avoided cost, with the cost savings to the utilities being passed on to the utilities' customers in the form of direct rate savings. They argued for this lower price by noting that PURPA required that the purchase price to be paid by the utilities should be "just and reasonable to the electric consumers of the electric utility and in the public interest," and that the interest of the consumers would be served by lower rates to them if the utilities could buy at lower rates from the cogenerators and small generators.

The United States Supreme Court, in *American Paper Institute, Inc. v. American Electric Power Service Corporation*,[25] upheld the "full avoided cost" purchase price regulation because it was a reasonable exercise of FERC's authority to provide an incentive for cogeneration and small power production facilities. Even though use of full avoided cost might mean that the utilities and their customers would pay more than the production costs plus a fair profit to the cogenerators and small power producers, any savings from paying less than full avoided cost would be insignificant for any individual consumer because there are large numbers of them among whom the overall savings would have to be allocated. On the other hand, letting the cogenerators and small power producers keep this extra amount might be a significant incentive to them because there are relatively few of them among whom the savings would be allocated. Also, in the long run, consumers of power would benefit from the decreased reliance on fossil fuel energy and the greater efficiency of energy production. Thus Congress, FERC, and the Supreme Court combined to use a price incentive to stimulate the production of electricity from alternative energy sources.

In the Energy Policy Act of 1992, Congress again used a price incentive to encourage energy production from renewable sources; however, instead of allowing the producer to charge more for the product, Congress provided a subsidy. Utilities will receive a 1.5 cent per kilowatt-hour subsidy for electricity generated through the use of solar, wind, biomass, or geothermal energy.[26]

In addition to encouraging alternative energy technology for electric power production, legislatures are also encouraging the use of alternative automobile fuels. These fuels are intended to reduce air pollution from automobiles, and here the state legislatures have taken the initiative. Pennsylvania is funding the conversion of some vehicles to use compressed natural gas and is also funding the development of technology to utilize methanol instead

---

25. 103 S. Ct. 1921 (1983).

26. P.L. 102–486 § 1212, 106 Stat. 2969.

of gasoline.[27] California is using its purchasing power to provide an incentive for development of alternative fuel automobiles. California law defines "low-emission motor vehicle" as including those that operate on methanol and other alternative fuels and create an improved air pollution result with respect to ozone. If low-emission motor vehicles meet standards such as availability, satisfying the performance needs for state-owned vehicles, and having sufficient servicing outlets for the vehicles, then the state is required to buy those low-emission vehicles in a quantity of at least 25% of the number of vehicles purchased by the state during the preceding year. That purchasing requirement applies so long as the low-emission vehicle does not exceed by more than 100% the average cost of comparable state vehicles purchased during the preceding year.[28] The state is therefore willing to spend a significantly greater amount of money for its vehicles if those vehicles will improve air quality. It is hoped that by the state providing a market for alternative fuel, low-emission vehicles, industry will be encouraged to develop and manufacture them. Following California's lead, Congress in the Energy Policy Act is requiring increased reliance on nonpetroleum-based fuels. By 1999, 75% of federally purchased cars and light trucks must be capable of operating on fuels such as natural gas, ethanol, methanol, propane, electricity, or hydrogen.[29]

Other incentives exist for alternative fuel use in automobiles including a tax credit of 55% of the costs of converting a car or truck to use alcohol fuels containing at least 85% methanol or ethanol.[30] There is, however, evidence that calls into question whether the use of alternative fuels such as methanol is environmentally and economically sound. Methanol-fueled vehicles, as currently constituted, emit three to five times more formaldehyde than gasoline vehicles, and formaldehyde, in addition to its carcinogenic nature, is an agent that produces ozone which is the pollutant that methanol use is intended to reduce.[31] Also, because of methanol's lower energy content, it only gets about half the miles per gallon of gasoline. This means the possibility of larger fuel tanks and less usable vehicle space.[32] Another problem concerns the source of methanol. It can be distilled from coal or

---

27. "Pennsylvania Announces Alternative Fuels Program," *Environment Reporter* (Washington, DC: Bureau of National Affairs, Inc., August 4, 1989) p. 645.

28. California Health and Safety Code, § 43800 et seq., as amended by Senate Bill 1123, 1989.

29. 106 Stat. 2871.

30. California Revenue and Taxation Code, § 17052.11(a).

31. Mobil Corporation, "Methanol: Panacea with Problems," *Time* (September 18, 1989) p. 18.

32. Ross, Philip E., "Cleaner Fuels For the '90s," *Popular Science* (January, 1990) p. 47.

natural gas, but using coal appears to create more carbon dioxide in the process of making the methanol than is saved in car emissions. The use of natural gas to make methanol precludes the release of large quantities of carbon dioxide and also has the advantage of widespread sources of supply, making price controls by one or a small group of countries impossible.[33]

Mixed reviews similar to those voiced about methanol are also given for other alternative fuel vehicles such as electric automobiles. The main operational problems are range before the batteries need recharging (less than 100 miles) and time for recharging (15 minutes to 6 hours); however, the day to day cost of operation may be much cheaper than a gasoline powered car. From the environmental perspective, there are no exhaust fumes; however, when the air pollution and other environmental detriments associated with the power plants that generate the electricity for battery recharging are considered, the net environmental benefit may be small or nonexistent.[34] Although there is both support for and doubts about alternative automobile fuels, the enactment of the federal and state legislation discussed above shows a clear government commitment to replacing the gasoline engine as the norm for automobiles.

As our last example of government efforts to stimulate energy supply, let's consider what is and is not being done to obtain energy from the vast amount of federally owned land and other areas over which the federal government has authority, such as the Outer Continental Shelf (OCS). Energy is obtained from those locations primarily by the government leasing the sites to private enterprise. The conditions of the leases are used to ensure that the federal energy resource actually provides a supply to the consumer. For example, leases of federal land for the mining of coal contain provisions requiring diligent development and continued operation of the mine.[35] The Code of Federal Regulations defines "diligent development" as developing the coal source such that coal is actually produced in commercial quantities (1% of the reserves of the source) by the end of the tenth year of the lease. "Continued operation" requires that an average of 1% of the reserves be produced in succeeding years.[36] Thus, those who might seek to enter into a long-term lease of the federally owned coal source for the purpose of speculating on increasing prices rather than to bring the coal to market are discouraged from doing so.

---

33. Firestone, M.J., "Alternative Fuels," unpublished paper (December, 1989).

34. Firestone, A.A., "Should Electric Cars Replace Gasoline Cars?" unpublished paper (November, 1992).

35. 30 U.S.C.S. § 207(b).

36. 43 CFR § 3400.0–5.

With respect to the Outer Continental Shelf, the leasing mechanisms have also been adjusted by Congress for the purpose of encouraging greater production of energy. In amendments to the Outer Continental Shelf Lands Act, Congress declared that it is national policy that the OCS should be made available, subject to environmental safeguards, for expeditious and orderly development.[37] The legislative history of the statute, as contained in the report of the House of Representatives, said that our dependence on foreign oil must be reduced, and that the basic purpose of the legislation was to "promote the swift, orderly and efficient exploitation of our almost untapped domestic oil and gas resources in the Outer Continental Shelf."[38] One mechanism that the statute uses to expedite the development of the OCS is to provide new bidding procedures for leases. Prior to the amendments, all leasing used a "front-end bonus system" that required a potential lessee to secure a large amount of capital to be available for payment to the government immediately upon acceptance of the winning bid for the lease. Alternative bidding and leasing procedures which do not require the making of a large front-end payment are allowed under the amendments.[39] The intent is to make leasing more attractive to producers and thus encourage greater production. Whether in part because of the above legislation or for other reasons, the Secretary of the Interior reported that new leasing records were set for the OCS in the years following the amendments, with over two million offshore acres leased to energy companies and over $9.8 billion obtained as federal revenue.[40] Huge volumes of oil and gas remain at offshore sites and on land, and industry remains eager to find this energy and bring it to market; however, increased public awareness of the environmental consequences of offshore drilling and land drilling in sensitive areas has led to a reduced willingness of government to lease wherever oil or gas drillers want to go. While the original versions of the Energy Policy Act of 1992 provided for oil and gas leasing of land in the Arctic National Wildlife Refuge in Alaska, Congress removed those provisions of the bill prior to passage.

Having considered examples of how Congress has encouraged production of more energy, let us next look at how it and state governments have attempted to handle some of the competing factors involved with encouraging energy production—the environmental problems that energy production cre-

---

37. 92 Stat. 629 at 635.

38. The material referred to here is from Vol. 3, 95th Congress, Second Session, p. 1460 of *United States Code Congressional and Administrative News*. A substantial amount of the history behind a piece of legislation may be found in the *United States Code Congressional and Administrative News*.

39. 43 U.S.C.S. § 1337(a) and (b).

40. *Energy Users Report* (Jan. 21, 1982) p. 66.

ates and the controls that have been enacted to deal with those problems. Congress' awareness of and concern about environmental problems associated with energy production can be seen by looking at qualifying language that exists in many of the statutes that seek to stimulate energy production. While the purpose of the Outer Continental Shelf Lands Act Amendments is to exploit the oil and gas reserves of the OCS, the statute calls for "expeditious and orderly development, subject to environmental safeguards." Also, although the Biomass Energy and Alcohol Fuels Act[41] encourages the use of biomass for energy production, the Congressional findings in the statute ask for a biomass energy program "that does not impair the Nation's ability to produce food and fiber on a sustainable basis for domestic and export use."

In addition to the somewhat nonspecific language seen in our last two examples, specific provisions for environmental protection may be found both in statutes whose primary goal is to encourage production and in those that are addressed primarily to environmental issues. An example of the former is Congress' loan guarantee program for the purpose of developing new underground coal mines. That "production enhancement" statute appears to recognize that burning low-sulfur coal creates less air pollution than burning high-sulfur coal. The statute thus leans in the direction of low-sulfur coal by prohibiting more than 20% of the loan guarantee funds issued in any fiscal year from being used to open new mines which produce coal which is not low-sulfur coal.[42]

Looking at our "production enhancement/environmental control" balance from the direction of statutes whose specifics are addressed primarily to environmental controls, we come to the Surface Mining Control and Reclamation Act[43] which, while recognizing that coal supply is essential to the nation's energy requirements, looks at the mining of coal primarily from the viewpoint of environmental protection. The federal surface mining statute concerns itself with past harm to the environment from coal mining as well as prevention of future harm. An abandoned mine reclamation fund is established to be used largely for the reclamation and restoration of land and water resources adversely affected by past coal mining.[44] The money for this fund comes from reclamation fees imposed on current production of coal. A fee of 35 cents/ton of surface mined coal and 15 cents/ton of underground mined coal or 10% of the value of the coal at the mine,

41. 42 U.S.C.S. § 8801 et seq.

42. 42 U.S.C.S. § 6211(b)(3).

43. 30 U.S.C.S. § 1201 et seq.

44. 30 U.S.C.S. § 1231 et seq.

whichever is less, is deposited in the fund. The geographic allocation of money in the fund takes into account the geographic area (state or Indian reservation) from which the revenue was derived.

The basic statutory mechanism for addressing present and future threats to the environment from surface coal mining is the permit system.[45] Surface coal mining is prohibited unless a permit is obtained. In a manner similar to its approach in the Clean Air Act, Congress has given primary responsibility for administering its surface mining program to the states if the states want to accept that responsibility. Thus permits to surface mine coal may be issued by the state if the state has a program that is approved by the Secretary of the Interior. In the absence of an approved state program, a federal program with federally issued permits is implemented. For a state program to be approved, the state must show that it is capable, through use of a permit system and by other means, of carrying out the environmental protection purposes and provisions of the federal statute. Among these are having and enforcing a reclamation plan that will restore the affected land to a condition capable of supporting its prior use or a better use and restoring the land to its approximate original contours.

Various provisions of the Surface Mining Control and Reclamation Act have been challenged on many grounds in the courts, but the validity of the statute has been upheld. In *Hodel v. Virginia Surface Mining & Reclamation Association*,[46] it was contended that the performance standards of the statute which required that on "steep slopes" an operator must return the site to its "approximate original contour" were unconstitutional as a violation of the Tenth Amendment to the United States Constitution. The Tenth Amendment says: "The powers not delegated to the United States by the Constitution, nor prohibited by it to the States, are reserved to the States respectively or to the people." It was claimed that the regulation of land use was a traditional function of the states under the states' "police powers" and that the Tenth Amendment limited the power that Congress would otherwise have had under the Commerce Clause of the Constitution to regulate private land use activities that affect interstate commerce.[47] The United States Supreme Court decided, citing many cases involving other statutes, that the scope of the Tenth Amendment did not limit Congress' interstate commerce authority with respect to the activities of private individuals and businesses. The steep slope provisions of the statute apply only

---

45. 30 U.S.C.S. § 1251 et seq.

46. 425 U.S. 264 (1981).

47. Article II, Section 8 gives Congress the power to "regulate Commerce . . . among the several states. . . ."

to private activity and do not regulate "States as States." An attempt to regulate the latter would violate the Tenth Amendment. The Court thus reaffirmed that the exercise by Congress of its authority under the Commerce Clause in a manner that displaces the states' exercise of their police powers over private activity does not invade areas reserved to the states by the Tenth Amendment.

Another court challenge to the surface mining statue concerned the "prime farmland" provisions of the act. With respect to obtaining a permit to mine most surface mining sites, the statute requires that there be a reclamation plan to put the land back into a reasonable use, but not necessarily its prior use, after mining occurs. Congress' concern that we do not lose our prime agricultural land led it to impose stricter reclamation requirements for that type of land. An applicant for a permit for mining on prime farmland must show that it has the capacity to restore the land, within a reasonable time after the completion of mining, to the productivity level of nonmined prime farmland in the surrounding area. The posting of a bond to ensure that the plan will be completed is also required. In *Hodel v. Indiana*,[48] it was claimed that the prime farmland provisions were a taking of private property by government without the payment of just compensation as required by the Fifth Amendment to the United States Constitution. The District Court had concluded that there was an unconstitutional taking of private property because "it is technologically impossible to reclaim prime farmland in a postmining period so that equal or higher levels of yield under high levels of management practice can be achieved."[49] The Supreme Court found that the prime farmland provisions are not a taking of private property since they do not prohibit surface mining but merely regulate the conditions under which the activity may be conducted. And even if the District Court is factually correct in its determination, there would still not be a taking that requires the payment of just compensation unless the landowner could show that there were no economically beneficial uses for his property besides mining.[50]

The Surface Mining Control and Reclamation Act is federal legislation, but it allows states to regulate surface mining so long as the state programs provide for implementation of the federal requirements. If a state chooses to have more stringent land use or environmental controls on surface mining, the statute specifically allows it to do so.[51] Let us consider a situation where

48. 425 U.S. 314 (1981).

49. 501 F. Supp. at 470.

50. A more detailed discussion of the "taking" clause of the Fifth Amendment is given in Chapter Four.

51. 30 U.S.C.A. § 1255.

states appear to want to be more environmentally cautious and where they have sometimes been allowed to and sometimes been precluded from imposing their own controls by the existence of federal controls.

The method of energy production that has spurred the most impassioned opposition is nuclear energy. Perhaps that is because the harm from a nuclear energy mishap is so direct in its impact on humans or because the type of harm is so distasteful or because of the large numbers of people who could be affected. In addition, it might be because of a belief that adequate environmental protection with respect to nuclear power is less of a certainty than protection against oil spills or protection against the harms that might result from coal mining. While other issues are relevant to the dispute concerning the desirability of nuclear power, protection from radiation hazards appears to be the major item of public concern.

The bulk of the responsibility for regulating nuclear power in general and providing protection against radiation hazards in particular is vested by the Atomic Energy Act[52] in the federal Nuclear Regulatory Commission (NRC), the successor to the Atomic Energy Commission. This authority includes the licensing of nuclear power facilities. In response to some of the above-mentioned concerns, various states have indicated dissatisfaction with the sufficiency of the protection provided by federal control of nuclear power and have enacted various types of state legislation to provide additional control over or protection from nuclear power. The leading case on this topic is *Northern States Power Company v. State of Minnesota.*[53]

In *Northern States*, the federal Atomic Energy Commission (AEC) had issued an operating license to the power company. Minnesota sought to impose more stringent conditions than the AEC on the allowable level of radioactive discharge. Minnesota argued that, while the Atomic Energy Act did not expressly allow more stringent state controls with respect to the radioactive waste releases, it neither expressly nor implicitly disallowed more stringent state control; i.e., it did not preempt the state's authority to more strictly regulate such waste releases. The United States Court of Appeals for the Eighth Circuit found that, although there was no express declaration in the Atomic Energy Act that federal control of radiation emissions is to be sole and exclusive, Congress had manifested an intent to displace all state regulation in that field, and preemption of state authority was thus implied. The implication of the preemption was based on the legislative history and pervasiveness of the federal regulatory scheme. This determination was further supported by the nature of the subject matter involved and by a finding

---

52. 42 U.S.C.S. § 2011 et seq.

53. 447 F.2d 1143 (1971).

that there is a need for uniform nationwide controls in order to effectuate the objectives of Congress under the Atomic Energy Act. Among those objectives are encouraging development and use of atomic energy to foster industrial progress, benefit the general welfare, and increase the standard of living. State controls that would affect the purchase and sale of power in commerce might interfere with attaining these objectives. States efforts to regulate nuclear power plants with respect to radiation hazards were therefore held to be invalid. The Eighth Circuit's decision was affirmed without an opinion by the United States Supreme Court.[54]

The reader may want to question the justification, if any, for the federal government expressly allowing states to regulate the mining of coal in ways that are more stringent than the federal controls and yet refusing to allow the states to enact stricter provisions to protect their citizens from nuclear power-related radiation hazards. Congress has not in any way explicitly rejected the implied intentions that were attributed to it in the *Northern States* case; however, the issue of what control states may exercise over nuclear power facilities was further contested in the courts in *Pacific Gas and Electric Co. v. State Energy Resources, Etc.*[55] *Northern States* had said that there can be no state regulation with respect to radiation hazards. In *Pacific Gas*, the question was whether a California statute is invalid due to its having been preempted by the federal Atomic Energy Act because the statute conditions nuclear power plant construction on findings by a state commission that adequate storage facilities and means of disposal are available for high-level nuclear waste. The Ninth Circuit Court of Appeals in *Pacific Gas* decided that this California statute was not preempted since it was based on the economic aspects of nuclear waste disposal rather than on radiation safety concerns. The United States Supreme Court, by a 9 to 0 vote, upheld California's right, as a state, to prevent nuclear power plant construction for economic reasons even if the federal government would license a plant as being safe.[56] If a state wants to regulate such areas as nuclear fuel disposal or other areas involving radiation hazards, could it not frame its statutory purposes and legislative history to show economic or other legitimate concerns rather than radiation hazard concerns and thus circumvent the federal preemption that Congress was found to have intended in the *Northern States* case?

In addition to the legal problem of some states trying to stop construction of new nuclear power plants, nuclear power encountered several economic

---

54. 405 U.S. 1035 (1972).

55. 659 F.2d 903 (1981).

56. 461 U.S. 190 (1983).

problems of cost competitiveness in the 1980s. While in the early 1980s, nuclear power plants provided almost one third of all the new electrical generating capacity being built in the United States, construction of new nuclear capacity was virtually non-existent in the late 1980s and projected to continue that way in the 1990s.[57] There are those who argue that America's current importing of almost 50% of its oil is asking for another energy crisis that could once again hold our economy hostage. They further contend that the appropriate way to achieve energy independence is by building new nuclear power plants;[58] however, public sentiment appears not to support additional nuclear plants. Yet, with increasing concerns about global warming from the use of fossil fuels and with reactor builders claiming that they have safer designs, nuclear power could make a comeback in the future. Indeed, the Energy Policy Act of 1992 seeks to give a boost to nuclear power by streamlining the licensing procedure to allow for the issuing of a combined construction and operating license for a nuclear power plant.[59] Thus, the Energy Policy Act takes quite a broad approach to the types of energy supplies it seeks to stimulate. Nuclear energy, as well as solar, wind, hydro, biomass, and methanol, is part of the package to reduce use of fossil fuels.

D.   ENCOURAGING CONSERVATION OF ENERGY

There are numerous legal mechanisms at both the federal and state levels of government that seek to encourage conservation of energy. Some of the approaches are directed solely at reducing the amount of energy being used, while others, although they may have the effect of reducing overall use, are directed more at changing the form of energy used from a less available supply to one that is more abundant. In addition, the mechanism of removing government imposed price controls (deregulation) has the duel objectives of stimulating supply, as we have already discussed, and of diminishing consumer demand for energy or at least for the type of energy whose price is deregulated.

Our examination of governmentally created conservation measures will focus on those of the federal government, although we note in passing that states can have significant regulatory input into the conservation process. One example of state influence is that states control the price structure of

---

57. *Independent Energy Producers: The New Electric Generating Sector* (Washington, DC: National Independent Energy Producers, 1989).

58. Statement of the U.S. Council for Energy Awareness, P.O. Box 66103, Washington, DC 20035 (1989).

59. 106 Stat. 3120.

electric power. Historically, electric power rate structures used the "declining-block" rate design, which said higher-quantity users paid a lower price per unit of power used than did lower-quantity users. The basis for this approach is that it is said that it costs the utility company less per unit to get power to a large-volume user than to a small-volume user. The "declining-block" structure is, however, claimed by some to provide a disincentive for user conservation of electricity. States can choose alternative structures such as "flat rates" with a constant price per unit consumed, or "inverted rates" with a higher price per unit as consumption increases. These rate structures are claimed to be more conservation oriented than the declining-block approach and also to more fairly account for actual costs of power production, since additional output capacity needed to meet high demands results in the cost per unit of electricity produced increasing as output increases. Thus, in setting the rate structure for electric power, states are left with a number of questions. Among them are: (1) which rate structure is economically more reflective of the true costs of supplying power to the high-volume and low-volume users; (2) whether it is fair to a high-volume user to make it pay more per unit consumed if the costs to provide power to it are lower than for a low-volume user; and (3) do flat rates or inverted rates really result in significantly greater conservation of energy than declining-block rates, or are large-volume users' consumption patterns independent of the rate structure?

Having noted a state role in energy conservation through the mechanism of rate setting, we begin our discussion of the federal role in conservation by looking at some examples of federal tax advantages for those who take steps toward conservation. For many years, the Internal Revenue Code (IRC) allowed as an annual credit against one's income tax liability 15% of the energy conservation expenditures made for residential insulation or other energy-conserving components such as storm windows.[60] This credit, which would be subtracted from one's tax bill, served as an incentive to make energy conserving improvements. Perhaps because Congress thought that what could be done had been done to retrofit old residences for conservation, the residential energy credit was repealed; however, the Internal Revenue Code continues to contain tax provisions to encourage desired energy related activities of business. Businesses are entitled to a general business credit against their tax liability for various expenditures, one of which is expenditures for "energy property."[61] Energy property is equipment using solar energy or geothermal energy. After tentatively repealing this energy credit

---

60. § 44C of the Internal Revenue Code, redesignated § 23, and subsequently repealed as of 1990.

61. IRC § 48, 26 U.S.C. § 48.

in 1991, in the 1992 Energy Policy Act,[62] Congress permanently extended the credit of 10% of the amount spent. This credit is designed to stimulate use of alternative energy rather than the approach of reducing overall energy consumption, regardless of source, which the focus of the residential energy credit. Another tax credit adopted by the Energy Policy Act to encourage the switch from one form of energy use to another is a credit against tax liability of 10% of the cost of an electric vehicle placed in service after mid-1993.[63] The approach of trying to actually reduce overall energy use also was taken in the Energy Policy Act by, for example, allowing employers to provide employees with mass transit passes and carpooling incentives like parking without those fringe benefits being income to the employee which would be subject to income tax.[64]

Congress has made extensive use of tax incentives to foster its conservation objectives; however, it must be kept in mind that the tax incentives approach to conservation is not free. Administrative costs aside, there is the direct reduction in the flow of revenue to the federal treasury. Let us next examine some examples of federal conservation mechanisms that work in ways that do not directly reduce the treasury's income. We will consider three examples in increasing order of the degree of federal government interference with the actions of private parties.

Our first example is energy conservation initiatives for federal buildings. A process begun in the 1970s of planning for energy conservation in buildings owned or leased by the federal government[65] has evolved into the 1990s requirement of energy standards for new federal buildings. Such buildings must have "those energy efficiency measures that are technologically feasible and economically justified," and the Secretary of Energy has the duty to establish federal building energy standards that meet this statutory directive.[66] These steps are taken not only for the purpose of reducing energy use by the country's largest energy consumer, but also for purposes of acting as an example to other consumers of energy and to stimulate energy conservation technology by stating that there is a large customer for such technology. The above steps involve government action with respect to energy conservation, but they create no direct interference by government with the actions of those outside of government.

Our second example, the federal labeling requirements imposed on man-

---

62. 106 Stat. 3024, § 1916.

63. 106 Stat. 3019, § 1913.

64. 106 Stat. 3012, § 1911.

65. 42 U.S.C.S. § 6361(a)(2).

66. 106 Stat. 2784.

ufacturers of automobiles and certain other consumer products such as refrigerators and television sets, interferes with manufacturers to the extent of requiring the labeling, but they do not prohibit the manufacture or the purchase by consumers of inefficient or high energy consumption products.[67] Rather, the labeling requirements operate on a theory of exposing the public to information about energy consumption with the belief that such information will lead to demand for and hence the production of more energy-efficient products.

When we come to our third example, the federal imposition of average fuel economy standards on automobile manufacturers, we have reached the level of government involvement where failure to conform to federal policy is unlawful and carries penalties with it. The average fuel economy standards require that the average of the fuel economy of all the passenger automobiles manufactured by a manufacturer shall not be less than a stated number of miles per gallon in a given model year.[68] Thus, the average fuel economy for all passenger automobiles manufactured by an individual manufacturer in 1980 was required to be 20.0 miles per gallon. The general standard for 1985 and thereafter is 27.5 miles per gallon. Violation of these fuel conservation requirements subject the manufacturer to the possibility of large civil penalties. Congress has not, however, gone to the level of saying that production of all inefficient automobiles is prohibited entirely or that failure to meet the average standards will result in a prohibition on the sale of any of a manufacturer's automobiles. Depending on factors such as the level of industrial cooperation, new technology, and the available supply of fuel, it is possible that conservation controls of a more mandatory nature than those described above may be imposed. Perhaps, however, even the conservation controls and incentives that exist now may become unnecessary because the cost of energy itself may provide the best measure of the appropriate level of conservation.

As a final point concerning encouraging conservation of energy, let's note the growing worldwide interest in an energy tax. The European Community is seeking to impose a "carbon tax" of $3 per barrel of "oil equivalent" to rise to $10 per barrel by 2000. One of the early proposals of the Clinton administration was for an energy tax based on a fuel's energy content as measured in Btus. Japan is also interested in taxing energy.[69] Energy taxes provide significant potential for encouraging conservation of energy. They

---

67. 15 U.S.C.S. § 2006 (automobiles); 42 U.S.C.S. § 6296 (other consumer products).

68. 15. U.S.C.S. § 2002.

69. *International Environment Reporter* (Washington, DC: Bureau of National Affairs, Inc., February 24, 1993) p. 115.

could also result in a major reduction of greenhouse gas emissions. This double benefit is very appealing, even leaving aside the increased revenue which government would obtain and which may have been a motivating factor behind the Clinton proposal. It is, however, appropriate to ask whether the details of a specific energy tax proposal will put the burden of energy conservation, pollution reduction, and government deficit reduction on those who can best afford the burden of these environmental and economic improvements.

ADDITIONAL READINGS

Annual Energy Outlook (Washington, DC: Energy Information Administration).

Energy Law Journal (Washington, DC: Federal Energy Bar Association).

Federal Energy Guidelines: Federal Energy Regulatory Commission Reports (Washington, DC: FERC).

Tester, J. et al, *Energy and the Environment in the 21st Century* (Cambridge, MA: MIT Press, 1991).

Tomain, J. et al, *Energy Law and Policy* (Cincinnati, Ohio: Anderson Publishing, 1989).

Yergin, D., *The Prize: The Epic Quest for Oil, Money & Power* (New York: Simon & Schuster, 1991).

CHAPTER 8

POPULATION

A. STIMULATION OF POPULATION GROWTH AND THE NEED FOR POPULATION REGULATION

1. Upper Limits on Population Growth and Lower Limits for Species Existence

Did you ever wonder how there got to be so many fleas, mosquitoes, Mediterranean fruit flies, cattle, and people everywhere and so few Atlantic salmon, Indiana bats, and elephants anywhere? There are numerous hypotheses to account for these observations, but, before we examine some of them, let us take a look at how a species population grows. The four processes—birth, death, immigration and emigration—and their relation to the size of a localized population are depicted in Figure 1. Taking the planet earth as a whole eliminates immigration and emigration as processes that influence population size. On the other hand, a localized population, such as the people of the United States, caddis flies in a temporary pool, or the Furbish louseworts of Maine, may all be influenced not only by births and deaths but also by immigration and emigration of individuals.

People who keep track of population size, growth, diversity, and distribution, as well as other vital population statistics are called demographers (demographers are usually assumed to keep track of only human populations, but some keep track of plants and animals). Demographers who keep track of population growth use mathematical techniques to help them understand how a population grew and what the population *could* grow to be. In word form, the size, N, to which a population *could* grow between time, t, and some future time, t + 1, is determined by the size of the population at time

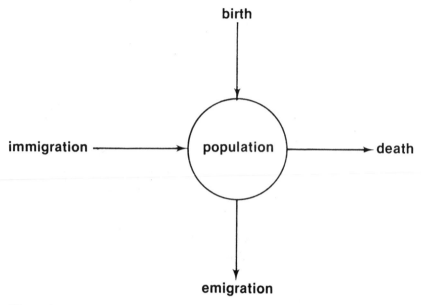

Figure 1. Processes that may add or subtract from the size of a local population.

t and the intrinsic rate of increase (r) over the time period in question.[1] In a mathematical manner, this could read as follows:

$$N_{t+1} = N_t + rN_t$$

The intrinsic rate of increase r is the difference between the birth rate b and death rate d of the population in question (r = b-d). Therefore, two populations that start at the same size could have two totally different sizes after the same time period if each has a different intrinsic rate of increase r for each time interval and each reproduces in a similar time domain (Table I). Conversely, two species populations with the same intrinsic rate of increase, but reproducing over different time intervals (one population reproduces every year while the other reproduces every two years), will also never reach the same population size over the same period of time.

If one were to graph either of the above situations through numerous time periods, the result would be a curve that rises exponentially and shows *no* upper limit to growth, a concept that was rejected in principle by some researchers referred to in Chapter 1. Instead, it was recognized that the growth

---

1. The term intrinsic rate of increase has, unfortunately, several indistinct meanings that have created some confusion among population scientists. We use the term here to mean only the rate of increase of a population based on historical perspective.

Table I.   An Example of How Two Populations with
Very Different Intrinsic Rates of Increase Grow over Time

Time Period	Population 1 (r = 0.2)	Population 2 (r = 0.6)
1	100	100
2	120	160
3	144	256
4	173	410
5	208	656

in a population reaches a limit of support after an elapsed time. Therefore, over any period of time, there is a limit imposed on the size that a population can reach, and this is a function of the space used by the population. Space contains the resources used by the population (food, shelter). In population studies, this upper limit is conceptualized as the "carrying capacity" of that environment, at that time, for the population in question. There is also another limit—the lower limit for a population to continue to exist. These limits are depicted in Figure 2.

What all this means is that, if a population exceeds the carrying capacity of the environment, there will be a decline of some proportion that "causes" the population numbers (number of living individuals) to decrease to some point below the carrying capacity for the population in question. If the population numbers fall even further and go below the lower limit, then the probability of that population becoming extinct is equal to 1.0, *i.e.*, the population has a 100% chance of becoming extinct. This lower limit could be a rather large actual number like 10,000 or a relatively small number like 100. The numerical level of the lower limit is determined by the occurrence of intraspecific reproductive encounters that give at least enough viable offspring such that the number of individuals in the species population can remain stable or increase under *any* circumstances (the worst case analysis). Therefore, a population that will survive under basically "any" circumstances is one whose numbers remain between the upper and lower limit (see Figure 2). The upper limit (carrying capacity) is not really a definite number, bur rather a group of numbers representing various limiting environmental parameters. The carrying capacity itself may vary because of many environmental factors external to the population in question, and it could converge with the lower limit. This would be a very precarious position for any species population. For example, suppose that one "family" of pileated woodpeckers needed 10 acres of woodlot to survive. Suppose further, that 5000 contiguous families of pileated woodpeckers were needed in order to have an indefinitely sustained population of woodpeckers. If there were not any woodlot of 50,000 contiguous acres for pileated woodpecker habitat,

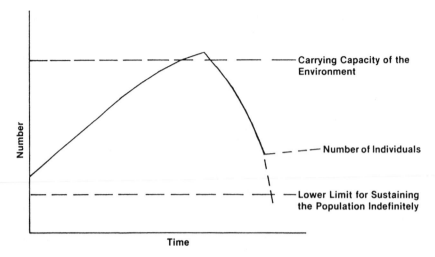

Figure 2.   Hypothetical growth curve for a population passing its carrying capacity.

then there could be no pileated woodpecker population sustained indefinitely. In other words, even if there were 10,000 noncontiguous woodlots of 2500 acres each, although the overall population of woodpeckers could currently be very high, the number of families close to each other would be too small to continue the species indefinitely.

2.   Stimulation of Population Growth

What stimulates a population to grow? More importantly, what could stimulate a population to grow to a number larger than the carrying capacity for that population? Contrary to what might be one's first thought, at least with respect to humans, it is not *increased* birth rates that stimulate a population to grow as much as it is *decreased* death rates. Remember, populations increase faster when the intrinsic rate of increase (r) increases, and this increase is usually caused by a reduction in death rates. Modern medicine has contributed substantially to the stimulation of population growth by reducing infant mortality as well as preserving the lives of individuals who would have died from some disease such as heritable diabetes or hemophilia. These people may now live and reproduce. Some believe that this artificial selection (keeping people alive through medical practices until reproductive success) will not only result in a larger population but will also eventually lead to a physical weakening of the human population by perpetuating "disease" traits. Under normal circumstances, it is believed that most of these people would die before experiencing reproductive success.

In addition to medicine, religion has also been implicated as a stimulus to population growth. By specifically forbidding the use of contraception and encouraging reproductive output, religion does indeed stimulate population growth. This religious attitude, coupled with the medical advances noted, creates an overwhelming stimulus to population growth. Other factors that have been implicated in stimulating population growth include increased food supplies, greater mobility of the populace, industrialization, and changes in moral standards. Some have voiced the idea that when people get more to eat and thus are healthier, they tend toward more reproduction. Also, the idea has been espoused that if individuals can get more food with the same effort or even less effort than previously made, then individuals will have more time for reproduction. Industrialization, which usually is thought of as reducing population growth, has sometimes been said to stimulate population growth. The argument is that industrialization (any advancement that is similar could substitute) gives people more leisure time, and therefore they spend more time engaged in reproductive activity, which eventually creates a population increase. While medicine and food can be viewed as manipulating death rates, religion and industrialization probably manipulate birth rates. Whichever of these one would choose to emphasize as the "cause" or "causes" of any perceived population growth problems, the fact is that the human population is increasing and therefore approaching the carrying capacity. To many people, this condition calls for some form of regulation. The questions are: Should population be regulated and, if so, what form should such regulation take?

3.   Population Regulation—Do We Need It?

There are basically two attitudes concerning population regulation—regulate and do not regulate. Since humankind as a whole is unsure about whether we really need to regulate ourselves, we have turned to an examination of nonhuman populations with the hope that, by understanding the population behavior of other animal species, we can shed light on our questions relating to the human population. Though at first this seems to be a fruitful endeavor, the controversy over what regulates populations of other animals is itself unresolved.

Current notions about animal population regulation take two fundamental approaches. One school of thought believes that populations regulate themselves by the density of the population itself. In other words, the number of individuals within the population dictates the size to which a population grows (internal control). This idea suggests that each individual, or perhaps each dominant individual, has a territory. When the total territory, summed over all individuals possessing a territory, approximates the total amount of

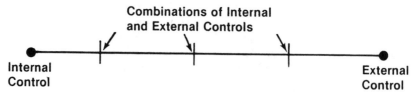

Figure 3.   Hypothetical continuum describing the relation between internal and external control of population density.

territory available, then the species population has regulated itself. Another way of viewing this idea is that every population has some space that it can inhabit. When the number of individuals in the population has comfortably inhabited all the available space that members of the population can use, the population has reached the carrying capacity, and regulation (internal) keeps increased reproductive effort at a minimum. The other school of thought argues that a species population size is independent of the population density and is a function of the environment (external control). What this means is that some external force such as temperature, wind speed, food availability, daylight period, or some other factor regulates population size rather than it being regulated by density. These ideas are really the opposite poles of a continuum that allows population regulation to be a combination of the two notions (Figure 3).

The major objection to either of these possibilities or a combination of them is that the operation of each of these regulating mechanisms is supposed to occur when the carrying capacity is about to be reached. Therefore, although we know that no natural population has ever annihilated itself, we do not know whether that statement will be applicable to humans and whether the mechanisms will operate to preclude humankind's self-annihilation due to it having reached or exceeded the carrying capacity. Furthermore, even if upon reaching the carrying capacity there is no total annihilation of humans, drastic consequences short of annihilation may occur, such as widespread famine. Yet another constraint on our thinking is that we do not know what form the real regulation among other species takes; rather, we know the result and speculate about the causes. While some scientists have attempted to study this question in experimental situations, these are generally artificial situations that examine segments of a species population. Some insight into whether we need to regulate our human population will likely be gained by studying non-human populations, but it is safe to say that no definitive answer has yet been provided.

Let's consider the need to regulate from another perspective. Every species population is assumed to start out small and grow larger over time. People keep track of localized human populations in terms of not only the number

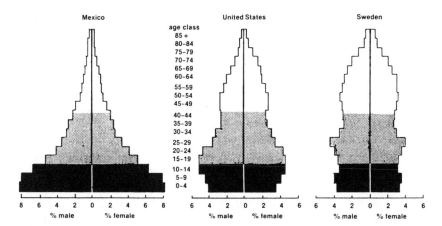

Figure 4.   Population pyramid graph for Mexico, United States, and Sweden. [Adapted from Miller, *Living in the Environment*, Wadsworth Publishing Co., 1982).

of individuals but also the distribution of individuals among age classes. Diagrammatically, this effort produces a population picture like that in Figure 4. As one can see by examining the age distributions in Figure 4, the population on the left (Mexico) is and will be expanding rapidly, and the population on the right (Sweden) is almost stable in population growth. The population in the middle diagram of Figure 4 (United States) is growing slowly and apparently approaching the structure of the population on the right (Sweden). The country on the left has a short time of doubling its population (approximately 30 yrs.), while the country on the right has a longer doubling time (approximately 125 yrs.). Two things are important to consider when examining diagrams such as these. One is the doubling time and thus the number of people. A second consideration is the age structure of the population. With respect to its numbers, any localized human population, as well as a global human population, places demands on our resource of space. People use space to domicile themselves, for recreation, and to provide food and other products for living. Since there is a finite amount of space that can be used for the above activities, the amount of available space per individual in each category decreases as the number of people increases. Therefore, the population may eventually stabilize itself once all the available space is used up. This may take place peacefully through mechanisms such as people reproducing less so as not to have to share space with their offspring, or it may happen through wars fought for space. If one wants to avoid the possible harsh consequences of nearing or exceeding our carrying capacity for human beings, one may opt for regulation of the growth of our population size. With respect to the age structure of population, society may need to concern itself with the burden placed on the younger members of the population in having to support the older members. As a population growth pattern becomes more stable (Figure 4), the percentage of older members within that population increases. Therefore, in stable populations where older individuals are supported by younger individuals (such as by a social security system), the financial burden on younger individuals increases. Soon it necessitates that the fewer younger individuals be supporting more older people.

Working against the idea of stable population or zero population growth (ZPG) is the expanding industrial society. As more jobs are created, more people are needed to fill these jobs. Since younger workers are preferred by industry, there may be a consequent shift in reproductive patterns to provide more younger available workers. Thus a stable population structure such as that shown for Sweden in Figure 4 may tend to change toward that shown for Mexico. When the industrial demands are met or the industrial demand for population declines, the structure may respond by gravitating away from the Mexican model toward the Swedish model. However, the response of industry to economic forces and the response of population to industrial forces are not necessarily equally as rapid. Population responses are usually less rapid compared to industrial responses. Therefore, some regulation to keep these responses in line with society's needs at a particular time may be appropriate.

Issues pertaining to immigration and emigration also raise the question of the need for control mechanisms. A sonnet, written by Emma Lazarus, is preserved on a tablet inside the pedestal of the Statute of Liberty on Liberty Island in New York Harbor. The sonnet says, in part:

> Give me your tired, your poor, your huddled masses yearning to breathe free, the wretched refuse of your teeming shore. Send these, the homeless, tempest-tost to me, I lift my lamp beside the golden door!

A noble motto for a young and struggling country such as the United States was in 1886 when the Statute of Liberty was dedicated in remembrance of our revolutionary alliance with France. In fact, since the United States began keeping records in 1820, over 50 million individuals have immigrated through the "golden door" of the United States. When there was much land to be settled and much work to be found, the idea of large-scale immigration, regardless of whether it was motivated by economic, political, or religious goals, was not considered burdensome. But, since land resources have become scarcer, food resources in some countries even more scarce, and the demands for workers in an organized labor market have become stressed, the need for and the tolerance for immigrants in many countries has begun to cause at least localized if not national negative reaction. Episodes in the United

States following the Vietnam War and the more recent mass immigrations from Latin American countries have demonstrated that, within the United States at least, the attitude embodied in Ms. Lazarus' sonnet is under reconsideration. The United States has implemented a policy of forced repatriation of illegal immigrants, and, although the action has been widely criticized and challenged in court, many Haitians who fled Haiti following a violent overthrow of the government there were returned to Haiti as economically motivated immigrants rather than those fearing political persecution.[2]

The United States, as well as other countries, is also becoming more selective regarding the quality of immigrants. In a sense, nations are discriminating more closely among immigrants. What this could eventually lead to is an even greater distinction between the nations that "have" and those that "have not." In terms of the overall regulation of the human population, what this suggests is a form of density-dependent population regulation among nations based on the quality of contribution a potential immigrant might make to the overall goals of a receiving nation. Conversely, nations might counter the loss of high-quality individuals to higher-quality nations by restricting emigration, much as Britain did with scientists in recent years. While the actions described above may seem not only inconsistent with Ms. Lazarus' thoughts but also inconsistent with the historical underpinnings of our society, the institution and maintenance of immigration quotas and the calls to tighten up on enforcement of immigration laws attest to the realistic nature of the situation.

To summarize, population size relative to the carrying capacity of its surroundings, matters such as age distribution of population, population size relative to society's contemporary need for people, and immigration and emigration are all issues which could be the subject of affirmative regulation. Again the questions are: Should there be regulation and, if so, in what form? Though regulation of human population issues by legislation may seem repugnant, the alternative regulatory mechanisms may be no less acceptable. For example, internal control of the human population by birth regulation and even death regulation may prove a more acceptable alternative than waiting until the use of space through time becomes limiting. This latter alternative may foster famine, wars, infanticide, and other more barbaric methods of population regulation. The question then becomes: Do we regulate before a critical density is reached, or do we wait and see what happens when and if a critical density is reached? The decision is further complicated

---

2. "U.S. Starts Return of Haiti Refugees After Justices Act," *New York Times* (Feb. 2, 1992) p.1. Petition for review of lower court decisions allowing deportation was denied by the Supreme Court. *Haitian Refugee Center v. Baker*, 1992 U.S. Lexis 1125.

by our inability to know how long one can play "wait and see" and when we will pass a "point of no return." Therefore, one must ask not only what are the real options for population regulation but also when should such options be implemented and how will they be enforced. We will now examine some methods which might be used to regulate population and some legal issues the resolution of which may substantially affect population issues.

B.   LEGAL ISSUES INVOLVING POPULATION

1.   Matters Where Population Regulation Is the Primary Issue

When the topic of population law is raised, issues that often come to mind first are contraception, abortion, and sterilization. In many countries, these issues have been addressed largely from the viewpoint of the utility of these tools as means of controlling population. For example, in India the national government uses media advertising to promote small families and has established medical camps where women and men receive cash payments for submitting to sterilization procedures. India has gone to the brink of imposing compulsory sterilization to try to control its mushrooming population, but the government which had been seriously considering compulsory sterilization was removed from power before the program was ever put into effect. Government policy of slowing population growth can also be seen by noting that in the countries containing 80% of the population of the developing world, there is some form of government-supported family planning. In some countries, abortion policy has been established based largely on the effects that abortion would have on population. For example, in 1955 the Soviet Union enacted a decree that legalized abortion on request. The purposes were to reduce harm to women from abortions performed outside of hospitals and to give women the opportunity to decide questions of motherhood for themselves. Most of the then socialist countries of eastern Europe soon followed suit; however, in more recent years some of these countries have become more restrictive about allowing abortions. This restrictiveness is said to be a response to those countries' concerns about low birth rates. Thus while most decisions concerning population issues that have been made on the basis of policies about population have resulted in governments acting to slow population growth, some decisions on population issues have been made with an eye toward increasing population.

In the United States, while issues such as population size, geographic distribution, and age distribution have been the subjects of much government action intended to impact on these issues, the issues of contraception, abortion, and sterilization have not really been "population" issues but have been disputed and decided primarily on grounds other than their effects on population. The political and judicial decisions on these topics have been made in the context of constitutional rights of privacy, due process, and equal protection. They have also been made in the context of religion and varying thoughts on what is appropriate morality and what is the appropriate relationship between government and morality. We will begin by first discussing a few examples of our own government acting for primarily population-related purposes. We will then discuss abortion and contraception in a separate section, thereby emphasizing that in the United States these issues have not really been "population" issues.

Our first example will be a governmental entity acting to control the number of people that will be allowed to live within the geographical area of that entity. Many communities have experienced huge increases in population during very short periods of time. This has resulted in stress being placed on a community's ability to provide municipal facilities and services. Towns such as Ramapo, New York, have sought to alleviate these population pressures by enacting ordinances to control the growth of the community.[3] Ramapo's ordinance tied development by residential subdivision to the availability of municipal facilities. Before a permit to subdivide would be issued, certain municipal facilities would have to be available. The facilities were to be provided in accordance with an 18-year plan or capital program. Growth would thus be allowed, but it would be slowed down to the pace at which facilities were provided. Ramapo's ordinance raised the general question of whether a town should have the right to control its growth, but in the *Ramapo* case the question was whether the town did in fact have that right. The town's ordinance was attacked on the grounds that it was a "taking" or confiscation of private property by the government without the just compensation required by the constitution[4] and also that Ramapo's action was an unjustifiable exclusion of people from the community.

The court's answer to the taking without compensation argument was that the restriction on any individual piece of property was only temporary rather than permanent because the property would be able to be subdivided sometime during the 18 years. Also, the property could be used prior to its qualifying for a subdivision permit—it just could not be subdivided. A detailed discussion of what is an unconstitutional "taking" without just compensation may be found in Chapter 4. It is there shown that what will be called a "taking" by the courts is very narrow, and that governments

---

3. *Golden v. Planning Board of Town of Ramapo*, 285 N.E. 2d 291 (1972).

4. 5th Amendment: ". . . nor shall private property be taken for public use, without just compensation."

such as the Town of Ramapo have a great deal of latitude in regulating and controlling the use of land and ultimately controlling population through land use controls. On the issue of whether the ordinance amounted to an unjustifiable exclusion of people from Ramapo, the court said that the ordinance was not exclusionary but was merely the implementation of sequential development and timed growth. The court said it would not countenance exclusion, but that timed growth was acceptable. Since timed growth is, however, temporary exclusion and results in fewer people in an area for a period of time, governmental control over the size of the population within its boundaries was found to be allowable at least to some extent.

In contrast to controlling the number of people who live in an area, some states have opted to regulate the quality of land development through planning legislation. Vermont's Growth Management Act provides that towns that adopt plans consistent with the act are eligible to receive money from the state planning fund.[5] Also, municipalities with approved plans are authorized to charge developers impact fees to cover the costs of services such as roads or schools that will be necessitated by the development.[6] Although this state statute does not directly limit population growth in an area, some contend that the effects of provisions such as the impact fees will result in less availability of housing and thus lower population growth in many locations.

Our second example of government acting for a population-related purpose involves not only numerical control but also control of the type or classification of people involved. That example is U.S. immigration laws. In our early history there were very few restrictions on immigration. We had frontiers to settle and a demand for labor by our expanding industries. These needs dovetailed nicely with our concern for economically, politically, and religiously oppressed people in other parts of the world. Later on came a desire to retain the racial and ethnic composition of our population, and the Immigration Act of 1924 established quotas and formulas restricting immigrants from certain countries as the method of implementing that policy. Today's complex immigration laws are based in part on humanitarian factors such as the needs of refugees, but they also take into account the availability and competition for our country's resources such as jobs and the government's ability to provide for the needs of those who cannot provide for themselves. The Immigration and Nationality chapter of the United States Code[7] has overall numerical limitations on the number of immigrants and thus addresses itself to numerical population control. It also provides a hierarchy for selection

---

5. Vermont Public Act No. 200, 1987 Adjourned Session, §§ 3 and 15.

6. 24 V.S.A. Chapter 131, Impact Fees.

7. 8 U.S.C.S. Chapter 12, § 1101 et seq.

which accords preferential treatment for factors such as being a member of a profession, having ability in the arts or sciences, being sought by an employer in the United States, or being capable of performing labor, not of a temporary or seasonal nature, for which a shortage exists in the United States. Therefore, in addition to numerical control, the statutory framework also addresses itself to controlling the types of people that we are willing to add to our country's population.

While United States law has sought to regulate the number and types of immigrants to this country, there continues to be a largely uncontrolled influx of illegal aliens across U.S. borders. In 1986, Congress enacted the Immigration Reform and Control Act[8] in an attempt to handle this problem. Employers who knowingly employ illegal aliens can be subjected to fines and other penalties. In an effort to resolve the status of illegal aliens who had resided in the United States for many years, amnesty and legal immigrant status was granted to certain illegal aliens who could document that they had resided in the United States continuously, albeit illegally, since January of 1982. By the termination date for the amnesty program, approximately 1.5 million applications had been received. Over 70% of them came from Mexican immigrants. With respect to the effectiveness of the legislation in achieving Congress's purpose, a study by the Rand Corporation found that the flow of illegal immigrants had been reduced by less than 20% over a three year period.[9] Whether immigration should or should not be limited is, of course, a debatable question. The question of whether illegal immigration has been effectively curtailed appears to have a clear negative answer.

As our last example of population parameters being directly related to actions taken by government, let's consider age. In contrast to our immigration example where the law sought to control the population parameters of "how many" and "who," the population parameter of age is not what is being controlled, but rather it may be used to control something else. To illustrate, if we want to reduce the size of the federal workforce and/or reduce unemployment by removing people from the working population, we can lower the age at which one will qualify for retirement benefits. If, however, our concern is the financial viability of the Social Security system in light of the fact that people are living longer and the percentage of older people eligible for social security is increasing, this age distribution pattern could result in pressure to raise the age at which one could qualify for retirement benefits. From these illustrations we can see that the age dis-

---

8. Pub. L. 99–603, 100 Stat. 3359, Nov. 6, 1986.

9. "Study Finds Mild Gain in Drive on Illegal Aliens," *New York Times* (April 21, 1990) Section I, p. 24.

tribution of our population could strongly influence what we might establish as the age for retirement with government benefits.

Having considered a few examples of laws specifically intended to control population matters or being subject to possible influence by population factors, let's next turn to issues where, although their resolution will have substantial effects on population, the population aspects of the issues have not had much effect on how these issues are resolved in the United States.

2. Matters Where Population Regulation is Not the Primary Issue—Contraception and Abortion

On one level the issues of contraception and abortion involve answering the substantive question of whether the state can legally interfere with the choice of the individual. On a second level are the problems that result from the lack of a clear answer about whether the state can so interfere. If, for example, performing an abortion violates a state criminal statute, and if it is not clear whether that statute is constitutionally valid or invalid, physicians will be deterred from performing abortions. The existence of the doubt will have itself provided an answer to the substantive question, and that answer may or may not be the correct answer. The doubt may also place physicians and patients in a precarious position. Thus, if performing or obtaining an abortion is a crime after the fetus has reached the state of "viability," what is the time of viability given the medical profession's ability to sustain life outside the womb at ever-earlier stages of fetal development? In this section we will consider some of the substantive answers that the courts have provided to the question of what a legislature can do in the way of interfering with an individual's desire to obtain contraceptives or an abortion. Where contraception or abortion is sought to be prohibited or regulated by state government, the interests that the state may have in controlling a type of conduct are brought into conflict with the interest of the individual in her or his own privacy. That the individual has a constitutional right to privacy was first recognized in a case involving contraceptives, and that is where we will begin.

a. Contraception

A Connecticut statute which was in existence in 1961 made it a crime to use drugs, articles, or instruments for the purpose of preventing conception or to counsel others in the use of contraceptives. A physician and an official of Planned Parenthood gave information, instruction, and medical advice to married persons as to the means of preventing conception. In the case of

Griswold v. Connecticut,[10] they were found guilty in the Connecticut courts as accessories to the violation of the state statute, and they asked the United States Supreme Court to reverse that conviction. The Supreme Court reversed the conviction saying that the Connecticut statute interfered with the fundamental right of privacy contained in the United States Constitution. The Court recognized that nowhere in the Constitution could one find a "right of privacy" explicitly stated; however, it found that various parts of the Bill of Rights created a "zone of privacy" which could be invaded by government in only extremely limited ways and only under extremely limited circumstances. An example of how the Court saw parts of the Bill of Rights as creating a "zone of privacy" is the First Amendment's protection of the freedom to associate and the privacy of one's associations. Although the First Amendment does not mention freedom of association, the Court said freedom of association was a peripheral First Amendment right and that the First Amendment has a "penumbra" where privacy is protected from governmental intrusion.

Other facets of the privacy penumbra can be found in places such as the Third Amendment's prohibition on quartering soldiers in people's houses in time of peace and the Fourth Amendment's prohibitions against unreasonable searches and seizures. The Court further noted that the Ninth Amendment provides: "The enumeration in the Constitution, of certain rights, shall not be construed to deny or disparage others retained by the people . . . ." A concurring opinion focused more heavily on the Ninth Amendment and said: "To hold that a right so basic and fundamental and so deep-rooted in our society as the right of privacy in marriage may be infringed because that right is not guaranteed in so many words by the first eight amendments in the Constitution is to ignore the Ninth Amendment and to give it no effect whatsoever . . . ." Thus, without it being stated in express terms in the Constitution, the "right of privacy" was recognized as a fundamental constitutional right.

The *Griswold* case involved contraceptive advice to married couples, and the opinions in the case repeatedly spoke of marriage and the marriage relationship. In *Eisenstadt v. Baird*,[11] the Supreme Court was called upon to determine whether the "zone of privacy" with respect to contraceptives extended beyond the marital relationship. *Eisenstadt* concerned Massachusetts statutes that prohibited the distribution of materials for the prevention of conception unless such distribution was to married persons and by a physician or a pharmacist. With respect to the right of privacy, the Court found that

---

10. 381 U.S. 479 (1965).

11. 405 U.S. 438 (1972).

this right is a right of the individual, not a right of the marital relationship or the marital couple. It said that the marital couple is not an independent entity but rather an association of two individuals, each with a separate intellectual and emotional makeup, and that the right of privacy is the right of the individual to be free from unwarranted governmental intrusion. The Court found that the Massachusetts statutes violated the Equal Protection Clause[12] of the Fourteenth Amendment of the United States Constitution because they provide dissimilar treatment for married and unmarried persons who are similarly situated and that there is no ground or difference that rationally explains the different treatment accorded married and unmarried persons. The Court's position was based on its findings that the statutes' unequal treatment could not be justified as either a deterrent to fornication or as a health measure when viewed in terms of what the statutes and their exceptions prohibited and what they did not prohibit.

While the right of privacy led to the invalidation of the Connecticut and Massachusetts regulatory efforts discussed above, it should be emphasized that individual rights may be subjected to governmental interference in some situations. Even "fundamental" rights such as the right of privacy or freedom of speech may be interfered with, but for governmental interference with a "fundamental" right to be found to be constitutional, there must be a very strong reason to support the interference. The required strength of the reason has been referred to as a "compelling state interest" or a "significant state interest" rather than merely a "valid state interest." In *Carey v. Population Services International*,[13] the Supreme Court examined various aspects of a New York statute to see if the strength of the state interest was sufficient to justify the interferences with the right of privacy that the statute created. The New York statute in *Carey* made it a crime: (1) to distribute contraceptives to minors under the age of 16, (2) for anyone other than a pharmacist to distribute contraceptives to persons over 16, and (3) for anyone to advertise or display contraceptives. All three provisions were found to be unconstitutional since a sufficient degree of state interest was not present to justify interference with a fundamental right. With respect to distribution to those under 16, the Court found that minors as well as adults have constitutional rights such as the right of privacy. It did, however, reaffirm that the power of the state to control the conduct of children is greater than the scope of its authority over adults. The minors' right to privacy in connection with procreation decisions could be restricted, but only if the restrictions served a significant state interest that is not present in the case

---

12. " . . . nor [shall any state] deny to any person within its jurisdiction the equal protection of the laws."

13. 431 U.S. 678 (1977).

of an adult. The state contended that it had a significant interest in that by restricting access of minors to contraceptives it could decrease sexual activity of minors. Without deciding whether a state could act to discourage sexual activity of minors, the Court found that the state had presented no evidence supporting a link between the availability of contraceptives and increased sexual activity of minors. The Court noted that the state had conceded that there was no such evidence and, further, that evidence had been presented to indicate that unavailability of contraceptives did not have a deterrent effect on sexual activity of minors. There was thus no significant state interest to justify the state's interference with the minors' right to privacy.

The Court handled the distribution by a pharmacist requirement in a similar fashion. It found that the alleged state interest of allowing purchasers to inquire into the relative quality of products was perhaps not even a factually valid state interest and certainly did not reach the compelling level of state interest that would be necessary to justify restricting the distribution channel of contraceptives to licensed pharmacists. Such a restriction on access could place a burden on the freedom to make the decision of whether to bear or beget a child, and the freedom to make that decision is what the right of privacy in this area is all about. Lastly, with respect to the New York statute's prohibition on advertising or displaying contraceptives, the Court acknowledged that such activity might be offensive or embarrassing to some people; however, that is not sufficient justification for interference with another fundamental right, the First Amendment right of freedom of expression. The dissemination of information about contraceptives, even in a commercial context, is protected from suppression under the First Amendment unless there is strong justification for such suppression. Embarrassment and offensiveness do not provide the required justification.

Given the above court decision, the general availability of contraceptives has overcome the major legal hurdles that have been placed in its way. Public debate with respect to contraceptives now focuses on issues such as whether or not secondary schools should play a role in the distribution of condoms. Some public school systems, including that of the City of New York, have formulated plans to distribute condoms in the schools.[14] While the plan was initiated as part of a comprehensive AIDS education and prevention program, the distribution of condoms to students may have the secondary effect of reducing teenage pregnancies. In an experiment in Baltimore, a school-linked clinic dispensed condoms along with comprehensive health care advice for over three years. It recorded a 30% reduction in the pregnancy rate as

---

14. "School Board Approves Plan for Condoms," *New York Times* (Feb. 28, 1991) Section B, p.1.

compared to a 58% increase in the pregnancy rate in a control group.[15] New York type condom distribution plans will continue to spark heated debates. Opponents condemn the plans for condoning immorality and abandoning or undermining parents' moral authority. Proponents firmly support the plans in order to protect a segment of the population that is particularly vulnerable to and experiencing a large increase in the spread of the AIDS virus. Although there will likely be disagreement about contraceptive issues in the future, it will certainly be small when compared to the battles concerning our next area of inquiry, abortion. We will see that court cases have upheld the right to privacy as applied to abortion; however, continuing legislative efforts and litigation leave open the question of whether a woman will always have a right to an abortion in the United States.

b.   Abortion

As with the contraception issues, the right of privacy has played the pivotal role with respect to abortion. In 1973, while a few states had removed most restrictions on abortion, 30 states had statues either prohibiting all abortions or any abortion not for the purpose of saving the life of the woman. The United States Supreme Court decided the case of *Roe v. Wade*[16] in 1973 on the basis of the constitutional right of privacy and invalidated a Texas statute making it a crime to procure or attempt an abortion unless it was to save the life of the mother. The court approached the question of the constitutionality of the Texas statute by balancing the interests of the mother on the one hand with the interests of the state on the other.

The state interests alleged to be served by prohibiting abortions were to discourage illicit sexual conduct (this was dismissed by the Court as not a serious argument), to protect the mother from a hazardous surgical procedure, and to protect prenatal or potential life. Against these interests are the woman's interests—her constitutional right of privacy. The Court said that, because of factors like possible mental and physical health problems of child care and distress associated with an unwanted child, her right of privacy was broad enough to encompass a woman's decision of whether or not to terminate her pregnancy. While the right of privacy is not an absolute right, it is a fundamental right and thus could be infringed upon by the state only to serve "compelling" state interests. In *Roe*, the Court found that the state's interests in protecting the mother's health and in protecting prenatal life are compelling state interests and thus not all statutes restricting or

---

15. *Westlaw United Press International Database* (Oct. 13, 1986) Section: General News, Story Tag: Contraceptives.

16. 410 U.S. 113 (1973).

prohibiting abortions are invalid. Why, if the state interests were found to be "compelling," was the Texas statute invalidated?

The Texas statute was held invalid because it was "overbroad"—it prohibited some conduct that it could validly prohibit, but it also prohibited conduct that it could not constitutionally prohibit. Although the state has an interest in protecting the mother's health, that interest does not allow prohibiting an abortion in the first trimester of pregnancy because it was factually shown that during the first trimester abortion is a less hazardous medical procedure than childbirth. Thus to prohibit abortion beyond the first trimester (or beyond whatever point in time abortion might become a greater health hazard to the mother than childbearing) might protect the mother and be allowed. Prior to that time, the statute does not protect the mother and does not serve the state interest. It therefore outlaws too much—it is overbroad—and is unconstitutional.

A similar analysis resulted in the statute being overbroad with respect to the state's interest in protecting potential life. The Court acknowledged that there are different religious, philosophical, and scientific views about when life begins. It went on to say that the time at which the state's interest in potential life becomes "compelling" is the time when the fetus has reached the point of viability (24–28 weeks), i.e., it presumably has the capability of meaningful life outside of the mother's womb. After the time of viability was reached, the Court said that there was both logical and biological justification for a state to prohibit abortion. Since the Texas statute prohibited abortions not only subsequent to the time of viability of the fetus but also prior to viability, it was overbroad and invalid.

Roe v. Wade did not tell states that they could not prohibit abortions under any circumstances, but it was the turning point in abortion law because it told states that some abortions could not be prohibited and that attempts to limit or regulate abortion would be closely scrutinized by the courts. A state would have to provide substantial justification for its restraints—it would have to show a compelling state interest. Since the *Roe* decision, the Supreme Court has used lesser standards of judicial scrutiny than the "strict scrutiny/compelling state interest" standard to determine whether a state statute seeking to regulate abortion is constitutional. In *Hodgson v. Minnesota*,[17] instead of asking whether a Minnesota requirement that a minor wait 48 hours after notifying a parent of her intention to get an abortion served a "compelling state interest," the Court found the requirement was constitutional since it reasonably furthered the "legitimate state interest" of ensuring that the minor's decision is knowing and intelligent. Indeed, in *Webster*

---

17. 110 S. Ct. 2926 (1990).

v. Reproductive Health Services,[18] four of the nine Supreme Court Justices showed a clear willingness to overrule *Roe* and give the states broad and perhaps unfettered authority to control abortion. They certainly would not have required that the state demonstrate a "compelling" state interest.

The opinions in *Webster* and *Hodgson* set the stage for the United States Court of Appeals for the Third Circuit to conclude in *Planned Parenthood v. Casey*[19] that the Supreme Court had already abandoned the holding of *Roe* which said that, because abortion is a fundamental right, any government controls that interfere with it must be justified by a compelling governmental interest. *Casey* involved challenges to 1988 and 1989 amendments to the Pennsylvania Abortion Control Act requiring that prior to an abortion there had to be certain information provided to the woman by the physician such as risks of abortion, gestational age of the fetus, and risks of carrying a child to term. A physician or counselor had to provide information about obtainable medical assistance benefits if the pregnancy continued and liability of the father for support of the child and also make available information describing the fetus at various stages of development. In addition, the statute included a mandatory waiting period, requirements of parental consent or court approval for women under 18, and spousal notification with respect to married women.

The 3rd Circuit's interpretation of the drift of Supreme Court cases prior to *Casey* was apparently correct. When *Casey* was heard and decided by the Supreme Court, the Court explicitly rejected *Roe*'s rigid trimester system and abandoned the strict scrutiny/compelling state interest test. It adopted the undue burden test. While the Court in *Casey* clearly backed off from the protection of a woman's right to choose that had been provided by *Roe v. Wade*, it did not, as many had anticipated, overrule *Roe* and allow states a free hand in restricting abortion. Yet four of the nine Justices seemed firm in their belief that *Roe* should be overturned entirely. Under *Casey*, the law now is that state regulation of abortion is valid unless it places an undue burden on a woman's right to choose. The Court stated that: "the undue burden standard is the appropriate means of reconciling the State's interest with the woman's constitutionally protected liberty."[20] It affirmed the 3rd Circuit's decision that the provisions of the Pennsylvania law involving informed consent (information giving), parental consent or court approval for minors, and the 24-hour waiting period were not undue burdens and were

---

18. 109 S. Ct. 3040 (1989).

19. 947 F.2d 682 (1991).

20. *Planned Parenthood v. Casey*, 112 S. Ct. 2791 at 2820 (1992).

valid. They also found that the spousal notice requirement was an undue burden and was thus invalid.

The spousal notice requirement was found to create an undue burden in *Casey* because of the large number of different situations in which women may reasonably fear dire consequences from notifying their husbands about a contemplated abortion. That fear is likely to dissuade many from seeking an abortion, and the notice requirement thus creates an undue burden on a woman's abortion decision. In the 1976 case of *Planned Parenthood v. Danforth*,[21] the Supreme Court had faced the father's rights issue: Should a father have the right to veto an abortion? In *Danforth*, a Missouri statute required prior written consent of the spouse unless the abortion was to save the life of the mother. The Supreme Court found that the statute was unconstitutional. The Court's opinion was grounded on logic and precedent relating to *Roe v. Wade* and also on practical reality. The Court reasoned that since *Roe* had decided that a state did not have the power to prohibit at least a first trimester abortion if the mother wanted it, a state could not delegate to the spouse a power that the state itself did not have. On the pragmatic level, the court recognized that where mother and father disagreed, only one of them can physically prevail. The Court in *Casey* quoted its own language from *Danforth* saying:

> We recognize that a husband has a ''deep and proper concern and interest . . . in his wife's pregnancy and in the growth and development of the fetus she is carrying.'' . . . [but] ''Inasmuch as it is the woman who physically bears the child and who is the more directly and immediately affected by the pregnancy, as between the two, the balance weighs in her favor.''[22]

Another ''consent'' issue with respect to abortion that the Court considered in *Casey* arises in the context of a state seeking to require parental consent prior to a minor obtaining an abortion. In *Danforth*, the Supreme Court had held that a state may not impose a blanket provision requiring such parental consent as a condition on an abortion. Subsequent to *Danforth*, Massachusetts attempted to reconcile its interests in encouraging parental advice in abortion situations with the right of a woman to choose to terminate her pregnancy. Massachusetts required the seeking of parental consent, but if that consent were refused, authorization for the abortion could be obtained through a court order with the judge basing his decision exclusively on what would serve

---

21. 428 U.S. 52 (1976).

22. 112 S. Ct. 2791 at 2830.

the minor's best interests. The Supreme Court, in *Bellotti v. Baird*, [23] found that although the Massachusetts statute was not a "blanket prohibition," the requirement that the minor first consult with her parents imposed "an undue burden upon the exercise by minors of the right to seek an abortion" because of the vulnerability of a minor to having her parents obstruct her going to the court or having an abortion.

In *Bellotti*, the Court's opinion stated:

> . . . every minor must have the opportunity—if she so desires—to go directly to a court without first consulting or notifying her parents. If she satisfies the court that she is mature and well-enough informed to make intelligently the abortion decision on her own, the court must authorize her to act without parental consultation or consent.

Even without this independent competency showing, the court must permit an abortion if the minor shows it would be in her "best interests." Following the *Bellotti* decision, Massachusetts enacted legislation to conform to the *Bellotti* requirements of access to the courts without parental involvement. Since *Bellotti*, a wide variety of parental consent and parental notification statutes have been found to be constitutional so long as they contain an appropriate "judicial bypass" of access to the Courts without parental knowledge for mature minors.[24] The Court in *Casey* held that the Pennsylvania requirement of parental consent with a judicial bypass procedure was valid. The judicial bypass approach may be fatally flawed in practical terms from the perspective of both those who favor some control over a minor's abortion decision and those who favor no control.

Those who favor control would cite a review of the post-*Bellotti* statute that appeared in the *Boston Globe* newspaper on March 31, 1982. That review found that 647 pregnant minors had received court permission for abortions while none had been refused permission. If the minor showed maturity, the abortion must be allowed. In situations where maturity is not shown, even those judges who oppose abortion could see no way to substantiate a judicial determination that the forcing of a clearly immature minor to have her baby against her wishes would be in her "best interests." Those who oppose any approval requirements prior to a minor undergoing an abortion also criticize the statute because of the traumatic and inhibiting effects that it produces. Should a 16-year-old girl have to go to a courthouse and appear in front of a male judge and answer questions pertaining to her sex life and abortion?

---

23. 443 U.S. 622 (1979).

24. *Hodgson v. Minnesota*, 110 S. Ct. 2926 (1990); *Ohio v. Akron Center for Reproductive Health*, 110 S. Ct. 2972 (1990).

Besides the inhibition on the exercise of her constitutional right which the prospect of such a proceeding may create for the girl, seemingly insignificant concerns such as having to go to court during school hours and possibly having her parents find out may inhibit the exercise of her rights. The practical results of the statute may include discouraging minors from asserting their constitutional right to an abortion, encouraging them to go to another state to have an abortion, or encouraging them to seek an illegal abortion.

Let's further consider the practical effect and the scope of the "constitutional right" to have an abortion by looking at the issue of public funding of abortions. Connecticut participated in the federal Medicaid program and paid for childbirth but refused to pay for nontherapeutic abortions as part of the program. In *Maher v. Roe*,[25] an indigent woman who wanted a nontherapeutic abortion contended that by paying the medical bills of women choosing childbirth, but refusing to pay the bills of those choosing abortion, Connecticut was establishing discriminatory classifications in violation of the Equal Protection Clause of the Fourteenth Amendment[26] to the United States Constitution. The Court in *Roe v. Wade* had found that the right to have an abortion was a fundamental right. In *Maher*, the Court found that there is no fundamental right to a free abortion. Without there being any interference with a fundamental right, and without there being any discrimination against an "inherently suspect classification" of people (race is an inherently suspect classification, but poverty is not), the state did not need to have a "compelling state interest" for treating "childbirth women" and "abortion women" unequally. Different treatment would be acceptable under the Equal Protection Clause so long as a "reasonable basis" for the classification is shown. Making references to the state's interests in encouraging normal childbirth and in choosing among competing demands for limited public funds, the Court found that there was a "reasonable basis" for the classification.

Maher said that a state was not required to fund nontherapeutic abortions through Medicaid, but it specifically said that a state was free to provide such benefits if it so decided. Federal law, in the form of various versions of the Hyde Amendment to appropriations bills, has precluded the use of Medicaid funds even for medically necessary abortions in all but limited situations, such as those threatening the life of the woman. The question of abortion funding thus moved from the state legislative forum to Congress, and Congress's 1979 Hyde Amendment[27] was challenged with respect to

---

25. 432 U.S. 464 (1977).

26. See footnote 12.

27. P.L. No. 96–123, § 109.

its constitutionality in *Harris v. McRae*.[28]

In *McRae*, a Medicaid recipient in the first trimester of a pregnancy that she wished to terminate contended that the Hyde Amendment's prohibition on the use of Medicaid funds to pay for an abortion for her, even if the state wanted to so use the funds, was unconstitutional. She claimed that the prohibition was unconstitutional as a denial of Equal Protection, as a violation of the Due Process Clause of the Fifth Amendment,[29] and as an establishment of religion in violation of the First Amendment.[30] The Supreme Court found that the Hyde Amendment was constitutional. It rejected the Equal Protection argument along lines similar to those discussed above with respect to *Maher*. Responding to the Due Process argument, the Court said that although the "liberty" protected by the Due Process Clause affords protection against governmental interference with freedom of choice in certain personal situations, it does not confer an entitlement to the funds that may be needed to realize the advantage of that freedom. Just because government may not prevent parents from sending a child to private school does not mean that government has an affirmative constitutional obligation to provide the funding to allow all persons to implement such a decision. Concerning the Establishment of Religion argument, the Court said that even though the Hyde Amendment may incorporate into the law a doctrine of the Catholic Church, the fact that a law may coincide with the tenets of a religion does not, without something more being present, constitute an "establishment of religion," i.e., the aiding of religion in general or the preferring of one religion over another.

The issue of the use of public funds in relation to obtaining an abortion arose in a different context in the 1991 case of *Rust v. Sullivan*.[31] Instead of a congressional or state prohibition on the use of public funds to pay for an abortion, *Rust* involved regulations of the federal Department of Health and Human Services that prohibited any family planning service which received federal funds, such as Planned Parenthood, from engaging in abortion counseling, referral, or activities advocating abortion as a method of family planning. The regulations were challenged on the grounds that they interfered with the free speech rights of the family planning services, their employees, and their patients; that they violated a woman's right to choose whether to terminate a pregnancy; and that they infringed on the doctor/patient

---

28. 100 S. Ct. 2671 (1980).

29. "No person shall be . . . deprived of life, liberty, or property, without due process of law . . . ."

30. "Congress shall make no law respecting an establishment of religion. . . ."

31. 111 S.Ct. 1759 (1991).

relationship. The Supreme Court, adhering to its approach in *Maher* and *McRae*, found no unconstitutionality. It said that the regulations did not restrict speech about abortion; they simply refused to subsidize it. Similarly, the regulations did not restrict a woman's ability to exercise her constitutionally protected freedom of choice; they simply refused to subsidize her. The court quoted from *McRae* saying:

> The financial constraints that restrict an indigent woman's ability to enjoy the full range of constitutionally protected freedom of choice are the product not of governmental restrictions on access to abortion, but rather of her indigency.

The Supreme Court vote in *Rust* was 5–4.

Arguments have been made that the practical effect of the Court's upholding the administrative regulations in *Rust* is that family planning clinics and counselors who receive federal funds will be caught in a trap. If they choose to continue receiving public funding, they will not be able to provide a full range of accurate medical information. That is wrong from the patient's perspective and may even expose the provider to liability. If they choose to turn down public funding, they will find it impossible to provide services to women who cannot afford to pay for medical and family planning advice. Congress responded by passing legislation that would have blocked implementation of the "gag rule" regulations that had been upheld in *Rust*. Although Congress passed the legislation, President Bush vetoed it, and there were not enough votes in Congress to override the veto.[32] Prior to implementing the "gag rule," the Department of Health and Human Services modified it to allow doctors, but not nurses or counselors, to provide complete medical information including advice about abortion. The guidelines allowed federally funded family planning projects to refer women "to full-service health providers that perform abortions but not to providers whose principal activity is providing abortion services."[33] Further evidence of the continuing volatility of abortion issues is seen in one of President Clinton's first actions after taking office. On the 20th anniversary of *Roe v. Wade*, President Clinton signed a memorandum that repealed the administrative agency ban on abortion counseling at federally funded clinics.[34]

---

32. "Bill to Let Clinics Discuss Abortion is Vetoed by Bush," *New York Times* (Nov. 20, 1991) p. 1.

33. "Implementation of Title X Abortion Regulation," March 20, 1992, Internal Memorandum of the Department of Health and Human Services clarifying Title X issues raised by the "gag rule" provisions of 42 CFR §§ 59.7–59.10.

34. "Settling In: Easing Abortion Policy; Clinton Orders Reversal of Abortion Restrictions Left by Reagan and Bush," *New York Times* (Jan. 23, 1993) p. 1.

The closeness of the Supreme Court's votes on abortion cases over the years, the tendency of the Court to swing from one position to another, the closeness of votes concerning abortion issues in the legislatures, and the changing position of agencies depending on who is President emphasize the question of whether any part of government should be involved with sensitive moral questions such as abortion. One can say that even if there is to be any governmental involvement in such an area, it should at least be by the elected legislature. On the other hand, it can be said that a major purpose of the Constitution is to protect individuals from the imposition of the political majority's judgment of what is morally acceptable and socially desirable. Freedom of speech, freedom of religion, as well as the right of privacy are protections against the majority's elected legislature, and those protections are entrusted by the Constitution to the care of the courts. Even if one advocates the position that the courts, by use of the Constitution, are supposed to protect the individual from the majority, one must be aware that the protection only exists so long as the Constitution contains the source of protection. If a constitutional amendment were enacted to prohibit abortion, the rules would all change, since a validly enacted constitutional amendment cannot be declared unconstitutional. Similarly, a constitutional amendment allowing abortion could not be declared unconstitutional. While no such amendments currently exist, many efforts have been made to incorporate some form of prohibition on abortions into the United States Constitution due to the absence of any longstanding and unwavering commitment by the courts to allow states to restrict or prohibit abortions. Conversely, a definitive commitment by the courts to allow state restrictions on abortion could lead to efforts to amend the Constitution to explicitly recognize a woman's right to determine whether her pregnancy should continue. At the same time that the Supreme Court was considering whether to accept the case of *Planned Parenthood v. Casey* as a vehicle for either reaffirming the right to an abortion under *Roe v. Wade* or for overruling *Roe*, full page national newspaper advertisements announced a campaign to enact a "federal statute or if necessary a Constitutional amendment" that would "explicitly guarantee the right to reproductive choice, leaving no room for restrictive interpretation by a hostile Court."[35] The Freedom of Choice Act was then introduced in both the House and the Senate.[36] The Supreme Court's undue burden test in *Planned Parenthood v. Casey* does not satisfy either those who oppose abortion or those who favor a woman's choice. Perhaps the only thing that can be said with certainty about the abortion issue in the United States is

35. American Civil Liberties Union, *New York Times* (Jan. 19, 1992) p. E20.

36. American Civil Liberties Union/Reproductive Freedom Project, *Reproductive Rights Update* (Vol. IV, No. 4, Feb. 28, 1992).

that, regardless of what courts decide, what Congress or state legislatures enact, or even what might be expressed in an amendment to the Constitution, abortion will continue to be a political and legal issue, as well as a moral issue, for many years to come.

ADDITIONAL READINGS

Annual Review of Population Law (New York: United Nations Population Fund).

Bean, F.D., Vernez, G. and Keely, C.B., *Opening and Closing the Doors: Evaluating Immigration Reform and Control* (Washington, DC: Urban Institute Press, 1989).

Ehrlich, P.R. & A.H., *The Population Explosion* (New York: Simon and Schuster, 1990).

Hartmann, B., *Reproductive Rights and Wrongs: The Global Politics of Population Control and Contraceptive Choice* (New York: Harper & Row, 1987).

Population and Environment: A Journal of Interdisciplinary Studies (New York: Human Sciences Press).

Salvatore, D., *World Population Trends and Their Impact on Economic Development* (New York: Greenwood Press, 1988).

Santos, M.A., *Managing Planet Earth: Perspectives on Population, Ecology, and the Law* (New York: Bergin and Garvey Publishers, 1990).

Wattenberg, B.J., *The Birth Dearth* (New York: Pharos Books, 1989).

CHAPTER 9

GLOBAL ENVIRONMENTAL LAW

A. SUBSETS OF GLOBAL ENVIRONMENTAL LAW

When many people refer to environmental law in a context that encompasses matters outside their own country, they generally use "international environmental law" as the title of their topic. A better title might be "global environmental law" because international environmental law is only one of three subsets of global environmental law. The other two are comparative environmental law and extraterritorial application and effects of national environmental law. Let's begin by seeing how these parts of the global environmental law matrix are different from each other. We will then consider the importance of having environmental control mechanisms in each of the subsets of global environmental law along with specific examples of what those control mechanisms are and how they work.

International environmental law is law which is applicable to more than one country. The most common example is where nations become parties to a treaty such as The Montreal Protocol which concerns stratospheric ozone depletion.[1] When the required number of countries stated in the treaty become parties to the treaty and the treaty thus "enters into force," those countries have expressly created international law. International law can also be created implicitly. This happens when there is a uniform practice followed by most nations, when general principles of law are recognized by nations, or when judicial decisions and writings by respected scholars indicate that nations have agreed, albeit without a treaty. This is known as customary international law.

An interesting example of customary international law is one of the early disputes involving transboundary air pollution and the newly discovered

---

1. 26 International Legal Materials 1541 (1987) and 1990 Amendments.

possibility of the phenomenon of acid rain. An arbitral tribunal was constituted to decide what should be done about the Trail Smelter in Canada whose emissions were going to the State of Washington in the U.S. and causing damage. The damage may have been greater than usual when the emissions mixed with precipitation. The tribunal said:

> no State has the right to use or permit the use of its territory in such
> a manner as to cause injury by fumes in or to the territory of another
> or the properties or person therein . . . .[2]

A nation's sovereignty over activities in its territory is therefore limited by its responsibility to not cause damage outside of its territory. This customary international environmental law principle of limiting sovereignty was also stated in Principle 21 of the Declaration of The United Nations Conference on the Human Environment which said that countries have the "responsibility to ensure that activities within their jurisdiction or control do not cause damage to the environment of other States or of areas beyond the limits of national jurisdiction."[3] Customary international law does play a role in international environmental law, but most international environmental law involves treaties. These will be discussed in Section C of this chapter.

International environmental law usually pertains to situations where activities in one country cause effects in other nations or to the global commons. Our second subset of global environmental law, extraterritorial application of national environmental law, also has effects outside the borders of the nation in which the activity takes place, but this body of environmental law is not international. It is not composed of treaties and customary international principles. Rather, it is the law of an individual country, but it may have environmental effects on other countries. Two examples of national law with extraterritorial effects that have been discussed earlier in this book are U.S. law with respect to the export of solid waste and pesticides. Concerning solid waste export, U.S. law is largely passive. By having no law, we allow the potentially adverse extraterritorial effects of export. In the pesticide area, we go beyond being passive. Our federal pesticide legislation explicitly allows unregistered and banned pesticides manufactured in the U.S. to be exported. Although this is a hotly debated topic and many efforts have been made to change this law, we do, with respect to pesticide export, specifically allow extraterritorial effects which may be adverse but which some people say

---

2. 35 Am. J. International 684 at 716 (1941).

3. U.N. Doc. A/Conf. 48/14/Rev. 1. This language is also part of Article 3 of the 1992 U.N. Framework Convention on Biological Diversity.

are not adverse and may even be beneficial.[4] Three additional examples of national laws or non-laws with significant possibilities for extraterritorial effects will be discussed in Section B. These will be the U.S. National Environmental Policy Act (NEPA), Brazil's allowing of rainforest cutting, and the labeling laws of Austria and the European Community which are designed to encourage environmental protection through the use of consumer buying power.

Our third subset of global environmental law is comparative environmental law. This facet of global environmental law also involves national as opposed to international law. Comparative law asks how do two or more individual nations, each using its own national law, deal with the same or similar factual situations that exist in their nations. While a fact situation in a country may have extraterritorial effects, comparative law is primarily interested in the differences and similarities with respect to the approaches that nations would use to handle the situation. If an environmental dispute involving land use exists between neighbors, how will it be resolved in the People's Republic of China compared to in the United States? Will the Russian government, like the U.S. government, conduct a site specific analysis to value the actual harm that an oil spill has caused to a natural resource? Might the culture of some nations allow them to successfully achieve environmental protection without the use of law? Comparative environmental law looks at the differences and similarities in approaches and asks questions such as are the differences explainable and appropriate in view of different cultures, geography, economics, etc., or should efforts be made to determine which is the "best" approach and to encourage uniform use of that approach. These comparative environmental law examples and issues will be discussed in Section D.

B. EXTRATERRITORIAL APPLICATION AND EFFECTS OF NATIONAL LAW

There are many activities that take place within the borders of one nation but have very significant effects outside that nation—effects on other nations directly or effects on parts of the global commons such as air and oceans. Unless there is international law like a treaty, these activities are subject only to the national law of the country in which they are located. If the national law of that country does not apply to environmental effects outside the country and if the activity does not produce environmental effects within

---

4. 7 U.S.C. § 136o, discussed in Chapter 6.

the country that trigger environmental controls, the activity is not subject to any environmental controls. In the United States, the National Environmental Policy Act (NEPA) is the most common context that raises the issue of whether extraterritorial effects will trigger U.S. environmental control mechanisms.[5] As discussed in Chapter 2, NEPA requires that all agencies of the federal government prepare an environmental impact statement (EIS) for any major federal action significantly affecting the quality of the human environment. Do environmental effects outside of the United States which would result from federal agency action fall within NEPA's EIS requirement, or are those effects not subject to NEPA's environmental controls?

The extraterritorial application of NEPA issue has arisen in numerous factual situations including highway construction in Central America involving the U.S. Department of Transportation,[6] the exporting of nuclear power plant components to the Philippines,[7] and, more recently, the U.S. Army's transporting 100,000 artillery shells containing nerve gas in Germany[8] and the National Science Foundation's plan to incinerate its waste at its facility in Antarctica.[9] NEPA appears to have a domestic orientation since it asks the federal government to "assure for all Americans safe, healthful, productive, and aesthetically and culturally pleasing surroundings."[10] It also, however, says that all agencies of the federal government shall:

> recognize the worldwide and long-range character of environmental problems and, where consistent with the foreign policy of the United States, lend appropriate support to initiatives, resolutions, and programs designed to maximize international cooperation in anticipating and preventing a decline in the quality of mankind's world environment.[11]

The courts have often not provided clear answers concerning NEPA's extraterritorial applicability. Thus, an EIS was required for the military to

---

5. Other contexts include the Resource Conservation and Recovery Act with respect to extraterritorial disposal of hazardous waste by private parties—not applicable, *Amlon Metals, Inc. v. FMC Corp.*, 775 F. Supp. 668 (1991) and the Endangered Species Act—applicable by Circuit Court of Appeals decision although the case was reversed on other grounds by the Supreme Court, *Defenders of Wildlife v. Lujan*, 911 F.2d 117, 125 (1990), 112 S. Ct. 2130 (1992). See McDougall, M., "Extraterritoriality and The Endangered Species Act of 1973," *80 Georgetown Law Journal 435* (1991).

6. *Sierra Club v. Adams*, 578 F.2d 389 (1978).

7. *Natural Resources Defense Council, Inc. v. Nuclear Regulatory Commission*, 647 F.2d 1345 (1981).

8. *Greenpeace USA v. Stone*, 748 F. Supp. 749 (1990).

9. *Environmental Defense Fund, Inc. v. Massey*, 1993 WL 11633.

10. PL 91–190, § 101(b)(2).

11. PL 91–190, § 102(F).

conduct a simulated nuclear explosion on a Pacific atoll, but, at least in part, the decision was based on the site being in a U.S. Trust Territory.[12] In the cases discussed above involving export of nuclear power plant components and the transportation of nerve gas, the courts' decisions not to require an EIS reflected concern about interference with U.S. foreign policy. Making the situation even murkier is Executive Order 12114, issued by President Carter.[13] E.O. 12114 establishes on environmental review process for extraterritorial effects of government actions, but it is expressly stated to be based on the President's independent authority rather than on NEPA. It therefore takes the position that NEPA does not have extraterritorial applicability. This might be irrelevant if the E.O. environmental review process were the same as the EIS requirement of NEPA, but it differs significantly.

Although an EIS is required under the Executive Order for federal actions affecting the global commons (e.g. the oceans or Antarctica), lesser evaluations, "environmental studies" or "concise reviews of the environmental issues," are sufficient for effects in countries that are not participating or involved with the U.S. agency action, and no environmental evaluation is required for effects in a country that is "participating."[14] While this non-review position may be defended on the grounds of not wanting to interfere with the sovereignty of another nation, one should at least question the degree to which an impoverished Third World country, dependent on foreign aid, can be said to be "voluntarily" agreeing to a U.S. activity that may result in environmental harm.

Another important difference between NEPA and E.O. 12114 is that the Executive Order says:

> This Order is solely for the purpose of establishing internal procedures for Federal agencies . . . and nothing in this Order shall be construed to create a cause of action [in a court].

This provision led the court in the 1993 Antarctica incineration case, *Environmental Defense Fund, Inc. v. Massey*,[15] to say:

> Thus, what is at stake in this litigation is whether a federal agency may decide to take actions significantly affecting the human environment in Antarctica without complying with NEPA and without being subject to judicial review.

---

12. *People of Enewetak v. Laird*, 353 F. Supp. 811 (1973).

13. 3 CFR 356.

14. E.O. 12114, § 2–4.

15. 1993 WL 11633.

In *Massey*, the National Science Foundation (NSF) contended that it did not need to do an EIS prior to operating its incinerator in Antarctica because NEPA does not apply to federal agency actions outside the U.S. It also contended that E.O. 12114, which it said covers extraterritorial environmental analysis, does not create a cause of action, and, therefore, courts do not have jurisdiction to hear cases alleging that an agency has not followed the E.O. procedures. The Federal District Court granted NSF's motion to dismiss the case, clearly stating that "NEPA does not apply extraterritorially and Executive Order 12114 does not provide for a private cause of action."[16] The U.S. Circuit Court of Appeals for the District of Columbia found that NEPA did apply to the Antarctica incineration proposal, and it reversed the District Court decision.

The Circuit Court in *Massey*[17] noted the U.S. Supreme Court's general presumption against extraterritorial application of statutes and the primary purpose of that presumption as being "to protect against the unintended clashes between our laws and those of other nations which could result in international discord."[18] The court in *Massey*, however, found this presumption to be inapplicable because to apply NEPA would not tend toward international discord. First, the NEPA EIS process is designed to control decisionmaking by an agency, not the substance of the agency decision. The decisionmaking process is done in the U.S., regardless of the fact that the incineration would be in Antarctica. Thus there are no issues of extraterritoriality and international conflict. Second, since Antarctica, under the Antarctic Treaty of 1961, is not subject to the sovereign rule of any nation, there is no potential for conflict between U.S. law and that of other nations. The conflict avoidance purpose of the presumption against extraterritorial application is not present.

The Circuit Court found that NEPA is applicable to agency action in Antarctica. It barely mentioned E.O. 12114 and certainly did not find it reduced the agency's responsibility to comply with the EIS requirements of NEPA. Not long after the Circuit Court's decision, the Clinton Administration announced it would not appeal the decision to the Supreme Court.[19] So where does the issue of the extraterritorial application of NEPA stand? The *Massey* decision is not a broad declaration that NEPA applies extraterritorially. In fact the court concluded: "[W]e do not decide today

---

16. 772 F. Supp. 1296, 1298 (1991).

17. 1993 WL 11633.

18. *Equal Employment Opportunity Commission v. Arabian American Oil Co.*, 111 S. Ct. 1227 (1991).

19. "Clinton Accepts Landmark Environmental Ruling," *The Reuter Library Report* (March 16, 1993) NEXIS; LBYRPT.

how NEPA might apply to actions in a case involving an actual foreign sovereign . . . ." The court also noted that NEPA's EIS requirement may yield where overriding policy concerns such as national security and foreign policy are present. While not a broad declaration of extraterritorial applicability, *Massey* and the Executive Branch's apparent acceptance of its result indicate a trend toward extraterritorial application, yet, after all the years of controversy, shouldn't NEPA be amended to clarify its application to environmental impacts abroad? With respect to the substance of such a clarification, shouldn't the environmental evaluation required by NEPA be the same regardless of whether the environmental effects of government action will be outside or inside the borders of the United States?

Our second example of the extraterritorial application and effects of national law is the cutting and burning of the rainforest in Brazil. The issue of extraterritorial application of the national law of Brazil is much less developed than that of our NEPA scenario, but the extraterritorial effects on the global commons may be more important, more difficult to ascertain, and more difficult to control than those from a relatively small incinerator activity in Antarctica. Until recently, there were virtually no controls in Brazil to prevent rainforest destruction. In fact, there were government incentives that encouraged deforestation. From the 1960s through the 1980s, Brazil tried to develop the Amazon by exempting farmers and ranchers from income and other taxes.[20] Those who cleared the rainforest for agriculture were the beneficiaries of the tax incentives, while the losers are said to be global climate and global biological diversity.

Burning the rainforest has produced billions of tons of carbon dioxide which climate experts contend builds up in the atmosphere and traps the earth's heat. This is the greenhouse effect and results in global warming. In addition, with fewer trees due to burning or cutting of the rainforest, less CO_2 is taken out of the atmosphere and converted to oxygen in the photosynthesis process. This may also contribute to the greenhouse effect. Besides global climate effects, rainforest deforestation destroys some of the world's richest areas of biological diversity. This leads to a vast array of environmental consequences, known and unknown in both types and magnitudes. Among these are destruction of the ecological processes that keep the Earth in balance and fit for life and destruction of genetic stocks which may be important for the future health and nutrition of humans.[21] Indeed, the importance of the topics of global warming and biological diversity, both

---

20. "Slower Rate of Amazon Deforestation Due to Economic Crisis, Expert Says," *International Environment Reporter* (April 22, 1992) p. 241.

21. *Caring for the Earth: A Strategy for Sustainable Living* (U.N. Environment Programme, 1991).

related to rainforest destruction, is underscored by their being the subject of the two treaties that came out of UNCED, the United Nations Conference on Environment and Development, held at Rio de Janeiro in 1992 and known as the Earth Summit.[22]

The tax incentives that encouraged deforestation in Brazil were discontinued beginning in 1989. Deforestation in Brazil today is largely caused by land speculation, which may be fueled by highway construction paid for by the government or by international organizations such as the World Bank. The Brazilian government notes that the area cleared during one year dipped by 20% after the removal of the tax incentives, yet over 11,000 square kilometers are still being cleared annually.[23] Why, with the huge potential for global impacts, does Brazil not enact national law that would stop rainforest destruction and prevent extraterritorial adverse effects? The question is largely one of rich nations and poor nations, developed countries and the less developed countries, north and south.

The poorer, developing countries take the position that the richer, developed nations achieved their success without environmental restrictions or concern for the rest of the world. Now the "haves" want the "have nots" to be environmentally responsible for the good of all. The people of the developing countries also have a different view of what are the significant environmental problems. This is not a new conflict. In the 1972 Declaration of The United Nations Conference on the Human Environment (Stockholm Conference), it was proclaimed that:

> 4. In the developing countries most of the environmental problems are caused by under-development. Millions continue to live far below the minimum levels required for a decent human existence, deprived of adequate food and clothing, shelter and education, health and sanitation. Therefore, the developing countries must direct their efforts to development, bearing in mind their priorities and the need to safeguard and improve the environment. For the same purpose, the industrialized countries should make efforts to reduce the gap between themselves and the developing countries. In the industrialized countries, environmental problems are generally related to industrialization and technological development.[24]

The 1992 United Nations Framework Convention on Climate Change contains a similar perspective:

---

22. U.N. Framework Convention on Climate Change and U.N. Framework Convention on Biological Diversity, *International Environment Reporter Reference File 1*, 21:3901 and 21:4001.

23. "Slower Rate of Amazon Deforestation Due to Economic Crisis, Expert Says," *International Environment Reporter* (April 22, 1992) p. 241.

24. U.N. Doc. A/ Conf. 48/14/Rev. 1.

7. The extent to which developing country Parties will effectively implement their commitments under the Convention will depend on the effective implementation by developed country Parties of their commitments under the Convention related to financial resources and transfer of technology and will take fully into account that economic and social development and poverty eradication are the first and overriding priorities of the developing country Parties.[25]

The ability to close the gap between the highly divergent standards of living in developed and developing countries is complicated by the tremendous foreign debt owed by Third World countries. This debt load puts great pressure on poor nations to expand their economies at the expense of environmental concerns. With respect to Brazil and its rainforest, proposals have been made to Brazil to swap some of its over $100 billion foreign debt for commitments to protect rainforest land (debt-for-nature swaps).[26] To Brazilians, this approach raises the issue of loss of sovereignty over their resources, and loss of sovereignty may be far worse than being in debt. The real answer to Brazil's preventing the extraterritorial impacts from destruction of its rainforests is probably its becoming able, with help from those outside of Brazil who all have a major stake in rainforest protection, to provide sustainable income to its people. If a poor nation is to be expected to take action to protect its land from being depleted of its economically valuable resources, it must be able to provide for the current needs of its people and for improving their standard of living. It must be assisted in achieving sustainable development of its resources.

Our third example of national law with extraterritorial effects is labeling of products to indicate their consistency with environmental protection. Here we do not have to stray from our discussion of tropical forests to find an example to begin our discussion. Austrian law requires a label showing the origin of tropical wood and tropical wood products.[27] This law will presumably allow consumers to make their purchasing choices with awareness that obtaining the wood may have contributed to adverse environmental effects. On a broader scale, the European Community, a group of nations but acting as a single nation under law established by the Community, has adopted an "eco-label" to tell consumers that the product with the label is less damaging to the environment than other products. With 340 million EC consumers, there is great potential for market forces to provide significant

---

25. *International Environment Reporter Reference File 1*, 21:3901.

26. "Playing with Fire," *Time* (Sept. 18, 1989) p. 76.

27. "Government Called on to Alter Law Requiring Labels on Tropical Wood, Products," *International Environment Reporter* (March 10, 1993) p. 176.

environmental protection.[28] As an example of the extraterritorial effect of EC eco-labeling, imported leather for shoes and bags will be judged based on how the leather was tanned and dyed. Leather tanning is an extremely polluting business, and non-EC suppliers from Turkey to Morocco may decide to use more "environmentally friendly" processes in order to be able to sell in the EC. Indications are that eco-labeling does result in greater environmental protection. Since Germany began eco-labeling, those manufacturers who have gotten the eco-label have reported a 10 to 30 percent increase in sales. Also, both German and non-German manufacturers have been redesigning their products to comply with the standards for obtaining an eco-label. In this instance, national law appears to be having a positive effect on the environment beyond the borders of the nation that enacted the law.

C. INTERNATIONAL ENVIRONMENTAL LAW

The most commonly discussed subset of global environmental law is international environmental law. International law also holds the greatest promise for solving environmental problems if the nations of the world can agree on what the problems are and on unified action to prevent or remedy those problems. The paramount example of international law's ability to recognize a problem, enact a solution, and apparently achieve success is the Montreal Protocol on Substances That Deplete the Ozone Layer.[29] The Montreal Protocol is a treaty, and treaties are the most meaningful form of international environmental law. We noted customary environmental law earlier as a way of implicitly establishing principles such as a nations responsibility to not cause damage outside its territory, and we will later consider United Nations' resolutions and programs as part of international environmental law, but our focus in this section will be treaties—express agreements by more than one country to establish law that is applicable to more than one country.

There are many ways to categorize treaties such as: (1) are they between two countries (bilateral) or are they multilateral, (2) do they use financial liability to remedy problems or do they create a system of preventative controls, (3) do they establish a separate entity with power to act in a situation or do they rely on the individual parties to the treaty to each act themselves, (4) are they merely statements of cooperative intentions, are they frameworks

28. "12 Countries, 340 Million Shoppers, One Planet," *New York Times* (April 11, 1993) Section 4, p. 5.

29. 26 International Legal Materials 1541 (1987) and 1990 Amendments.

for future treaties but non-binding in and of themselves, or do they establish substantive mechanisms to control an environmental problem, and (5) are they treaties directed specifically at environmental issues or are they treaties that are directed at other subject matter like trade but have significant environmental implications? We will discuss a number of treaties that are examples of these various approaches of international environmental law. Let's begin with what is hoped will be a dramatic international environmental success story—The Montreal Protocol.

The significance of The Montreal Protocol begins with the magnitude and timing of the stratospheric ozone layer depletion issue. Although possible depletion of the ozone layer that shields Earth from ultraviolet radiation was raised in 1974,[30] it only became widely publicized in 1985. By 1989, a treaty, The Montreal Protocol to protect the ozone layer, had been drafted, agreed to, and formally ratified by 29 countries and the European Community— enough to have the treaty enter into force.[31] In the international environmental law timeframe, this time period between problem acknowledgement and "in force" standards to solve the ozone problem is unrivaled in its brevity. A short explanation of the process and effects of ozone layer depletion will indicate why the international community was motivated to act so quickly.

Photochemical reactions in the stratosphere constantly create and destroy ozone, but the presence of CFCs, halons, and other gases alter the balance. These gases, having been produced at ground level, migrate to the stratosphere where they are broken down due to ultraviolet radiation, and the breakdown releases chlorine. Chlorine atoms react with ozone to destroy the ozone without destroying themselves. Thus the chlorine remains to continue destroying more ozone. A small amount of chlorine can destroy a large amount of ozone.[32] Figure 1 shows the increased levels of global CFC releases over the years.

Increased ultraviolet radiation because of lack of protection from the ozone layer has numerous possible effects. Among the more publicized are skin cancer, depression of the human immune system, and reduced crop yields due to a decrease in photosynthesis. Others include fading paint, cataracts, and harm to phytoplankton which are the source of food for most fish. The type, variety, and magnitude of the effects of ozone layer depletion make it easy to understand the need for quick action.

30. Molina and Rowland, "Stratospheric Sink for Chlorofluoromethanes: Chlorine Atom— Catalyzed Destruction of Ozone," *Nature* (1974) pp. 910–12.

31. 26 I.L.M. 1541.

32. Mintz, J., "Keeping Pandora's Box Shut: A Critical Assessment of the Montreal Protocol on Substances that Deplete the Ozone Layer," 20 *U. Miami Inter-Am Law Review*, (1989) pp. 566–68.

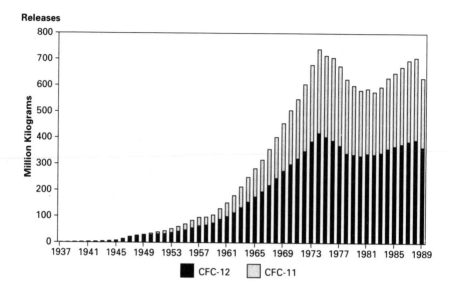

Figure 1.   Global Releases of Chlorofluorocarbons (CFCs).[33]

The Montreal Protocol is a multilateral treaty that contains specific control measures to stop ozone layer depletion and allow its "regrowth." It requires that each party to the treaty act to create its own national law to achieve the targets and timetables established in the treaty. As amended in 1990, it has control measures and control levels in Articles 2, 2 A-E, and Article 3 with respect to the production and consumption of CFCs, Halons, Carlon Tetrachloride, and other ozone depleting substances. For example, with respect to CFCs, Article 2 provides in part:

> Each Party shall ensure that for the twelve-month period commencing on 1 January 1995, and in each twelve-month period thereafter, its calculated level of consumption of the controlled substances in Group I of Annex A does not exceed, annually, fifty percent of its calculated level of consumption in 1986. Each Party producing one or more of these substances shall, for the same periods, ensure that its calculated level of production of the substances does not exceed, annually, fifty percent of its calculated level of production in 1986.

---

33. Council on Environmental Quality, *Environmental Quality 1991, 22nd Annual Report* (Washington, DC: March, 1992) p. 124.

More stringent phaseout levels are provided for subsequent years, culminating with annual calculated levels of consumption and production of zero for the Group I, Annex A CFCs.

In our discussion of the issue of rainforest protection, we noted the divergent economic situations and thus divergent perspectives held by the developed as opposed to the developing countries. The Montreal Protocol about ozone seeks to account for the "Special Situation of Developing Countries"—the title of Article 5. For example, a developing country whose annual level of consumption of Annex A controlled substances is less than 0.3 kilograms per capita is entitled to delay its compliance with the control measures for 10 years. In addition, Articles 10 and 10A require that developing countries be provided with financial and technological assistance including the transfer "under fair and most favorable conditions" of "the best available, environmentally safe substitutes and related technologies." Further, Article 5 notes that for developing countries to meet even the delayed compliance schedule will depend upon the effective implementation of financial co-operation and transfer of technology. The Montreal Protocol thus seeks to achieve unity by not demanding uniformity for all nations regardless of their ability to take steps toward environmental protection.

The Montreal Protocol establishes targets and timetables for phasing out ozone layer depleting chemicals, but each party to the treaty is left to implement its treaty obligations through its own national law. Thus different nations can use different approaches to meet the treaty requirements. As discussed in Chapter 3, the United States enacted a phaseout schedule for production of CFCs and halons in its 1990 Clean Air Act.[34] The phaseout was to be complete by 2000, as mandated by the Montreal Protocol; however, concern over new scientific data that showed likely ozone depletion in highly populated northern hemisphere areas led the U.S. President to use the power that had been given to him in the Clean Air Act to accelerate the phaseout. CFC and halon production in the U.S. was required to halt entirely by the end of 1995.[35]

The massive northern hemisphere ozone depletion that was predicted for the winter of 1992 and that led the U.S. and other nations to accelerate their phaseout of CFCs did not occur.[36] Stratospheric temperatures were warmer than expected, and the ice that is essential for ozone destruction was absent that year. There are, however, other winters. Measurements at the end of the winter of 1993 found that ozone levels were down 10–20%

---

34. 42 U.S.C. § 7671 and § 7671c.

35. *Weekly Compilation of Presidential Documents* (Washington, DC: Office of the Federal Register, Feb. 17, 1992) p. 249.

36. "Ozone Loss in Northern Hemisphere Averted: Chemicals Still Seen Posing Depletion Threat," *Environment Reporter* (May 8, 1992) p. 283.

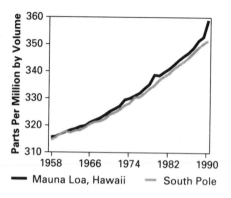

Figure 2. Atmospheric concentrations of carbon dioxide.[39]

from their normal range in the middle latitudes of the northern hemisphere,[37] and the threat of ozone layer destruction is continuing to increase. That is the bad news. The good news is that scientists expect the threat of ozone layer destruction to peak in 2000 and think that the ozone layer should begin to slowly get thicker after that. Even scientists working for environmental public interest groups such as the Environmental Defense Fund say: "The current and projected levels of ozone depletion do not appear to represent a catastrophe."[38] If this is true, it will indeed be good news. It is also good news to see that the world community was capable of quickly addressing an environmental problem and implementing a solution. Perhaps the success of the Montreal Protocol will serve to boost our ability to solve other global environmental problems through international law. It is important, however, to remember that the evidence was quite clear with respect to ozone layer depletion and that the adverse effects would be of a catastrophic nature and include at least one effect to which everyone can relate—cancer. Let's consider another worldwide environmental issue, global warming, and note a few of the differences between it and ozone layer depletion that may explain

37. "Northern Hemisphere Ozone at 14-Year Low," *New York Times* (April 23, 1993) p. A26.

38. "After 2000, Outlook for the Ozone Layer Looks Good," *Washington Post* (April 15, 1993) p. A1.

39. The Carbon Dioxide Information Analysis Center, Oak Ridge National Laboratory, *Trends '91: A Compendium of Data on Global Change*, pp. 15, 19, 23, 27, (Oak Ridge, TN: DOE, 1991), cited in Council on Environmental Quality, *Environmental Quality 1991, 22nd Annual Report* (Washington, DC: March, 1992) p. 116.

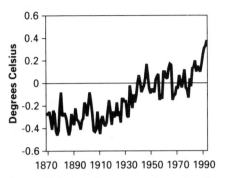

Note: Global surface temperature is relative to a 1950-1979 reference period mean.

Figure 3.   Global surface temperature variations.[40]

why, instead of targets and timetables, we have only a framework treaty with respect to global warming.

Many authors have written about scientific evidence pointing to significant increases in global temperatures due to increases in greenhouse gases such as carbon dioxide in the atmosphere. Data concerning atmospheric concentrations of carbon dioxide and global surface temperature variations is shown in Figures 2 and 3. Predicted mean temperature increases of 1.5 to 4.5 degrees centigrade could result in changes in agricultural patterns, reduced supplies of fresh water, and the rise of sea levels.[41] Other scientists offer contrary evidence. NASA has said that its measurements show no global warming trend, and a number of university researchers claim that global warming is either nonexistent or of insignificant magnitude.[42] The scientific community appears to be not nearly as united about global warming as about ozone layer depletion. In addition, the predicted effects of global warming present a different image. People think of changing agricultural patterns, but they don't

40. The Carbon Dioxide Information Analysis Center, Oak Ridge National Laboratory, *Trends '91: A Compendium of Data on Global Change*, pp. 516–17, (Oak Ridge, TN: DOE, 1991), cited in Council on Environmental Quality, *Environmental Quality 1991, 22nd Annual Report* (Washington, DC: March, 1992) p. 116.

41. Zaelke, D. and Cameron, J., "Global Warming and Climate Change—An Overview of the International Legal Process, *5 American Univ. Journal of International Law and Policy* (1990) p. 249.

42. Brooks, W., "Climate Debate Heating Up," *The Detroit News* (Feb. 5, 1991) p. 7A.

envision worldwide famine. Rising sea levels would be critical for some. The author's visit to the near sea level Republic of the Marshall Islands in the Pacific showed no topic of greater interest there, and coastal businesses and residents in every country would suffer severely from rising sea levels. Most people do not, however, feel directly threatened by rising sea levels, and there is also the perception that, if it happens at all, it will be gradual and adjustments in lifestyle can be made. It's not quite like cancer looming with nowhere to hide. Whatever the reasons, while there is much concern about global warming and much study being done of it, and while the issue has resulted in a treaty which is open for signature but not yet in force, that treaty is a "framework convention" rather than one with specific numerical obligations such as are contained in the Montreal Protocol.

The U.N. Framework Convention on Climate Change[43] encourages national action to reduce the emission of greenhouse gases. It does not, however, provide international law in the form of a specific approach like a phaseout or of targets and timetables which nations would be committed to meeting. Thus, Article 4 states:

> All Parties, taking into account their common but differentiated responsibilities and their specific national and regional development priorities, objectives and circumstances shall: . . . Formulate, implement, publish and regularly update national . . . programmes containing measures to mitigate climate change. . . . Each of [the developed] Parties shall adopt national . . . policies and take corresponding measures on the mitigation of climate change, by limiting its anthropogenic emissions of greenhouse gases and protecting and enhancing its greenhouse gas sinks and reservoirs.

The principle reason why the Climate Change Convention did not adopt targets and timetables was opposition to that approach by the United States. President Bush took the position that targets and timetables for CO_2 emissions are not adequate to deal with the complex dynamics of climate change[44] and that it might be too expensive to set strict limits on emissions of greenhouse gases.[45] President Clinton, in his first major environmental policy speech as President, repudiated the Bush policy and committed the U.S. "to reducing our emissions of greenhouse gases to their 1990 levels by the year

---

43. *International Environment Reporter Reference File 1*, 21:3901.

44. "Bush Remains Opposed to Target Schedule for Cutting Emissions of Greenhouse Gases," *Environment Reporter* (March 27, 1992) p. 2640.

45. "Clinton Supports Two Major Steps for Environment," *New York Times*, (April 22, 1993) p. 1.

2000."[46] The questions remain, of course, of whether U.S. law will be enacted to reflect President Clinton's statement of policy and, if so, will that law produce the appropriate results. In addition, from the perspective of international environmental law, regardless of any action now taken by the U.S., the Climate Change Convention is a treaty whose approach is to be a framework for national law and for future treaties instead of requiring a specific control mechanism to achieve a specific result within a specific time.

Another substantive area where the Bush and Clinton Administrations have differed is with respect to the Biological Diversity Convention produced by the Earth Summit at Rio de Janeiro. President Bush rejected the treaty which was signed by about 150 countries on the grounds that it would unfairly penalize some American companies. President Clinton pledged that the U.S. would sign the treaty.[47] Although President Clinton said he was concerned about the treaty's provision requiring that countries share profits from products developed from native plants or animals because that might weaken patent protections for biotechnology companies and might discourage research and innovation, he said that an interpretive statement attached to the U.S. signature would reduce the negative effects on research. The profit sharing approach in the treaty is designed to encourage conservation in developing countries by giving them a share in the profits obtained from their biodiversity.

The Biological Diversity Convention[48] is of relatively recent vintage compared to another treaty designed to protect the components of nature, the Convention on International Trade in Endangered Species of Wild Fauna and Flora, commonly known as CITES.[49] While the Biological Diversity Convention emphasizes entire ecosystems, CITES emphasizes individual species. CITES came into force in 1975, and today over 110 nations participate in its species protection process. CITES has been in force for a long enough time to allow for the development of a substantial amount of law to implement its provisions. Let's consider the operative mechanisms of CITES and the various types of national law in the United States that implement its provisions—statutory law, administrative regulations, and court proceedings.

Endangered species often need protection because, whether for reasons of real usefulness, fashion, superstition, or just because they are rare, these species may fetch high prices in the marketplace. The exotic wildlife trade

---

46. Ibid.

47. Ibid.

48. *International Environment Reporter Reference File 1*, 21:4001.

49. 27 UST 1087, TIAS No. 8249, 993 UNTS 243.

is estimated to be worth $5 billion per year, and examples of the financial incentives to participate include giant pitcher plants from Borneo at $1000 each, Peruvian butterflies at $3000 each, rhinoceros horn at $13,000 per pound, and leopard coats selling for over $100,000.[50] The Endangered Species Convention (CITES) divides those species that are to be protected into three categories according to the degree of threat to the species and lists those species in Appendices I, II, and III. CITES says that Appendix I shall include "all species threatened with extinction which are or may be affected by trade." Appendix II includes all species which "although not necessarily now threatened with extinction may become so" unless trade is subject to strict regulation. Species of Appendix I plants and animals, dead or alive, may only be traded upon the granting of both an export permit and an import permit. Each of these permits may only be granted upon the advice of a Scientific Authority of the respective state which certifies that trade will not be detrimental to the survival of that species. For these most threatened species, CITES has thus provided that even if the exporting nation and its Scientific Authority succumb to economic or political pressure to allow export, the importing nation may have an independent responsibility to prevent trade. For the less threatened species listed in Appendix II, an export permit, but not an import permit, is required. Therefore, with respect to the primate order of mammals, the Golden Langur (P. geei) listed in Appendix I is subject to a higher level of protection than the Nilgiri Langur (P. johnii) listed in Appendix II. Amendments to Appendices I and II listing additional species, or perhaps delisting species, are authorized to be made by agreement at periodic conferences of the parties to the treaty. A third list, Appendix III, consists of those species which any one party to the treaty designates as being subject to regulation within its jurisdiction and as needing co-operation of other parties to control trade. These species are not in the threatened or may be threatened with extinction categories but are listed by a country for the purpose of helping it prevent or restrict exploitation. If a species is listed in Appendix III, it may not be imported without an export permit, and an export permit will only be granted if the specimen was not obtained in violation of the laws of the exporting country and the specimen will be handled so as to minimize risk of injury, damage to health, and cruel treatment.

As discussed above, CITES has specific control mechanisms to protect endangered species. Those controls are implemented through national law in the countries that are parties to the treaty. Import and export permits are required under CITES and may be issued only upon the advice of a designated

---

50. Fitzgerald, S., *Whose Business Is It?* (World Wildlife Fund, 1989).

Scientific Authority of a country. U.S. statutory law designates the Secretary of the Interior, acting through the U.S. Fish and Wildlife Service, as the Scientific Authority.[51] CITES requires that the parties take appropriate measures to enforce the treaty and prohibit trade in violation thereof. These measures must include penalties for conducting such trade and provisions for confiscation or return of specimens traded in violation of the treaty.[52] U.S. statutory law provides for civil penalties, criminal sanctions, and forfeiture of the illegally traded plants or animals.[53] The day to day implementation of U.S. responsibilities under CITES such as issuing permits and dealing with enforcement is carried on by the Interior Department pursuant to its statutory authority. This agency is responsible for issuing import and export permits. Its regulations for obtaining a permit include the process for getting a permit and the information which must be provided such as how transport will occur, care during transport, and expertise of the persons who will provide care.[54] Enforcement proceedings are also initiated by Interior or other administrative agencies, and the U.S. District Courts and the U.S. Magistrates may issue enforcement orders.

One example of an enforcement proceeding that also involved an issue of interpretation of the U.S. law implementing CITES is *United States v. 3,210 Crusted Sides of Caiman Crocodilus Yacare*.[55] In *Crusted Sides*, 10,875 hides of partly tanned (thus "crusted sides") *Caiman Crocodilus Yacare*, an endangered species, were being sent from Bolivia to France by way of Florida. The CITES permit described the shipment as 3,210 hides of *Caiman Crocodilus Crocodilus*, an Appendix II species. During a routine inspection by the U.S. Fish and Wildlife Service, the discrepancies were discovered. The court found that the government had established probable cause to institute a forfeiture action due to violation of CITES controls on trade in endangered species as implemented by 16 U.S.C. § 1538(c)(1) which says:

> It is unlawful for any person subject to the jurisdiction of the United States to engage in any trade in any specimens contrary to the provisions of the Convention or to possess any specimens traded contrary to the provisions of the Convention. . . .

51. 16 U.S.C. § 1537a.(a).
52. CITES, Art. VIII.
53. 16 U.S.C. § 1540.
54. 50 CFR § 23.15.
55. 636 F. Supp. 1281 (1986).

It also found that the CITES export permit was improper regardless of which species was involved because it did not contain the proper number of hides. Forfeiture was thus appropriate. The parties claiming the hides argued that forfeiture should only be of the number of hides that exceeded the amount declared on the CITES permit. In deciding that all the hides were subject to forfeiture, the court said that the purpose of CITES is to prevent extinction of certain species by over-exploitation through international trade, and, to accomplish that aim, the penalties for violation of CITES must be stringent. Forfeiting only the offending hides, those in excess of the permit, would only serve to thwart the intent and undermine the effectiveness of CITES.

Has CITES worked? To some extent, yes, but in one of the most visible endangered species situations, the answer is either no or not yet. The demand for ivory has resulted in the death of almost half of all elephants,[56] and this demand is almost exclusively for decorative use in products that could be made with highly satisfactory substitutes. Until 1989, elephants had been listed in Appendix II of CITES and, therefore, importing countries did not feel the Appendix I responsibility to independently consider the adverse effects of allowing importing of ivory. The exporting countries, mostly impoverished, view the elephant as a resource, and, even with responsible governments in exporting countries, impoverished citizens have a great financial incentive for illegal poaching. Today, elephants are listed in Appendix I, and importing nations have banned or reduced ivory imports. It is hoped that this change in international environmental law, along with heightened awareness of the elephant issue, will reduce the demand for ivory to the point where its price no longer makes exporting nations interested in conducting a legal ivory trade and no longer makes illegal poaching and trading worthwhile.

The treaties we have considered thus far in our discussion of international environmental law have all been multilateral treaties open to all countries to become parties if they so choose. Other treaties are multilateral but are limited with respect to their membership. The Treaty of Rome, as amended by the Single European Act, is a multilateral treaty of the Member States of the European Economic Community (EEC).[57] This treaty also differs from the other treaties we have discussed in that it establishes institutions and confers powers upon those institutions whereas our other treaties left future action to each party individually or to a reconvening of all the parties. The institutions of the EEC are the European Parliament, a Council, a Commission, and a Court of Justice.

---

56. Glennon, M., "Has International Law Failed the Elephant," *84 Amer. Journal of Int. Law 1* (1990).

57. Carter, B. and Trimble, P., *International Law, Selected Documents*, (Boston: Little, Brown and Co., 1991).

The original Treaty of Rome did not expressly provide authority for environmental protection. Instead, in a manner analogous to the U.S. Congress enacting environmental controls under its power to regulate interstate commerce,[58] the Council would issue Directives concerning environmental issues under its power to:

> issue directives for the approximation of such provisions laid down by law, regulation or administrative action in Member States as directly affect the establishment or functioning of the common market.[59]

By this "approximation" process which could only happen with unanimous action of the Council, the Council would create uniformity in European environmental law as Congress creates uniformity in U.S. environmental law. For example, the early Council Directive of 4 May 1976 set up a process for imposing numerical restrictions on discharge of dangerous substances into the aquatic environment.[60] That process led to quantitative discharge limits and quality objectives for hexachlorocyclohexane being established later in the Council Directive of 9 October 1984.[61]

The Treaty of Rome was amended by the Single European Act (SEA). The SEA allows the Council to exercise its approximation powers by qualified majority rather than only unanimously,[62] and it expressly states that environmental protection is within the power of the Community. The Commission, in making its proposals to the Council, is told that concerning the environment it is to take as a base a high level of protection.[63] Also, Title VII, Environment, was added to Part Three, the "Policy of the Community." Among the provisions of Title VII are that action by the Community relating to the environment shall have the objectives of preserving, protecting, and improving the quality of the environment and of ensuring a prudent and rational utilization of natural resources. In addition, the principles of preventative action, rectifying damage at the source, and payment by the polluter are expressly stated.[64] The amending of the charter document of the European Community to expressly provide for environmental protection rather than to rely on implicit powers has been cited by some people as a precedent

---

58. Discussed in Chapter 1, Section C.

59. Treaty of Rome, Article 100.

60. 76/464/EEC.

61. 84/491/EEC.

62. Treaty of Rome, Article 100a.

63. Ibid.

64. Treaty of Rome, Article 130r.

that the U.S. should follow. The issue of amending the U.S. Constitution to expressly provide for environmental protection is discussed in Chapter 2.

The Treaty of Rome differs from the treaties we previously discussed because it involves only a limited number of nations and it operates through a set of treaty created institutions. Also, as opposed to the others which are largely single issue treaties (ozone layer, species protection), it pertains to a wide range of environmental issues. EC law is applicable to air pollution, water pollution, pesticide use, food additives, waste disposal, and numerous other topics. Our next treaty example involves a limited number of nations and utilizes a treaty created institution; however, that institution is administrative rather having the legislative capabilities of the EC Council, and the treaty is basically single issue oriented. This is the U.S.-Canada Agreement on Great Lakes Water Quality.[65]

The U.S.-Canada Great Lakes Water Quality Treaty addresses the quality of a huge system of waters along an international boundary. It is a bilateral treaty—only two nations are eligible to be parties—and the institution that the treaty creates and uses for implementation is the International Joint Commission (IJC). The IJC is responsible for the collection, analysis, and dissemination of data and information concerning Great Lakes water quality and human activities that affect it such as toxic, nutrient, and heat discharges. The IJC is also responsible for making recommendations to the parties about legislation, standards, and other regulatory measures relating to water quality; however, legislative implementation is to be done by the parties themselves. The parties explicitly commit themselves to enacting necessary legislation in their countries, including the appropriation of funds, to implement the protection programs and measures provided for in the treaty. Those programs include abatement, control, and prevention of pollution from municipal and industrial sources, agricultural sources such as pesticides and animal wastes, and shipping activities. The programs contain components like construction of waste treatment facilities with target dates for their being operational, effluent limitations, and evaluation processes to determine progress being made and identify emerging problems.

The primary thrust of the U.S.-Canada Great Lakes Water Quality Treaty and all the other treaties we have discussed thus far is to prevent harm by legislative and regulatory action. Other treaties take a much different approach to preventing harm and also have a goal besides prevention that is considered to be of at least equal importance—compensation for harm that has taken place. The example of a compensation treaty approach that we will consider is actually a pair of treaties that provide a system of compensation for harm

---

65. 30 UST 1383, TIAS 9257, Amended by Protocol, TIAS 10798.

caused by oil pollution from tanker ships. These are the Civil Liability Convention and the Fund Convention.

Concern about oil pollution from ships has a long history.[66] It is widely accepted, however, that the *Torrey Canyon* incident was the precipitating force in the creation of the modern international matrix for dealing with the issue of oil pollution from ships. The *Torrey Canyon*, carrying approximately 118,000 tons of oil, impaled herself on the rocks off the English coast in March, 1967, resulting in oil pollution expenses of an extent previously unknown, about $15,000,000. Decades later, the oil tanker industry itself estimates that 400,000 metric tons of oil are annually spilled into the marine environment by tankers,[67] and the potential costs of cleanup and harm to humans and natural resources can be in the billions of dollars as was the case in the *Exxon Valdez* oil spill in Alaska.[68] Although there are treaties that focus directly on oil pollution prevention such as by banning or limiting discharges of oil,[69] the Civil Liability Convention (CLC) and the Fund Convention (FC) have providing compensation for harm done by tanker oil spills as their primary goal.

The CLC[70] and the FC[71] combine to form a system whereby damage caused by an oil tanker spill is paid for by the tanker owner and by the owner of the cargo, the oil. The CLC provides that the tanker owner is strictly liable for harm done. Strict liability means that if the oil caused damage, the tanker owner is liable for that damage even if the tanker owner was not negligent. Strict liability is liability without fault and is often the standard of liability used by the law with respect to harm that results from participating in dangerous activities like using dynamite or using toxic substances. If the activity causes the harm, that is itself sufficient to impose liability even if there is no wrongdoing like negligence and the harm came about due to an unpredicted storm blowing a tanker off course and onto the rocks. By providing for strict liability, the CLC is saying that transporting oil will inevitably result in some spills which are not the fault of anyone and that

---

66. Soni, R., *Control of Marine Pollution in International Law* (Johannesburg, Juta & Co., Ltd., 1985) p. 175.

67. *Response to Marine Oil Spills* (London, International Tanker Owners Pollution Federation Ltd., 1986) pp. 3–4.

68. "Oil Companies Rethink Risk of Having Tankers," *New York Times* (June 13, 1990) p. A26.

69. The International Convention for the Prevention of Pollution from Ships (MARPOL). Printed in: Timagenis, *International Control of Marine Pollution* (New York: Oceana Publications, 1980) Vol. 2, pp. 699–710 and 807–824.

70. 9 International Legal Materials 45.

71. 11 I.L.M. 284.

victims of those spills must be compensated by the businesses doing the transporting. The tanker owners bear the costs of compensation or of purchasing insurance that will compensate victims.

Although under the CLC the tanker owner is held liable even if it is not at fault (strict liability), the tanker owner's liability is limited. The maximum amount of liability is expressed in the treaty in terms of SDRs, Special Drawing Rights of the International Monetary Fund. Based on recent rates of exchange, the limits are approximately $175 per ton of the ship's tonnage, up to a maximum of $18 million. Thus, while the tanker owner is held strictly liable, the owner is given some protection with a ceiling on that liability. If, however, the owner is negligent, the limited liability protection does not apply.

The Fund Convention (FC) enters the CLC picture in two ways. One is to provide supplementary compensation to victims if they are not compensated fully under the CLC because the harm done by the oil spill exceeds the limited liability amount. The second interface between the FC and the CLC is that the FC provides money to indemnify the tanker owner for a portion of the tanker owner's liability under the CLC. The heart of the FC is the International Oil Pollution Compensation Fund that it established. The Fund is financed by contributions from the cargo owners—those who receive the oil after it has been carried on the sea. The cargo owners pay a levy of a given amount per ton of oil received, and the amount per ton is set annually so as to cover the anticipated need for revenue to keep the Fund viable. If a tanker spill incident causes harm in excess of the CLC limit of liability payable by the tanker owner, money from the Fund is used to provide supplementary compensation to victims so that the aggregate of compensation payable under the CLC and FC is about $79 million. In addition, money from the Fund is used to indemnify or reimburse the tanker owner for part of what the tanker owner had to pay to compensate for harm caused by the spill. The combination of the CFC and the FC thus results in sharing of the cost of compensating victims between the tanker owner whose ship was involved in the incident and the Fund composed of money collected from all cargo owners of all oil transported.

More than 65 countries are parties to the CLC, and over 40 are parties to the FC, but the United States is not a party to either treaty. Instead, the U.S. has a national liability system to cover oil spills. This is the Oil Pollution Act discussed in Chapter 3. A number of reasons have been advanced for why the U.S. should not be a part of the international system of oil pollution liability, but there are many people who think that the U.S. should not refuse to join an international arrangement that has won widespread international acceptance even without U.S. participation and which would likely be joined by many more nations if the U.S. became a party. These people contend that if the U.S. wants to obtain overall international cooperation from other nations, it must be willing to go along with reasonable international law about a specific topic even if it is not necessarily what the U.S. would prefer. Among the reasons for the U.S. not becoming a part of the international liability matrix are the actual amounts of liability provided by the CFC/FC and the types of damage for which the CFC/FC mandate compensation.

Although only one tanker oil spill has given rise to claims that exceeded the liability limits of the CFC/FC, the U.S. thinks the limits are too low and furthermore, if the U.S. were to become a party, getting the other nations to agree to raise the limits in the future would be nearly impossible. To induce the U.S. to join, protocols or amendments to the CFC/FC were drafted in 1984 raising the CFC liability to about $550 per ton and the combined CFC/FC limit to $262 million.[72] This is still nowhere near the $1200 per ton and the $1 billion compensation fund provided by the U.S. Oil Pollution Act. In addition, and of great political significance in the U.S. decision not to join the CFC/FC, the Oil Pollution Act does not preempt state laws that provide for unlimited liability for oil spills. Joining the CFC/FC would have meant that a coastal state in the U.S. that wanted to impose unlimited liability could not have done so.

Intertwined with the U.S. concern about the CFC/FC liability limits being too low is the issue of the types of damage covered by the treaties. The CFC/FC pays compensation for cleanup operations and for economic losses. It does not pay for non-economic environmental damage or for pre-spill preventative measures. The U.S. Oil Pollution Act does provide for payments for damage to natural resources. The 1984 Protocols also tried to induce U.S. acceptance by making changes about these matters. Pre-spill preventative measures might be compensable, as would be costs for reasonable measures to restore the contaminated environment, but these protections are still not as broad as the compensation umbrella provided in the Oil Pollution Act, and it is highly unlikely that the U.S. will become a CFC/FC party in the near future.

The treaties we have discussed up to this point have been created or later amended to specifically address environmental problems. While the Treaty of Rome that established the European Economic Community was a trade oriented treaty, it was amended by the Single European Act to expressly include environmental matters. We will now consider two trade treaties that recognize the environment in only limited ways in their language but where, in one instance, the environment is having substantial impact on the treaty's administration and, in the second, environmental concerns are highly relevant to its coming into force. The two trade treaties we will explore are the General

---

72. International Maritime Organization documents LEG/CONF. 6/66 and 6/67, 25 May 1984.

Agreement on Tariffs and Trade (GATT)[73] and the North American Free Trade Agreement (NAFTA).[74]

The objectives of the GATT, as expressed in its preamble, are economic— develop full use of resources, expand production and exchange of goods, raise standards of living. The GATT seeks to achieve its goals by precluding barriers to trade. Article XI prohibits parties from imposing restrictions, other than duties, taxes, etc., on imports and exports. Thus measures such as import prohibitions and quotas and import licenses are not allowed. Article XX does, however, provide exceptions for nondiscriminatory measures "necessary to protect human, animal or plant life or health" or "relating to the conservation of exhaustible natural resources . . . ." The best known example of the GATT interplay between encouraging trade and protecting a natural resource is the tuna/dolphin dispute.

Because dolphins and yellowfin tuna swim in close proximity to each other, when the tuna are caught in large seine nets, dolphins also become part of the catch.[75] Pursuant to a U.S. statute that banned importing tuna caught in this type of net[76] and a U.S. court decision to enforce the statute,[77] the U.S. embargoed tuna caught by Mexican fishermen. Mexico contested the U.S. action before a GATT dispute resolution panel claiming that it violated the GATT prohibitions on import quotas and discrimination against foreign products. The panel found that the embargo violated Article XI and that it did not fall within the exceptions of Article XX.[78] The panel concluded that the prohibition was not "necessary" as required under Article XX because the U.S. had not pursued the alternate approach of attempting to negotiate an international agreement to protect the dolphins. The panel came out strongly against "unilateral prescription," i.e., one nation imposing restrictions to protect the environment outside of its own borders, and it used that position to also narrowly interpret the "global commons" exception in Article XX to not apply outside of a nation's territorial jurisdiction.

It is certainly within the realm of reasonability to contend that the interests of free trade and the interests of environmental protection should be reconciled by the international community as a whole rather than unilaterally. Otherwise Canada could prohibit the importation of U.S. products made with

---

73. 55 U.N.T.S. 187.

74. LEXIS, GENFED-EXTRA database; WESTLAW, NAFTA database.

75. Dunoff, J., "Reconciling International Trade with Preservation of the Global Commons: Can We Prosper and Profit?" *Washington and Lee Law Review* (Fall, 1992) p.1407.

76. 16 U.S.C. § 1371(a)(2)(B).

77. *Earth Island Institute v. Mosbacher*, 746 F. Supp. 964 (1990), 929 F.2d 1449 (1991).

78. Tuna/Dolphin Panel Report, 30 I.L.M. 1594 (1991).

energy from high sulfur coal based on its belief that burning high sulfur coal excessively pollutes the global commons. However, it is also reasonable to contend that a nation whose people have a high level of commitment to global environmental protection should be able to advance environmental protection outside of its borders by responsibly controlling actions such as consumption inside its borders. Whether what appears to be the dominance of the trade aspects of the GATT will continue in the face of greater global environmental concern has only recently begun to be tested.

The GATT, originally a document of the 1940s, has raised environmental issues in the 1990s, but the GATT is firmly in place with over 100 nations as parties. It is certainly open to environmentally oriented amendments and interpretations, but few doubt that it will remain in force as a worldwide treaty. With respect to a recent trade treaty, the North American Free Trade Agreement (NAFTA), the environmental issues were raised long in advance of the treaty ratification process in the U.S. Congress.[79] The NAFTA, which seeks to eliminate trade barriers among Canada, Mexico, and the U.S., has had the support of both the Bush and Clinton Administrations. It has been supported on the grounds that free trade would be of economic benefit to all the countries and that environmental problems can be prevented. It has been opposed because many people think that either legally or by way of lack of enforcement the environmental protection standards in Mexico will be significantly lower than in Canada or the U.S., and, therefore, dirty industries, instead of becoming cleaner and solving their environmental problems, will move to Mexico and simply relocate the center of those problems. Labor interests in the U.S. are concerned that moves to Mexico will result in a net loss in jobs, and both labor and environmentalists are concerned that the potential for industry to move to Mexico could ultimately result in the weakening of environmental standards in the U.S. The ultimate test of Congressional approval of the NAFTA and of the treaty's effect on the environment and jobs is the content of "side agreements" among the parties to protect the environment and jobs. These were negotiated in an effort to win Congressional approval prior to the treaty's stated effective date of January 1, 1994.[80]

Our discussion of international environmental law, besides making brief note of customary international law, has considered examples of categories of treaties such as preventative vs. compensating for harm, multilateral vs. bilateral, and working through an independent entity vs. working through nationally enacted laws. A far less binding form of international environ-

---

79. "Symposium: Free Trade and the Environment in Latin America," *Loyola of Los Angeles Int. and Comp. Law Journal* (Dec., 1992).

80. "Trade-Pact Opposition Eases a Bit," *New York Times* (May 11, 1993) p. D1.

mental law exists as formal documents that are not treaties. One example of this is United Nations Conference reports and resolutions such as those that pertain to the topic of desertification in Africa. Typical operative words of these types of documents are the General Assembly "requests," "recommends," "endorses," and "urges." With respect to coping specifically with problems of the desertification of the Sahelian region of West Africa, the U.N. has held conferences, passed resolutions, and drafted a Plan of Action to Combat Desertification.[81] These action were taken in the late 1970s, and although some progress was seen by the late 1980s,[82] the growth of the desert continues. Reasons include a very high population growth rate of 2.6%, deforestation because most of the area's energy needs are supplied by wood, and the difficult climatic working conditions that discourage experts from working in the area. Aside from these logical explanations, one should also ask whether racial, cultural, or commerce factors enter into the failure to successfully stop the desertification process. If a white, western culture of 37 million people were similarly threatened by processes of nature, would more be done? How about if a significant trading partner of developed nations were threatened—would more money be forthcoming from those developed nations? The possibility that racial and cultural discrimination interfere with solving a technologically solvable environmental problem is not, however, all one-sided. A country that has had notable success at reclaiming desert land and putting it to profitable agricultural use is Israel. A case study, "The Negev: a desert reclaimed,"[83] which was submitted by Israel to the Desertification Conference was formally denounced by a resolution of the conference, with most nations of the Sahel region voting to denounce the report.

D. COMPARATIVE ENVIRONMENTAL LAW

The comparative environmental law subset of global environmental law looks at how the national law of individual countries would handle a given environmental problem. Why is the same issue resolved differently in different countries? When should a problem be approached in different ways in different nations, and when should one nation move toward adopting the approach of another? Let's consider three examples of how different countries

---

81. A/Conf. 74/36.

82. "Some Gains in West Africa's War on the Desert," *New York Times* (Sept. 13, 1987) p. 22.

83. A/CONF. 74/20.

deal with specific environmental problems: (1) what should be the result of a dispute between neighboring landowners due to one having negligently caused environmentally related economic harm to the other, (2) how should we value the harm to a natural resource so that we can require the cause of that harm to pay for it, and (3) how should we get people to conserve energy?

In Chapter 6, we discussed negligence law in the U.S. We saw that if someone applied a pesticide so that it went onto his or her neighbor's property and caused economic harm such as to crops or livestock, unless compensation was voluntarily paid, the injured party would likely sue the negligent party in a court and obtain compensation for the harm that was caused. Let's consider the same situation in the People's Republic of China. In the PRC, rural agricultural workers are members of communes or collectives, but they may also have private enterprises and grow produce for individual profit. Suppose X and Y are neighboring rural operators of private adjoining plots of land. X uses a chemical pesticide in a manner that allows it to drift onto Y's land, and it destroys Y's commercial cabbage crop. In such a situation, the injured party, Y, would take the dispute to the head of the collective for mediation. While there is the right to go to court in China, one goes through mediation first, and ending up in court is rare.

China strongly emphasizes mediation to bring about a reconciliation of the parties.[84] It is to be principled peacemaking which may use persuasion and education, but not coercion. There are many possible outcomes of the mediation process with respect to X and Y.[85] X may be responsible to pay for all of the lost cabbage crop, but if X can't afford to pay the entire amount, part of the loss may be paid to Y by Y's collective. There is a notion of suretyship or insurance by the collective that says Y will be protected when another collective member harms Y but cannot be given the burden to pay. Another possible result is that the victim, Y, may be left to bear part of the loss because, as a member of the collective, one is subject to some risk from actions of other members, especially if the victim does not really "need" full compensation for the destroyed cabbages. Yet another alternative would be for the collective to provide Y (the victim) with extra work so Y could have the opportunity to recover the economic loss.

Of relevance to the mediation process and to the results concerning X and Y is the undercurrent of traditional law and Confucian ideology which stress social harmony and the restoration of society's peace rather than

---

84. Chan, Peter P.F., *China Modernization and its Economic Laws* (Hong Kong: Hong Kong Economist Newspaper Limited, 1982) Chap. 7.

85. These are based on a discussion with Xiao Zhi yue, lawyer and Lecturer in Law, Hangzhou University, PRC.

stressing which party is legally right or wrong.[86] The goal is to have X and Y walk away from the situation with as much harmony between themselves and between each of them and the community as possible. Ill will should be minimized. This is far different than the usual American process for dispute resolution which gives us a "winner take all" court decision or a settlement of a lawsuit based on factors like economic power of the parties—could the victim afford to wait for a just remedy, or was quick settlement a matter of necessity? The "winner take all" decision and the economic power settlement scenarios tend to maximize rather than minimize ill will. Is the Chinese dispute resolution process and its result as far removed from American law as it sounds? Historically, yes. More recently, no. As noted in Chapter 3, the use of environmental mediation and negotiation has grown greatly in recent years. Also discussed in Chapter 3 was the *Spur Industries* case involving an existing cattle feedlot that became a nuisance when a newly developed housing project was being built. The court ordered the feedlot to close but also ordered that its relocation costs be paid by the housing developer who stood to make large profits if the feedlot closed. The result seemed to take into account many of the factors discussed in our X-Y example above and perhaps gave a result designed to minimize ill will and restore the peace of society. From a different perspective, however, as China seeks more foreign investment, it is going to have to provide the greater legal protection that such investors are likely to demand. In addition to social harmony, the investment community is very concerned with who is legally right or wrong.

Having considered the resolution of private disputes in different legal systems, let's, as our second comparative environmental law example, see how administrative agencies in the U.S. and in Russia answer the question of how to value damage to natural resources in order to obtain payment for those damages from the party responsible for causing the harm. The legal systems of most nations have a long history of methodologies for valuing economic harm done to individual victims, but only recently has the law tried to value harm to natural resources like a coastal ecosystem or wildlife habitat. If there is an oil spill or other hazardous substance release which damages or destroys a coastal ecosystem, how can we determine the amount to charge the party responsible for the harm? If the ecosystem can be restored or replaced, perhaps the cost of the work is an appropriate measure; however, not all ecosystem losses can be replaced, and there is often a long time lag even if replacement is possible. How then do countries assess the monetary value of natural resource damages resulting from an oil spill?

---

86. Merryman and Clark, *Comparative Law: Western European and Latin American Legal Systems* (Charlottesville, VA: Michie Co., 1978) p.8.

The Russian system, established under the former Soviet Union, gives a quick answer and costs very little.[87] First, the amount of oil spilled is determined such as by looking at the documents to see how much the ship was carrying and then noting what the ship still holds. The spilled oil is then assumed to disperse to a concentration of 50 parts oil to one million parts water, and the hypothetical volume of impacted water is determined. The 50 parts per million concentration is considered to be 1000 times greater than acceptable, and the cost to restore a unit volume of impacted water to acceptable condition is obtained from cost tables which specify restoration costs for waters in different coastal regions. The amount of damage is calculated by multiplying the volume of impacted water by the restoration cost for each unit volume. The above process is done by a government administrative agency and, once you know how much oil was spilled, it is basically a simple arithmetic problem to get the damage amount. Data gathering at the site is not needed.

The U.S. system for assessing damages to natural resources is provided in the Superfund Act[88] and Department of Interior regulations.[89] For "minor" releases of hazardous materials, a "Type A" assessment is required. This is to be done with minimal fieldwork and is to use existing data and computer models relating to units of discharge or units of affected area. This approach sounds quite similar to the Russian system; however, in the U.S., when a release is large or unusually damaging rather than minor, site-specific damage assessment is undertaken. In these situations, the individual site is evaluated to determine the type and extent of short- and long-term injury, destruction, or loss. Factors to be considered include replacement value, use value, and the ability of the ecosystem or resource to recover. While some aspects of site-specific damage assessment such as replacement or restoration costs can be relatively precise, others are more questionable. For example, in determining use value of a natural resource, "travel cost methodology" may be employed. A person's incremental travel costs to an area are used as a proxy for the price of the services of that area, and damages to the area are the difference between its value with and without the hazardous substance release. Presumably, fewer visitors willing to pay the price of getting to the area will help to measure the lost use value of the area. The cost of travel and people's interest in visiting particular areas are, however, subject to many

---

87. *Summary and Analysis of State and Selected Foreign Procedures for Determining the Costs of Natural Resource Damages From Releases of Oil or Hazardous Materials* (Washington, DC: Office of Ocean Resources and Assessment, National Oceanic and Atmospheric Administration) p. A-193.

88. 42 U.S.C. § 9651(c).

89. 43 CFR Part 11.

variables other than the damage to the area caused by a substance release. Does the use of these types of approaches provide a more precise valuation of natural resource damage, or is there only an increase in the time and money spent on valuations with no meaningful increase in the precision of the amount determined?

The ease of the Russian and Type A U.S. approaches to natural resource damage assessment allow available time and money to be spent on environmental enhancement instead of on bureaucratic investigation of the amount of loss. On the other hand, if site-specific evaluation is done, the ability to accurately determine actual loss in a given situation may develop over time. Also, discussing the issues involved in site-specific evaluation may lead to a better understanding of what should be considered "natural resource damage." Furthermore, much of the work done to value the resource loss may provide information that can be used in the process of deciding what to do with the damaged site and in implementing that decision. Perhaps the question of spending money on site-specific evaluation of natural resource damage is a question of a country's ability to spend the capital to do such an evaluation. Russia clearly does not have the financial ability to do so. Whether the U.S. does or does not is a matter of opinion, just as is the question of what we will get for our money if we spend it.

Our comparative law examples thus far have involved alternative approaches for dispute resolution and administrative alternatives for placing a value on a harm done to society. Our last comparative law example raises the fundamental issue of whether law in any form is the way to solve environmental problems or, instead, should societies use other means to achieve their desired environmental ends. In Chapter 7, we discussed how different legal mechanisms have been used in the U.S. to conserve energy. Included in our discussion were mandatory constraints on the amount or type of energy that could be used and "voluntary" constraints such as tax savings for those who chose to conserve. These mechanisms were provided by federal and state law in the form of statutes and administrative regulations. There are those who contend that law is often not the best way to deal with environmental problems, and that other tools such as culture, tradition, and religion may be better suited to achieving environmental goals.[90] Islam teaches that humankind is the Viceregent of Allah on earth, and, as such, humankind should live in harmony with nature. Perhaps the teachings of Islam could be used to convince people in Islamic countries to conserve energy. Chinese culture and tradition—Confucian, Taoist, and Buddhist—

---

90. Sulaiman, A., "Citizens' Rights and Enforcement of Conservation Law: A Plea for a Comparative and Multi-Faceted Approach," *Journal of Malaysian and Comparative Law* (1983) pp. 33–43.

urge people to live in harmony with their environment. Perhaps these sources could be used to raise social consciousness and encourage real estate developers to respect wetlands and endangered species habitat rather than try to find ways to build in those areas. In the U.S., some aspect of culture, religion, or the tradition of family farming might be called upon to raise the social consciousness of surface mine owners so that they would respect prime agricultural land rather than our having to rely on the Surface Mining Control and Reclamation Act to keep prime agricultural land from being turned into wasteland. If we are willing to learn from Native American culture, wildlife conservation could be increased while at the same time decreasing the administrative and enforcement costs of wildlife conservation. Can social consciousness raising work along with or maybe better than law to solve environmental problems? It is at least arguable that non-smokers may be exposed to less tobacco smoke due to the heightened social awareness of smokers than due to laws that restrict smoking. Law is critical to environmental protection, but attention should be paid to non-law approaches which might significantly contribute to that protection. In some situations, they may be less costly and even more effective.

ADDITIONAL READINGS

Brown, L., *The World-Watch Reader on Global Environmental Issues* (New York: W.W. Norton & Co., 1991).

Caldicott, H., *If You Love This Planet* (New York: W.W. Norton & Co., 1992).

Caldwell, L., *International Environmental Policy* (Durham, NC: Duke Univ. Press, 1990).

DeBardeleben, J., *To Breath Free: Eastern Europe's Environmental Crisis* (Washington, DC: Woodrow Wilson Center Press, 1991).

Editors of the Harvard Law Review, *Trends in International Environmental Law* (Washington, DC: American Bar Association Section of International Law and Practice, 1992).

Wallace, R., *International Law, A Student Introduction* (London: Sweet & Maxwell, 1986).

APPENDIX A

CEQ GUIDELINES
FOR ENVIRONMENTAL
IMPACT STATEMENT
40 CFR 1502 et seq.

Sec.
1502.23 Cost-benefit analysis.
1502.24 Methodology and scientific accuracy.
1502.25 Environmental review and consultation requirements.

AUTHORITY: NEPA, the Environmental Quality Improvement Act of 1970, as amended (42 U.S.C. 4371 *et seq.*), sec. 309 of the Clean Air Act, as amended (42 U.S.C. 7609), and E.O. 11514 (Mar. 5, 1970, as amended by E.O. 11991, May 24, 1977).

SOURCE: 43 FR 55994, Nov. 29, 1978, unless otherwise noted.

§ 1502.1 Purpose.

The primary purpose of an environmental impact statement is to serve as an action-forcing device to insure that the policies and goals defined in the Act are infused into the ongoing programs and actions of the Federal Government. It shall provide full and fair discussion of significant environmental impacts and shall inform decisionmakers and the public of the reasonable alternatives which would avoid or minimize adverse impacts or enhance the quality of the human environment. Agencies shall focus on significant environmental issues and alternatives and shall reduce paperwork and the accumulation of extraneous background data. Statements shall be concise, clear, and to the point, and shall be supported by evidence that the agency has made the necessary environmental analyses. An environmental impact statement is more than a disclosure document. It shall be used by Federal officials in conjunction with other relevant material to plan actions and make decisions.

§ 1502.2 Implementation.

To achieve the purposes set forth in § 1502.1 agencies shall prepare environmental impact statements in the following manner:

(a) Environmental impact statements shall be analytic rather than encyclopedic.

(b) Impacts shall be discussed in proportion to their significance. There shall be only brief discussion of other than significant issues. As in a finding of no significant impact, there should be only enough discussion to show why more study is not warranted.

(c) Environmental impact statements shall be kept concise and shall be no longer than absolutely necessary to comply with NEPA and with these regulations. Length should vary first with potential environmental problems and then with project size.

(d) Environmental impact statements shall state how alternatives considered in it and decisions based on it will or will not achieve the requirements of sections 101 and 102(1) of the Act and other environmental laws and policies.

(e) The range of alternatives discussed in environmental impact statements shall encompass those to be considered by the ultimate agency decisionmaker.

(f) Agencies shall not commit resources prejudicing selection of alternatives before making a final decision (§ 1506.1).

(g) Environmental impact statements shall serve as the means of assessing the environmental impact of proposed agency actions, rather than justifying decisions already made.

§ 1502.3 Statutory requirements for statements.

As required by sec. 102(2)(C) of NEPA environmental impact statements (§ 1508.11) are to be included in every recommendation or report.

On proposals (§ 1508.23).

For legislation and (§ 1508.17).

Other major Federal actions (§ 1508.18).

Significantly (§ 1508.27).

Affecting (§§ 1508.3, 1508.8).

The quality of the human environment (§ 1508.14).

§ 1502.4 Major Federal actions requiring the preparation of environmental impact statements.

(a) Agencies shall make sure the proposal which is the subject of an environmental impact statement is properly defined. Agencies shall use the criteria for scope (§ 1508.25) to determine which proposal(s) shall be the subject of a particular statement. Proposals or parts of proposals which are related to each other closely enough to be, in effect, a single course of action shall be evaluated in a single impact statement.

(b) Environmental impact statements may be prepared, and are sometimes required, for broad Federal actions such as the adoption of new agency programs or regulations (§ 1508.18). Agencies shall prepare statements on broad actions so that they are relevant to policy and are timed to coincide with meaningful points in agency planning and decisionmaking.

(c) When preparing statements on broad actions (including proposals by more than one agency), agencies may find it useful to evaluate the proposal(s) in one of the following ways:

(1) Geographically, including actions occurring in the same general location, such as body of water, region, or metropolitan area.

(2) Generically, including actions which have relevant similarities, such as common timing, impacts, alternatives, methods of implementation, media, or subject matter.

(3) By stage of technological development including federal or federally assisted research, development or demonstration programs for new technologies which, if applied, could significantly affect the quality of the human environment. Statements shall be prepared on such programs and shall be available before the program has reached a stage of investment or commitment to implementation likely to determine subsequent development or restrict later alternatives.

(d) Agencies shall as appropriate employ scoping (§ 1501.7), tiering (§ 1502.20), and other methods listed in §§ 1500.4 and 1500.5 to relate broad and narrow actions and to avoid duplication and delay.

§ 1502.5 Timing.

An agency shall commence preparation of an environmental impact statement as close as possible to the time the agency is developing or is presented with a proposal (§ 1508.23) so that preparation can be completed in time for the final statement to be included in any recommendation or report on the proposal. The statement shall be prepared early enough so that it can serve practically as an important contribution to the decisionmaking process and will not be used to rationalize or justify decisions already made (§§ 1500.2(c), 1501.2, and 1502.2). For instance:

(a) For projects directly undertaken by Federal agencies the environmental impact statement shall be prepared at the feasibility analysis (go-no go) stage and may be supplemented at a later stage if necessary.

(b) For applications to the agency appropriate environmental assessments or statements shall be commenced no later than immediately after the application is received. Federal agencies are encouraged to begin preparation of such assessments or statements earlier, preferably jointly with applicable State or local agencies.

(c) For adjudication, the final environmental impact statement shall normally precede the final staff recommendation and that portion of the public hearing related to the impact study. In appropriate circumstances the statement may follow preliminary hearings designed to gather information for use in the statements.

(d) For informal rulemaking the draft environmental impact statement shall normally accompany the proposed rule.

§ 1502.6 Interdisciplinary preparation.

Environmental impact statements shall be prepared using an inter-disciplinary approach which will insure the integrated use of the natural and social sciences and the environmental design arts (section 102(2)(A) of the Act). The disciplines of the preparers shall be appropriate to the scope and issues identified in the scoping process (§ 1501.7).

§ 1502.7 Page limits.

The text of final environmental impact statements (e.g., paragraphs (d) through (g) of § 1502.10) shall normally be less than 150 pages and for proposals of unusual scope or complexity shall normally be less than 300 pages.

§ 1502.8 Writing.

Environmental impact statements shall be written in plain language and may use appropriate graphics so that decisionmakers and the public can readily understand them. Agencies should employ writers of clear prose or editors to write, review, or edit statements, which will be based upon the analysis and supporting data from the natural and social sciences and the environmental design arts.

§ 1502.9 Draft, final, and supplemental statements.

Except for proposals for legislation as provided in § 1506.8 environmental impact statements shall be prepared in two stages and may be supplemented.

(a) Draft environmental impact statements shall be prepared in accordance with the scope decided upon in the scoping process. The lead agency shall work with the cooperating agencies and shall obtain comments as required in part 1503 of this chapter. The draft statement must fulfill and satisfy to the fullest extent possible the requirements established for final statements in section 102(2)(C) of the Act. If a draft statement is so inadequate as to preclude meaningful analysis, the agency shall prepare and circulate a revised draft of the appropriate portion. The agency shall make every effort to disclose and discuss at appropriate points in the draft statement all major points of view on the environmental impacts of the alternatives including the proposed action.

(b) Final environmental impact statements shall respond to comments as required in part 1503 of this chapter. The agency shall discuss at appropriate points in the final statement any responsible opposing view which was not adequately discussed in the draft statement and shall indicate the agency's response to the issues raised.

(c) Agencies:

(1) Shall prepare supplements to either draft or final environmental impact statements if:

(i) The agency makes substantial changes in the proposed action that are relevant to environmental concerns; or

(ii) There are significant new circumstances or information relevant to environmental concerns and bearing on the proposed action or its impacts.

(2) May also prepare supplements when the agency determines that the purposes of the Act will be furthered by doing so.

(3) Shall adopt procedures for introducing a supplement into its formal administrative record, if such a record exists.

(4) Shall prepare, circulate, and file a supplement to a statement in the same fashion (exclusive of scoping) as a draft and final statement unless alternative procedures are approved by the Council.

§ 1502.10 Recommended format.

Agencies shall use a format for environmental impact statements which will encourage good analysis and clear presentation of the alternatives including the proposed action. The following standard format for environmental impact statements should be followed unless the agency determines that there is a compelling reason to do otherwise:

(a) Cover sheet.
(b) Summary.
(c) Table of contents.
(d) Purpose of and need for action.
(e) Alternatives including proposed action (sections 102(2)(C)(iii) and 102(2)(E) of the Act).
(f) Affected environment.
(g) Environmental consequences (especially sections 102(2)(C)(i), (ii), (iv), and (v) of the Act).
(h) List of preparers.
(i) List of Agencies, Organizations, and persons to whom copies of the statement are sent.
(j) Index.
(k) Appendices (if any).

If a different format is used, it shall include paragraphs (a), (b), (c), (h), (i), and (j), of this section and shall include the substance of paragraphs (d), (e), (f), (g), and (k) of this section, as further described in §§ 1502.11 through 1502.18, in any appropriate format.

§ 1502.11   Cover sheet.

The cover sheet shall not exceed one page. It shall include:

(a) A list of the responsible agencies including the lead agency and any cooperating agencies.

(b) The title of the proposed action that is the subject of the statement (and if appropriate the titles of related cooperating agency actions), together with the State(s) and county(ies) (or other jurisdiction if applicable) where the action is located.

(c) The name, address, and telephone number of the person at the agency who can supply further information.

(d) A designation of the statement as a draft, final, or draft or final supplement.

(e) A one paragraph abstract of the statement.

(f) The date by which comments must be received (computed in cooperation with EPA under § 1506.10).

The information required by this section may be entered on Standard Form 424 (in items 4, 6, 7, 10, and 18).

§ 1502.12   Summary.

Each environmental impact statement shall contain a summary which adequately and accurately summarizes the statement. The summary shall stress the major conclusions, areas of controversy (including issues raised by agencies and the public), and the issues to be resolved (including the choice among alternatives). The summary will normally not exceed 15 pages.

§ 1502.13   Purpose and need.

The statement shall briefly specify the underlying purpose and need to which the agency is responding in proposing the alternatives including the proposed action.

§ 1502.14   Alternatives including the proposed action.

This section is the heart of the environmental impact statement. Based on the information and analysis presented in the sections on the Affected Environment (§ 1502.15) and the Environmental Consequences (§ 1502.16), it should present the environmental impacts of the proposal and the alternatives in comparative form, thus sharply defining the issues and providing a clear basis for choice among options by the decisionmaker and the public. In this section agencies shall:

(a) Rigorously explore and objectively evaluate all reasonable alternatives, and for alternatives which were eliminated from detailed study, briefly discuss the reasons for their having been eliminated.

(b) Devote substantial treatment to each alternative considered in detail including the proposed action so that reviewers may evaluate their comparative merits.

(c) Include reasonable alternatives not within the jurisdiction of the lead agency.

(d) Include the alternative of no action.

(e) Identify the agency's preferred alternative or alternatives, if one or more exists, in the draft statement and identify such alternative in the final statement unless another law prohibits the expression of such a preference.

(f) Include appropriate mitigation measures not already included in the proposed action or alternatives.

§ 1502.15   Affected environment.

The environmental impact statement shall succinctly describe the environment of the area(s) to be affected or created by the alternatives under consideration. The descriptions shall be no longer than is necessary to understand the effects of the alternatives. Data and analyses in a statement shall be commensurate with the importance of the impact, with less important material summarized, consolidated, or simply referenced. Agencies shall avoid useless bulk in statements and shall concentrate effort and attention on important issues. Verbose descriptions of the affected environment are themselves no measure of the adequacy of an environmental impact statement.

§ 1502.16   Environmental consequences.

This section forms the scientific and analytic basis for the comparisons under § 1502.14. It shall consolidate the discussions of those elements required by sections 102(2)(C)(i), (ii), (iv), and (v) of NEPA which are within the scope of the statement and as much of section 102(2)(C)(iii) as is necessary to support the comparisons. The discussion will include the environmental impacts of the alternatives including the proposed action, any adverse environmental effects which cannot be avoided should the proposal be implemented, the relationship between short-term uses of man's environment and the maintenance and enhancement of long-term productivity, and any irreversible or irretrievable commitments of resources which would be involved in the proposal should it be implemented. This section should not duplicate discussions in § 1502.14. It shall include discussions of:

(a) Direct effects and their significance (§ 1508.8).

(b) Indirect effects and their significance (§ 1508.8).

(c) Possible conflicts between the proposed action and the objectives of Federal, regional, State, and local (and in the case of a reservation, Indian tribe) land use plans, policies and controls for the area concerned. (See § 1506.2(d).)

(d) The environmental effects of alternatives including the proposed action. The comparisons under § 1502.14 will be based on this discussion.

(e) Energy requirements and conservation potential of various alternatives and mitigation measures.

(f) Natural or depletable resource requirements and conservation potential of various alternatives and mitigation measures.

(g) Urban quality, historic and cultural resources, and the design of the built environment, including the reuse and conservation potential of various alternatives and mitigation measures.

(h) Means to mitigate adverse environmental impacts (if not fully covered under § 1502.14(f)).

[43 FR 55994, Nov. 29, 1978; 44 FR 873, Jan. 3, 1979]

§ 1502.17   List of preparers.

The environmental impact statement shall list the names, together with their qualifications (expertise, experience, professional disciplines), of the persons who were primarily responsible for preparing the environmental impact statement or significant background papers, including basic components of the statement (§§ 1502.6 and 1502.8). Where possible the persons who are responsible for a particular analysis, including analyses in background papers, shall be identified. Normally the list will not exceed two pages.

§ 1502.18   Appendix.

If an agency prepares an appendix to an environmental impact statement the appendix shall:

(a) Consist of material prepared in connection with an environmental impact statement (as distinct from material which is not so prepared and which is incorporated by reference (§ 1502.21)).

(b) Normally consist of material which substantiates any analysis fundamental to the impact statement.

(c) Normally be analytic and relevant to the decision to be made.

(d) Be circulated with the environmental impact statement or be readily available on request.

§ 1502.19   Circulation of the environmental impact statement.

Agencies shall circulate the entire draft and final environmental impact statements except for certain appendices as provided in § 1502.18(d) and unchanged statements as provided in § 1503.4(c). However, if the statement is unusually long, the agency may circulate the summary instead, except that the entire statement shall be furnished to:

(a) Any Federal agency which has jurisdiction by law or special expertise with respect to any environmental impact involved and any appropriate Federal, State or local agency authorized to develop and enforce environmental standards.

(b) The applicant, if any.

(c) Any person, organization, or agency requesting the entire environmental impact statement.

(d) In the case of a final environmental impact statement any person, organization, or agency which submitted substantive comments on the draft.

If the agency circulates the summary and thereafter receives a timely request for the entire statement and for additional time to comment, the time for that requestor only shall be extended by at least 15 days beyond the minimum period.

§ 1502.20   Tiering.

Agencies are encouraged to tier their environmental impact statements to eliminate repetitive discussions of the same issues and to focus on the actual issues ripe for decision at each level of environmental review (§ 1508.28). Whenever a broad environmental impact statement has been prepared (such as a program or policy statement) and a subsequent statement or environmental assessment is then prepared on an action included within the entire program or policy (such as a site specific action) the subsequent statement or environmental assessment need only summarize the issues discussed in the broader statement and incorporate discussions from the broader statement by reference and shall concentrate on the issues specific to the subsequent action. The subsequent document shall state where the earlier document is available. Tiering may also be appropriate for different stages of actions. (Section 1508.28).

§ 1502.21   Incorporation by reference.

Agencies shall incorporate material into an environmental impact statement by reference when the effect will be to cut down on bulk without impeding agency and public review of the action. The incorporated material shall be cited in the statement and its content briefly described. No material may be incorporated by reference unless it is reasonably available for inspection by potentially interested persons within the time allowed for comment. Material based on proprietary data which is itself not available for review and comment shall not be incorporated by reference.

§ 1502.22   Incomplete or unavailable information.

When an agency is evaluating reasonably foreseeable significant adverse effects on the human environment in an environmental impact statement and there is incomplete or unavailable information, the agency shall always make clear that such information is lacking.

(a) If the incomplete information relevant to reasonably foreseeable significant adverse impacts is essential to a reasoned choice among alternatives and the overall costs of obtaining it are not exorbitant, the agency shall include the information in the environmental impact statement.

(b) If the information relevant to reasonably foreseeable significant adverse impacts cannot be obtained because the overall costs of obtaining it are exorbitant or the means to obtain it are not known, the agency shall include within the environmental impact statement:

(1) A statement that such information is incomplete or unavailable; (2) a statement of the relevance of the incomplete or unavailable information to evaluating reasonably foreseeable significant adverse impacts on the human environment; (3) a summary of existing credible scientific evidence which is relevant to evaluating the reasonably foreseeable significant adverse impacts on the human environment, and (4) the agency's evaluation of such impacts based upon theoretical approaches or research methods generally accepted in the scientific community. For the purposes of this section, "reasonably foreseeable" includes impacts which have catastrophic consequences, even if their probability of occurrence is low, provided that the analysis of the impacts is supported by credible scientific evidence, is not based on pure conjecture, and is within the rule of reason.

(c) The amended regulation will be applicable to all environmental impact statements for which a Notice of Intent (40 CFR 1508.22) is published in the FEDERAL REGISTER on or after May 27, 1986. For environmental impact statements in progress, agencies may choose to comply with the requirements of either the original or amended regulation.

[51 FR 15625, Apr. 25, 1986]

§ 1502.23 Cost-benefit analysis.

If a cost-benefit analysis relevant to the choice among environmentally different alternatives is being considered for the proposed action, it shall be incorporated by reference or appended to the statement as an aid in evaluating the environmental consequences. To assess the adequacy of compliance with section 102(2)(B) of the Act the statement shall, when a cost-benefit analysis is prepared, discuss the relationship between that analysis and any analyses of unquantified environmental impacts, values, and amenities. For purposes of complying with the Act, the weighing of the merits and drawbacks of the various alternatives need not be displayed in a monetary cost-benefit analysis and should not be when there are important qualitative considerations. In any event, an environmental impact statement should at least indicate those considerations, including factors not related to environmental quality, which are likely to be relevant and important to a decision.

§ 1502.24 Methodology and scientific accuracy.

Agencies shall insure the professional integrity, including scientific integrity, of the discussions and analyses in environmental impact statements. They shall identify any methodologies used and shall make explicit reference by footnote to the scientific and other sources relied upon for conclusions in the statement. An agency may place discussion of methodology in an appendix.

§ 1502.25 Environmental review and consultation requirements.

(a) To the fullest extent possible, agencies shall prepare draft environmental impact statements concurrently with and integrated with environmental impact analyses and related surveys and studies required by the Fish and Wildlife Coordination Act (16 U.S.C. 661 *et seq.*), the National Historic Preservation Act of 1966 (16 U.S.C. 470 *et seq.*), the Endangered Species Act of 1973 (16 U.S.C. 1531 et seq.), and other environmental review laws and executive orders.

(b) The draft environmental impact statement shall list all Federal permits, licenses, and other entitlements which must be obtained in implementing the proposal. If it is uncertain whether a Federal permit, license, or other entitlement is necessary, the draft environmental impact statement shall so indicate.

APPENDIX B

CONTENTS AND SUMMARY FOR ENVIRONMENTAL IMPACT STATEMENT ON LOON MOUNTAIN SKI AREA PROJECT

TABLE OF CONTENTS, Continued

TABLE OF CONTENTS, Continued

TABLE OF CONTENTS, Continued

TABLE OF CONTENTS, Continued

TABLE OF CONTENTS, Continued

TABLE OF CONTENTS, Continued

LIST OF APPENDICES

APPENDIX A - LOON MOUNTAIN EIS SKIER DEMAND STUDY
APPENDIX B - LOON MOUNTAIN EROSION CONTROL PLAN
APPENDIX C - SOIL CHARACTERISTICS OF ECOLOGICAL LAND TYPES
APPENDIX D - AQUATIC BIOLOGY IFIM ANALYSIS RESULTS
APPENDIX E - VISUAL RESOURCE DEFINITIONS
APPENDIX F - WATER QUALITY MONITORING RESULTS
APPENDIX G - WATER RESOURCES MITIGATION PLAN
APPENDIX H - WILDLIFE MITIGATION PLAN

EXECUTIVE SUMMARY

BACKGROUND AND PURPOSE AND NEED

Loon Mountain Recreation Corporation (Loon) operates Loon Mountain Ski Area under a special use permit located in part on the White Mountain National Forest (Figure 1.1). Loon has applied for an amendment to their permit to allow an expansion onto South Mountain, an area of National Forest System land located on the west side of the existing ski area.

A Draft Environmental Impact Statement (Draft EIS) was prepared and released to the public in February 1989. Following review and comment, a Supplement to the Draft EIS was released in November of 1989 and addressed issues not included in the Draft. A Revised Draft EIS was issued in January 1991 and replaced the previous Draft and Supplement to the Draft and contained all information found in those two documents, as well as additional information on alternatives, alternatives considered but eliminated from detailed consideration, and cumulative impacts.

The Final EIS contains two volumes. Volume I updates and clarifies the Revised Draft EIS, and Volume II is the public comments, and response to comments, on the Revised Draft EIS. The Record of Decision will be issued approximately 45 days following release of this Final EIS.

The White Mountain National Forest Land and Resource Management Plan (Forest Plan-USDA-Forest Service 1986a) and Record of Decision (USDA-Forest Service 1986b) determined that future skier demand on the Forest would exceed supply, and that the Forest would meet the demand by expanding existing downhill ski areas rather than building new areas. A more recent study has indicated that demand may be greater than predicted. The Forest Plan designated part of the forest adjacent to existing ski areas, including South Mountain, as 9.2 Management Areas, which are set-asides for potential ski area expansion. The Forest Plan states that future ski area expansion could result in environmental impacts and that it will be necessary to assess the impacts on a case-by-case basis in accordance with the National Environmental Policy Act.

This document evaluates the potential impacts of Loon's proposed expansion on the environment. The decision to be made is whether or not to approve the proposed action, and, if not, whether to offer an alternative kind or degreee of expansion. The decision will be made in a Record of Decision which will be released approximately 45 days after issuance of this Final EIS.

The purpose of the proposed expansion is to meet the increased demand for downhill skiing at Loon Mountain Ski Area on the White Mountain National Forest. In the last few years, Loon has averaged over 20 sell-out days from mid-December to mid-March. Use of lifts and runs has been 5 to 10 percent over the rate used by the ski industry to indicate when expansion is needed to provide a quality skiing experience.

SCOPING AND IDENTIFICATION OF ISSUES

The White Mountain National Forest conducted scoping and initiated an environmental analysis in 1987. Based on public response, the Forest Service announced its intent to prepare an EIS on March 14, 1988. In preparation for the EIS, a Joint Review Committee comprised of federal, state, and local agency representatives was formed. Environmental groups and individuals were also invited to participate in the joint review process.

Additional scoping meetings were held in May 1988, and issues and concerns were received from the public and the Joint Review Committee. A total of 284 letters were received following publication of the original Draft EIS. Additional letters were received following publication of the Supplement. These comments were included as part of scoping for this EIS. Following release of the Revised Draft EIS, 218 individual comment letters were received and about 80 people spoke at public meetings. Although the comments were extensive, and are responded to in Volume II of the Final EIS, no new issues were raised in comments on the Revised Draft EIS The issues considered significant for this Final EIS, therefore, did not change from those of the Revised Draft EIS, and are summarized as follows:

Water Resources - There is a concern that the construction and operation of additional facilities would reduce the water quality and quantity of the East Branch of the Pemigewasset. Specifically, there is concern about sedimentation from ski slopes, roads, water lines, housing, and base facilities. Other concerns are that runoff from parking lots would result in heavy metal, salt, or petroleum contamination of the river. Another concern is the effect of snowmaking withdrawals on aquatic habitat, especially for the Atlantic salmon and brook trout. Still others are concerned about the effects of Loon's total water needs competing with other water uses such as municipal use by the town of Lincoln.

Socioeconomics - A number of those who commented are concerned about the increased rate of growth both at Loon and in surrounding communities, particularly Lincoln and Woodstock. Some people see the expansion as an acceleration that would detract from the quality of life. People are concerned about increased traffic, noise, demand for housing, and demand for public services such as drinking water, solid waste disposal, sewage treatment, schools, and police and fire protection. Others see this as an opportunity to increase job choices, expand secondary services, and increase the local tax base. Some see this as an opportunity to improve the quality of life through added recreation facilities and cultural opportunities that accompany the type of development proposed. Several people expressed concern when they started businesses, remodeled or expanded existing ones, or started new regional attractions such as the North Country Center for the Arts that they had relied on the Forest Plan and Loon's expressed intention to grow. Failure to increase skier capacity may threaten the viability of these endeavors.

Skier Demand - Some of the public are concerned whether there is sufficient future skier demand to warrant the Forest Service's permitting further development of the Loon Mountain Ski Area. People want to know what the options are and whether the demand is real. Others want to see Loon expand so they too can enjoy the quality of recreational experience Loon now provides without concern of overcrowding or being denied a ticket.

Alternative Sites for Meeting Skier Demand - A number of people think that skier demand on the Forest could be met at sites other than Loon. Some are concerned that the alternatives considered in detail should include expansions at other sites in New England, or the White Mountain region in general, and not be restricted to Loon Mountain. Other people indicated that skiers had site-specific preferences and that other sites would not be reasonable alternatives to expansion at Loon Mountain.

Wildlife Resources - In addition to the potential impacts on aquatic habitat from changes in water quality and quantity, several people are concerned that there may be a loss of deer habitat, bear mast trees, or other impacts due to the conversion from a forest to open slopes.

Competing Uses - Some people express concern that further ski development would so change the area's aesthetics that visual quality would be reduced; that there would be a major shift in the type of recreation experience in this part of the Forest; or that it would change the land's character, reducing local residents' quality of life.

ALTERNATIVES

The following six alternatives were analyzed in detail: No Action, Loon's Proposed Action, Limited Development, Smaller Permit Area, Expansion on the Existing Permit Area Only, and Consolidated Development. A number of other alternatives were considered including sites off the White Mountain National Forest, sites considered in earlier Forest Service planning studies, and other existing ski areas on the Forest. In addition, other alternatives at Loon Mountain were suggested during scoping, including night skiing, no snowmaking, other configurations on South Mountain, and other configurations on the existing permit area. All of these other potential alternatives were eliminated from detailed analysis because they were not reasonable or feasible alternatives. Still other alternatives were suggested but eliminated because they had already been analyzed in the Forest Plan. These other potential alternatives included whether or not skiing was an acceptable use of National Forest System lands, whether or not skier demand could best be met on National Forest System lands, or whether demand should be met by expansion of existing facilities or development of new facilities.

Alternative 1 - No Action

If this alternative were selected, the special use permit amendment would be denied. It is assumed that recreation-oriented growth would occur in the Lincoln-Woodstock area. Existing ski area operations would continue as in the past. Loon could develop some of their private land for recreation or for increased recreational housing.

Alternative 2 - Loon's Proposed Action

Under this alternative the Forest Service would grant Loon a 930-acre permit expansion onto South Mountain. Loon's expansion would be conducted in two phases (Figure 2.8). Phase I facilities on National Forest System lands would include three lifts, thirteen trails, a new snowmaking system using Loon Pond, and an up-mountain lodge. Facilities on private land would include one lift, a South Mountain base lodge, maintenance buildings, parking lots, a golf course, and additional housing units. Additional facilities on National Forest System lands during Phase II would include four more lifts (one on the existing permit area) and sixteen trails. Loon would also build a small base area lodge and more housing on private land. The Proposed Action would provide for a variety of skiing terrain from beginner to advanced. Skiing between the existing area and South Mountain would be facilitated by crossover trails.

Water for snowmaking for the proposed expansion would come from Loon Pond. Loon would drill into the side of the pond 15 feet below the top of the dam (Figure 2.9) and use gravity to provide water to the ski trails. Loon would continue to use the East Branch, Boyle Brook, and Loon Pond as the sources of snowmaking water for the existing ski area (Figure 4.1). Loon Pond would be refilled from the East Branch if needed.

In total, Phases I and II would add 7,600 skiers to Loon's present capacity of 5,800 skiers while expanding the base area facilities. Cost of the total expansion would be approximately $27 million, and would create 180 winter jobs and 40 full-time jobs at Loon. Summer use in the Lincoln area would be slightly greater than under No Action. If the Forest Service permitted full expansion, the decision on the timing and extent of Phase II would involve several factors, including economics, skier demand, available water, and the successful mitigation of Phase I impacts.

Alternative 3 - Limited Development

This alternative has been substantially revised since the Draft EIS was issued in order to reflect public concerns about the size of the proposed South Mountain expansion. A major difference between this alternative and the Proposed Action is limitations on withdrawals of water for snowmaking use from the East Branch and Loon Pond. When flows in the East Branch are above 85 cfs, Loon would use the East Branch and Boyle Brook to make snow on the existing mountain and withdraw water from Loon Pond for South Mountain and the upper portion of the existing ski area. When flows in the river drop below 85 cfs, Loon would withdraw snowmaking water only from Loon Pond for all portions of both the existing ski area and South Mountain (Figure 4.1). Loon would not be able to draw Loon Pond down below 15 feet from the top of the dam, and would ensure that the pond is full during the first week of December and by May 15 of each year. It assumes that only Phase I of Loon's Proposed Action would be permitted, but limited to an additional 3,200 skiers at one time and with a reduced South Mountain base area development. This alternative would involve a 930-acre ski area permit expansion. Housing development on Loon's private land would still continue at the same level as in their Proposed Action. The alternative would include three lifts, thirteen trails, a new snowmaking system, and an up-mountain lodge on National Forest System lands. One lift, parking lots, a golf course, and housing development would be on private land. This expansion on South Mountain would be connected to the existing ski area with ski trails to go both directions, and would provide a mix of skier terrain from beginner to advanced intermediate. The cost of construction would be about $17 million.

Alternative 4 - Smaller Permit Area

This alternative was developed due to concerns that the Limited Development Alternative was too large of an expansion. This alternative would allow an increase of 2,600 skiers at one time, and would include three lifts and nine trails. The ski area permit expansion would be about 370 acres. Skiers could ski from Loon to this expansion, but would need to take a shuttle bus back. Skier terrain would be primarily beginner and low intermediate. A lodge would be constructed at the base of the expansion, along with a maintenance building and a 750-car parking lot. This alternative would also include the private housing and golf course located on private land as discussed for the Proposed Action. Snowmaking water for the expansion would come from Loon Pond and limitations on withdrawals from the pond and the East Branch would be the same as included in Limited Development.

Alternative 5 - Expansion on the Existing Permit Area Only

This alternative represents the smallest expansion possible at Loon Mountain Ski Area and was developed in response to concerns that existing demand could be met within the existing permit area. This alternative would include one lift and two advanced trails on the eastern side of the ski area that would provide an additional 900 skiers at one time. Additional parking and limited base area facilities would be provided at the South Mountain base area. A shuttle bus would take skiers from the South Mountain parking lot to Loon. Additional snowmaking water would come from Loon Pond. Limitations on withdrawals from the pond and the East Branch would be the same as discussed for Limited Development.

Alternative 6 - Consolidated Development Alternative

This alternative was developed following release and comment on the Revised Draft EIS. It responds to concerns about meeting the demand for additional skiing capacity at Loon and about the magnitude of potential impacts related to expansion on South Mountain. To meet skier demand, this alternative would include improving and upgrading most of the existing lifts at Loon Mountain, widening many existing trails, developing six new trails, and one new lift on private land on the existing ski area. This would reduce the need for a large expansion on South Mountain, and resulted in only lift G and associated trails being proposed on South Mountain adjacent to the existing ski area. The special use permit area would be enlarged by 581 acres. Existing lodge/restaurant facilities would also be enlarged, a lodge would be built at the base of lift G, and parking would be provided at the base of South Mountain. Shuttle buses would transport skiers from the parking lot to lift G and the existing base area. This alternative would increase skier capacity to the same level (9000 CCC) as Alternative 3. The snowmaking system and water withdrawal limitations would be the same as Alternative 3, but the intake system to Loon Pond would use the current pumping facilities rather than drilling through the side of the pond. Construction would likely occur over a 5 to 7 year period and cost would be about $17.5 million.

ENVIRONMENTAL IMPACTS AND MITIGATION

The alternatives vary in the level of development on National Forest System lands and private land. The major variables are summarized by alternative in Table 1.

Numerous issues were identified during the environmental analysis review and public scoping. Six of these issues were determined critical to the permit expansion decision. They are Alternative Sites for Meeting Skier Demand, Water Resources/Aquatic Biology, Socioeconomics, Skier Demand, Wildlife Resources, and Competing Uses. This section summarizes the six major issues and how they were addressed in this EIS. The issue of alternative sites was discussed in Chapter 2 of the Final EIS. The impact analysis presented in Chapter 4 of the Final EIS indicates that impacts between the six alternatives analyzed in detail differ considerably. The alternatives vary in the amount and location of land area that would be impacted, and therefore, the resources that would be affected. Hence, these six alternatives also vary in how the six major scoping issues would be resolved.

Alternative Sites for Meeting Skier Demand

The alternatives analysis in this chapter indicated that there were no other reasonable or feasible alternative sites for meeting the skier demand at this time. A thorough analysis using existing information indicated that expansion of other ski areas on the White Mountain National Forest may meet some of the skier demand, but none of these sites would have substantially less environmental impact associated with its expansion, none are ripe for a decision, none would meet the demand better than at Loon, and all four other ski areas may be permitted to expand in the future even if Loon or another area were permitted to expand.

Water Resources/Aquatic Biology

Water quality in the East Branch and mainstem is e*cellent at present except for occasional periods in the summer. Alternatives 2, 3, 4, and 6 have the potential to create water quality impacts due to increased erosion and sedimentation of the tributary streams that drain South Mountain. Of the South Mountain alternatives, Alternative 4 would have the least impact since only one crossover trail would cross Loon Pond Brook. Alternative 6 would have less impact on Loon Pond Brook than Alternatives 2 and 3 since it would cross the stream in a less sensitive area. Alternative 5 would have the lowest potential sedimentation impact of any of the action alternatives since it would not involve construction on South Mountain, or cross Loon Pond Brook. Best management practices and a State Alteration of Terrain Permit would reduce water quality impacts under all alternatives to acceptable levels. A monitoring program would assure that water quality remains excellent in the rivers and streams.

Under the No Action Alternative (Alternative 1), Loon would deplete water from the East Branch and Boyle Brook for snowmaking at a maximum combined rate of 3 cfs (1 cfs from Boyle Brook, 1 cfs from the East Branch, and 1 cfs from the Loon Pond system). This maximum rate of depletion would remain the same under all of the other five alternatives since no new snowmaking pumping system is planned. What would vary between alternatives is the total amount of water used per ski season, varying from the 67 million gallons used at present and for Alternative 1,

TABLE 1

COMPARISON OF ALTERNATIVES FOR MAJOR VARIABLES

	Current	Alt 1	Alt 2	Alt 3	Alt 4	Alt 5	Alt 6
Additional comfortable carrying capacity	0	0	7,600	3,200	2,600	900	3,200
Total comfortable carrying capacity	5,800	5,800	13,400	9,000	8,400	6,700	9,000
Acres of National Forest under permit	785	785	1,715	1,715	1,155	785	1,366
Additional acres of clearing for ski area	0	0	400	200	125	32	150
Additional acres served by snowmaking	0	0	354	189	99	32	195
Total acres served by snowmaking	185	185	540	374	284	217	380
Total annual snowmaking water demand (million gallons)	67	67	193	134	118	78	138
Peak snowmaking water demand (cfs)	3	3	4**	4**	4**	4**	4**
Lifts on South Mountain	0	0	8	4	3	0	1
Winter peak visitation	14,500	22,000	25,000	25,000	25,000	22,000	25,000
Additional cars in lots	0	0	1,800	900	700	250	900
New base facilities (ft^2)	0	0	51,000	37,500	10,000	5,000	43,500

*   cfs = cubic feet per second, No Action domestic water demand will increase if the town used the river for more water than at present.
** This number reflects conditions when pumping to refill Loon Pond.

to the 193 million gallons used under full development of Alternative 2 (Loon's Proposed Action). Alternative 3 would require 134 million gallons; Alternative 4, 118 million gallons; Alternative 5, 77 million gallons; and Alternative 6, 138 million gallons. This rate of depletion would potentially impact Atlantic salmon habitat in the East Branch, but a 32 cfs minimum flow mitigation measure would minimize impacts to fish for Alternative 2. The 85 cfs minimum flow (after the phase-in period) of Alternatives 3, 4, 5, and 6 would provide even better protection for Atlantic salmon. The total amount of water used would, under all alternatives, not affect downstream users since the amount is a very small percent of the total flow of the stream, even under Alternative 2. Under Alternatives 2, 3, 4, 5, and 6, Loon would deplete the East Branch by a maximum of 4 cfs while refilling Loon Pond (3 cfs from the East Branch and Boyle Brook combined plus 1 cfs from the Loon Pond system).

The amount of water withdrawn from Loon Pond would also vary among alternatives. Under Alternative 2, Loon could draw the pond down 10 feet below the normal full level of the pond, with another 5 feet reserved for an emergency supply for the town of Lincoln. Under Alternatives 3,

4, 5, and 6, Loon would have the potential of drawing the pond down 15 feet, with an additional 5 feet for the Town. This would be accomplished by drilling a pipe into the side of the pond under Alternatives 2, 3, 4, and 5, and by pumping the water out under Alternative 6. The 10-foot drawdown limit for Alternative 2, and the 15-foot limit for Alternatives 3, 4, 5, and 6 would protect the ecology of the pond since most of its inhabitants would not be affected by a winter drawdown. Alternative 5 would use very little additional water from Loon Pond, so withdrawals would generally be about the same as present operations (No Action).

The town of Lincoln is planning a new water treatment system that would utilize the East Branch as its primary water source. The rate of withdrawal of water from the East Branch would be 3 cfs under all six alternatives, and all alternatives would have a 5-foot emergency water supply in Loon Pond for the town of Lincoln. The total amount of water withdrawn would be greatest under Alternative 2, especially during the winter, due to increased numbers of skiers. All alternatives would see greater water usage in the future, but this usage would be relatively minor in comparison to the total flow of the river and would not affect downstream users. The Corps of Engineers has placed a 30 cfs minimum flow requirement for withdrawals by the town to protect Atlantic salmon habitat.

Socioeconomics

The towns of Lincoln and Woodstock, and to a much lesser degree, surrounding towns would grow under all alternatives. The primary source of the growth is a projected continued increase in summer recreation associated with this area of the White Mountains. Alternatives 2, 3, 4, 5, and 6 would have increased winter growth also due to expansion of the ski area. Under No Action (Alternative 1), the area is projected to have about 25,000 peak summer visitors within 20 years. This level of summer visitation would be reached in 15 years under both Alternatives 2, 3, and 6, and in between 15 and 20 years by Alternatives 4 and 5. Winter visitation would reach 25,000 also under Alternative 2 in 15 years, and about 20,000 under Alternatives 3 and 6 in 15 years. Alternatives 4 and 5 would see lower numbers of winter visitors. Hence, the infrastructure in the Lincoln-Woodstock area would need to support 25,000 visitors under all alternatives, but this level of visitation would be reached much sooner under Alternatives 2, 3, and 6. This rate of growth would stress local planning, traffic, demand for housing, and the demand for public services. Both Lincoln and Woodstock officials have indicated they are prepared for the growth, but other members in the communities are not as sure. Present problems with Lincoln's sewage treatment lagoons and water supply system suggest these areas may not be able to handle the rapid growth, although state and local officials feel the town's systems can handle the growth.

The Forest Service would work closely with the state and the towns to ensure that the rate of growth of the ski area does not exceed the capacity of the towns to keep up with the growth. If needed, the Forest Service would delay or deny portions of the ski area expansion to prevent serious problems with the infrastructure.

The growth of the area would provide additional jobs in the area, both summer and winter. Alternative 2 would provide the best balance between winter and summer jobs, with a greater likelihood that people could use two or three seasonal jobs to provide year-round employment. The tax base generated by the development proposed in Alternatives 2, 3, and 6 would support the infrastructural needs of the communities, although taxes would lag behind the need for the services requiring bonding or other methods to provide services.

Alternative 4 would also provide additional winter jobs but due to its small size and poor skier mix, would be the least likely of the alternatives to be financially feasible. Recent trends in the ski industry show that skiers favor larger resort-type areas with a good balance of skier mix. Alternative 4 would provide only beginner and lower intermediate skiing, not the type of skiing most of Loon's present customers are seeking. Alternative 5 would add little economic benefits or adverse impacts due to the small size of its expansion, and its poor skier mix. Alternative 5 would add only expert skiing terrain to Loon, rather than a mix of skiing terrain. Alternative 6 would add skier capacity to the present ski area, which is presently quite crowded. Planned trail widening, improvements in the lifts and facilities should reduce the crowding.

Skier Demand

Skier demand studies have shown there is sufficient skier demand to warrant construction of Alternative 2, which would provide for an additional 7600 skiers at one time. None of the other alternatives would meet this demand better than Alternative 2, since the increase in skiers at one time for Alternatives 3, 4, 5, and 6 are 3,200, 2,600, 900, and 3200, respectively. Alternatives 2, 3, and 6 would provide the best opportunities to add additional skiing similar to that presently provided at the existing ski area since these alternatives would provide beginner to advanced intermediate skiing. Alternative 4 would provide novice and intermediate skiing only, and Alternative 5 would provide advanced skiing only, but would add to present congestion and parking problems at the ski area.

Wildlife Resources

Alternatives 2, and 3 would directly impact a deer wintering area along lower Loon Pond Brook through construction of a crossover ski trail. This deer wintering area has been impacted by past ski area development and would be indirectly impacted to a lesser degree by housing construction on Loon's private land under all Alternatives. Mitigation of enhancing and protecting a nearby deer wintering area would mitigate the impacts under Alternatives 2, 3, 4, and 6. Bear mast trees and cavity trees would also be lost due to clearing of ski trails under all alternatives except No Action, with the greatest loss in Alternative 2. This impact would be minimized by avoiding cavity trees and mast trees to the extent possible during the layout of trails. Clearing for ski trails under Alternatives 2, 3, 4, 5, and 6 would increase fragmentation of dense forested areas that is preferred by some bird and mammal species. Clearing would provide additional edge habitat for other species of birds and mammals. Alternative 2 would result in the most habitat fragmentation, and greatest loss of bear mast and cavity trees, and the amount of these habitats lost would be reduced in Alternatives 3, 4, 5, and 6.

Competing Uses

Alternative 2 would create the greatest change in visual resources, as well as the greatest change in character of the land since it is the largest expansion of the four action alternatives. Alternatives 3, 4, and 6 would also have substantial visible change on South Mountain since they would all develop portions of the mountain that are most visible from the Lincoln area and I-93. Alternative 5 would be hardly noticeable to most visitors in the area. A major expansion of the ski area as proposed in Alternatives 2, 3, and 6 would have the most potential for changing the recreational experience of visitors to the area, although the type of growth that would occur under Alternative 1 is unknown and could result in considerable change to the private lands in Lincoln for additional summer tourist attractions. Some residents would feel their quality of life was reduced under Alternative 1, and others' quality of life would be reduced under Alternatives 2, 3, 4, or 6.

Mitigation

The impact analysis indicates that without mitigation, environmental consequences from permitting expansion of ski facilities onto South Mountain could result in significant impacts due to degradation of water quality in the East Branch by non-point sources, likely loss of deer winter habitat along Loon Pond Brook, accelerated growth in the Lincoln-Woodstock area, and traffic and parking problems in the Lincoln area. Permitting the expansion would also have beneficial consequences, including meeting present skier demand and some of the future skier demand, and increasing the local and regional economic activity by creating a year-round resort balance.

A number of other impacts were also noted in the analysis that were not significant, but were adverse. These impacts included small amounts of erosion to Loon Pond Brook; disturbance to less than one acre of wetland; noise from snowmaking which would affect a few people; water quality degradation would occur more frequently when flows are reduced below the seven-day, ten-year low flow (7Q10) on the East Branch; disturbance to raptor nests, cavity trees, and mast trees during construction of ski trails; alteration of the area's visual characteristics; and some social dissatisfaction. Beneficial impacts would include some social satisfaction, especially among skiers, and alleviation of present skier congestion at Loon.

On the other hand, the impact analysis indicates that denial of the expansion could result in continued skier congestion at Loon, failure to meet the current and projected skier demand at Loon, additional impacts to deer winter habitat that would not be mitigated, and less economic activity in Lincoln-Woodstock and the region, as well as a less balanced year-round economy.

A number of mitigation measures were developed that, in combination with Forest Plan standards and guidelines, would minimize or eliminate adverse impacts of the five action alternatives. Most of the mitigation measures have been successfully applied by Loon and other ski/resort permittees on the White Mountain National Forest. The Forest Service will monitor the effectiveness of the proposed mitigation measures.

ENVIRONMENTALLY PREFERRED ALTERNATIVE

The environmentally preferred alternative would be the No Action Alternative, Alternative 1. Substantial impacts would still occur under this alternative, primarily due to the continued growth in the summer recreation-based economy of the Lincoln-Woodstock area. Therefore, many of the socioeconomic and infrastructural impacts would occur under this alternative, although they would occur later than under any of the other alternatives.

FOREST SERVICE PREFERRED ALTERNATIVE

Alternative 6 (Consolidated Development) is the Forest Service's preferred alternative. This is a change from the preferred alternative described in the Revised Draft EIS. This alternative, if implemented, would result in conversion of Loon's special use permit to a new permit and adoption of Alternative 6 as the Master Development Plan for the ski area. This alternative would allow Loon, subject to the mitigation discussed with the alternative, to expand its downhill ski facilities. New facilities on National Forest System lands would include one lift, fifteen trails, expanded lodges, and a new snowmaking system. Facilities on private land could include one lift, expansion of existing base facilities, a base lodge at lift G, parking lot at South Mountain, and additional housing units.

A final decision will follow public review of this Final EIS.

Mitigation for the Preferred Alternative

Erosion/Sedimentation

o Loon will obtain a New Hampshire Alteration of Terrain Permit prior to construction or disturbance in order to determine and implement best management practices for sedimentation and non-point pollution sources as outlined in Appendix G.

o The Forest Service will have an employee on-site during construction activities to insure that mitigation measures are being fully implemented and are effective.

Noise

o Loon will use the best available technology to reduce noise impacts from snowmaking operations.

Water Resources

o No construction on National Forest System lands will be allowed until the town of Lincoln has installed a new water treatment facility or suitable alternative approved by the state of New Hampshire.

o Until Loon's snowmaking system has been converted, by 2003 or twelve years after issuance of the permit at the latest, water withdrawals for snowmaking will cease at river flows of 40 cfs, and withdrawal for refilling Loon Pond will cease at 62 cfs. Water withdrawals from the East Branch of the Pemigewasset River will not be permitted when flows are less than or equal to 85 cubic feet per second (cfs) following Loon's conversion of their snowmaking system, by 2003 or twelve years after issuance of the permit at the latest. Depletion from the East Branch and Boyle Brook combined will not exceed 2 cfs for snowmaking and 3 cfs for refilling Loon Pond. Maximum depletion of the East Branch will, therefore, be 3 cfs for snowmaking and 4 cfs for refilling Loon Pond when 1 cfs depletion due to use of Loon Pond is added to the depletion amounts for snowmaking and refilling Loon Pond.

o Loon will develop a water quality monitoring program in cooperation with the Forest Service, state of New Hampshire, Environmental Protection Agency, town of Lincoln, and other interested agencies to document future water quality changes and to determine if predictions in this environmental impact statement were accurate. Should water quality problems be identified, the Forest Service will require Loon to conduct appropriate additional mitigation.

o Loon will install recording strip charts or their equivalent to meter snowmaking water pumps and will cooperate with the town of Lincoln in installing a gauge in the East Branch in order to monitor withdrawals and flows.

o Loon will assure the Forest Service that Loon Pond will be filled each year it is used for snowmaking during the first week of December and by May 15 to prevent wetland or visual impacts, and there will be a drawdown limit on Loon Pond of 15 feet for snowmaking.

o Loon Pond refill withdrawals will not be permitted when turbidity in the East Branch exceeds 5 nephelometric turbidity units, or the coliform bacteria count is above 50 per 100 ml., or other requirements prescribed by the State to prevent degradation of Loon Pond are not met.

o Loon, the New Hampshire Department of Environmental Services, and the town of Lincoln will develop an acceptable plan for assuring an adequate emergency water supply for the town from Loon Pond.

Wildlife

o The Loon Pond Brook deer wintering area will be replaced with a suitable alternative site, and be managed according to the mitigation plan.

o Cavity trees and mast trees will be avoided during clearing operations, where feasible.

o Raptor nest surveys will be conducted prior to forest clearing. Nesting areas will be left undisturbed until nesting and rearing is complete.

Visual Resources

o All structures and clearings will meet Forest Service visual quality objectives.

Socioeconomics/Transportation

o The Forest Service may delay or deny authorization of construction of any component of the expansion if, in consultation with Lincoln-Woodstock and the state, the group determines that the area's infrastructure is unable to meet any increased demand for municipal services which would result from such construction.

o The Forest Service will not approve clearing of land or construction of facilities until the state of New Hampshire certifies that the town of Lincoln's sewage lagoons are operating properly.

o Loon will build the new proposed South Mountain access road to be serviceable as soon as practical but in no case later than the start of the third season of operation of South Mountain, subject to the approval of the town of Lincoln and the state of New Hampshire.

o Loon will be required to continue to use a traffic officer during peak use times at the Loon Mountain Road/Highway 112 intersection. The Forest Service will not approve additional development of the ski area if other intersections in Lincoln fall below a LOS C due to Loon Mountain traffic and are not mitigated to the satisfaction of the New Hampshire Department of Transportation.

Additional detail on these mitigation measures can be found in Chapter 4 of the Final EIS, and in the detailed mitigation plans included in the Appendix of that document. This detail includes estimated costs, agencies responsible for the mitigation, locations for the mitigation, and implementation plans for all of the mitigation proposed. The Forest Service will monitor the effectiveness of the mitigation measures.

APPENDIX C

STATUTE AND REGULATIONS FOR MOTOR CARRIER NOISE EMISSION STANDARDS. STATUTE: NOISE CONTROL ACT 42 U.S.C.S. § 4917 REGULATIONS: 40 CFR, PART 202

§ 4917. Motor carrier noise emission standards

(a) Regulations; standards; consultation with Secretary of Transportation.

(1) Within nine months after the date of enactment of this Act [enacted Oct. 27, 1972], the Administrator shall publish proposed noise emission regulations for motor carriers engaged in interstate commerce. Such proposed regulations shall include noise emission standards setting such limits on noise emissions resulting from operation of motor carriers engaged in interstate commerce which reflect the degree of noise reduction achievable through the application of the best available technology, taking into account the cost of compliance. These regulations shall be in addition to any regulations that may be proposed under section 6 of this Act [42 USCS § 4905].

(2) Within ninety days after the publication of such regulations as may be proposed under paragraph (1) of this subsection, and subject to the provisions of section 16 of this Act [42 USCS § 4915], the Administrator shall promulgate final regulations. Such regulations may be revised from time to time, in accordance with this subsection.

(3) Any standard or regulation, or revision thereof, proposed under this subsection shall be promulgated only after consultation with the Secretary of Transportation in order to assure appropriate consideration for safety and technological availability.

(4) Any regulation or revision thereof promulgated under this subsection shall take effect after such period as the Administrator finds necessary, after consultation with the Secretary of Transportation, to permit the development and application of the requisite technology, giving appropriate consideration to the cost of compliance within such period.

(b) Regulations to insure compliance with noise emission standards. The Secretary of Transportation, after consultation with the Administrator shall promulgate regulations to insure compliance with all standards promulgated by the Administrator under this section. The Secretary of Transportation shall carry out such regulations through the use of his powers and duties of enforcement and inspection authorized by the Interstate Commerce Act and the Department of Transportation Act. Regulations promulgated under this section shall be subject to the provisions of sections 10, 11, 12, and 16 of this Act [42 USCS §§ 4909–4911, 4915].

(c) State and local standards and controls. (1) Subject to paragraph (2) of this subsection but notwithstanding any other provision of this Act, after the effective date of a regulation under this section applicable to noise emissions resulting from the operation of any motor carrier engaged in interstate commerce, no State or political subdivision thereof may adopt or enforce any standard applicable to the same operation of such motor carrier, unless such standard is identical to a standard applicable to noise emissions resulting from such operation prescribed by any regulation under this section.

(2) Nothing in this section shall diminish or enhance the rights of any State or political subdivision thereof to establish and enforce standards of controls on levels of environmental noise, or to control, license, regulate, or restrict the use, operation, or movement of any product if the Administrator, after consultation with the Secretary of Transportation, determines that such standard, control, license, regulation, or restriction is necessitated by special local conditions and is not in conflict with regulations promulgated under this section.

(d) Definitions. For purposes of this section, the term "motor carrier" includes a common carrier by motor vehicle, a contract carrier by motor vehicle, and a private carrier of property by motor vehicle as those terms are defined by paragraphs (14), (15), and (17) of section 203(a) of the Interstate Commerce Act (49 U.S.C. 303(a)).
(Oct. 27, 1972, P. L. 92-574, § 18, 86 Stat. 1249.)

PART 202—MOTOR CARRIERS ENGAGED IN INTERSTATE COMMERCE

Subpart A—General Provisions

AUTHORITY: Sec. 18, 36 Stat. 1249, 42 U.S.C. 4917(a).

Subpart A—General Provisions

§ 202.10 Definitions.

As used in this part, all terms not defined herein shall have the meaning given them in the Act:

(a) *Act* means the Noise Control Act of 1972 (Pub. L. 92-574, 86 Stat. 1234)

(b) *Common carrier by motor vehicle* means any person who holds himself out to the general public to engage in the transportation by motor vehicle in interstate or foreign commerce of passengers or property or any class or classes thereof for compensation, whether over regular or irregular routes.

(c) *Contract carrier by motor vehicle* means any person who engages in transportation by motor vehicle of passengers or property in interstate or foreign commerce for compensation (other than transportation referred to in paragraph (b) of this section) under continuing contracts with one person or a limited number of persons either (1) for the furnishing of transportation services through the assignment of motor vehicles for a continuing period of time to the exclusive use of each person served or (2) for the furnishing of transportation services designed to meet the distinct need of each individual customer.

(d) *Cutout or by-pass or similar devices* means devices which vary the exhaust system gas flow so as to discharge the exhaust gas and acoustic energy to the atmosphere without passing through the entire length of the exhaust system, including all exhaust system sound attenuation components.

(e) *dB(A)* means the standard abbreviation for A-weighted sound level in decibels.

(f) *Exhaust system* means the system comprised of a combination of components which provides for enclosed flow of exhaust gas from engine parts to the atmosphere.

(g) *Fast meter response* means that the fast dynamic response of the sound level meter shall be used. The fast dynamic response shall comply with the meter dynamic characteristics in paragraph 5.3 of the American National Standard Specification for Sound Level Meters, ANSI S1. 4-1971.

This publication is available from the American National Standards Institute, Inc., 1420 Broadway, New York, New York 10018.

(h) *Gross Vehicle Weight Rating* (GVWR) means the value specified by the manufacturer as the loaded weight of a single vehicle.

(i) *Gross Combination Weight Rating* (GCWR) means the value specified by the manufacturer as the loaded weight of a combination vehicle.

(j) *Highway* means the streets, roads, and public ways in any State.

(k) *Interstate commerce* means the commerce between any place in a State and any place in another State or between places in the same State through another State, whether such commerce moves wholly by motor vehicle or partly by motor vehicle and partly by rail, express, water or air. This definition of "interstate commerce" for purposes of these regulations is the same as the definition of "interstate commerce" in section 203(a) of the Interstate Commerce Act. [49 U.S.C. 303(a)]

(l) *Motor carrier* means a common carrier by motor vehicle, a contract carrier by motor vehicle, or a private carrier of property by motor vehicle as those terms are defined by paragraphs (14), (15), and (17) of section 203(a) of the Interstate Commerce Act [49 U.S.C. 303(a)].

(m) *Motor vehicle* means any vehicle, machine, tractor, trailer, or semitrailer propelled or drawn by mechanical power and used upon the highways in the transportation of passengers or property, or any combination thereof, but does not include any vehicle, locomotive, or car operated exclusively on a rail or rails.

(n) *Muffler* means a device for abating the sound of escaping gases of an internal combustion engine.

(o) *Open site* means an area that is essentially free of large sound-reflecting objects, such as barriers, walls, board fences, signboards, parked vehicles, bridges, or buildings.

(p) *Private carrier of property by motor vehicle* means any person not included in terms "common carrier by motor vehicle" or "contract carrier by motor vehicle", who or which transports in interstate or foreign commerce by motor vehicle property of which such person is the owner, lessee, or bailee, when such transportation is for sale, lease, rent or bailment, or in furtherance of any commercial enterprise.

(q) *Sound level* means the quantity in decibles measured by a sound level meter satisfying the requirements of American National Standards Specification for Sound Level Meters S1.4-1971. This publication is available from the American National Standards Institute, Inc., 1430 Broadway, New York, New York 10018. Sound level is the frequency-weighted sound pressure level obtained with the standardized dynamic characteristic "fast" or "slow" and weighting A, B, or C; unless indicated otherwise, the A-weighting is understood.

[39 FR 38215, Oct. 29, 1974]

§ 202.11 Effective date.

The provisions of Subpart B shall become effective October 15, 1975, except that the provisions of § 202.20(b) and § 202.21(b) of Subpart B shall apply to motor vehicles manufactured during or after the 1986 model year.

[51 FR 852, Jan. 8, 1986]

§ 202.12 Applicability.

(a) The provisions of Subpart B apply to all motor carriers engaged in interstate commerce.

(b) The provisions of Subpart B apply only to those motor vehicles of such motor carriers which have a gross vehicle weight rating or gross combination weight rating in excess of 10,000 pounds, and only when such motor vehicles are operating under the conditions specified in Subpart B.

(c) Except as provided in paragraphs (d) and (e) of this section, the provisions of Subpart B apply to the total sound produced by such motor vehicles when operating under such conditions, including the sound produced by auxiliary equipment mounted on such motor vehicles.

(d) The provisions of Subpart B do not apply to auxiliary equipment which is normally operated only when the transporting vehicle is stationary

or is moving at a speed of 5 miles per hour or less. Examples of such equipment include, but are not limited to, cranes, asphalt spreaders, ditch diggers, liquid or slurry pumps, air compressors, welders, and trash compactors.

(e) The provisions of Subpart B do not apply to warning devices, such as horns and sirens; or to emergency equipment and vehicles such as fire engines, ambulances, police vans, and rescue vans, when responding to emergency calls; or to snow plows when in operation.

(f) The provisions of § 202.20(a) and § 202.21(a) of Subpart B apply only to applicable motor vehicles manufactured prior to the 1986 model year.

(g) The provisions of § 202.20(b) and § 202.21(b) apply to all applicable motor vehicles manufactured during or after the 1986 model year.

[39 FR 38215, Oct. 29, 1974, as amended at 51 FR 852, Jan. 8, 1986]

Subpart B—Interstate Motor Carrier Operations Standards

§ 202.20 Standards for highway operations.

(a) No motor carrier subject to these regulations shall operate any motor vehicle of a type to which this regulation is applicable which at any time or under any condition of highway trade, load, acceleration or deceleration generates a sound level in excess of 86dB(A) measured on an open site with fast meter response at 50 feet from the centerline of lane of travel on highways with speed limits of 35 MPH or less; or 90 dB(A) measured on an open site with fast meter response at 50 feet from the centerline of lane of travel on highways with speed limits of more than 35 MPH.

(b) No motor carrier subject to these regulations shall operate any motor vehicle of a type to which this regulation is applicable which at any time or under any condition of highway grade, load, acceleration or deceleration generates a sound level in excess of 83 dB(A) measured on an open site with fast meter response at 50 feet from the centerline of lane of travel on highways with speed limits of 35 MPH or less; or 87 dB(A) measured on an open site with fast meter response at 50 feet from the centerline of lane of travel on highways with speed limits of more than 35 MPH.

[39 FR 38215, Oct. 29, 1974, as amended at 51 FR 852, Jan. 8, 1986]

§ 202.21 Standard for operation under stationary test.

(a) No motor carrier subject to these regulations shall operate any motor vehicle of a type to which this regulation is applicable which generates a sound level in excess of 88 dB(A) measured on an open site with fast meter response at 50 feet from the longitudinal centerline of the vehicle, when its engine is accelerated from idle with wide open throttle to governed speed with the vehicle stationary, transmission in neutral, and clutch engaged. This section shall not apply to any vehicle which is not equipped with an engine speed governor.

(b) No motor carrier subject to these regulations shall operate any motor vehicle of a type to which this regulation is applicable which generates a sound level in excess of 85 dB(A) measured on an open site with fast meter response at 50 feet from the longitudinal centerline of the vehicle when its engine is accelerated from idle with wide open throttle to governed speed with the vehicle stationary, transmission in neutral, and clutch engaged. This paragraph shall not apply to any vehicle which is not equipped with an engine speed governor.

[39 FR 38215, Oct. 29, 1974, as amended at 51 FR 852, Jan. 8, 1986]

§ 202.22 Visual exhaust system inspection.

No motor carrier subject to these regulations shall operate any motor vehicle of a type to which this regulation is applicable unless the exhaust system of such vehicle is (a) free from defects which affect sound reduction; (b) equipped with a muffler or other noise dissipative device; and (c) not equipped with any cut-out, bypass, or similar device.

§ 202.23 Visual tire inspection.

No motor carrier subject to these regulations shall at any time operate any motor vehicle of a type to which this regulation is applicable on a tire or tires having a tread pattern which as originally manufactured, or as newly retreaded, is composed primarily or cavities in the tread (excluding sipes and local chunking) which are not vented by grooves to the tire shoulder or circumferentially to each other around the tire. This § 202.23 shall not apply to any motor vehicle which is demonstrated by the motor carrier which operates it to be in compliance with the noise emission standard specified for operations on highways with speed limits of more than 35 MPH in § 202.20 of this Subpart B, if the demonstration is conducted at the highway speed limit in effect at the inspection location, or, if speed is unlimited, the demonstration is conducted at a speed of 65 MPH.

[39 FR 38215, Oct. 29, 1974]

APPENDIX D

PORTIONS OF A DISCHARGE PERMIT FORM FOR WATER POLLUTANTS

Permit No. _____
File No. _____

AGENCY OF ENVIRONMENTAL CONSERVATION
NPDES Permits Section State Office Bldg.
MONTPELIER, VERMONT 05602

Application Number: _____

Name of Applicant: _____

_____

Expiration Date: _____

DISCHARGE PERMIT

In reference to the above application for a permit to discharge in compliance with the provisions of the Vermont Water Pollution Control Act as amended (hereinafter referred to as the "Act"), _____

_____

_____

(hereinafter referred to as the "permittee") is authorized by the Secretary, Agency of Environmental Conservation, Montpelier, Vermont, to discharge from _____

_____

to _____
in accordance with the following general and special conditions:

I. SPECIAL CONDITIONS

A. *Effluent Limits*

1. Until _____, the permittee is authorized to discharge
   from_____
   to the _____
   an effluent whose characteristics shall not exceed the values listed
   below.

	Discharge Limitations					
	kg/day (lbs/day)			(specify units)		
Effluent Characteristic	Monthly Average	Weekly Average	Maximum Day	Monthly Average	Weekly Average	Maximum Day
Flow, cu. M/day (MGD)	**	**	**	(1)	**	**
Biochemical Oxygen Demand, 5-day, 20°C						
Total Suspended Solids						
Settleable Solids						
Total Coliform Bacteria						

(1)   Annual Average

2. From _____ until _____, the permittee
   is authorized to discharge from _____
   to the _____
   an effluent whose characteristics shall not exceed the values listed
   below.

	Discharge Limitations					
	kg/day (lbs/day)			(specify units)		
Effluent Characteristic	Monthly Average	Weekly Average	Maximum Day	Monthly Average	Weekly Average	Maximum Day
Flow, cu. M/day (MGD)	**	**	**	(1)	**	**
Biochemical Oxygen Demand, 5-day, 20°C						
Total Suspended Solids						
Settleable Solids						
Total Coliform Bacteria						

(1)   Annual Average

   a. The pH of the effluent shall not be less than 6.0 nor greater than 8.5
at any time.

b. The chlorine residual shall not be greater than 4.0 MG/L. The total chlorine residual of the effluent shall not result in any demonstrable harm to aquatic life or violate any water quality standard which has been or may be promulgated. Upon promulgation of any such standard, this permit shall be reviewed or amended in accordance with such standard, and the permittee shall be so notified.

c. The effluent shall contain neither a visible oil sheen, foam, nor floating solids at any time.

d. The discharge shall not cause visible discoloration of the receiving waters.

e. The discharge shall not cause a violation of the water quality standards of the receiving waters.

f. The monthly average concentrations of BOD and total suspended solids in the discharge shall not exceed 15 percent of the monthly average concentrations of BOD and total suspended solids in the influent into the permittee's wastewater treatment facilities. For the purposes of determining whether the permittee is in compliance with this condition, samples from the discharge and the influent shall be taken with appropriate allowance for detention times.

g. When the effluent discharged for a period of 90 consecutive days exceeds 80 percent of the permitted flow limitation, the permittee shall submit to the permitting authority projected loadings and a program for maintaining satisfactory treatment levels consistent with approved water quality management plans.

h. Maintenance activities or emergencies which cause reductions of effluent quality below effluent limits as specified herein shall be considered a violation of the conditions of the permit, unless the permittee shall immediately apply for an emergency pollution permit under the provisions of 10 VSA Chapter 47, Subchapter 1, Section 1265 (f). Application shall be made to the Secretary of the Environmental Conservation Agency, State Office Building, Montpelier, Vermont 05602.

i. Any action on the part of the Agency of Environmental Conservation in reviewing, commenting upon or approving plans and specifications for the construction of wastewater treatment facilities shall not relieve the permittee from its responsibility to achieve effluent limitations set forth in this permit and shall not constitute a waiver of, or act of estoppel against any remedy available to the Agency, the State of Vermont or the federal government for failure to meet any requirement set forth in this permit or imposed by state or federal law.

II. GENERAL CONDITIONS

A. All discharges authorized herein shall be consistent with the terms and conditions of this permit. The discharge of any pollutant more frequently than, or at a level in excess of, that identified and authorized by this permit shall constitute a violation of the terms and conditions of this permit. Such a violation may result in the imposition of civil and/or criminal penalties as provided for in Section 1274 and 1275 of the Act. Facility modifications, additions and/or expansions that increase the plant capacity must be reported to the permitting authority and this permit then modified or reissued to reflect such changes. The permittee shall provide notice to the Secretary of the following:

1. any new introduction of pollutants into the treatment works from a source which would be a new source as defined in Section 306 of the Federal Water Pollution Control Act if such source were discharging pollutants;

2. except as to such categories and classes of point sources or discharges specified by the Secretary, any new introduction of pollutants into the treatment works from a source which would be subject to Section 301 of the Federal Water Pollution Control Act if such source were discharging pollutants, and

3. any substantial change in volume or character of pollutants being introduced into the treatment works by a source introducing pollutants into such works at the time of issuance of the permit.

The notice shall include:

1. the quality and quantity of the discharge to be introduced into the system, and

2. the anticipated impact of such change in the quality or quantity of the effluent to be discharged from the permitted facility.

B. After notice and opportunity for a hearing, this permit may be modified, suspended, or revoked in whole or in part during its term for cause including, but not limited to, the following:

1. violation of any terms or conditions of this permit;

2. obtaining this permit by misrepresentation or failure to disclose fully all relevant facts; or

3. a change in any condition that requires either a temporary or permanent reduction or elimination of the permitted discharge.

INDEX

global environmental law
  acid rain 244
  alternatives to law 274–275
  biological diversity 249–250, 259
  comparative 245, 270–275
  desertification 269–270
  developing nations 15–16, 78,
    146–147, 250–251, 255, 262, 270
  energy 192, 213–214
  endangered species 259–262
  environmental labeling 251–252
  extraterritorial effects 244–252
  global warming 146, 192, 249,
    257–269
  international (*See also* specific
    topics) 14, 243–244, 252–270
  natural resource valuation 267,
    272–274
  NEPA 246–249
  ozone depletion 14, 74–75, 243,
    253–257
  pesticides 181–183, 244–245
  population 14, 220–224
  rainforests 249–251
  regional controls 251–252, 262–264
  solid waste 145–147, 244
  trade and the environment 267–269
  United Nations 269–270
  water pollution 264–267, 272–274
growth 5–10, 16–17, 64–65, 120,
  215–226

hazardous waste (*See* solid waste)

international environmental law (*See*
  global environmental law)

judicial review 40–42
jurisdiction 31–32, 86–88

land use
  cropland 103
  developed land 103, 108
  easements 111–113
  eminent domain 120–126,
    175–176, 225–226
  energy 194
  exclusionary practices 111–112,
    118, 226
  federal lands 108, 130–136
  forest land 108–109, 132–136
  land and soil classification 99–107
  land reclamation 194–195
  land trusts 114–116
  land uses 103–110
  nonconforming use 119
  public trust doctrine 126–130
  rangeland 109–110, 195
  restrictive covenants 111–113
  subdivision approval 119–120,
    225–226
  variance 118–119
  wetlands 86–88, 101, 108
  wildlife 130–136
  zoning 116–119, 141

mediation 96–97, 271–272
multi-media environmental protection
  48–52

National Environmental Policy Act
  (NEPA) and environmental
  impact statement (EIS)
  alternatives to proposed
    action 36–37, 278, 281,
    294–296
  cost–benefit analysis 36–37, 284
  Council on Environmental Quality
    29, 37, 277
  does it work? 43–44
  EIS content 36–39, 277–284
  EIS example 285–302
  environmental assessment 41–42
  extraterritorial effects 246–249
  human environment 32–33
  major federal actions 29–32, 134
  national security 46–47
  private sector 33–34
  remedies 46–48
  relationship to other statutes 44–45
  role of the courts 40–42
  segmentation 38–39